globalizing eastern europe

globalizing eastern europe

politics, culture and economics from the 18th to the 21st century

Gilad Ben-Nun, Katja Castryck-Naumann and Lena Dallywater

BLOOMSBURY ACADEMIC
LONDON • NEW YORK • OXFORD • NEW DELHI • SYDNEY

BLOOMSBURY ACADEMIC
Bloomsbury Publishing Plc, 50 Bedford Square, London, WC1B 3DP, UK
Bloomsbury Publishing Inc.,1359 Broadway, 12th Floor, New York, NY 10018, USA
Bloomsbury Publishing Ireland, 29 Earlsfort Terrace, Dublin 2, D02 AY28, Ireland

BLOOMSBURY, BLOOMSBURY ACADEMIC and the Diana logo are trademarks of
Bloomsbury Publishing Plc

First published in Great Britain 2025

Cover design by Catherine Wood
Cover image © Valentyn Chernetskyi / Unsplash

A catalogue record for this book is available from the British Library.

A catalog record for this book is available from the Library of Congress

ISBN: HB: 978-1-3502-6431-1
       PB: 978-1-3502-6532-5
       ePDF: 978-1-3502-6433-5
       eBook: 978-1-3502-6432-8

Typeset by RefineCatch Limited, Bungay, Suffolk
Printed and bound in Great Britain

For product safety related questions contact productsafety@bloomsbury.com.

To find out more about our authors and books visit www.bloomsbury.com
and sign up for our newsletters.

Contents

Part II Impacts on Cultures and Societies

Part III Forays into Global Economic Processes

Illustrations

Preface

The Central German region surrounding Leipzig, Halle and Jena has long been understood as a centre for research on Eastern Europe. Following German unification, the commitment to revive this tradition took shape in various forms – primarily by continuing training at universities, as well as establishing new extra-university research centres with clear regional focuses. Three Leibniz Institutes emerged in Leipzig alone: one on the History and Culture of Eastern Europe (GWZO); one on regional geography and its features particular to Europe's East (IfL); and one on the global historical impact of Jewish intellectual and material lives (DI). The universities of Halle and Jena have joined forces in the establishment of an interdisciplinary centre for Polish Studies, and two Leibniz Institutes in Halle, which analyse the development of agriculture and food production in the post-Soviet Middle East, alongside the transformation of post-socialist economies in the former Eastern bloc. A great contribution to this research was the Max Planck-Institute in Halle which held for more than a decade a clear focus on the anthropology of societal transformation in post-socialist societies. While this list is far from inexhaustive, it highlights a central aim initiated by federal German science policy, to specialize the region in knowledge production about the East, an area that remained widely unknown to many Westerners at the end of the Cold War. The general attitude was one of curiosity, accompanied by a great willingness to say farewell to the confrontative patterns of the Cold War. Exchanges with individual scholars and academic institutions from across the vast and only vaguely defined area of Eastern Europe intensified enormously in both directions.

A second trend has emerged, one particularly observable at Leipzig University. Grown out of a historic interest in world history and a broad spectrum of Area Studies institutes sedimented since the late 1890s, it has materialized as an interdisciplinary research centre (first on transregional studies and now on global dynamics, both new and historical) and the Graduate School Global and Area Studies (GSGAS), with more than two hundred students from all over the world. A Master's programme in Global Studies was complemented by one in European Studies with a strong emphasis on Eastern European developments, especially inspired by the 2004 and 2007 enlargement waves of the European Union, considering the implied necessity for orientational knowledge.

This textbook draws upon the abundance of largely new research carried out over the past fifteen years within these different research institutions, programmes and study capacities. Much of this research has been channelled into the workings of the Leibniz ScienceCampus 'Eastern Europe – Global Area' (EEGA), whose research agenda has significantly encouraged new perspectives on this region's changing role within processes of globalization. Its primary focus concerns how Eastern European societies have positioned themselves historically and continue to position themselves in relation to global challenges, conflicts and tensions.

The EEGA became very important in providing an agile, and simultaneously stable, framework for the interplay between the two research traditions on Eastern Europe and global history for almost a decade. As a result, it has ensured that the specializations of the participating institutions have been channelled into fruitful cooperation oriented towards useful products.

It is of course to be expected that the central issues have undergone changes that can be attributed to both general historiographical developments and, to a particular extent, political events. Initially, research on Eastern Europe was confronted with widespread neglect, if not complete absence, in research on globalization. At best, Eastern Europe and the Soviet Union appeared to be the opposite of a world globalizing along North American lines: anti-capitalist, closed off, and critical of any free circulation of capital, ideas and movement of people – with the exception of importing urgently needed consumer goods and exporting its own raw materials. This simultaneously meant that Eastern Europe remained stuck in the trap of extractivism, when the transition from an industrial to a service society had long since been heralded.

However, with consideration to the extent that research on Eastern Europe opened up to the omnipresent questions of globalization research, the picture has changed considerably. This can be seen in two respects: 'red globalization', as Oscar Sanchez-Sibony has called it, now appears much more multifaceted and omnipresent than was acknowledged in earlier sketches of the contemporary history of Eastern Europe. In particular, the involvement of Eastern European states in the so-called Third World has attracted a growing community of researchers and produced many new insights into the ambitions of the actors and their (often much more limited) scope for action. For some authors, this socialist globalization also had certain unexpected neoliberal traits in the organization of their own societies and in the organization of cooperation with the countries of the so-called global South. Overall, it was a recognizably significant part of the globalization processes that have shaped the world in waves since the later 19th century. The emerging global condition since then cannot be understood without reflecting on the role of Eastern Europe.

What is more controversial is the extent to which it was simply a single part of a globalization that integrated this world or whether it represented a fundamental alternative. This, of course, is a question that cannot be answered without assessing the historical balance of the 20th century. Some emphasize that Eastern Europe also belonged to a world that was increasingly striving for integration, with all the conflicts, contradictions and asymmetries that this implied. Others underline that the existence of the socialist camp not only inspired the hopes of many people around the world for an alternative to exploitation and oppression, but also imposed the character of a welfare state on Western globalization. Since the collapse of the Soviet Union, these issues have not only moved into the realm of highly committed politics of remembrance, but also influence ideas about how future challenges should be met.

But regardless of this contentious issue, which of course includes the question of the legacy of socialist globalization that continues in a very different way in several countries in East and South East Asia, the journey of discovery through the entanglements of Eastern Europe has provided many new empirical findings and enriched our picture of the diversity of globalization projects. This volume draws on some of these research findings, which have been achieved in numerous disciplines.

However, the fascination with connections has now given way to a new interest in the non-linearity of the history of entanglements. An ever more entangled history is obviously not a goal in itself. This has significantly changed the debates on globalization. The simplistic belief in the omnipotence of globalization, which continues to integrate the world so that sooner or later there will be trickle-down effects for civilization as a whole, has given way to a new disillusionment. The war that Russia has launched against Ukraine is contributing significantly to the broader trend towards a more sceptical assessment of globalization. Some speak of deglobalization as companies have been shortening their value chains since the crisis of 2008–10 and bringing some previously outsourced production back or at least closer to their headquarters. The lack of geopolitical stability as well as the fragility of logistics are recognizably at play here. Others emphasize the tendencies towards decoupling initiated by populist politicians such as Donald Trump. Such assessments sound dramatic but we should not forget that the omnipresent division of labour across continents and regions produces cost advantages with which political intentions to decouple have to compete.

Similarly, the penetrable nature of the internet leaves hardly any areas untouched. It is still a new challenge for the study of global dynamics that cannot simply be approached with the old instruments and approaches.

The academic landscape has changed radically. Many academic cooperative relationships, especially in Eastern Europe, have been frozen or interrupted in the wake of the Russian aggression of February 2022. The focus has shifted to explaining the military confrontation and rejecting Russian propaganda about the lack of a Ukrainian nation's right to exist. This is linked to the further fate of the European project and its integrative effects on their immediate neighbouring countries. The unity of an Eastern Europe, which was previously less problematized as a working hypothesis, is now assessed much more critically, and the many divisions, divergent strategies and coalitions are analysed with great attention.

However, this new orientation does not lead to Eastern Europe disappearing once again from global historical considerations. On the contrary, it clearly motivates a new round of empirical interest in societal transformation inside Eastern European countries in relation to their connectedness with other parts of the world. This is to be welcomed. After all, general knowledge about these region(s) is still insufficient compared to its significance in global processes.

The environment within which EEGA is working has significantly changed as research on Eastern Europe has undergone significant structural and intellectual transformations within a very short period of time. However, this has not made the EEGA's research paradigm obsolete – quite the opposite! The question of how and in which alliances, with which motives and with which results, the actors between Poland and the Caucasus, between the Balkans and Central Asia, position themselves in and towards globalization – if there is a single one – and which globalization projects they pursue, remains of central interest precisely because the idea that it is simply a matter of an eternally progressing all-encompassing rapprochement has dissolved. This invites the search for answers for how we evaluate the next steps of those involved in Eastern Europe's conflict history and what we can expect from these steps for the position of Eastern European globalization projects in a world of ongoing interaction.

Matthias Middell, Pro-rector, Leipzig University
December 2023

Acknowledgements

'It takes two flints to make a fire,' wrote Louisa May Alcott, born in 1832 in Germantown (now a part of Philadelphia), almost two centuries ago. Alcott, herself from a family with a transnational history, knew that it is the combination of different people and their idiosyncrasies that often trigger human creation. In our case, it took many hands, eyes, thoughts and experiences to make this book possible – not to mention hours, places with ample coffee cups, from cafes to seminar rooms, to conference halls. Emulating Alcott, we would like to highlight and warmly thank the people who endeavoured with us in this volume's making. First, we wish to thank the contributors to this textbook, our chapter authors and the authors of bracketed contributions. It is only through their intellectual capacities and hours of work on their respective texts that this book could come into being.

The textbook, from its first conception back in 2019, through all its editorial phases, not to mention COVID-19 challenges, and up to the point of layout and printing, was wholeheartedly supported and generously funded by the Leibniz Association within the framework of the Leibniz ScienceCampus 'Eastern Europe – Global Area' (EEGA 2016–25). Our first debt is to EEGA's two spokespersons: Prof. Sebastian Lentz from the Leibniz Institute for Regional Geography in Leipzig and Prof. Matthias Middell from Leipzig University. It was they who first suggested and advocated for the need and merit of this advanced-research textbook. Their advocacy allowed us to bank on EEGA's network and gain access to its range of collaborating institutions from where most of this book's chapters have emerged. EEGA's funding and administrative and coordinative back-up has supported the production of texts via fee contracts and contracts for work, made proofreading possible, and organized the acquisition of rights for many of this volume's visualizations. A heartfelt thanks to Melanie Mienert and Clara Seeber for these efforts.

One of EEGA's key partner institutions, the Leibniz Institute for the History and Culture of Eastern Europe (GWZO), deserves special mention, as two of the editors, and a number of the chapter contributors, have emerged from within the walls of this warm-hearted and research-savvy institution. Towards the last stages of production, GWZO provided much-needed supplementary funds for editing and rights acquisition, and we thank especially Frank Hadler, head of Department III ('Entanglements and Globalization'), for the opportunity he gave us to present and discuss our ideas within the framework of the institute's meetings.

This book would have not been possible in its current form – print and e-book with coloured images and creative maps – without the work of our visualizations team, led by Jana Moser, head of the Department Cartography and Visual Communication and Coordinator of the Research Area 'Geovisualisations' at the Leibniz Institute for Regional Geography Leipzig. Jana's long-standing expertise in developing and editing of maps and atlases, map design, and the history of cartography helped us as she counselled and supervised the overall design. We thank her for checking chapters for their cartographic accuracy and adequacy. Kristin Bolanz, trained in geoinformation, cartography and graphic design, provided the innovative map creations and layout which have brought so much of our research to life, as she shaped the book's visual appeal.

At Bloomsbury, we thank Tomasz Hoskins and Atifa Jiwa for their unwavering trust in this rather specific project. They and their team made the entire process from concept note to clearance review a pleasant, constructive and cooperative endeavour. From our side, we can say with certainty that the book proposal's review process, as this was steered by Bloomsbury, benefited it considerably, not least due to the intellectual acumen and rigour which our reviewers brought forth, and which they kindly shared via their views on the publication proposal, and their blessed attention, especially with regard to their requests for additional chapters on literature and Islam, which have made this volume much richer.

Without the careful editing of Ian McDonald, Timothy Jones and Deniz Bozkut Pekar much would have been 'lost in translation'. We thank them for their watchful eyes and sensibility for language (and for their generous spirit).

Last but not least we wish to thank Martina Keilbach, academic director of the Graduate School Global and Area Studies (GSGAS) at Leipzig University for helping us share initial chapter drafts at the school's doctoral seminar, where our authors presented their work, and duly received some very precious feedback.

We hope we can ignite a small spark with this book and initiate further steps towards understanding actors in Eastern Europe, their agencies and their global embeddedness, both in further research but especially in academic teaching.

Gilad Ben-Nun, Katja Castryck-Naumann and Lena Dallywater
Leipzig, February 2025

Introduction

Gilad Ben-Nun, Katja Castryck-Naumann and Lena Dallywater

Dis:locating 'Eastern Europe'

The global historian and scholar of Islam Marshall Hodgson famously called his colleagues to investigate 'interregional configurations of interrelated things'. 'No region or period of human life has, in the long run, been so isolated that it has not had its effects in turn on the rest of us' – so he wrote, back in the early 1970s.[1] Nowadays, regionally focused inquiries centre on interactions and entanglements within and beyond regions. This is certainly true for Eastern Europe's past and present. Consequently, because of the focus on entanglements, a perennial question so often posited has moved into the background: Where exactly is 'Eastern Europe' located? Does it begin at the river Oder or further westwards? Does it end at the Volga or as far east as the Urals? Does Turkey belong to it perhaps more than to Hodgson's 'Islamic world', or is it rather a part of a 'South-eastern European' region?

Critical geographers, in particular, have argued that spaces, including regions and continents, are not given but human-made – construed by people via their activities, concerns and relations. They are changeable, and changing, and usually are not neatly bounded but rather overlap.[2] Locating 'Eastern Europe' has therefore become a challenge that goes beyond a mere demarcation upon a map. For many contemporary scholars, this term broadly denotes the area between Berlin and Kazan from east to west, and from the Baltic to the Aegean on a north–south axis. It serves as focal point for investigations that follow people and their doings, both within and beyond the region itself.

Locating 'Eastern Europe' today involves more than turning a seemingly stable geographical category into a social one. The term 'Eastern Europe' carries different associations in different tongues. *Osteuropa*, *L'Europe orientale* and *l'Europe de l'Est*, *vostochnaia Evropa* or *Europa wschodnia* – all these terms differ, pursuant to the divergent socio-political and academic landscapes from which they emanate.[3] Yet whether originating from within the region or from abroad, most of these terms connote vestiges and associations of Eastern Europe as seen through the eyes of its subjugators: as a place where social, political and strategic objectives are executed over and above the will, freedoms or choices of this region's populaces. Taking a different approach, this textbook recognizes agency and scopes of action more than subordination; it acknowledges interactions as well as entanglements. It explores Eastern Europe as a dynamic and global area, not in isolation but in the context of constant exchanges, by revealing the multiple ways in which its societies have positioned themselves in and towards global processes from the 19th through to the 21st century.

The chapters in this book trace the responses offered by people from Eastern Europe to the resulting challenges of, and interactions with, the emerging global sphere. They unpack the multitude of intertwinements and circulations by which these people have shaped the 'global', and where in turn that 'global' has reciprocally shaped them. Indeed, many of the findings presented here provide testimony to the considerable imprints that Eastern Europeans have exerted upon our contemporary connected world.

Examples of such impacts abound; they range from economic to social spheres, and from legal systems to international politics – even prompting a rethinking of art in a global framework.[4] From the late 19th century until after the First World War, for example, global grain supply, along with the rules for its trade and the determination of its prices, was influenced by producers emanating from Eastern Europe as much as by those from the American Midwest. Since the 1917 Bolshevik Revolution and largely until today, women's rights over their bodies, as manifested in their freedom to opt for foetus abortion, has stemmed from legal freedoms originally first enshrined under Soviet family law. It is due to the abolition of that Soviet family law in countries such as Poland, Hungary and Slovakia three decades ago that a considerable deterioration in women's reproductive choice has been recently observed there. Stemming from forward-thinking conceptions of children as free individuals, in contrast to Western ideals of childhood, it was Polish diplomats who were largely responsible for the elaboration of the United Nations (UN) Convention on the Rights of the Child (1989) for the benefit of children the world over. The development of international law as we know it today runs from the UN Charter (1945) to the Genocide Convention (1948), and from the 4th Geneva Convention for Civilians (1949) to the 1951 Refugee Convention and the 1954 Convention on Statelessness; these instruments were elaborated after the Second World War in large part by East European international jurists. The promotion of the world's health agenda, as in the introduction of the concepts and infrastructures of so-called 'social medicine' and 'public health', was largely undertaken by experts from Warsaw, Prague and Belgrade, who ultimately shaped the League of Nations' Health Organisation. International shipping, which carries 90 per cent of international trade, has been placed under international control with the help of Polish jurists and economists.

These findings, along with many others published in this book, might not be known to the readership to whom this volume caters. Indeed, until our elaboration of these and other occurrences compiled in the following chapters, even we as its editors did not fully grasp the intriguingly broad scope of connectedness between Eastern Europe and the global sphere – nor did we sufficiently appreciate this region's various impacts on the so-called global condition.[5] The authors of this textbook took into account the fact that different people in different places have different visions of Eastern Europe. A student from Prague might harbour a very dissimilar view to that voiced by an engineer in Shanghai; a political-programme officer in Washington, DC; a trader from the Arab Gulf; a private banker from London; or a scholar based in Leipzig. 'Eastern Europe', this region which seems to be both near and far, and which frequently appears in world news – especially nowadays – has evoked a variety of viewpoints. Relegated to a buffer zone or viewed as a claimed part of Russia's empire-building, as in the case of Ukraine, or seen as fundamental opponent, in the case of the Soviet Union, some scholarship has viewed this area as backward and retrograde. Others have seen socialist Eastern Europe as a place that has considerably impacted upon the world in the post-Second World War decades – a 'global region' so to speak.[6] Still others see the region in an intermediary manner, as having influenced while being considerably shaped by other world regions for centuries – notably, the Middle East; the Mediterranean; and (postcolonial) Africa, Latin America and South East Asia.[7] Being aware of these divergent views as to its positioning, we have sought to put seemingly clear positions of the region in global relation aside, and have opted to bring forth contributions that demonstrate the region's interconnectedness with, and imprints upon, the global sphere, while acknowledging the reciprocal impacts that these engagements brought about in Eastern Europe itself.

This textbook offers global perspectives on and from the region by giving telling examples of the ways in which people have found their own way of positioning in what they perceive as a state of globalization. We portray them as being globalized and as globalizing the world; and, accordingly, we present Eastern Europe as both a globalized and a globalizing region.[8] Seeing and acknowledging the different visions and conceptions of Eastern Europe – the different understandings of actors inside and outside the region, which change and reconfigure over time depending on the goal and point of view in question – we also realize that this textbook is about the diversity of different 'Eastern Europe*s*': the plurality of what the region meant and means, and, accordingly, the impressive variety of its connectedness with the world. Acknowledging this plurality goes hand in hand with our understanding of the elasticity of the term 'Eastern Europe', which we embrace as we emphasize its multiplicity through the actor-centred prism we have opted for.

Just as different actors in different places and times have different understandings, so our authors each consider a temporally and geographically distinct Eastern Europe. Each chapter brings out a different facet of the larger spectrum. So, when we speak of 'Eastern Europe' in what follows, we have this plurality in mind. This textbook presents research from a wide range of disciplines, including legal studies, geography and literary studies, and for that reason discipline-related vocabulary has been retained. Beyond informing the reader about discipline-specific ways of thinking, it also acknowledges that research regarding Eastern Europe as a global region continues to adopt different vocabulary sets. While some scholars make use of terms such as 'pre-/modern' or 'peripheral' to denote the thorny issue of development, other scholars, notably in area studies and global history, have criticized those very ideas of peripheralization as being Eurocentrically driven. We faced similar challenges with terms such as 'Global South', 'Global North', 'Global East', 'Third World', 'West' and 'postcolonial', all of which represent certain views of world order. These have been accepted in a wide range of disciplines as relevant or adequate to describe phenomena from such worldviews. Yet, such terminologies are similarly perceived as essentializing. Correspondingly, in this book we have chosen to vest the authors with the freedom to use these terms as they see appropriate to their subject matters. We call on the reader to engage with such terminologies cautiously. Yet, regardless of divergent disciplinary conventions, what affirmatively unites all this book's chapters is both its actor-centred approach, and its attention to the notion of 'transregional connections' as this is explained below.

The volume's contributions form a sequence that highlights three core features of this region's global connectedness, which also form the book's sequential parts:

1 its involvement in international political and legal spheres (Part I)

2 its global impacts on cultures and societies (Part II)

3 its interweaving into global economic processes (Part III)

Accompanied by numerous maps and infographics produced in association with its chapters' authors, along with images and text boxes, the book shows Eastern Europe in all its richness, variety, and relevance for the global sphere. The empirical findings presented here on the economy, law, literature, climate change, regional development, international organizations, childhood and migration call into question visions of backwardness and subjugation. The facts, on the contrary, confirm notions of interconnectedness, of diversity and alterity, and of interdependence towards other world regions. At the same time, they reveal periods and spaces of disconnection, of fading and recurring connectivity, and of an unequal partaking in global processes. Entanglements are time- and space-bound, never all-encompassing. If we, in this book, focus on the multitude of connections and exchanges, we also take care not to leave out borders, boundaries and other countering forces.

Human actors

At the heart of the book, and our choice of its chapters, lies the idea of understanding Eastern Europe through its peoples' agency. Put simply, when one is looking through the lens of agency, one chooses to focus on the actions, activities, affirmative stances, struggles and concrete deliberations of people and social groups, carried out under given structures of politics and power. Correspondingly, we use an actor-based prism. Connectedness comes into being as a result of people's activities, as they preconfigure, articulate, delimit and transcend the initial spaces allocated to them while 'carving out' new spaces and scopes of interactions for themselves. This 'carving out' process as conducted by Eastern Europe actors progressively and actively enhanced their dovetailed engagement with the global sphere. In terms of global entanglements, our textbook traces the ways in which, via their actions, the region's actors have addressed cross-border problems that they faced by pushing towards relations with actors from other world regions. Virtually all chapters explain agendas that these actors pursued (within their varying domains of activity) at the individual or group level, from local, regional, national, cross-border, sub-regional and international spheres.

We keep in mind the fact that agency enfolds under structures of politics and power; entanglements are carried out within political entities, in social structures and institutions, as well as in asymmetrical worldwide power relations. Some of these contexts seem to enable connectivity, others to delimit it; at certain times, it seems, spaces of action were larger than in other periods.

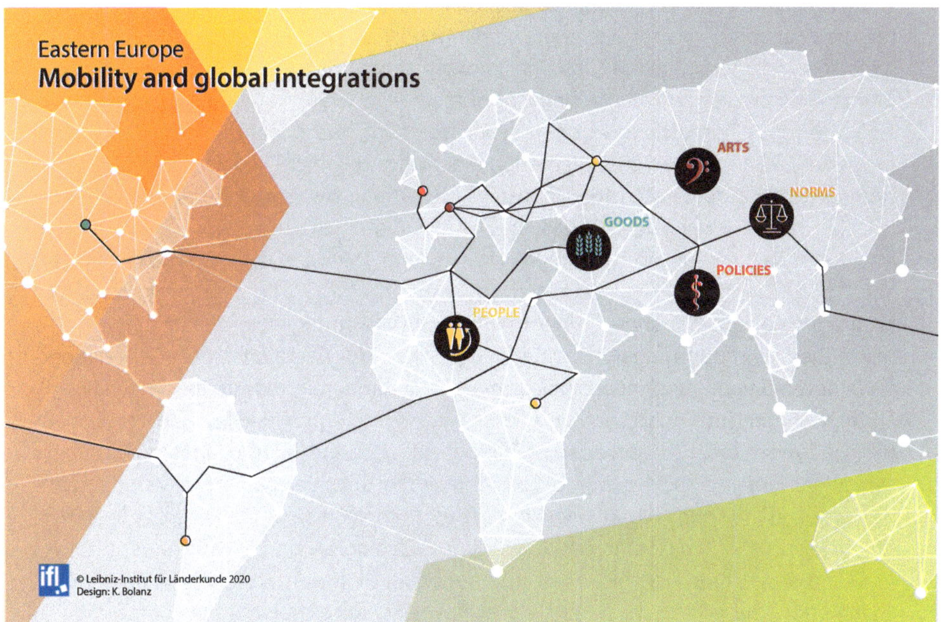

Figure 0.1 Eastern Europe: Mobility and global integrations.
This map provides examples of global interconnections between Eastern Europe and other world regions, including aspects such as policies of global health (Ch. 3 by Castryck-Naumann), grain export (Ch. 10 by Müller), migrations across the Atlantic (Ch. 8 by Esch), legal norms (Ch. 4 by Aliyev), and economic thinking (Ch. 11 by Trecker).

Progressive initiatives in the socialist bloc?

Beáta Hock

For a period of some two decades after the collapse of the Iron Curtain, the cultural-social history of socialist Eastern Europe has been typically captured in broad stereotypes about atrocious dictatorial regimes, their well-designed ideological manipulation, and the subjugation of art and culture to political propaganda and censorship. In more recent years, however, there seems to have been a growing interest in retrieving the social and cultural history of 'really existing socialism' in less antagonistic or ideologically biased ways. This new strand of research contributes towards rendering the historical realities of socialist countries visible in mainstream international scholarly literature. Several authors place socialist Eastern Europe in a transnational context, and thus shed light on the Soviet bloc's often pioneering role in the global conflicts of the Cold War.

Women's and gender history was perhaps the first field of study that came to acknowledge the relatively progressive nature of socialist arrangements. Feminist social scientists took the recognition that at the core of the Cold War was an international battle over how to modernize society as their starting point and argued that the programme for women's emancipation implemented in socialist Eastern Europe created, to some extent, the material conditions for achieving global gender equality. From this vantage point, researchers demonstrated a 'lead in modernization' [*Modernisierungsvorsprung* in German] in comparison with Western societies prior to 1990.

Some recent research has gone beyond assessing the benefits of domestic social provisions, as it surveyed the international activities of official women's organizations from Eastern Europe. As Kristen Ghodsee's (2019) and my own archival research have revealed, socialist delegates defined the debates during the three world congresses of the United Nations (UN) Decade for Women in 1975 (Mexico City), 1980 (Copenhagen) and 1985 (Nairobi). They advocated for women's rights in a globally conceived programme of social change. Rather than limiting the struggle to equality between the sexes, they also fought against military aggression, the persistence of racist relations, underdevelopment, and neocolonialism (at the time referred to as 'imperialism'). Through setting such goals, women's issues were tightly embedded in – and occasionally overshadowed by – the broader politics of the 'Second World'. In tandem, these aspirations largely coincided with propositions set forth by delegates from world regions belonging to the 'Third World' back then. Thus, in the course of this UN Decade (1975–85), women from developing countries forged ideological bonds with representatives from the Soviet bloc. The history of international law is another research area within which efforts have been made in the past few years to re-evaluate the contribution of Cold War-era socialist experts. Whereas dominant legal history has generally interpreted the role of the socialist bloc as mere roadblock to fulfilling the ideals of Western liberalism, the conference 'State Socialism, Legal Experts and the Genesis of International Criminal & Humanitarian Law after 1945' (Humboldt University, Berlin, November 2016) set out to adjust this simplified view. The speakers underlined the fact that, far from being 'impediments to progress', initiatives from the socialist world were often timelier than those put forth by 'Western' representatives in that they led the way in codifying issues that had been formerly treated as local conflicts (violations of peace and the crimes of the apartheid regime, for example) as international crimes.

It is fairly clear that the socialist bloc's progressive initiatives were inseparable from political and propagandistic agendas. That said, taking the Cold War as an interpretive framework helps us to realize that such oversaturation with ideology was the usual state of international affairs in those decades. The interventions of Eastern European socialist experts were nevertheless important as they significantly shaped the development of global projects and transnational epistemic communities.

The reassessment of artistic and cultural production in socialist societies can look back on a similar record. After the political changes of 1989, art historiography paid almost exclusive attention to the so-called unofficial artistic sphere of Eastern European communist regimes, framing this cultural arena as a site of political opposition, intellectual dissent and cultural resistance. A widening research agenda now devotes scholarly attention to other segments of cultural life as well, including state-supported 'official' art. As this internationally emerging field of study of the 'Cultural Cold War' has revealed, artistic and cultural life was strongly shaped by politics and ideology on both sides of the Iron Curtain.

From this perspective, the kind of 'universal art history' (*vseobshchaya istorija iskusstv*) that was introduced in the countries of the socialist bloc under the aegis of a socialist internationalism is worth revisiting. It is fairly well known that being part of the Soviet sphere of influence demanded a great degree of uniformity across the various countries in terms of the administration of artistic life and the nature of prevalent art that demonstrated a critique of historical discourses. Less discussed has been the fact that belonging to the Soviet bloc also implied an enforced allegiance towards 'friendly states' in other continents, in the name of solidarity between communists of all countries and international peoples struggling for common goals. The transfers and exchanges resulting from this socialist internationalism powerfully shaped the world of early socialism, and beyond, during the Cold War. Viewed from this perspective, a tentative link between internationalism as a political and cultural-diplomatic principle and as a proposed framework for art-history writing and teaching can be interrogated.

Since the 2000s, 'Global Art Studies' and 'World Art History' have been buzzwords promising to renew art history through an attempt to dispel the discipline's persistent Eurocentrism and Western biases, some of which still bear the marks of colonial-era beliefs in cultural superiority. Kitty Zijlmans and Wilfried Van Damme (2012), renowned proponents of the World Art Studies model, would reach back to the early 1990s when identifying the roots of this approach and methodology. Hans Belting similarly connected the emergence of Global Art to the contemporary period, linking it to the geographical shift that the art market has witnessed under the conditions of a globalized world economy. But what if the genealogy of a global approach to art and its historiography could be traced further back in time, to the partly politically determined model developed and practised in socialist countries after 1945?

This proposition inspires a range of new research questions: Did 'universal art history' and 'world art history' – as practised in the Soviet world – operate with aspirations, concepts, frameworks and methodologies comparable with those put forth more recently by Global Art Studies? Or, was this knowledge production in an internationalist paradigm a mere foil for communist rhetoric? Did socialist scholars engage in innovative knowledge projects, or devise a geographically more inclusive canon? Conferences such as 'Socialist Internationalism and the Global Contemporary' (Leipzig, November 2017) set out to discuss some initial answers to these questions.

Rather than following preconceived notions about what hindered Eastern Europe's global connectedness and when it did so, the studies presented here offer exciting new views. For example, the region's history during the Cold War is traditionally presented as being caught in the power struggle between the 'West' and the 'East', and individual actors are typically rendered passive. Yet, as this book's chapters repeatedly demonstrate, the Cold War was equally a period catering for and enabling individual action within existing structures of power and politics. The region was globalized on its own terms, becoming the 'Eastern bloc' – a space of action *and* global interaction.[9]

What emerges from this actor-based and historically informed optic is an Eastern Europe that, rather than being an abstract and pre-given entity, becomes an actor-related category: a region that has been actively defined and articulated by the variety of people and social groups who shaped it, in their responses to processes of globalization. This actor-related view is directed against fixed ideas about what and where 'Eastern Europe' ought to be, or how it ought to look, or operate. Alongside other perceptions of the region, to its own actors, it has been first and foremost an enabling social space not a given geographical position. Infographic 0.2 (pp. 9–10) depicts actors from each chapter and examples of their origins as well as their local, regional and transregional interconnectedness.

Transregional connections

A term repeatedly referred to in this textbook carries a global perspective, namely 'transregional' connection. Commonly, when it comes to region-transcending dynamics, an *inter*-regional relationship between two or more continental world regions – such as 'Africa' or 'Eurasia' – is highlighted. This is a dialogue that takes place between agents, who are thinking in these regional terms, representing their region (and not just their nation-state or city) as they interact with other actors from other regions who also conceive of themselves as representatives of their respective world regions. From the perspective of 'Eastern Europe', an example of a transregional connection conceived in this traditional sense would be the dialogue between an 'East European' and a 'West African', as opposed to one between say a 'Russian' and an 'Ivorian'. Yet, we advance a wider understanding than the shift from the 'national' to the 'regional' or 'meso-regional' level. Entanglements are spatial in nature: they take on different scales and stretch also across localities, empires, nation-states, cultures and sub-regions. Focusing solely on the inter-regional dimension would blend out the multidirectional and parallel scales of interactions on different levels – all co-constituting Eastern Europe as a frame of reference, meaning and action. Distinguishing between three dimensions of 'transregionality' – the formation of regions, transfers between regions and region-transcending dynamics – helps us to recognize the broad spectrum of connections that have emerged in and shaped this part of the world.[10]

Accordingly, the transregional perspective, as we understand it, does not contradict or undermine interest in the inner-regional or inter-regional connectedness; rather, it complements and contextualizes them. It opens our eyes to Eastern Europe's multilayered spatiality. This includes references that these actors made to meso-regions, as in sub-regions within

Figure 0.2 Eastern Europe's actors and their connections. Locations are an exemplary selection.

Figure 0.2 (Continued).

Tatar exile poet, publicist, and political activist **Ayaz Ishaki** (1878–1954) in the circle of his North Caucasian, Azeri, Ukrainian, Turkestani as well as Polish colleagues in Warsaw on 15 October 1937. The meeting took place in accordance of Ishaki's active participation at the Polish-backed anti-Communist and anti-Soviet Promethean movement in the interwar period.
Picture Credits: Wikipedia. 2022. "Джабагиев, Вассан-Гирей Ижиевич." Wikimedia Foundation. Last modified December 14, 2022, retrieved 01.03.2023
Location: Kazan, St. Petersburg, Warsaw

Arshak Makichyan studied violin and is a climate youth activist based in Russia, originally from Armenia. In 2019 he staged a solo school strike for the climate every Friday on Pushkin Square, Moscow, for more than 40 week, inspiring others across Russia to take part in school strikes for the climate. He was jailed in December 2019 for six days, hours after returning from the COP 25 Madrid. Currently he lives in exile.
Picture Credits: Arshak Makichyan (private twitter account)
Location: Jerewan, Moscow, Berlin

Gertruda Sekaninová Čakrtová (1908–1986) was a lawyer, diplomat, and communist politician. Due to her Jewish descent, she was sent to Theresienstadt Ghetto and deported to the extermination camp Auschwitz-Birkenau. After 1945 she made a steep political career in socialist Czechoslovakia and became permanent delegate in the UN, working on colonial issues, social, labor, and women's right. Supporting the reform movement in 1968, she became a prominent dissident and co-initiated the Charta 77.
Picture Credits: Muzeum Vysočiny Havlíčkův Brod, Fotoarchiv, F2008/268
Location: Havlíčkův Brod

Fuad Abdurahmanov's statue of a liberated woman errected 1960 in Baku, Azerbaijan. Abdurahmanov was inspired by the Jafar Jabbarli's play "Sevil" (1928). Sevil is a symbolic figure of a young Soviet woman, who took off her veils and stood up against the supressions of her former husband. Female emancipation advanced in Azerbaijan already during the short period of the first independent Democratic Republic (1918–1920) as women received election rights. Progressive Soviet family and labour law facilitated this development tremendously. This Chapter shows the Socialist law as a complex and paradoxical system, which denied the fundamental principles of modern law (rule of law and democracy) but provided for most progressive approachs in specific areas. It also shows that Eastern Europe in legal sence can include great parts of Asia and some patterns of Socialist law remain quite resilienteven 30 years after the dissolution of the Eastern bloc.
Picture Credits: Mursel at English Wikipedia, CC BY 3.0 <https://creativecommons.org/licenses/by/3.0>, via Wikimedia Commons.
Location: Baku

Children
This Soviet postage stamp (circa 1960) is from a series called 'Drawings by Soviet Children'. It has the slogans 'Friendship!' and 'Peace!' on it, as well as the name USSR.
Picture Credits: Alexander Mitrofanov / Alamy Stock Photo
Location: Moscow

Jacob Robinson (1889–1977) was Jewish jurist, historian, and politician, born in Seirijai (today Lithuania), educated in Warsaw, who fled to the US in 1940. The picture taken during the time when he worked for the League of Nations shows him clearly as a diplomat from Europe's East, since diplomats from Western Europe always wore long ties, and the sort of unofficial "dress code" was for Eastern European diplomats to wear bow ties.
Picture Credits: Archives of the Institute for Jewish Affairs, Hebrew Union College Cincinnati (1958)
Location: Warsaw, Geneva, New York

You see a photo of the Petőfi-bust in Satu Mare/Szatmárnémeti/Sathmar (Romania). **Sándor Petőfi** is perceived as a national poet of Hungary but he is also remembered outside of the country. There are about 250 depictions of Petőfi, an important number of which are placed all over the globe.
Picture Credits: (c) Stephan Krause 2017
Location: Satu Mare, Budapest, Vienna, Buffalo

Samuel Šolem Švarcbart (1886–1938) on trial in Paris in 1926. Born into a Jewish family in Bessarabia, he fought in the Russian Revolution of 1905 before moving to Vienna where he became an anarchist. Expulsed for bank robbery, he went to Paris and fought for France in WW I. Joining the October Revolution he became disappointed with Bolshevik politics and returned to Paris. In 1926 he shot Petljura, former Ukrainian president who had fled after the Ukraine was incorporated into the Soviet Union. Švarcbart held Petljura responsible for pogroms committed by Ukrainian nationalists in Paris. Acquitted of trial for the murder, Švarcbart wrote for Jiddish anarchist papers in France and the US.
Picture Credits: wikipedia
Location:

Ignacy Jan Paderewski (1860–1941) was the most famous pianist of his time, touring globally from the late 1880s up to the 1930s. He was also one of the rare musicians who also entered politics, signing the Treaty of Versailles and becoming a symbol of Poland's resurrection in 1918/19.
Picture Credits: dreamtime.com
Location: Krakow, Berlin, Warsaw, Strasbourg, Vienna, New York

József Bognár (1917–1996) was one of the most influential economists and policy advisors in Hungary between the failed Hungarian Revolution (1956) and the end of state socialism (1989). As founder of the Afro-Asian Research Center and the Institute of World Economy at the Hungarian Academy of Sciences, he forged a multitude of contacts and facilitated intellectual exchange between Eastern and Southern scholars and politicians
Picture Credits: MTVA Archívum, MTI Fotó: Molnár Edit
Location: Budapest

Virgil Traian N. Madgearu (1887–1940) was a Bucharest-based social scientist, journalist, and left-wing politician, who became a leading figure and theorist of the Romanian Peasants' Party. He served as Minister for Industry and Trade, for Finance, and for Agriculture while he also represented Romania at the League of Nations conferences on economy. Madgearu was murdered by the fascist "Iron Guard" during WW II.
Picture Credits: Wikipedia. 2023. "Virgil Madgearu." Wikimedia Foundation. Last modified January 12, 2023. https://en.wikipedia.org/wiki/Virgil_Madgearu
Location: Leipzig, Bucharest, Geneva

Dagnis Straubergs (*1969), former Chairman of Riga Planning Region Development Council, relates the successful European and global integration of Latvia's capital to the wellbeing of the whole country: "The city of Rīga, together with range of the adjacent territories, is a pronounced metropolis area […], which can be felt across the whole of Latvia." Such growth-based policies stand in contrast to a growing divides between urban and rural areas in Eastern Europe and in other parts of the world.
Picture Credits: Rīgas plānošanas reģions (Riga Planning Region Sustainable Development Strategy 2030, https://www.varam.gov.lv/sites/varam/files/04_riga_eng.pdf, page 5)
Location: Riga

Unknown Protester
The picture shows a protest against building a satellite campus for China's Fudan University in Budapest (in June 2021), which called on the government to invest in local universities. The analysis of Chinese investments in Eastern Europe often centres on inter-state relations and decisions of national political elites. Yet, investment plans are often contested by local civil societies.
Picture Credits: dpa, Motiv 244002225
Location: Budapest

Eastern Europe's larger spatial realm between Berlin, Kazan, Tallin and Thessaloniki. Terms such as 'East Central Europe' (*Ostmitteleuropa*), 'South-eastern Europe', Transcarpathia, or the 'Trans-Ottoman realm' denote sub- or meso-regions that were given their names either by Eastern Europeans or by outside agents, so as to imbibe these sub-regions with certain qualities that could demarcate them from the broader 'Eastern European' area.[11] What we might intuitively associate with say an 'East-Central' European city such as Prague (for example, an accumulation of Art Nouveau architecture) could equally apply to cities further to the east, such as Riga, or Odesa. Yet by carving out and insisting on the term 'East-Central Europe', actors have sought to distinguish Prague from areas further to the east (or the north).[12] In doing so, they endowed their region with certain characteristics, loading it with a meaning that might be equally salient for other areas of Eastern Europe, yet which they wished to be first and foremost identified with their own space.

We have done our best to recognize regions' multilayered spatiality – articulated by a plurality of actors who, serving their own agendas, came to coin their own titles. Similar phenomena can be observed for other world regions; whether and to which degree the region of 'Eastern Europe' is nevertheless specific is a complicated question that deserves wider investigation than the scope of this volume permits. Yet, what is presented in the following text can be read fruitfully with a comparative perspective in mind. In fact, we hope to stir curiosity for future studies that explore the commonalities and specificities of Eastern Europe in a global framework.

Eastern Europe between 'newness' and the *longue durée*

A core idea that our textbook advances concerns the temporal aspect of Eastern Europe's *global connectedness*. Over the past two decades, much scholarly attention has been allocated to the concept of 'globalization'. In everyday usage and public parlance, globalization starts commonly with the 1990s, or at best the 70s, and appears as a somehow automated trend leading (seemingly) towards worldwide integration. Within academia, too, this understanding has been nourished for quite some years. In addition, the effects of the COVID-19 pandemic and the way in which it seems to have radically 'slowed down' the pace of globalization, from the suspension of rapid air travel to the reclosure of national borders to a return to autarkic economic modalities, have invoked a sense of newness – as if the world had never before lived through pandemics, with all the contradicting dynamics resulting from them. A policy of quarantining the sick so as to protect society at large, for example, is nothing new; it had already appeared four thousand years ago in the Jewish Torah,[13] and has regularly recurred since that time. Furthermore, it behoves us to speak of 'globalization*s*' (plural) as people from around the world, rather than natural forces, have forged and countered ties with the world at large – as they have done for many centuries, not only recently.[14]

Historians have thoroughly criticized and refuted a-historical views of 'globalization' and claims for newness, regardless of whether they are linked to the 1970s, 90s or 2020s.

The historian's turn against the discourse of newness, with which the first elaborations of the concept of globalization were imbued, has accompanied a focus on the emergence of our current, global age – roughly from the late 18th or early 19th century onwards. This age is seen in somewhat of a stark comparison to previous historical eras. So much attention has been given to this recent period of globalization that, at times, connected histories before the emergence of Eric Hobsbawm's *Age of Capital* seemed to have been overshadowed.[15] Granted that during the 19th to 21st centuries, humanity has indeed departed from what came before the age of electricity and the era of the internet, historians working on older periods have insisted on the need to contextualize these developments of the last two centuries, and set them within their longer historical patterns.[16] Viewing our age from a *longue durée* perspective helps to point towards the many aspects that we assume to be 'new', yet which, in fact, have been around for a very long time. We build on this argument for the global perspectives on Eastern Europe that this textbook offers. China might be building new 'belts and roads' in Eastern Europe, for instance, yet these still very much resemble the geographical and social trajectories of the ancient Silk Road.

Notwithstanding the wisdom of viewing Eastern Europe's historical trajectories in their *longue durée* patterns, one would be hard pressed to disregard *qualitative* differences that are inherent to the global condition under which we live. For example, only since the 2010s has the majority of humanity resided in urban areas.[17] Correspondingly, the rise of disparities between rural and urban developments is a challenge now facing virtually all societies around the world, with special relevance for Eastern Europe.

When we speak of globalization in this textbook, we do so from the historical vantage point. This phenomenon – which we believe began sometime during the late 18th century, and whose 'onslaught' accelerated from the late 19th century to the present – parallels the terminological emergence of the phrase 'Eastern Europe'.[18] Characteristic of this new epoch of global integration are large-scale interactions, transfers and shifts of people, goods and ideas. Dovetailing these changes were political crises and conflicts. Woven together, these larger-scale interactions, coupled with the political crises they helped trigger, all eventually generated a new quality of connectedness of all parts of the world – which scholars now call the 'global condition', in which 'globality proved the tangible context of action, of political decisions and social practice, for all'.[19]

Recognizing 'newness': Effects of climate change in Eastern Europe and in the world

Gilad Ben-Nun, Katja Castryck-Naumann and Lena Dallywater

So profound do current changes in the age of our so-called 'globalization' seem, for the first time in the earth's 4.5 billion years of history, it is humankind that is changing the planet's climatic conditions. Notwithstanding the very valid argument for the need to look to longer historical patterns of Eastern Europe's entanglements with the world, the fact that mankind is changing the planet's weather patterns points at a qualitative difference of our time, in relation to previous periods. The following info graphic visualizes the consequences of climate change in Eastern Europe, especially focusing on the vast area of the Russian Federation.

Up until roughly two decades ago, and for the past 650,000 years, some 65 per cent of Russia's surface has been covered with permafrost, whereby the ground remains permanently frozen, thus locking in it an immense amount of metric carbon. The risks inherent to the thawing of this massive permafrost layer in the regions of Russia, Alaska, Greenland and Canada are considered as some of the most detrimental in terms of their climate change associated dangers (Kertysova and Ramnath 2021). In tandem, the retreat of permafrost and the release of the locked carbon gasses are seen as one of the key initiators and exacerbators of massive forest fires in Russian Siberia, and as influencing globally weather conditions.

Yet as with many processes of globalization, the retreat of permafrost also has unintended consequences which in turn might well increase the pace of interconnectedness. The melting of the icecaps, and especially the opening of the Arctic Ocean to shipping routes, now that their ice layers have become penetrable thanks to global warming, imply a significant shortening of maritime trade routes from the production metropoles of East Asia (China, Korea, Japan and Taiwan) towards Europe via the so-called 'Northeast passage' (represented with icon of the cargo ship on the top right corner of the info graphic). For centuries, polar explorers could only imagine the possibility of unlocking the global trade potentials associated with an opening of the Northeast passage as a permanent maritime shipping route. The effects of climate change, which have now rendered the maritime Northeast passage as a viable commercial trade route, would most probably mean a further rise in global trade.

Figure 0.3 Russia – Phenomena: Effects of climate change.

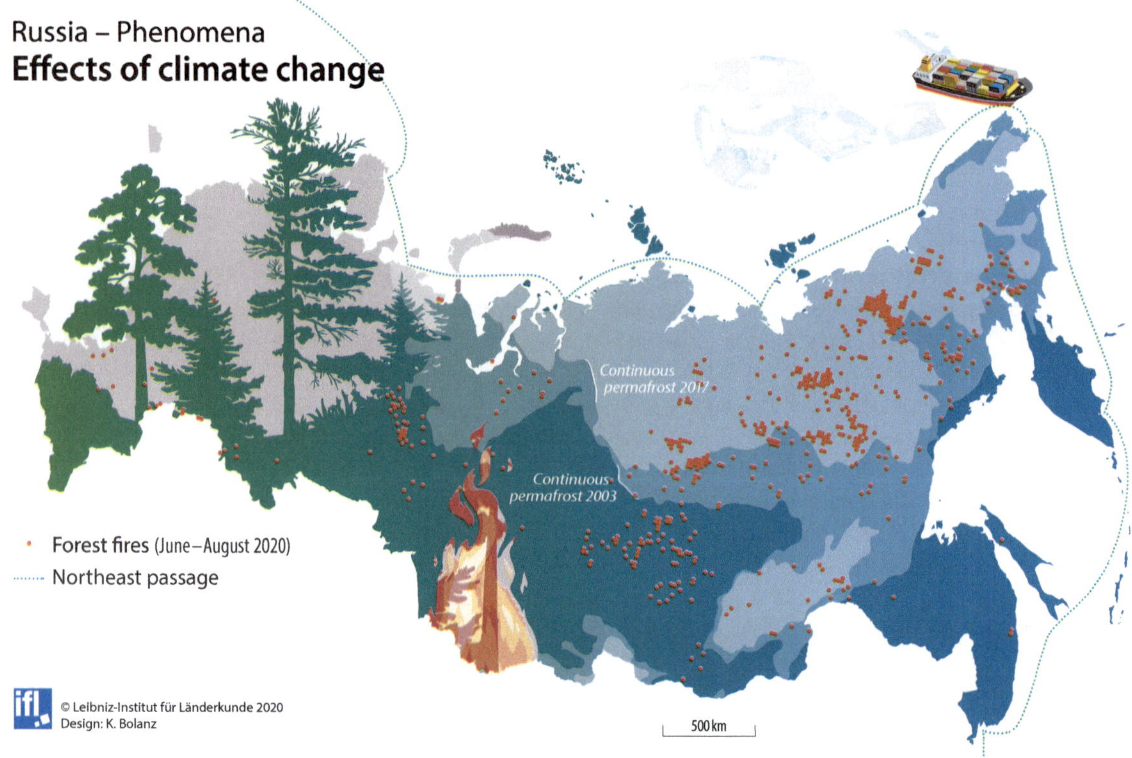

Yet, we also recognize the *longue durée* view of things that rightfully stresses the fact that human migrations such as those by Eastern Europeans from the Russian Pale of Settlement across the Atlantic were nothing new – mirroring, as it were, the great migrations of the 4th to 6th century bce by the Huns of Hungary, or by the Turkic and Mongol-Tatar Islamic migrations into Eastern Europe. Think also of the unbroken, rich legacy of Islam in Eastern Europe to this day.

As editors of this volume, we pay attention to both arguments – the one insisting on the 'global condition' by which Eastern Europe, among other regions, has been shaped, as well as the one pointing to the *longue durée* of the region's global connectedness. The vision we have subscribed to, and one which we would hope to bring forth, is a compromise of sorts between 'newness' and *longue durée*. This implies a recognition of the deep historical traits going back hundreds (and in some cases thousands) of years – albeit with an acceptance of the qualitative difference that began during the late 18th century, and which gathered pace from the second half of the 19th century onwards. On these grounds, we can also begin to consider caesuras within our own age – as the chapters in this textbook show, the 'global condition' might not be static but rather a period in which moments of greater entanglement alternate with moments of lessening integration.

Structure of the book: A guide to the reader

As mentioned earlier, the book's chapters are organized according to the three topical groupings they address: political and legal spheres; cultures and societies; economic processes.

Each part of the book opens with a preliminary 'cohesion note' written by us as editors. The aim of this introductory text is to point towards cross-cutting themes within each part and to explain the synergies between the topics covered by the chapters within that part, as well as the ways in which those themes relate to other parts of the book. All chapters share the same approach: each starts with a well-known preconceived notion of Eastern Europe and, countering those stereotypes, outlines a different picture based on fresh empirical material. Chapters vary in their historical depth and in terms of their spatial focus. In that way, each contribution brings to light one of the many different notions of 'Eastern Europe' that form the full spectrum of imaginations, social practices and political formations contained in this term.

Directly after this introduction follow two chapters that present the perspectives of both *longue durée* and contemporariness side by side. The chapter on the role of Islam in Eastern Europe and its links to neighbouring regions (the Caucasus, Turkey and Asia Minor) highlights a distinct feature of the region's *longue durée* entangled history. As Zaur Gasimov demonstrates, in contrast to 'Western Europe' – where, from the 15th until the late 19th century, Islam and Muslim people were largely absent – Islam has remained an integral part of Eastern Europe from the 13th century until today. As such, Gasimov's chapter challenges common perceptions of religious structures and communities in the region, as it shows Islam's deeply embedded nature within Eastern Europe as an overtly indigenous and integral part of this region's history, identity and cultural fabric. This autochthony of Islam in Europe's east contrasts rather sharply with Western Europe's total banishment of Islam in the 15th Century from Spain, to legacies of its occidental colonialism (e.g. France in Algeria, Britain in India/Pakistan) prior to the 20th century's influx of Muslim migrants into Western Europe. Showing how Polish intellectual Tatars came to forge Azerbaijan's formative governmental ruling as this new state emerged, while weaving into the chapter aspects of journalism and influences over architecture, Gasimov's writing conveys Islam's transregional reach from Eastern Europe across the Black Sea, and south towards Europe's long-standing and intimate relations with Turkey and the Caucasus.

In his chapter on climate change and Eastern Europe as a region of natural resources, Benjamin Beuerle presents the region's paramount importance to the world energy and trading system as well as the lasting importance of these resources in the socio-economic history and shaping of the region itself. He does so by introducing the reader to the discovery, usage and neglect of these resources, thus illustrating how natural conditions have played out in this region's making. His chapter shows the essential part that energy exports and infrastructures have played in the region's interrelations and connections with other parts of Europe, but also in its economic and political developments – not least, the stances of its various governments on the issue of climate change. Its focus is on the relevance of the region for the world's climate, via its huge permafrost grounds and forests; on the changes wrought on this region by climate change; and, correspondingly, the reciprocal contributions of its actors to the increase in climate change's effects over themselves given their widespread extraction of fossil fuels for burning (oil, gas and coal). These contributions include a considerable rise in devastating forest fires and the changing of ground conditions due to the melting of permafrost. In a country such as Russia – where permafrost still occupies almost two thirds of the land area of an immense territory, and where whole cities, pipelines and other vital infrastructure are built on ice – these ongoing changes bode ill, and risk accelerating worldwide climate change. Eventually, the chapter also illustrates that as these natural changes continue and the world reacts to climate change, the relationships of the region's societies and politicians to the climate emergency is a very dynamic one that continues to develop – even at time of writing.

The chapters in Part I examine Eastern Europe in relation to international political and legal spheres, via deeper explorations of the ways in which its actors came to participate in and heavily impact on international organizations (IOs) and structures of global governance. From the influential role played in the League of Nations and the United Nations to the making of international law, the chapters in this part demonstrate how this region shaped the so-called 'international sphere'.

From the emergence of international organizations in the late 1860s, actors from Eastern Europe played a substantial role in their crafting, development and policy. In her contribution Katja Castryck-Naumann traces the role played by Eastern Europeans in three crucial fields of international politics of the 20th century: health, disarmament and trade. She shows that agents rooted in or based in Eastern Europe initiated lasting changes: the shift in the international health agendas towards 'social medicine' and 'public health' which impacted epidemics control that has for long time been of urgent concern; the proposal of an alternative concept in nuclear disarmament based on regional agreements which was much more successful than efforts towards 'universal disarmament'; and the change of unequal global trade relations in the field of international shipping. The chapter makes clear that these agendas of international regulation were elaborated in reaction to political and social processes within Eastern Europe and that they were pursued by both Eastern Europe's official delegates to the League of Nations and the United Nations as well as by experts and international officials coming from the region.

The picture that emerges here is one of actors who, more often than not, go beyond representation of their own nation-state in favour of global purviews for the betterment of mankind and for changing the asymmetric global power relations.

In the next chapter, Azar Aliyev turns to Eastern European legal systems and explains their standardization in terms of Marxist-socialist law, which dates back to the Soviet era, as similar codes, procedures and legal rulings applied from Mongolia to the German Democratic Republic (GDR). The strongest influence on older legal systems stemmed from the Soviet Union's family law, which departed from the tsarist or imperial legal heritage, especially with regard to rights in marriage. Among its most important principles were the equality of men and women, the equality of legitimate and illegitimate children, the right to paid maternity leave, and the right to abortion. These rights were provided for in all socialist states regardless of religious and cultural particularities, including in Muslim Central Asia and strictly Catholic Poland. The political caesura of 1989 was accompanied by changes in legal systems. Nevertheless, many post-socialist states have largely been able to retain the basic structure of socialist family law to this day.

Elizabeth White, in her chapter, continues the exploration of children's rights in the socialist bloc, now with a focus on education and its impact on the international sphere (hereby connecting to Castryck-Naumann's chapter). While the field of education in socialist Eastern Europe has hitherto been viewed as tantamount to totalitarian indoctrination cut off from global developments, this chapter shows quite the contrary. It vividly demonstrates the internationalization of socialist childhoods and the ways in which the internationalizing of human rights did not, in fact, emanate solely from 'the West'. Educational models and concepts of childhood formed part of the strategic competition with the Western states during processes of decolonization in the mid-20th century, and the circulation of those models were part of the network of global entanglements between European socialism and postcolonial states. They formed part of Cold War rivalries. Children's rights, like women's rights, was an area in which socialist states believed they could demonstrate superiority over the West. White's chapter illustrates the historical developments, transformations and legacies of the Soviet model. First and foremost, the author clearly illustrates one thing: the interventions of Eastern bloc actors such as jurists and legal scholars, educators, political figures and socialist women activists in transnational networks and the internationalization that they drove onwards need to be evaluated in a completely new way.

In the following chapter, we return to law. One of the distinctive features of the global world is the consolidation of the international legal field, through the adoption of multilateral legal treaties under the aegis of international organizations with global mandates and purviews. Since the late 19th and especially during the 20th century, Eastern European state and non-state actors have been crucial to this process of consolidation of international law. International criminal law and the prosecution of war crimes, international humanitarian law within the laws of war, territorial-demarcation principles of borders under public international law (the *uti possidetis* principle), and many other international legal innovations were either the result of workings by Eastern European international jurists or were designed to deal with legal challenges that stemmed from this geographical region. In his chapter, Gilad Ben-Nun traces these Eastern European impacts on modern international law while pointing to other world regions where these principles were later applied. Beginning with the history of minority protections since the 19th century, this chapter traces the process by which this region's concepts 'went global' – from the Hague Regulations on the laws of war (1899–1907); through the interwar period's minorities' treaties under the League of Nations; to the 'treaties after trauma' post the Second World War (1946 Military Tribunal in Nuremberg, 1948 Genocide Convention, 1949 Geneva Convention for Civilians, 1951 Refugee Convention). Seen retrospectively, another important overarching theme explored here connects the region's history with international law's long march towards, and eventual revocation of, duress as a legitimate measure for the securement of international legal obligations under the law of treaties.

Part II of the book illuminates patterns and impacts over societies and cultures. It focuses on migrations from Eastern Europe to other world regions, while highlighting the region's global influences over literature and music, as much as over natural resources and climate change. The chapters in this part demonstrate the ways in which radical social, political and economic changes in the region have affected its cultural and social histories and also influenced the relationship of these shifts to Eastern Europe's visions of musical, literary and cinematographic aesthetics. They point to the relevance of the region for the world's climate and place natural resources in the socio-economic history and shaping of the region itself.

The analysis of literature and cinematographic aesthetics in regard to their global entanglements examines the region's contribution in the fields of literary prose, poetry, films and drama. As Moniká Dánél and Stephan Krause show in their chapter, Eastern and Central European writing is very much characterized by the multilingual spaces to which it relates as well as by regional microstructures wherein thematic and aesthetic entanglements can be observed. This literature's colourfulness and its accents, as well as its stylistic and medial differentiation within the region, testify to its permanent openness towards global subjects. These can be observed and heard in this literature's wording and 'worlding' of global interests so as to serve the image of the world depicted as a matter of literary language, which can be grasped at hand. In its ideal essence, although it conceives of itself very much according to the territory within which it is written, East and Central European literature advances and supports a transnational perspective on this region's cultural and literary production. The linguistic ontology of Eastern and Central European literature is first and foremost set apart by its multilingualism – which is the most important criteria used to describe it, as this literature can only be understood when it is seen to be 'written in many languages' while existing in parallel with, rather than in the necessary exclusivity of, national languages. This literature is not bound only to one language that is said to be nationally, politically, socially or historically dominant. Rather, it exists through its highly differentiated and diverse linguistic multidimensionality. In their chapter, Dánél and Krause provide keys to the successful value, and a sustainable understanding of, Eastern and Central European literary texts as poetical works of art. They help us to grasp why it remains imperative to continue interpreting and highlighting the autonomy of the aesthetic and literary attributes that widen, add to and embellish various other discourses and the ways in which they work.

In several respects, migration has been one of the signal tokens associated with Eastern Europe over the past one-and-a-half centuries. Tying in closely to other chapters in the volume, Michael Esch's contribution sets into context successive emigrations out of this region – starting with the Jewish departure from the Russian Pale of Settlement for the 'New World' (the United States, Latin America) and Palestine, followed by the Turkish targeting of the Armenians (undertaken through major, forced population transfers) and the population exchanges (Greeks, Turks, Bulgarians, Poles, Ukrainians, Romanians and so on) executed in the Balkans after the First World War under the auspices of the League of Nations. Stalin's ethnic re-engineering of the Soviet empire; the population shifts during the Ukrainian famine (1928–34); the Nazi relocation of populations before and during the Second World War; and, finally, the uprooting of some 12 million ethnic Germans from Eastern Europe westwards all come into this overview. This chapter concludes with a distinct example of how the varying and often widely diverging definitions of international bodies dealing with refugees (United Nations High Commissioner for Refugees, Council of Europe, European Union) have considerably recalibrated our understanding of the political and regional boundaries that we tend to associate with the term 'Eastern Europe'.

The status of music from Eastern Europe in international music historiography is rather ambivalent. Although many musicians from the region have played, and continue to play, a prominent role in international musical life – and although many important movements, especially in the 20th century, have received strong impulses from there – the main achievement explicitly attributed to 'Eastern European music' is that it introduced 'national traits' into art music. This narrative is highly problematic insofar as it reduces the great variety of musical trends originating in the region to a very one-sided, distorted 'sketch'. In his chapter on cultural exchanges and transfers in the field of music, Stefan Keym singles out areas of cultural production in which Eastern European actors exercised a considerable imprint on global cultural patterns, from the late 19th century to the present.

Part III of the book hones in on the ways in which global challenges have been addressed from within Eastern Europe, as seen through the perspectives of economy. Alternative ideas and models are presented that have been developed in the politically relevant fields of the world economy, agrarian development, transregional infrastructures and climate change. Many of these solutions have circulated widely, both within the region and beyond. In turn, these circulations eventually exerted considerable impact both within and beyond the region – especially as they triggered a re-questioning of Western economic orthodoxies and occidental neoliberal visions generally.

In his contribution on Eastern Europe's positioning strategies in world marketplaces, Uwe Müller examines the region's forays into global wheat markets. From the second half of the 19th century onwards, this important and ever-growing involvement manifested itself in Eastern Europe's production of grain, and particularly wheat, which 'went global' and was consequently confronted with competition from the Americas as well as Australia. After the First World War, the region's wheat producers tried to regain the now-contested Western European markets with new instruments (agreements among themselves, international cartels, etc.). Eastern Europe's erstwhile paramount role in grain export, which fluctuated significantly during the early 20th century, has been supplemented over the past fifty years by the cardinal role this region plays in the production of energy. Notwithstanding the mid-century disruptions in grain production brought about by the upheaval of the Second World War, and the problems of the communist economic system in establishing efficient agricultural practices, the resurgence of Eastern Europe's prominence in the generation of this critical commodity after 1989 testifies to the region's importance to a world whose food-security concerns grow by the day.

In his chapter concerning socialism's economic-developmental ethos, Max Trecker skilfully demonstrates the socialist alternative to the neoliberal economic model as this emanated from the thought and practices of Eastern Europe economic minds. As Trecker clearly shows, this alternative modality for generating equitable world economic growth, which was born following the 1917 October Revolution in Russia, has remained central to economic development thinking both for Eastern Europe and for other world regions. The Soviet experiment played a critical role in its attempted global appeal, in the effort to significantly challenge – even if only in theory – Western notions of capitalist development. Therein, Trecker pays special attention to Romanian economic thinkers who influenced Latin American and, later, UN debates on development. This chapter concludes with a discussion of the ways in which, after 1989 and throughout the 90s, it was Eastern Europe that became the par excellence experimental field for Western, neoliberal economic thinking as it was imposed upon the region's countries, and how, conversely, it triggered transformations of certain Western economies, at the side.

As mentioned earlier, in contrast to all previous periods of human history when the majority of the world's population lived in rural areas, at the turn of the 21st century that majority resides in cities and urban spheres. In his chapter, Thilo Lang emphasizes the impact that Eastern European metropolization exerted upon the region – and, more broadly, upon neighbouring regions. Somewhat in contrast to cities in other regions (most notably, the Levant and Western Europe), but quite in line with developments in other world regions such as Latin America, the emergence of several of today's Eastern European major cities (Odesa, Tiraspol, St. Petersburg, etc.) was the result of initial deliberate construction efforts *ex nihilo* around the turn of the 18th and 19th centuries. In much of the same manner, since 1989, a significant rift in economic and infrastructural development has emerged in Eastern Europe between metropoles and rural areas – often juxtaposing the economic 'take off' of capital cities such as Budapest, Riga, Bratislava and Kyiv with their 'left-behind' rural hinterlands. As Lang demonstrates, the growing developmental disparities between urban and rural areas in this region are intimately bound up with the ideological triumph of neoliberal economic-policy outlooks that were developed in the West, and which were adopted by emerging regimes in Eastern Europe from the 1990s onwards.

The unprecedented increase in Chinese investment in Eastern Europe's infrastructures over the past decade has sparked anxieties, prompting European Union (EU) institutions to take steps to constrain further efforts by the People's Republic (PRC) in these sectors. To some, this represents the entry of a Chinese 'Trojan Horse' into Eastern Europe's peripheries, which are seen as fertile ground for the PRC's 'authoritarian advance'. China's alleged use of 'divide and rule' strategies offers the possibility of increasing fissures between Western and Eastern Europe, as the latter develop new dependencies on the PRC. Lela Rekhviashvili's contribution elaborates on the contemporary realities of Chinese infrastructure investments in Eastern Europe, as she showcases the diversity of responses to this reality across Eastern Europe's different meso-regions. As Rekhviashvili stresses, the problematic overemphasis on China's efforts in Eurasia is exacerbated by the representation of the EU and other 'Western' developmental powers as benevolent, innocent or normatively superior to China's approaches. Rekhviashvili shows how research on Chinese investments in Eastern Europe needs to be linked with broader debates regarding the spatial reorganization of global capitalism.

Notes

1   Marshall G. S. Hodgson, *Rethinking World History: Essays on Europe, Islam, and World History* (Cambridge: Cambridge University Press, 1993), p. 75.

2   Martin W. Lewis and Kären Wigen, *The Myth of Continents: A Critique of Metageography* (Berkley: University of California Press, 1997).

3   Frithjof Benjamin Schenk, 'Eastern Europe', in *European Regions and Boundaries: A Conceptual History*, ed. Diana Mishkova and Balazs Trencsenyi (New York: Berghahn Books, 2017), pp. 188–209; Tomasz Zarycki, *Ideologies of Eastness in Central and Eastern Europe* (Oxford: Routledge, 2014).

4   Antje Kempe, Beáta Hock and Marina Dmitrieva (eds), *Universal - International - Global. Art Historiographies of Socialist Eastern Europe* (Köln: Böhlau Verlag, 2023).

5   On the notion of the global condition, see, for example, Charles Bright and Michael Geyer, 'Benchmarks of Globalization: The Global Condition, 1850-2010', in *A Companion to World History*, ed. Douglas Northrop (Malden, MA: Wiley-Blackwell, 2012), pp. 285–302; Matthias Middell and Steffi Marung (eds), *Spatial Formats under the Global Condition* (Berlin: de Gruyter Oldenbourg, 2019).

6   James Mark, Artemy M. Kalinovsky and Steffi Marung (eds), *Alternative Globalizations: Eastern Europe and the Postcolonial World* (Bloomington: Indiana University Press, 2020); Michael Müller, 'In Search of the Global East: Thinking between North and South', *Geopolitics* 25 (2020) 3, pp. 734–55.

7   See, for example, in history: Jane Burbank and Frederick Cooper, *Empires in World History: Power and the Politics of Difference* (Princeton: Princeton University Press, 2010); Jane Burbank, Mark von Hagen and Anatolyi Remnev (eds), *Russian Empire: Space, People, Power, 1700–1930* (Bloomington: Indiana University Press, 2007); Maria Todorova, *The Lost World of Socialists at Europe's Margins: Imagining Utopia, 1870s–1920s* (London: Bloomsbury Academic, 2020); Maria Todorova, *Imagining the Balkans* (New York: Oxford University Press, 1997); Diana Mishkova, *Приспособяване на свободата. Модерност-легитимност в Сърбия и Румъния през XIX век* [Domestication of Freedom. Modernity-Legitimacy in Serbia and Romania in the Nineteenth Century] (Sofia: Paradigma, 2001); Diana Mishkova and Roumen Daskalov (eds), *Entangled Histories of the Balkans*. Vol. II. Transfers of Political Ideologies and Institutions (Leiden: Brill, 2014). In politics: Balázs Trencsényi et al., *A History of Modern Political Thought in East Central Europe* (Oxford: Oxford University Press, 2015 (Vol. 1) and 2018 (Vol. 2)).

8   Doreen Massey, 'Imagining Globalization: Power-Geometries of Time-Space', in *Global Futures: Explorations in Sociology,* ed. A. Brah, M. J. Hickman and M. M. Ghaill (London: Palgrave Macmillan, 1999).

9   Jörg Scheller, 'Eastern Europeanizing Globalization: Polish Artists at the Venice Art Biennale and the Microcosms of Globalization', in *Globalizing East European Art Histories: Past and Present*, ed. Beáta Hock and Anu Allas (New York: Routledge, 2018).

10 On this notion of the 'transregional', see Katja Castryck-Naumann (ed.), *Transregional Connections in the History of East Central Europe* (Berlin: de Gruyter 2021); Matthias Middell (ed.), *The Routledge Handbook of Transregional Studies* (London: Routledge, 2019); Francis Onditi et al (eds), *Contemporary Africa in the Foreseeable World Order* (Lanham: Rowman & Littlefield, 2018).

11 Siegfried Huigen and Dorota Kołodziejczyk (eds), *East Central Europe between the Colonial and the Postcolonial in the Twentieth Century* (London: Palgrave Macmillan, 2023).

12 See Stefan Troebst, 'Historical Meso-Regions and Transregionalism', in *Handbook of Transregional Studies*, ed. Matthias Middell (London: Routledge, 2018), pp. 169–78.

13 Bible, Book of Numbers, Ch. 12, verses 10–17.

14 Middell, *Handbook of Transregional Studies*.

15 Eric Hobsbawm, *The Age of Capital 1848-1875* (New York: Weidenfeld & Nicolson, 1975).

16 Burbank and Cooper, *Empires in World History*; Peter Frankopan, *The Silk Roads: A New History of the World* (London: Bloomsbury, 2015). On the notion of an 'archaic globalization', see, for example, C. Bayly, 'From Archaic Globalization to International Networks, circa 1600–2000', in *Interactions, Transregional Perspectives on World History,* ed. Jerry H. Bentley, Renate Bridenthal and Anand A. Yang (Honolulu: University of Hawai'i Press, 2005). Cf. Osterhammel's framing of globalization in *Globalization: A Short History*, ed. Jürgen Osterhammel and Niels Peterson (Princeton: Princeton University Press, 2005).

17 Edward Glaeser, *Triumph of the City: How Our Greatest Invention Makes us Richer, Smarter, Greener, Healthier, and Happier* (London: Penguin Press, 2011).

18 Larry Wolff, *Inventing Eastern Europe: The Map of Civilization on the Mind of the Enlightenment* (Stanford: Stanford University Press, 1994).

19 Bright and Geyer, *Benchmarks of Globalization*, p. 290.

Bibliography

Ghodsee, Kristen. *Second World, Second Sex: Socialist Women's Activism and Global Soli-darity during the Cold War*. Durham, NC: Duke University Press, 2019.

Kertysova, Katarina and Akash Ramnath. 'How Permafrost Thaw Puts the Russian Arctic at Risk'. International Peace Institute (IPI) Press, 22 November 2021, URL: https://theglobalobservatory. org/2021/11/how-permafrost-thaw-puts-the-russian-arctic-at-risk/

Zijlmans, Kitty and Wilfried Van Damme. 'Art History in a Global Frame: World Art Studies'. In *Art History and Visual Studies in Europe: Transnational Discourses and National Frameworks*, edited by Matthew Rampley, Thierry Lenain and Hubert Locher. Leiden: Brill, 2012, pp. 217–29.

Longue Durée Connectivity: Islam in Eastern Europe

Zaur Gasimov

1

The story of Islam in Eastern Europe is driven by two forces that emerged successively from the 11th until the mid-15th century: those of the Tatars and the Ottoman Turks. These two 'carriers' of the mission of Islam are inextricably embedded into Eastern Europe's history, politics, economy, and its cultural identity.

Two beginnings: Tatars and Turks

The first Muslims to arrive in the region were the forefathers of Eastern Europe's Tatars. Russian military expeditions to Baku on the western shore of the Caspian Sea in the 11th century and the economic relations that the city of Novgorod forged with tradesmen from the Middle East set up a century-long interaction between Eastern Europe and Islamicate societies. Long before Turks conquered Constantinople, South Slavs fruitfully interacted with Arabs in trade as well as in military alliances against Byzantium. The same also goes for the Kievan Rus, who interacted both with Arabs and with Volga(-Kama) Bulgaria. Arab settlers, most probably from Syrian Aleppo, settled in the Balkans throughout the 14th century. The Cossacks of Zaporizhian Sich, on what is now Ukrainian territory, maintained various contacts with the Khanate of Crimea and frequently allied with it in its struggles against the Polish-Lithuanian Commonwealth.

The conquest of the Grand Duchy of Muscovy and Kievan Rus by Mongol troops in the 13th century established the so-called 'Mongol–Tatar yoke' on the lands settled by Eastern Slavs – and had a long-lasting and intense mutual influence on both Slavic and Turkic cultures and languages, and on Christian Orthodoxy and Islam. The weakening and ultimate dismemberment of the Chingizid state in the 13–14th centuries ushered in the fragmentation of that polity and its cultural legacy. It led to the emergence of the Crimean Khanate on the northern shore of the Black Sea, along with that of the Kazan and Astrakhan Khanates and other smaller entities. These Muslim presences in Eastern Europe dovetailed the European–Asian borderlands with the Sunni Muslim settlements found within the boundaries of the Polish-Lithuanian Commonwealth. By the 14th and early 15th century, Muslim khanates in both the Volga region and on the northern shore of the Caspian, along with the Polish-Lithuanian Tatars, had become prominent 'players' in European politics. This was especially so given the ongoing rivalry between the predominantly Catholic Polish-Lithuanian Commonwealth and the post-Mongol, mostly Orthodox Russian, state of Muscovy as well as the Orthodox Cossack settlements of Zaporizhian Sich.

By the middle of the 15th century, Eastern Europe's second group of Muslim forebears had emerged along the Black Sea's southern shores as the Ottomans finally subjugated the Byzantine capital of Constantinople and rapidly gained control over Southern Europe's Balkan region. Challenged by Shia-ruled Persia in the Caucasus, Sunni-Hanafi Ottomans turned the Black Sea into their own *mare nostrum* thanks to a massive construction spree. Ornate Sunnite mosques and flourishing educational institutions (*madrasa*s) sprang up all across 16th-century Asia Minor, in tandem with Russia's occupation of the khanates of Kazan (1552) and Astrakhan (1556). The expansion of Ottoman rule north-westwards brought Greece; the Balkans' Slavic regions; and also, following the victory of the army of Sultan Süleyman I (1520–66) at Mohács in 1526, Hungary into the Ottomans' governmental orbit – a condition which was partially sustained well into the 18th and even 19th century (the latter in the cases of Greece and the Balkans).

In the 17th century, further westward Ottoman expansion was halted in the vicinity of Vienna. Polish elites sent emissaries to Persia searching for alliances with its Shia-ruled monarchy against the Ottomans, who also challenged Persia in Anatolia and the Caucasus.

By the 18th century, Romanov-ruled Russia and the Ottoman empire had evolved into distinctly multiconfessional and multiethnic political entities with vast possessions in Eastern Europe. These were inhabited by millions of Orthodox Christians, Sunni Muslims and a mosaic of other confessions such as Jews, Armenians and Chaldean and Nestorian Christians. By this time, a distinctive Ottoman architectural landscape and cityscape had come into being – one which stretched from Istanbul to Budapest and Belgrade, and from Sarajevo to Szeged, and was filled with numerous mosques, municipal buildings, Ottoman wells, clock-towers and traditional baths (*hammams*). In parallel to this Ottoman development, in the more northern Tatar realms on the territory of the Polish-Lithuanian Commonwealth close to present-day Minsk and Vilnius, a number of extant Muslim cemeteries lay bare these regions' Islamicate past – a testimony to the Romanovs' tolerance for mosque-building in cities such as Kazan, Ufa and Astrakhan.

Cultural transfer from Western Europe

In the 17th century, the Russian empire continued its expansion as well as its policy aimed at forceful assimilation of the non-Orthodox population. A century after the conquest of the Tatar-populated entities of Kazan and Astrakhan, St. Petersburg liquidated the autonomy of the Qasim Khanate in today's city of Riazan and annexed it. According to legislation adopted by the Russian authorities in 1649, mosques could be built only at a great distance from churches and severe punishment for conversion to Islam was introduced. At the same time, the Tsarist authorities started to translate and publish overtly anti-Muslim literature from Western Europe that had been written from the 12th–13th centuries onwards. The scripts of the Dominican friar Vincent of Beauvais (1184/94–1264) gained particular popularity, and the Russian intellectual Simeon Polotskii (1629–80) played an important role as an intermediary and translator of these writings. The 'Anti alKoran', written by the Czech Protestant missionary Vaclav Budovec (1551–1621), was avidly read not only in his native region but also in Russia. At the start of the 18th century, Russia launched its 'Persian raid' (*persidskii pokhod*), which boosted publications aimed at discrediting the Islamic faith and legitimized the military operation itself. These developments formed the ideological background to the very first Russian translation of the Holy Quran. The basic text was the French translation prepared and published by the diplomat and Orientalist André du Ryer (*c.* 1580–*c.*1660) under the title 'L'Alcoran de Mahomet' in the mid-17th century, which was further translated by Russian diplomat Petr Postnikov (1666–1703) in the late 1690s. While his translation of du Ryer's text was superficial and lacked rigour, Postnikov's foreword warning of Islam's alleged menaces was of particular importance for Russian publishers.

In 1719, the forefather of Russian Oriental Studies, the Moldovan aristocrat and polyglot Dimitrie Cantemir (1673–1723), authored Latin writings that reflected, among other topics, on the 'false prophet' Muhammad. Backed by the Romanov court itself, this book was translated into Russian and published in 1722. These culturally biased and partial knowledge and narrative transfers from Western to Eastern Europe mirrored Western European colonialism and imperialism, impacting on the Eastern European perception of Islam and Muslims and giving impetus to Russia's own cultural and academic preoccupation with Islam.

The coming of modernity and globalization

The year 1783 served as a watershed moment in the history of Islam in Eastern Europe, as St. Petersburg annexed the Khanate of Crimea in what amounted to a momentous semi-colonial bond with the Ottoman empire. During the following decades, as Ottomans consequently lost control over Greece (which announced its independence in 1821) and numerous territories in Southern Europe, Russia annexed the weakened Kingdom of Eastern Georgia (1801) and the northern provinces of Persia (1813–28). Having thus expanded into the south Caucasus, Russia had come to obtain vast territories between the Black and Caspian seas housing millions of Sunni and Shia Muslims speaking mostly Turkic tongues. In 1878, Russian Orthodox cleric and Orientalist Gordii Sablukov (1803–80) published the first Russian translation of the Quran from Arabic into Kazan. In the 1880s–90s, in a move that contained the Ottoman empire on its the south-western edge and boosted its own home-grown version of the discipline of Oriental Studies, St. Petersburg annexed a vast portion of territory east of the Caspian Sea towards Central Asia. At a stroke, century-old centres of Islamic clerical learning and tradition such as Samarkand and Bukhara suddenly became parts of the same empire as Baku, Kazan, Crimea, Kyiv and Vilnius. The imperial framework accelerated mobility within its borders: for instance, attracted by industrial development in what is now Eastern Ukraine, Tatars from the Volga region moved into that territory, establishing local Muslim communities there. The start of the oil boom on the Absheron peninsula around Baku in the 1870s–80s attracted thousands of Christians, Jews and Sunni Tatars to this part of the Russian empire.

For Tatars in the territory of the former Polish-Lithuanian Commonwealth, the Russian conquest of Crimea had an additional effect. On the peninsula, St. Petersburg created the so-called Taurian Muslim Religious Authorities, and the Muslims at the western edge of the empire fell under their jurisdiction. Religious guidance for the formerly Polish-Lithuanian Tatars was therefore transmitted from the *muftiat* (Sunni Muslim authorities) of Orenburg in Central Russia to Crimea. Although part of the overall Sunni congregation, both Tatar communities lived in different cultural and linguistic contexts: those in Crimea had used Arabic as a service and sermon language for centuries and were Turkic-speakers, while Polish-Lithuanian Tatars had used the (highly Polonized) Byelorussian language for

Figure 1.1 Tatar mosque of Ivje, built c. 1882 in present-day Belarus.

© Digital Commons 2023

ecclesiastical purposes and Polish for intra- and intercommunal communication since the 16th century (Akiner 1978). While Crimean Tatars were closely bonded with the Ottoman empire – linguistically, culturally and geographically – Tatars in the neighbourhoods of Grodno, Minsk and Vilnius lived thousands of miles from the Mediterranean and Middle East, and had created local and distinct forms of folk Islam. The Tatar clergy produced specific prayer books (*khamail*) in Byelorussian, with explanatory texts, and shaped the original forms of wooden mosques, prayer houses and traditional cemeteries (*mizar*). In the 1850s, a Polish Tatar, Jan Murza Tarak Buczacki (1830–57), authored the Polish translation of the Quran in Warsaw by using previous fragmentary translations prepared in the 1820s–30s and, until then, censored by the authorities.

The mosque of Ivje

Zaur Gasimov

Similar to various types of Christian architecture, Islamic mosques offer a broad spectrum of exterior and interior design. Alongside the imperial grandeur of the Süleymaniye Mosque in Istanbul, there were countless, much smaller mosques on both sides of the former Ottoman capital as well as in the Balkans. Many of them were wooden – as was, initially, the Al Aqsa Mosque in Jerusalem – and fell victim to frequent fires as well as warfare.

However, a small wooden mosque situated in the tiny provincial town of Ivje, in the region of Grodno in present-day Byelorussia, survived both world wars. When these lands became part of the Byelorussian Soviet Socialist Republic, this town became a centre of the local Tatar community that travelled to Ivje – particularly, to this mosque – when celebrating religious holidays. In Soviet times, the mosque attracted the local non-Tatar Muslims – mostly Azeris, Uzbeks and Tajiks working or studying in Byelorussia. Both this mosque and the Belorussian Tatar community look back on centuries of political and cultural presence in these lands, and at an entangled history of confessional co-existence across the entirety of North-eastern and Eastern Europe.

Grodno was for centuries an integral part of the Polish-Lithuanian Commonwealth, and the arrival of the Tatars harks back to the recruitment policy of the Lithuanian Duke of the Commonwealth, Wytautas, who invited Tatars in the 14th century, offering them the possibility of settling in the borderland of the Moscow Principality and protecting the Commonwealth against possible intrusions from the East (Lederer 1995). And indeed, Tatars – called Polish, or Polish-Lithuanian, Tatars in the international scholarship – served the Polish-Lithuanian leadership, protecting the country and taking part in warfare as an integral part of the Polish-Lithuanian Army against Moscovians and the knights of the Teutonic Order. In the parts of the Polish-Lithuanian Commonwealth with a high Tatar population, mosques and Muslim cemeteries were set up (Weeks 1999). Grodno was one of the most prominent regions of the Polish-Lithuanian state to host a significant Tatar community. The lands around Ivje, like most eastern parts of the formerly Polish-Lithuanian state, became Russian after the third partition of 1795. The mosque of Ivje was erected in 1882, with financial support for the building of this Sunni place of worship being provided by the Polish noble Elvira Zamoyska – herself a Catholic. Evidently, she financed the erecting of the main body of the mosque, while Polish Tatar emigrants in the United States paid for the construction of its minaret.

> It should be mentioned that this Polish-Lithuanian, then Russian, town of Ivje, about 150 kilometres from the city of Grodno, was a prominent *shtetl* with a large Jewish community. During the Soviet period, when Grodno became a Soviet Byelorussian region, the mosque of Ivje was the only functioning mosque in the entire territory of Byelorussia. While the language of religious practices at the turn of the century was Polish, the Sovietization of these lands with its de-Polonization strategies – as well as the influx of Muslims from other Caucasian and Central Asian republics of the USSR – caused the Russification of the religious practices of the mosque of Ivje.

The withdrawal of Ottoman military power and bureaucracy from a large part of the Balkans in the first quarter of the 19th century was accompanied by the almost simultaneous conquest of the Caucasus by Russia. These developments resulted in a mass emigration of Muslims (*muhacir*) to the territorially diminished Ottoman empire from the territories of the new post-Ottoman states in the Balkans and Russian-controlled territories in the Caucasus and Central Asia. In the world view of 19th-century Greek, Serbian and Bulgarian nationalisms, Muslims in the Balkans – even those who were Slavic speakers and were not of Turkic background – were perceived as remnants of the Ottoman past: allegedly alien and hostile. Since that time, this pattern of extreme othering of these local Muslim communities despite obvious linguistic and cultural bonds has undergone a degree of evolution. However, in that part of the world, the dichotomy 'local, native Christian' vs. 'adversary, alien Muslim' played a significant role throughout the 20th century and continues to do so even today.

Taking its cue from Russia's expansion, the first wave of 19th-century globalization saw Crimean and Kazan Tatars, as well as Azeris in the Caucasus, pioneering modernist tendencies within a large Russian Muslim community. They did so via education reform under the aegis of a new, so-called jadidist (*jadid* in Arabic) type of secularist school, and through the emergence of a national press (*Akinchi* in the Azeri vernacular [Ploughman, 1875–7], *Tercüman-Perevodchik* [Translator, 1883–1914] in Crimean Tatar and Russian), both of which fed into the articulation of a new political, nationalist will, as evident in the Muslim-Congresses in Novgorod, and the rise in the number of Muslim candidates in the Russian Duma. By the turn of the 20th century, the number of Muslims at Russian universities had also grown steadily. Along with their growing enlightenment, education and professionalization, Russia's Muslim communities increased interactions with neighbouring countries, especially through their active engagement with the Ottoman empire. The reasons behind this increased interaction during the late 19th century are manifold. For one, in addition to Bosniaks and Albanians, the Ottoman Muslims in the Balkans (as well as the Turks of Thrace, Greece and Romania) were all Turkic-speaking – as were the majority of Russia's Muslim Crimean and Kazan Tatars, Azeris, Kumyks and Turkestanis (all of whom spoke different Turkic languages and dialects). This significant factor of mutual linguistic intelligibility and 'script unity' clearly eased communications between places such as Istanbul, Romanian Constanţa and Simferopol. Consequently, by the start of the 20th century, Tatar and Azeri intellectuals such as Yusuf Akçura (1876–1935), Ahmet Ağaoğlu (1869–1939) and Ali Bey Hüseyinzade (1864–1940) elaborated Pan-Turkist ideology and transplanted it into the space of ideas that was late Ottoman

Istanbul. The journal of the Crimean enlightener Ismail Gasprinski (1851–1914) *Tercüman-Perevodchik* enjoyed readership throughout the Russian Caucasus and the Volga region as well as Ottoman Anatolia. The same goes for the satirical journal *Molla Nasraddin*, which was set up by Azeri intellectual and journalist Jalil Mammed Quluzade (1869–1932) in 1906 in Tbilisi (Benningsen 1962; Keller 2011; Paksoy 2021; Afary and Afary 2021; Ocón

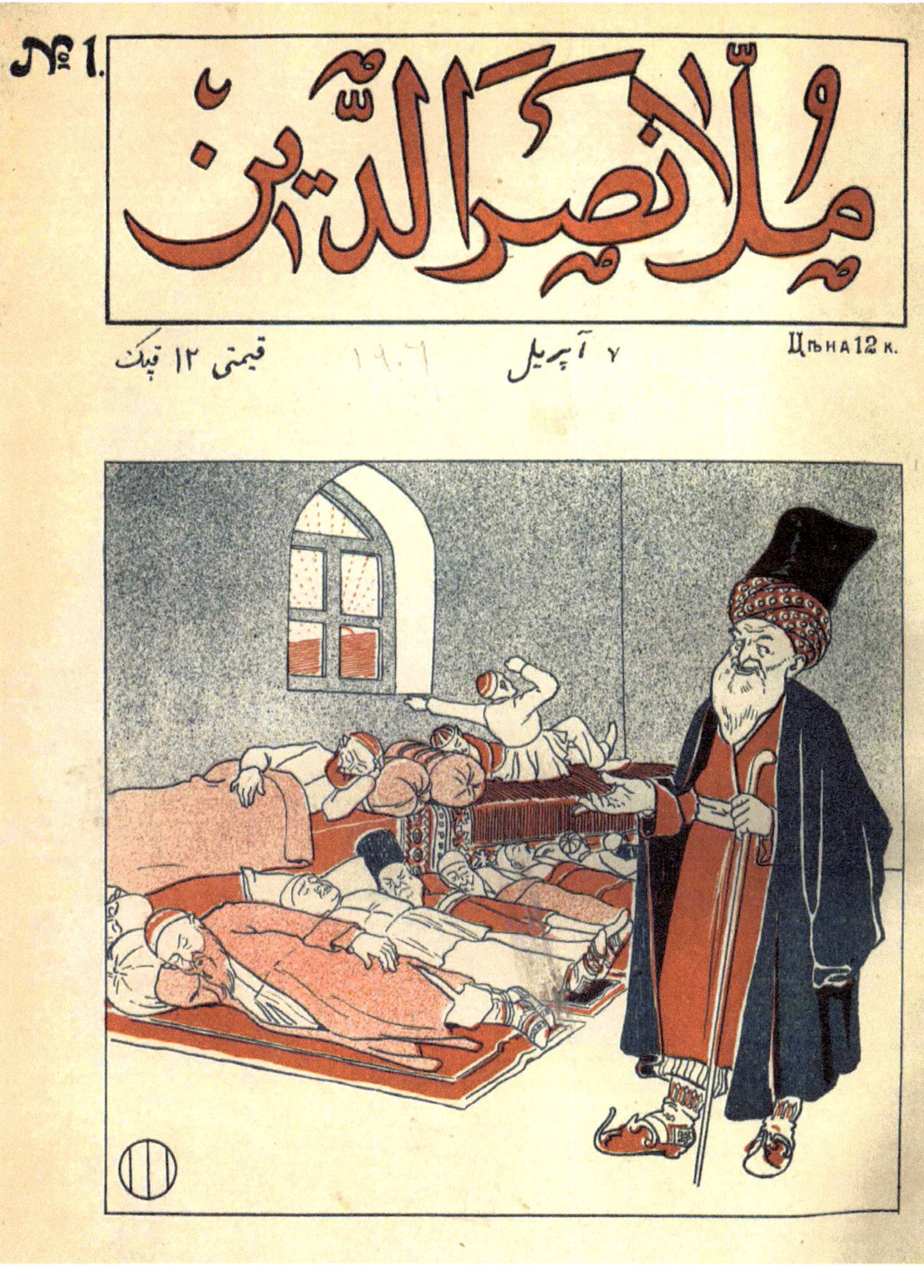

Figure 1.2 Front cover of the first issue of *Molla Nasraddin* (1906).

© Wikimedia Commons 2023

2021). Its short texts and ironic sketches and caricatures enjoyed popularity throughout the Russian Caucasia and Crimea but were attacked by conservative Muslim circles for the journal's overt critique of social, economic and cultural life in the Islamicate world – particularly of polygamy, early-age marriages and other phenomena. During this period, Russian Muslims reflected on reformism in the Ottoman empire (especially *Tanzimat*, 'constitutionalism') and boosted the ethnically delineated ideology of Pan-Turkism and Pan-Turanism, echoing the Pan-Slavist discourses in Russia and in the post-Ottoman Balkans. The Pan-Turanism of the Russian Muslims at the turn of the century embodied their intensive interaction with Hungarian Turanists represented by the prominent Orientalist Arminius Vambery (1832–1913) and the intellectual milieu around the Budapest-based journal *Turán*.

The satirical journal *Molla Nasraddin* (1906–31)

Zaur Gasimov

When discussing the history and textual influence of Islam in Eastern Europe, one is hard pressed to circumvent the allure of Islam's religious aspects. Majestic works such as M. Meša Selimović's *Death and the Dervish* (1966) offer an almost intuitive association between Eastern European Islamic literary traditions and a 'weighty seriousness' of sorts, wherein the region's Islam immediately translates into sombreness. Yet in fact, one could just as easily associate Eastern European Islam with notions of humour, witty sarcasm and a humourous sense of self-deprecation – the very essence of comedy, in fact. A keen example of this can be observed in the history of the first satirical journal in the Muslim world, *Molla Nasraddin* (1906–31).

Molla Nasraddin was set up at the margins of Europe, in the local centre of the Russian-ruled Caucasus, in the city of Tbilisi in 1906. Its founder was an Azeri journalist, writer of short stories and intellectual, Jalil Mammad Quluzade (1866–1932). Quluzade was originally from Nakhichevan, a historical landscape situated between the Ottoman and Persian empires, and he studied at the Teachers' Seminary in Gori in present-day Georgia. He cooperated closely with Omar Faiq Nemanzade (1872–1937), an Istanbul-educated Sunni Muslim from Western Georgia, and was able to acquire funding for the establishment of the journal from Nakhichevani tradesmen. Until its first closure by the Tsarist authorities in 1912, the periodical was based in Tbilisi – and Quluzade and other authors used it extensively to highlight issues as diverse as alleged regional backwardness, social and economic disaster throughout the entire Caucasus region, the poor working conditions of Iranian seasonal labourers, gender inequality, polygamy and paedophilia. The main focus of the journal's critique was the Islamic clergy: both Quluzade and the entire milieu of *Molla Nasraddin* indirectly blamed Muslim clerics for the asserted backwardness of the Caucasus, as well as of the neighbouring Ottoman empire and Persia. The periodical cooperated with the Tbilisi-based Russian painter of German descent, Otto Schmerling (1863–1938), who created impressive cartoons for *Molla Nasraddin* that gave an additional, very strong meaning to each article – making the paper's messages understandable even to illiterate Caucasians. The journal's language was the colloquial Azerbaijani spoken in Baku, and Quluzade was eager to take the fight to Azeri and Tatar intellectuals in the turn-of-the-century Russian empire who were eager to popularize Ottoman Turkish among Russia's heterogenic Turkophone community as a unique literary language and communication tool. The articles were relatively short; the language was very clear, partly radical and categorical. The readers of *Molla Nasraddin* lived not only in the Russian Caucasus but also in Crimea, in the Volga region and in Central Asia as well as outside of the Russian empire altogether – mostly in the northern part of Iran and in the Ottoman lands. Accordingly, the journal's authors covered not only political processes unfolding in the Caucasus but also news from the Ottoman and Persian empires. During the constitutionalist movement in Persia, in particular, *Molla Nasraddin* fully supported the reformism and even overtly articulated the necessity of similar reforms in the Russian empire. Along with its blatant critique of the Islamic clergy, both Shia and Sunni, in the Caucasus, the paper also attacked European imperialism – repeatedly mocking high-ranking German and French officers serving in the headquarters of the Ottoman Army, or European politicians trying to divide Iran into zones of control.

During the First World War, the journal was, on several occasions, closed down and reopened – and finally moved from Tbilisi to Karabakh. During the short-lived independence of the Caucasian republics (the North Caucasus, Georgia, Armenia and Azerbaijan), Quluzade and his *Molla Nasraddin* resettled in Tabriz and continued to publish. In April 1920, the Azerbaijani Democratic Republic was invaded by the Red Army and a Soviet Socialist Republic of Azerbaijan was founded on its ruins. The Azerbaijani communist leadership invited Quluzade to return and to settle in Baku. The new regime needed a strong and experienced, secularist publication organ, and *Molla Nasraddin* finally moved to Soviet Baku in 1922. There, the journal was instrumentalized by the ill-famed atheist movement, popularizing the ideas of aggressive atheism and persecution of the clergy. *Molla Nasraddin* became an important tool of the local Communist Party for its anti-Islamic propaganda, and existed until it was renamed *Allahsiz* ('Godless') in 1931 and finally closed down in 1933. In 1932, Quluzade died in Baku.

The satirical *Molla Nasraddin* thus existed for twenty-five years with short breaks. It was published first in Arabo-Persian and then, after the reform of Azerbaijani and the other Turkic languages in the Soviet Union, in the Latin script. It was avidly followed in Ottoman Turkey and particularly in Persia, and had an impact on the establishment of satirical journalism not only in the Russian Caucasus and Central Asia but also in Iran and Turkey.

Similar developments took place among Muslims in the post-Ottoman Balkans. In 1878, the Austro-Hungarian Monarchy occupied Bosnia and installed colonial control over it. By expanding southwards, Vienna and Budapest obtained control over numerous Slavic- as well as Turkish- and Albanian-speaking Muslim communities. Many Sunni Boshniaks, similarly to the Albanians, were adherents of Bektashi and other congregations and lodges (*tekke*) that interacted throughout the entire Balkans and the Middle East in a way that transcended boundaries. Indeed, Albanian Bektashis maintained active contacts with Egypt and the Levant. The Austro-Hungarian authorities created Muslim clerical institutions in order to diminish the influence of the Ottoman Sultan, who still acted as Caliph of all Muslims. Perceiving the reformist movement in late Ottoman Istanbul – for example, the writings of the Ottoman intellectual Ahmet Mithat Effendi (1844–1912) – and the publishing activities of Russian

Muslims, Bosnian Muslims set up their own newspapers like *Behar* ('Blossom', 1900–11), *Boshniak* ('Bosnian', 1891–1910) and several others both in their own Slavic vernacular language as well as in Ottoman-Turkish.

At the start of the 20th century, numerous Bosnian and Tatar clerics, journalists and intellectuals read humanities and technical sciences in Austria-Hungary, France and Germany, took up contacts with other parts of the former Ottoman lands, and studied at the famous al-Azhar University in Cairo. European universities as well as the educational institutions in Istanbul, the prestigious French-speaking Galatasaray Lyceum and the Istanbul University (*dar-ul-fünun*), became important spaces of interaction between East European Muslim students and Muslim intellectuals from the Ottoman empire and Persia.

The ruptures of 20th-century nationalism

The period 1917–18 was crucial for Europe in general, and for Eastern Europe in particular: thanks to the Russian Revolution (1917) and the endgame of the First World War, three empires (Russian, Austro-Hungarian and Ottoman) – all three with sizeable Muslim populations within their borders – were dismembered, or at least were torn apart by internal warfare. In 1918, Poland, Lithuania, Georgia, Armenia and Azerbaijan – as well as the northern Caucasus Republic of Gortsy ('Mountaineers'), Crimea and Ukraine – were proclaimed independent states atop the post-imperial ruins. For the community of Polish-Lithuanian Tatars, this state-building was a severe challenge: during the Polish partitions (1772–1918), all Tatar settlements had been in one administrative territory under Russian control. Before and during the Polish partitions, the Polish-Lithuanian Tatars could preserve their Muslim faith but became culturally and linguistically assimilated to Polishness in the 16th century. By 1918, the Tatars had become divided and had obtained citizenship of Poland (residents of Bialystok), Lithuania (Vilnius) or Soviet Belarus (Minsk). In 1919, Polish troops annexed Vilnius and it became the centre of the Polish Tatar community's cultural and cleric life during the interwar period. Well-educated, secularist and multilingual, many Polish Tatars arrived as specialists to assist the state-building in Crimea in 1918 and, after the collapse of the state independence of Crimea, in Azerbaijan. The high-ranking military commander Maciej Sulejman Sulkiewicz (1865–1920) and dozens of others played significant roles in army-building in Azerbaijan from 1918 to 1920. The brothers Leon and Olgierd Kryczyński embodied both the Polish-Tatar transfer of knowledge to Crimea and the Caucasus and Tatar and Muslim intellectual activity generally in interwar Poland. During the Polish-Soviet war (1919–21), Tatar military units sided with the Polish Army in their struggle against Soviet troops. In the 1930s, Petersburg-educated lawyer Leon Kryczyński (1887–1939) created the Tatar Folk Museum in Vilnius, and set up and published *Rocznik Tatarski* ('Tatar Yearbook', 1932–8). Polish Tatars assisted the political emigrant from the northern Caucasus, Vassan-Girey Dzhabagi (1882–1961), who established the journal *Przegląd Islamski* ('Islamic Overviews', 1930–7; see the front cover, Figure 1.3, below) in 1930 in Warsaw. Many

Figure 1.3 Front cover of *Przegląd Islamski* (1937) with a portrait of Leon Krzyczyński.

© Wikimedia Commons 2023

Polish Tatars, including the brothers Kryczyński, contributed to this Islam-related periodical.[1]

In 1920, the Bolsheviks reconquered formerly Tsarist Caucasia: the North Caucasian Republic, Crimea, Azerbaijan and Armenia became Soviet. In an attempt to export the proletarian revolution to the Middle East, Moscow organized the Muslim Congress in Soviet Baku in the autumn of 1920. At the same time, the communist parties both of Iran and of Turkey were established in the Azerbaijani capital. Moscow backed the Turkish national movement under the leadership of Mustafa Kemal Atatürk, who was able to oust the Entente troops, proclaim the Republic of Turkey in October 1923, and negotiate the Lausanne Treaty with the Western powers. In Moscow, the Communist University of Toilers from the East (*Kommunisticheskii Universitet Trudiashchikhsia Vostoka*, KUTV) was set up to train Communist cadres for the aforementioned countries, offering scholar-ships for hundreds of Arabs, Turks and Persians. In the early 1920s, the Soviet authorities supported the translation of Karl Marx's and Vladimir Lenin's theoretical books on communism and related topics into Arabic, Turkish and other languages widely spoken in the Islamicate world. Local Muslim intellectuals and Russian orientalists acted as signif-icant intermediaries within this knowledge-and-ideology transfer of European and Russian communism into the Middle East. Tatar communist Mirsaid Sultan-Galiev (1892–1940) and Azeri communists Nariman Narimanov (1870–1925) and Samed Agamali-ogly (1867–1930) were promoted to important positions within the party hierarchy in the same period. While Sultan-Galiev and Narimanov were invited to Moscow, Agamali-ogly stayed in the 'Red Mecca', Baku, and acted as the most arduous promoter of the Latinization of the Turkic and Iranian languages spoken by Soviet Muslims during the First Turkological Congress in Baku in 1926.

In 1924, the Caliphate was officially abolished and Turkey proclaimed secularism. In the Soviet Union, which preached so-called scientific atheism, members of the Muslim clergy were persecuted along with Christian and Jewish clerics. Numerous mosques in Crimea, throughout the Caucasus, in Belarus and Ukraine, in Kazan and Ufa were closed, repurposed or destroyed in the late 1920s – and particularly during the Stalinist purges in the following decade. Throughout the 1920s, several national branches of the so-called 'Union of Belligerent Atheists' (*Soiuz voinstvuiushchikh bezbozhnikov*) were set up in Tatarstan, Azerbaijan and other parts of the USSR. These institutions organized propagan-da-related and anti-religious and anti-clerical activity in factories, universities and schools. Accused of espionage and nationalism, numerous Tatar, Azeri and Turkestani Communist activists, intellectuals and Orientalists fell victims of Stalinist repression from 1937–8 onwards. The aforementioned high-ranking Tatar communist activist Sultan-Galiev, who also taught at the KUTV, was arrested in the mid-1920s and executed in 1940 in Moscow.

After the dismemberment of the Austro-Hungarian empire, the Kingdom of Serbs, Croats and Slovenes obtained vast territories populated with numerous Muslim commu-nities; Bosnia and Kosovo became parts of the Yugoslav state. The local Muslim community consisted mostly of Sunnis as well as of adherents of traditional lodges of Bektashi who were, linguistically, a very heterogeneous group of Slavic, Albanian and Turkish speakers. The Yugoslav authorities appropriated and partly reformed the Austro-Hungarian practices of Muslim clerical institutionalization by setting up different administrative bodies in Belgrade, in Sarajevo and other places. In 1925, the political party Islamic League for the Defence of Justice (*Islam Muhafaza-i Hukuk Cemiyeti*), which had been established in 1919, was banned. At the same time, the Yugoslav authorities prohibited the activities of traditional lodges (*tekke*) and appointed Bosnian imams to the communities in the predominantly Albanian and Turkish settlements in Kosovo and Macedonia. By integrating Bosnian, Albanian and Turkish Muslims into the Yugoslav state, Belgrade supported the linguistic assimilation of non-Slavic Muslims and encouraged their emigration to Albania and Turkey. According to the convention of 1938 that Yugoslavia arranged with Ankara and Tirana, close to 200,000 ethnic Turks and Albanians were forced to emigrate to neighbouring Albania and Turkey.

The Greek and Bulgarian authorities, in pursuit of their post-Ottoman state-building efforts, tolerated the hostile attitude of nationalist segments of the local society towards Ottoman architecture, including mosques and Muslim cemeteries. Tens of thousands of Sunni Muslims, both Turkic and non-Turkic speakers (Bosniaks, Goranis and Cherkessians, among others) migrated to the Ottoman empire in the 19th century, while Christians from Eastern Anatolia, mostly Armenians, migrated to the Russian-controlled Caucasus throughout the 19th century. In the 1920s, Greece and Turkey arranged the reciprocal repatriation of Orthodox Greeks and Muslims. It is worth mentioning that, like almost everywhere in the Balkans, and throughout the entirety of Eastern Europe, ethnicity did not always overlap with confession: while the majority of Kosovo Albanians were Sunni Muslims, 30 per cent of Albanians in Albania were Catholic or Orthodox Christians; the Gorani community in the Gora region of Kosovo and Macedonia was Muslim but spoke a Slavic language that differed from both the Bosnian and Pomak tongues, the latter a dialect of Bulgarian spoken by Bulgarian Muslims mostly in the area of Rhodope. The Russian authorities backed the emigration of Muslims from their borderlands, too; the Bolshevik conquest of the Caucasus in 1920 caused a new wave of emigration, mostly towards Turkey and partly to Iran.

The Second World War

The outbreak of the Second World War heavily impacted on the lives of Muslim communities in the Soviet Union – particularly in Crimea and the North Caucasus. Accusing entire communities of collaboration with the Third Reich, espionage, sabotage and betrayal, in 1944 Moscow initiated the mass deportation of Crimean Tatars, Chechens and Ingush to Central Asia and Siberia in freight trains under inhuman conditions: tens of thousands died during the deportation or shortly afterwards. Also in 1944, tens of thousands of Meskheti Turks, Muslim Armenians (*amshens*) and Muslim Kurds were deported from the southern region of Soviet Georgia to Central Asia. While Chechens and Ingush were allowed to return to Chechnya in the late 1950s, Crimean Tatars and Meskheti Turks struggled for the right to return to Crimea until Soviet premier Mikhail Gorbachev's programme of *perestroika* in the late 1980s. The 'internal' deportations of Muslims within the Soviet Union continued even after the Second World War: in the late 1940s, tens of thousands of Shia Muslims – mostly Azeris and Kurds – were forced to leave Soviet Armenia in the direction of Azerbaijan.

In September 1939, two weeks after the German assault against Poland, Soviet troops invaded the country from the east. After the outbreak of the German-Soviet war in June 1941, the Baltic regions, Ukraine and Belarus, as well as the territory of today's Moldova, became frontline and battlefield terrain. The entire area of settlement of the Polish-Lithuanian Tatars had thus far been under Soviet control, but mosques and prayer houses built in the late Tsarist period were heavily damaged or burnt down due to warfare as well as Soviet occupation policy. Most Polish-Lithuanian Tatars displayed solidarity with Poland and joined the Polish underground army, *Armija Krajowa*, that opposed both Soviet and Nazi occupiers. Many Polish-Tatar activists emigrated to the United Kingdom and joined the Polish government in exile there. In 1941, when the Soviet Union was attacked by Nazi Germany, Poland was no longer perceived by Moscow as an adversary but as an Allied Nation. Hundreds of thousands of Polish citizens had been imprisoned in the Soviet camps in Siberia since 1939; in 1941, those who had survived were allowed to join the Polish Army of General Anders stationed in the Middle East. In 1942, more than 200,000 Polish citizens were evacuated from Siberia by train across Soviet Central Asia and the Caspian Sea to Iran, which had been under British-Soviet occupation since 1941. While men joined the Army of Anders and were sent to the front, Polish refugees – mostly women, elderly persons, and, particularly, orphaned children – were settled in the camps in Tehran and Isfahan, and stayed in Iran until 1945, interacting with Iranian society on multidimensional levels. The book written in 1988 by Polish exile author Irena Stankiewicz (born 1925) and titled *Isfahan – miasto polskich dzieci* ('Isfahan – a city of Polish children') chronicles an interesting encounter of Polish refugees with the Middle East, Islamicate society in general and with Iran in particular. In 1945, some of these Poles resettled to communist Poland; a larger part, however, headed to Lebanon and then to London.

After the end of the Second World War, the Soviet Union became one of the world's two superpowers. Lithuania became Soviet and the eastern provinces of Poland were integrated into Soviet Ukraine and Belarus. The Polish-Lithuanian Tatars' encounter with Soviet communism had already begun in 1944–5 when the Soviet Army started a large-scale counter-offensive on the entire Western front. In the same period, Moscow still occupied the northern part of Iran and launched territorial claims against Turkey with regard to the Anatolian borderland with the Soviet Caucasus. In 1946, however, the only nuclear power at that time, the United States, was able to force Moscow to leave Iran, withdrawing its troops and thousands of military experts and translators. Numerous members of the Iranian Communist Party, mostly of Azeri and Kurdish background, were evacuated to Moscow, Baku and Dushanbe. Anti-Turkish rhetoric in Soviet diplomacy and public opinion resulted in Turkey's active participation on the Western side in the war in Korea (1950–3) and prompted Ankara to join NATO in 1952.

During the Second World War, hundreds of thousands of Soviet soldiers became prisoners of war (PoWs) on the Western front. The German military authorities, with the help of German Turkologists and Tatar and Caucasian political emigrants, made contact with those Soviet PoWs of non-Russian background. A large body of these PoWs started to collaborate with the Nazis, and were recruited into nationally organized divisions. In the early 1940s, several Tatar, Azeri and North Caucasian military units (among them, the Kaukasisch-Mohammedanische Legion) were set up along with Georgian, Armenian and other equivalents. These units were subordinated to the German military and were used both against Soviet troops and to oppress anti-German resistance in Eastern Europe. In order to gain more sympathy, the Nazi authorities permitted Muslim religious rituals to be performed in the ranks. The Soviet authorities flirted with the religious and, particularly, nationalist aspirations of Soviet Muslims in 1941–5 as well. On the one hand, the activities of the atheist movement were slowed down and partly even banned; on the other, Moscow was ready for more concessions in the field of nationalization of academic infrastructure in the non-Russian peripheries. During the Second World War, the Azerbaijani National Academy of Sciences was set up in Baku and thousands of Azeris were sent as semi-colonialists and party activists to Soviet-controlled parts of Iran. After the end of the conflict in May 1945 and the division of defeated Germany into zones, Soviet Muslim collaborators of the Wehrmacht tried to flee into the Western security zones – to emigrate to Italy and, particularly, to Turkey. Most of them stayed in Germany, however; some joined the Radio Free Europe station set up in Munich.

Hundreds of thousands of Soviet Muslims from across the entire USSR combatted German troops on the western frontline – meeting their deaths on the battlefields of Belarus, Ukraine or Czechoslovakia – and even joined the anti-German partisan movement in Yugoslavia. Soviet Central Asia became the settlement place for millions of deported Crimean Tatars, Chechens and Poles as well as hosting numerous Russian industry units, factories, and research and academic institutions that had been rapidly evacuated from the western parts of the country. The pressure on the civilian population in the Soviet Union during the war and the accompanying mobilization of mass production brought extreme hardship particularly for Muslim women, who were torn between the traditional, male-dominated frameworks of private/family life and Soviet-enforced working discipline under inhuman conditions in Baku's oil refineries or the factories of Kazan and Ufa.

Postwar

Romanian communist authorities, particularly the secret service Securitate, persecuted Tatar Muslim clergy in the 1950s, while communist Poland remained relatively tolerant towards its small Polish-speaking Muslim minority. In Bulgaria, under the leadership of Todor Zhivkov, the Turkish minority was faced with multidimensional assimilationist pressures, reaching their peak in 1989: hundreds of thousands of Bulgarian Turks decided to move to the Republic of Turkey and were settled in Thrace, in Istanbul's neighbour-hoods and in Bursa. Despite its announced solidarity of the working class and blatant critique of nationalism, the socialist leadership in Yugoslavia as well as the Soviet ruling elites contributed to a radical change and shift in the lives of local Muslim communities. While Kosovo Albanians became a 'double minority' in the Christian- and Slavic-dominated society of Yugoslavia, the Soviet authorities backed the linguistic and cultural russification of non-Russian nationalities. Contrary to the situation of the non-Russian Christian communities of Ukrainians, Latvians and Georgians, the languages of the mostly Turkic-, Iranian- and Caucasian-speaking Muslims were Latinized in the mid-1920s and, finally, Cyrillized in the 1930s. The Arabic-Persian script used for centuries was abandoned and the books written in it mostly expropriated from public libraries and even from personal possession. It is worth mentioning that the double alphabet changes (from Arabo-Persian script to Latin, then from Latin to Cyrillic) along with the persecution of Muslim clergy and closure of mosques damaged cultural ties between Soviet Muslims and the wider Islamicate world. The political self-isolation of Albania under the leadership of Enver Hoxha had a similar impact on Albanian Muslims, whose interconnection with the outside world was heavily restricted. The encouraged and forced emigration of Muslims from Yugoslavia, Bulgaria and Greece – and the mass deportations of Muslims from Crimea, the North Caucasus and the Soviet-Georgian borderland Samtskhe-Javakheti – changed the local demographic situation, diminishing Muslims' physical and cultural presence in those spaces.

The demolition of mosques during the communists' most ardent atheist policies in the early 1920s and the neglectful treatment of the Islamicate legacy throughout the Soviet Union chimed with Yugoslav, Bulgarian and Greek treatment of Ottoman architecture, wells and other cultural sites as well as local Muslim shrines. The development of relations between the Middle East and the countries of the socialist Bloc during the Cold War, particularly the rapprochement between the USSR and the Arab world, went hand in hand with a general liberalization in the post-Stalinist Soviet Union and in Yugoslavia after the latter politically drifted away from Moscow. While Bosnian students could once again obtain a theological education at Cairo-based al-Azhar University, some Soviet Muslims could make pilgrimage to Mekka and Medina. The interaction of these Muslims with the wider Islamicate world was highly bureaucratized and conducted seemingly under the surveillance of the security services, but it was possible. Arab countries, Turkey and Iran maintained embassies in the capitals of Eastern European countries and consulates even in some Soviet republics. From the 1950s onwards, tens of thousands of Syrian, Libyan, Iraqi and Lebanese students studied at the universities of Prague, Budapest, Łódź, Moscow, Kyiv and Bucharest. The Soviet authorities, particularly in the Caucasus, became more tolerant with regard to Muslim practices and rituals. Many Tatars, Azeris and other Soviet Muslims were sent as specialists to the countries of the Middle East and Africa in the framework of Soviet humanitarian aid and assistance. All these dimensions of interaction between Muslims in Eastern Europe and those from other countries within and outside of the bloc boosted knowledge, culture transfers and experience exchange. The Soviet invasion of Afghanistan and the ensuing war between 1979 and 1989 challenged these Soviet Muslim communities immensely by nourishing confessional solidarity towards the Afghan people and by forging an antipathy towards Soviet ideology.

The rapid modernization and industrialization in the Soviet Union after the Second World War eased and accelerated mobility between urban and rural areas and between republics. Soviet citizens of Muslim background from the Caucasus and Central Asia moved to the Baltics, Ukraine, Belarus and Soviet Russian cities. Numbers of interethnic and interreligious marriages grew rapidly, and in the 1970s–80s multi-ethnic Muslim communities appeared in most Ukrainian, Belarusian and Russian cities. The religious section of these 'newcomer' communities used private flats and houses for their rituals.

During *perestroika* (1985/6–91) in the Soviet Union, Muslims across the country underwent a certain religious awakening and the number of new mosques grew rapidly. However, it was neither Muslims nor Islam that 'exploded' the Soviet Union from within – contrary to the predictions of international Russia experts like the French historians Alexandre Bennigsen, delineated in his co-authored publication, and Hélène Carrère d'Encausse, who described this process in her seminal *L'Empire éclaté*.[2] Independence activists in the predominantly Muslim-populated Soviet republics like Azerbaijan or Chechnya were attentive but rather passive observers of political processes in the western republics of the Soviet Union. Ethnicity trumped religious identity among the members of the predominantly secularist Popular Front movement in Azerbaijan, which was formed in the late 1980s as a reaction to the outbreak of the Armenian-Azerbaijani conflict over the region of Nagorno Karabakh in February 1988 and the arrival of Azeri and Kurdish IDPs in Baku. The Azerbaijani Popular Front organized rallies in Baku in 1989, showing solidarity with Bulgarian Turks expelled from the country. Such support actions embodied ethnic solidarity of Azeris with linguistically kin Turks rather than any Pan-Islamic amity.

In 1991, the Soviet Union disintegrated, and all three South Caucasian republics proclaimed the restoration of their independence. Land-locked Tatarstan and Chechnya articulated distinct breakaway tendencies, and claimed far-reaching political autonomy and even independence from Moscow. In the early 1990s, however, post-Soviet Azerbaijan and post-socialist Albania were the two Muslim-majority states to register on Europe's political map. Chechen efforts to establish an independent state were frozen, while Tatar aspirations were dismissed. At the same time, Moscow tolerated Kazan's and, particularly, Grozny's search for religious identity – which involved establishing direct contacts with the outside world, building mosques and setting up Islamic Studies courses at the local universities. After the fall of socialism, Muslims in the former Yugoslavia, Albania and the ex-Soviet republics forged relations with the broader Islamicate world, opening up new vistas for different schools of thought as well as for both political Islam and extremist Islamism. The post-socialist transformation both in Yugoslavia and in the Russian North Caucasian republics of Chechnya and Dagestan was accompanied by ethnic clashes, a strong search for religious identity, and conflict.

In former Yugoslavia, these interethnic conflicts grew into overt warfare. Regular armies and paramilitary groups of Serbs and other nationalities combatted each other, and Belgrade tried to preserve the Serb-dominated state by force. While the war against Croatia and Slovenia was relatively short-term, the involvement of the Serbian Army and military units under the command of Serbian generals in Bosnia-Herzegovina (BiH) grew into a lasting and bloody conflict that clearly mirrored religious animosities and hatreds. The genocidal mass killing of more than 8,000 Bosnian Muslims by Serbian paramilitary troops in 1995 in the town of Srebrenica tragically marked both the post-socialist transition in the territory of the former Yugoslavia and the fiasco of the Dutch-led UN peacekeeping mission there.

Despite heavy international criticism of such massacres of Bosnian Muslims, the Muslim community was denied an autonomous entity within the new Bosnia-Herzegovina.

The amendments to the Dayton Treaty set up the multiconfessional entity of BiH and assigned international control over it; however, a post-Yugoslav state entity with a predominantly Muslim population was not established.

In 1991–2, the Russian Federation was challenged by the Chechen quest for national independence and, after severe military failures on the ground, the leadership in Moscow had to accept broader autonomy for the Chechens. During the first presidency of Vladimir Putin, however, Moscow decided to take back political and military control over the breakaway republic and invaded it militarily. Using terrorist attacks in Russian cities allegedly perpetrated by Chechen activists, Moscow initiated the Second Chechen War; partly expelled the territory's leadership into exile, partly persecuted them abroad; and appointed a new pro-Kremlin ruler, Ramzan Kadyrov. Tens of thousands of Chechen refugees left Russian-controlled Chechnya for Poland, the Scandinavian countries, Germany and France. The Second Chechen War resulted in stronger ties between the new pro-Kremlin Chechen authorities and Moscow. The severe political control established over Chechnya, and Russia's military victory, resulted in greater tolerance in Moscow towards Kadyrov's totalitarian rule in the entity as well as towards Islamic revival in the war-torn republic. In 2008, Kadyrov officially opened, in the presence of Vladimir Putin, one of Russia's largest mosques: the Ahmad Kadyrov Mosque in the centre of Chechnya's capital, Grozny. The building was named after Kadyrov's late father, and echoed Ottoman mosque architecture in general and that of the Blue Mosque (Sultan Ahmed Mosque) in Istanbul in particular.

To a large extent due to the warfare of the 1990s, Bosnia and Chechnya became two important centres of intensive interaction and the mobility of radical Sunni Islamists between Eastern Europe and the countries of the Middle East as well as Western Europe. The radicalization of political Islamism in that period boosted the popularity of extreme

forms of Wahhabism in those areas. Hundreds of international *mujahidin* from Afghanistan and Arab countries took part in battles in Bosnia and Chechnya, and forged contacts with local paramilitary organizations and Islamist milieus. In the 2000s, numerous Bosnians and Chechens joined the ranks of extreme Islamists across the Middle East. The wars in the 1990s and these interactions in the following years had an immense impact on Bosnian and Chechen Islam: national and folk features of Islamic rituals were overshadowed by purist aspirations and a willingness to 'return to the beginnings'.

Islam and Muslims in Eastern Europe look back on a millennium-old history. In the present-day region between the Baltic, Black and Caspian seas, broad-based Muslim communities live in Bosnia; Albania; Kosovo; Macedonia; Georgia; Azerbaijan; and, particularly, in Turkey and Russia. The initial interaction with the Islamicate world and the penetration of the Islamic faith, accompanied by the arrival of the first Muslim settlers, took place via the Grand Duchy of Muscowy and Kievan Rus. Tatars settled even in the Polish-Lithuanian Commonwealth and were used as mercenaries in the struggle of the Polish crown against predominantly Orthodox Muscowy. First challenged and then conquered by Mongol tribes under the leadership of the Chingizids, the East Slavic proto-states became spaces of intensive interaction between Sunni Muslims and Orthodox Christians and of their initial co-existence within one state. While East Slavs lived in the framework of various dependencies (with)in the Mongol empire, in the 14th–15th centuries, the Grand Duchy of Muscowy regained independence and captured post-Chingizid Muslim khanates. Leaving aside the issue of dominance, this experience introduced the continuity of co-existence and mutual social and cultural impacts. This process of active interaction between East Slavs and Islam was paralleled by Ottoman penetration into Anatolia, and then into the Balkans and South-eastern Europe, opening up the empire's 'second direction'. In the 17th–19th centuries, the Ottoman and Russian empires were mighty rivals in the region, combatting each other in the Black Sea region and in the Caucasus. Ottoman-ruled Thrace and Anatolia became important destinations for the mass emigration of Sunni Muslims from a Russian empire that annexed Crimea (1783) and the Caucasus (1801–28). At the turn of the 19th century, the Muslims of both empires were densely entangled, boosting the circulation of knowledge, Islamic practices, and nationalist and modernist views as well as ideologies like Pan-Turkism and Pan-Turanism. The linguistic Turkic-ness of the majority of Eastern European Muslims played an important role in easing communication between Baku and Istanbul, Kazan and Pazarcik.

Notes

1 Anna Cieslik and Maykel Verkuyten, 'National, Ethnic and Religious Identities: Hybridity and the Case of the Polish Tatars'. *National Identities* 8 (2006) 2, pp 77–93.
2 Alexandre Bennigsen and Marie Broxup, *The Islamic Threat to the Soviet State* (London: Routledge ,1990); Hélène Carrère d'Encausse, *L'Empire éclaté. La Révolte des nations en URSS* (Paris: Flammarion, 1978).

Further reading

Bustanov, Alfrid K. and Michael Kemper. 'Russia's Islam and Orthodoxy beyond the Institutions: Languages of Conversion, Competition and Convergence'. *Islam and Christian-Muslim Relations* 28 (2017) 2, pp. 129–39.
Clayer, Nathalie and Eric Germain (eds). *Islam in Inter-War Europe* (London: Hurst Publishing, 2008).
Gasimov, Zaur and Wiebke Bachmann. 'Transnational Life in Multicultural Space: Azerbaijani and Tatar Discourses in Interwar Europe'. In *Muslims in Interwar Europe. A Transcultural Historical Perspective*, edited by Bekim Agai, Umar Ryad and Mehdi Sajid (Leiden: Brill, 2016), pp. 205–24.
Hajdarpasic, Edin. 'Out of the Ruins of the Ottoman Empire: Reflections on the Ottoman Legacy in South-Eastern Europe'. *Middle Eastern Studies* 44 (2008) 5, pp. 715–34.
Kemper, Michael. 'Imperial Russia as Dar al-Islam? Nineteenth-Century Debates on Ijtihad and Taqlid among the Volga Tatars'. *Encounters* 6 (2015), pp. 95–124.

Recent Dynamics: Natural Resources, Environmental Policies and Climate Change

Benjamin Beuerle

2

Introduction

Among the challenges faced by humankind in the late 20th century and through the 21st, arguably no topic is more daunting and global in nature than climate change. Because of its global scope, climate change is among the core topics that link Eastern European societies with other parts of the world – and that in turn compel them to negotiate and find their position in the global community. This has been especially true for the late-era Soviet Union and post-Soviet Russia. Due to the sheer size of their territories and their richness in natural resources, *nolens volens* both have been – and should be seen as being – central actors with regard to climate change and to any chance of keeping it to a level bearable for future generations. The present chapter examines the Soviet Union's and Russia's complex relationship with the topic of climate change. For most of the time since the climate rose to the top of the global agenda, Russia has been out of the spotlight of attention. There are certain reasons for this, but the lack of attention is nevertheless unwarranted. Though diminished in size since the break-up of the Soviet Union in 1991, Russia remains by far the largest country on earth by territory. It stretches across a variety of climatic zones, and developments in this vast expanse inevitably affect the global climate.

In this sense, this chapter presents a specific aspect of globality within the present textbook, an aspect that is hardly mentioned in others, namely a global role – here played and to be played by the Soviet Union and Russia – conferred by sheer size and environmental conditions. Since the Second World War, the opportunity to satisfy a substantial share of European and Asian-Pacific countries' steadily rising demand for fossil fuel-derived energy, together with consequential decisions made by politicians and businessmen, has contributed greatly to Russian transnational and transregional interactions, entanglements and infrastructures as well as to the country's geopolitical leverage. This underlines the fact that like their counterparts elsewhere, Eastern European – in this case Soviet and Russian – actors operate and interact globally within a context that is co-defined by natural conditions. At the same time, changing natural conditions and the reaction of the global community to them inevitably affect Russia's international connections, its own socio-economic model and its future. The Soviet Union and Russia have themselves been part of transnational negotiations on dealing with climate change, and contemporary Russia continues to look for a seminal position in this regard.

This chapter will argue that it is impossible to understand Russia's complex relationship with climate change without taking into consideration its socio-economic structure and, above all, its richness in and dependence on hydrocarbons. This explains why fossil resources, their pivotal role in the Soviet and Russian past and present, and their impact on international relations are the focus of the first part of this contribution. This sets the stage for the second part, which takes a closer look at Soviet and Russian positions on climate change, and particularly at the Soviet Union's and Russia's role in international climate diplomacy. The third and last part deals with the most dramatic effects of climate change within Russia and their global repercussions. Due to Russia's very substantial areas of permafrost and forest, large parts of the country are seeing ever more palpable consequences of climate change, and this has started not only to affect how Russians perceive climate change but also to have an impact on the global climate.

As will become clear, the phenomenon of climate change and Russia's natural and socio-economic conditions link the country's fate and future closely with those of the whole world, for better or worse. In that sense, Russia is not merely a globally connected country; it is also a globally decisive area.

Underground: Fossil resources

Fossil resources have been the backbone of contemporary societies for some considerable time. Since the late 18th century, the energy stored at high densities in coal, oil and gas, and then set free via combustion has been combined with appropriate technologies and has driven economic growth and large-scale technological innovation to levels previously unseen in human history.

The Soviet Union and Russia have always been rich in fossil resources and have been among the leading producers – and reserve holders – for the most significant ones for decades. In recent years, Russia has swapped first and second place with Saudi Arabia on the list of the world's largest oil producers, and is currently second in known coal reserves and third in coal exports worldwide. Today, Russia holds by far the largest natural gas reserves in the world and ranks second in gas production (cf. Figure 2.1, below).

Taken as a whole, Russia's fossil resources have been far more than a simple source of energy or export commodity. They have been the backbone of the Soviet Union's and Russia's wealth and financial resources, and a powerful foreign policy instrument – from the oil contracts with Japan on Sakhalin in the 1920s, via the gas pipelines laid to Western Europe starting in the 1970s through to the gas wars with Ukraine and the new pipelines to China and other Asian-Pacific countries. The demise of the Soviet Union has been linked to falling oil prices in the 1980s; the rise of Putin and his popularity during his first decade in power were closely connected with the nationalization of major oil and gas companies and with rising oil prices. Several authors have analysed Russia's 'Petrostate' (Goldman 2008) and its 'hydrocarbon culture' (Tynkkynen 2019). The significance of these terms will become clear in the course of this section which will present a sketch of the history and significance of fossil resources in Russia and the Soviet Union, outlining how they became the cornerstone of the Russian economy, increased Moscow's geopolitical leverage, and instigated transregional and transnational connections and interdependencies of various sorts – infrastructural, commercial and human. At the end of the section, the potential for renewable energies, a different kind of natural resource, is touched upon.

Figure 2.1 Russia: Natural resources.

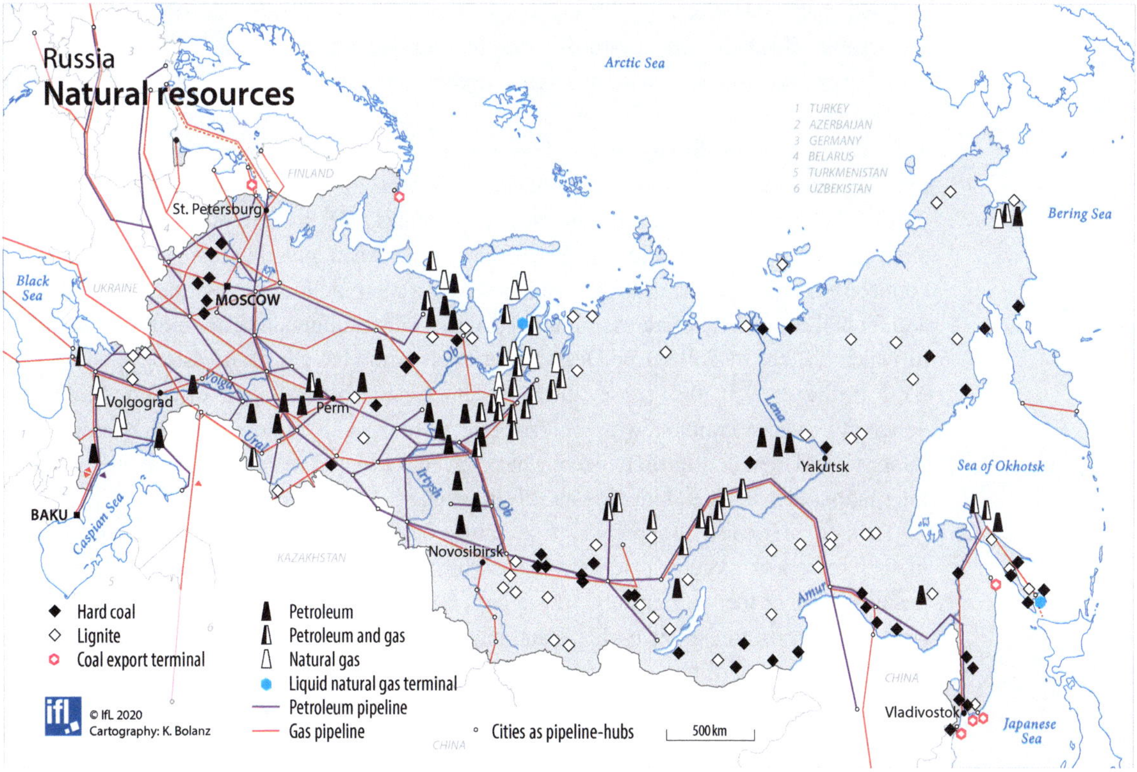

Fossil fuels: Cornerstone of domestic economy and initiator of transnational connections

Coal played a vital role in the industrialization of late tsarist Russia and the Soviet Union, with production rising steadily from the 1860s onwards. Traditionally, the Donbass region in eastern Ukraine was by far the most important mining area, but during the Soviet era numerous new fields were opened up. Most were in Siberia, but there were also operations on Svalbard, or Spitzbergen, in Norway, where the Soviet Union established several mines that are in Russian possession even today.[1] For a long time, the Soviet Union's rising energy demands made it a net importer of coal, but since 1991 Russian coal exports to European and to Asian-Pacific countries have been on the rise.

As in Europe, the Soviet Union saw a growth in the use of natural gas beginning in the 1940s. As in the case of coal, the biggest Soviet reserves of natural gas to be exploited initially were situated in Ukraine (though in this case in the western part of the republic). Plans for the Soviet Union to supply natural gas to Western Europe started to be discussed in the mid-1960s, in the middle of the Cold War. The combination of ever-growing demand in Western Europe and the discovery of large natural gas fields in western Siberia some years earlier led to a coalition of interests that spanned the Iron Curtain. When Willy Brandt and Leonid Brezhnev signed the ground-breaking Moscow Treaty in 1970, natural gas was a key component. In the following years, the foundations were laid for an extensive pipeline network stretching from Siberia to Western Europe, which has been expanded ever since and has been described by Thane Gustafson as "'The Bridge'.[2] Beyond instigating remarkable channels for day-to-day communication across the East–West divide and bringing in much-needed hard foreign currency, the gas business with Western Europe brought western (notably German and Austrian) construction and engineering equipment and technology to the Soviet Union. This was crucial not only for building the transnational pipeline network itself but also for connecting the western Siberian gas fields to the western parts of the communist empire. Oil and gas pipelines, and the intermediate actors responsible for the fossil fuel trade on both sides, have been pivotal to Soviet and Russian connections with Western Europe ever since. Building pipelines creates path-dependencies and mutual dependencies across political divides, constituting a transnational infrastructure in which billions of dollars (or Deutschmarks or euros) have been invested, thus incentivizing further use. In this sense, these pipelines have become part of a trans-European geography whose creation was the result of political conjunctures and mutual business interests, and their continued existence has proved a stronger factor in decision making than international tensions and ideological discrepancies.

The story of Russian oil exports stretches further back. In fact, the first drilling worldwide in the modern sense took place in 1846 near Baku, which had been acquired by the Russian empire at the beginning of the 19th century. The region became the cradle of the world's oil industry, attracting massive foreign investments and interest in the following decades. By the turn of the century, on the back of fast-growing global demand from a burgeoning automobile industry and other consumers, the Russian empire had become the world's biggest oil producer and was responsible for around one third of global output. This commanding position was lost within a quarter of a century, however, due to a lack of investment in plant modernization, on the one hand, and to the destructive turmoil of the First World War, revolution and the Civil War, on the other. Indeed, in its first years, the Soviet Union had to import oil for even its most basic needs, and it was only after 1923 that the by-then-nationalized Soviet oil industry returned to some semblance of normal production, and outputs began to increase again. Oil started to become a geopolitical tool shortly afterwards: in 1925, the Japanese agreed to (re)cede the northern part of Sakhalin, which they had occupied during the Civil War, to the Soviet Union – but they did so only in return for oil extraction concessions on the whole island (an agreement that would remain binding until the end of the Second World War). Soviet oil deliveries to Germany were an important component in the Soviet–German 'non-aggression' pact of 1939, and one of the chief aims of Operation Barbarossa was to capture the main Soviet oil fields, still centred on Baku and the Caucasus in general.[3]

In the decades after the war, new reserves were discovered and extraction began first in the Volga region and in the Urals, and later – from the 1960s onwards – in western Siberia; taken together, these brought a major increase in Soviet oil production. This had a considerable impact on the global oil price and was one of the main factors behind the founding of OPEC in 1960, which brought together major oil-exporting countries but excluded the Soviet Union. In the following decades, the USSR grew increasingly dependent on revenues from oil and gas exports. This was not a problem as long as the oil price went up, as was the case from 1973 until the end of the 1970s. Beginning in the 1960s, the gas price on the international market was directly linked to the oil price, meaning that fluctuations in the latter always affected both. Between June 1973 and May 1980, the price of a barrel of crude oil on the world market increased almost sixfold, from 21 US dollars to more than 125 US dollars.[4] Against that background, the Soviet Union could afford to expand consumer and welfare spending, and to import more and more agricultural and consumer goods while still investing in its mining and drilling industries and ramping up defence spending. This became a problem in the 1980s when oil prices fell – and especially so beginning in 1986 when they slumped, remaining under 50 US dollars per barrel for more than a decade with the short-lived exception of the First Gulf War in 1990. The Soviet Union had become heavily dependent on imports but could no longer finance them, and fell into economic stagnation and crisis. The causes of the collapse of the 'Red Empire' in 1991 are manifold, but the economic crisis that was related to low oil prices and high dependency on oil and gas exports was most certainly one of them.

In 1998, the Russian economic crisis reached its apogee with the devaluation of the ruble and a default on government debt – coinciding with the lowest oil price on the world market since 1973, at around 20 US dollars per barrel. From 1999 until the financial crisis in 2008, the oil price rose constantly, reaching more than 160 US dollars just before the crash. Over the same decade, Russia's GDP grew on average by about 7 per cent a year and GDP per capita more than doubled; this doubtlessly contributed to the popularity of Vladimir Putin, who became first prime minister and then president just when the economic upturn started (1999/2000). Putin renationalized large parts of the oil and gas industry – the oil-and-gas provider Yukos being the most prominent example – and put trusted persons in charge of them. The energy corporation Gazprom, for instance, has been headed since 2001 by Alexey Miller, who had already worked for Putin in St Petersburg in the 1990s. The same is true for Igor Sechin, the head of integrated-energy company Rosneft, who had followed

Putin to Moscow when the latter entered the presidential administration under Boris Yeltsin. Under Putin, who is known to be very well informed about the fossil fuel sector, investment in exploration, export facilities, and in crucial pipeline infrastructure, including in several European countries, has increased significantly.

In 2012, fossil resources accounted for more than 70 per cent of Russia's exports and for over 50 per cent of state revenue. Since then, these figures have varied from year to year, with the overall trend being modestly downward. Indeed, a declared goal of Russian governments for a number of years has been to reduce the Russian economy's dependency on fossil resources. However, both practical steps undertaken on the ground and other declarations by senior officials have run counter to this goal. Over the last two decades, the Russian leadership and state-owned companies – Gazprom most prominent among them – have expanded export capacity in various ways and continue to do so. The Nord Stream 1 and the highly controversial Nord Stream 2 pipelines have been built with the goal of delivering more gas to Germany and Western Europe by circumventing Ukraine. Blue Stream and Turk Stream were constructed to increase gas exports to Turkey and South-east Europe. LNG terminals have been constructed on the Yamal Peninsula and on Sakhalin to supply liquefied natural gas to Asian-Pacific and European countries. In December 2019, a first gas pipeline to China was inaugurated by Putin and Chinese president Xi Jinping. Its construction, via what was regarded largely as a deal overwhelmingly favourable to China, had been negotiated by the two leaders in 2014 in the wake of the imposition of Western sanctions against Russia. The clear Russian goal here is 'diversification', not away from fossil fuels but towards reducing Russia's dependency on European export markets. Building these infrastructures creates new geographical connections and interrelations, while others – notably the decades-old pipelines passing through Ukraine – are weakened.

The expansion of export facilities for fossil fuels has not only concerned natural gas. Starting in the second half of the 2010s, several ports in the Russian Far East have been enlarged to ship coal from the Kutznetsk Basin (or Kuzbas) in western Siberia and other coalfields to Asian-Pacific countries like China, Japan and South Korea. This has entailed significant environmental damage to Far Eastern ports like Nakhodka, where coal dust thrown up during the handling process has polluted the air to a point that has provoked protests – and this issue of airborne particulate matter has even been raised in the State Duma and by the president at various times. In addition, there are obvious problems with regard to the goals of the Paris Agreement on climate change. However, Russia has been trying to position itself as the main competitor to Australia and Indonesia with regards to coal exports within the Asia-Pacific region, and from the perspective of the Russian leadership this has obviously outweighed any potential environmental considerations.

Clinging to hydrocarbons vs. potentials for renewables

None of the above has contributed to diversifying Russia's economy. The long-standing Russian leadership has also made it abundantly clear that it is not ready to envision a future without fossil energy use. In 2019, Putin not only attacked renewable energies for being detrimental to nature but stated publicly that decarbonizing energy production would send humanity back to the Stone Age. While he called American shale gas exploration 'barbaric', he has shown no understanding whatsoever for any environmentalist turn against natural gas, branding it as clean.

Indeed, Russia is among the countries with the lowest shares of renewable energies in the national energy balance. This assessment does not take into account large-scale hydropower, which has played an important role in Russia since Soviet times, but which also has a number of negative side-effects on the regional environment. Overall, renewable energies (excluding large hydropower), though on the rise in recent years, still accounted for considerably less than 1 per cent of Russia's power generation in 2019. For background, in 2009 the government defined a goal of 4.5 per cent to be achieved by 2020. In 2013, the goal was postponed to 2024, but as of 2020 Russia was not on track to achieve this either. Meanwhile, it has been all but forgotten that the Soviet Union ran a large renewable energy development programme. Beginning in 1981, more than two hundred institutions throughout the Soviet Union coordinated efforts in researching and developing methods for producing electricity and heat from solar, wind, geothermal and biomass energy. As in Western countries around that time, the installed capacity remained relatively low and was limited mostly to test facilities. It is clear, however, that the potential for installing renewable energy in the Russian Federation is immense. The country's territorial expanse, with its different climatic conditions, lends itself to the installation of wind power and solar power facilities that could not only meet domestic energy needs but could be exported in various forms to energy-hungry countries both in the Asia-Pacific region and in Europe. Whether this potential is taken up will depend largely on changes being made to the energy strategy currently pursued by the Russian leadership, but also on signals from the demand side on the part of European and Asian countries.

The huge importance of fossil resources to Russia is an essential part of the explanation as to why Russia has had an uneasy relationship with the international climate change regime.

In the air: Climate change

The relationship between Eastern Europe, and more specifically the Soviet Union and Russia, and climate change has been an ambivalent one. As will be explained in this section, the very prominent role played by the Soviet Union in early international climate change research and diplomacy was followed by the incomparably more subdued role played by post-Soviet Russia. At the same time, Russian positioning on the matter has not been unequivocal; in fact, it has been subject to various changes and internal debates and, as will be argued, cannot be understood without taking into account the importance of fossil fuels as explained in the first part of this chapter. However, in part as a result of developments explained in the third part (below), as of late, change is under way.

Soviet scientists like Mikhail Budyko were among the first to discover the effects of anthropogenic (i.e. caused by human beings) greenhouse gases (GHGs) on the world's climate.[5] The Soviet Union was indisputably at the forefront of global climate science and was second only to the United States in nascent climate diplomacy from the 1970s until 1991. After 1972, Soviet scientists met annually with their American counterparts for intense exchanges on climate change within the framework of 'Working Group 8' set up under the Soviet–American environmental treaty and co-headed by Budyko until 1991. Soviet scientists were also prominently involved in the work of the International Institute for Applied System Analysis (IIASA), founded in 1972 near Vienna, in which they closely discussed topics like global climate change and its possible/probable anthropogenic origins with colleagues from the United States, Japan, West Germany and several other Western (and Eastern) countries, enhancing research and thought on the topic both internationally and at home.

In 1986, the Soviet Union hosted two international events at which climate change and its causes and consequences were discussed. The first was a five-day WMO-UNEP symposium on 'Climate and Human Health', the second the 7th session of the Brundtland Commission on sustainable development. At the latter gathering, the Soviet climatologist K. Y. Kondratiev, while more cautious than Norwegian prime minister Gro Harlem Brundtland herself about the probability of anthropogenic factors as leading causes of climate change, underlined the fundamental importance of investigating this possible causal link and suggested a global monitoring system in order to facilitate joint research on this question. In 1988, the Soviet Union's importance to and engagement in international efforts on climate change was also underscored by the fact that a Soviet representative was nominated to chair one of the three working groups of the newly founded Intergovernmental Panel on Climate Change (IPCC – the UN's main expert body on climate change) – namely, 'Working Group II', dealing with the potential socio-economic impacts of climate change. The role was taken by the prominent Soviet climatologist Yuri Izraėl', head of the Soviet hydrometeorological agency (*Goskomgidromet*).[6]

This is not to say that the Soviet Union's relationship with early international climate diplomacy was untroubled. Internal documents reveal some uneasiness about a growing politicization of climate change that was seen as a 'Western' agenda in the first place. This uneasiness was also rooted in language – with English as a working language in the IPCC and other bodies – and methodological issues – with modelling associated with Western science used as a tool for researching climate change. Due to a lack of investment, Soviet scientists simply did not have the supercomputers they would have needed to be able to keep up with their Western counterparts in climate modelling. They relied heavily instead on a paleo-analogic method that predicted climatic changes based on analogues in the past. For a number of years, the approach raised interest in the international scientific community, but towards the end of the 1980s it was increasingly seen as less reliable than the ever-advancing computer modelling.[7] Internal documents also testify to growing difficulties experienced by the Soviet Union in meeting international funding obligations, both in terms of sending participants to international meetings and in terms of paying contributions to participating international organizations. Despite all this, however, the late-era Soviet Union continued to play a very prominent role in practically all international climate change-related events, second only to the United States. This was in line with the USSR's status as a superpower and its role as one of the biggest GHG emitters worldwide.

In fact, an IPCC report from May 1990 expected that the Soviet Union's GDP would more than triple between 1985 and 2025, while its CO2 emissions (one fifth of global emissions in 1990) were forecast to almost double in the same period and to approach those of the United States by 2025. Taken together with its position as a superpower, these figures seemed to guarantee that the Soviet Union would be the second most important player in international climate diplomacy for decades to come. After 1991, much of this changed dramatically. In some sense, post-Soviet Russia has been consistently underrepresented in the international climate change regime – at first numerically and personally, then by its relatively passive and reactive role in climate negotiations. Clearly, some of the explanation lies in the very diminished power and international standing of the new Russia in comparison with the Soviet Union. The Russian Federation was no longer a superpower, and it seems obvious that this contributed to a reduction in attention to what Russian scientists had to say on the international scene, on the one hand, and to a reduction in ambition among leading Russian figures to play a principal role in developing international efforts to tackle climate change, on the other. However, as will be elaborated below, these international factors are not by themselves sufficient to explain the diminished role played by post-Soviet Russia in climate diplomacy. The Rio Conference in 1992, which had been prepared with Soviet participation and where the signing of the United Nations Framework Convention on Climate Change (UNFCCC) brought into being the international climate change regime, was symptomatic. More than a hundred heads of state were present – but Boris Yeltsin was missing. The US delegation numbered 200 – the Russian contingent comprised eleven people. During the first Conferences of the Parties (COPs) held under the UNFCCC framework, the Russian delegation's stance vacillated between passivity and obstruction to any ambitious commitments. Russia was in the middle of a painful transition to market liberalism, and environmental problems that had been a focus of attention in the last years of the Soviet Union were relegated to secondary concerns on the agenda of most Russian decision makers.

It was only after the turn of the millennium that Russia (suddenly) reacquired a central role: when the United States under its new president, George W. Bush, refused to join the Kyoto Protocol, the treaty's coming into force depended on its ratification by Russia. There were controversial debates within Russia, with the presidential adviser Yuri Izraèl', who had played a prominent role in Soviet climatology at home and on the international scene since the 1970s, maintaining that Kyoto would hinder Russia's development perspectives, while some influential business circles argued the contrary. In the end, Russia ratified the Protocol in 2004 after some hard negotiating. It gained not only the EU's support for Russia's commercially advantageous accession to the World Trade Organization (WTO) in return, but also very modest emission reduction targets for Russia that could be achieved without any substantial effort. In addition came the possibility of attracting foreign money via the Join Implementation and the Clean Development mechanisms, both of which enabled foreign actors to invest in (cheaper) Russian emissions-reduction projects instead of reducing GHG emissions at home. This could be seen as a very good deal for Russia. However, it can be argued that by very openly giving economic interests priority over environmental concerns, Russia missed an opportunity to increase its soft power by showing leadership in a field that affects an increasing number of people around the world.

In 2009 and 2010, the new president, Dmitry Medvedev, signalled on several occasions a readiness to take on a more ambitious position and role regarding climate change. More concretely, he signed the first 'Climate Doctrine' of the Russian Federation in 2009 – pointing out the necessity of taking action to mitigate climate change, and his willingness to do so. During the Copenhagen climate conference (COP15) in the same year, Medvedev underlined Russia's readiness to take the lead in reducing emissions and to help poorer countries to move towards the common aim of protecting the world's climate. However, any optimism stirred by these signals was soon damped by a lack of substantial Russian steps in this direction and, in 2011, the Russian government announced that Russia would exit the Kyoto Protocol in 2012, along with Japan and Canada.

At the historic Paris Climate Summit (COP21) in December 2015, Putin surprised the world by stressing publicly that climate change was among the biggest challenges for mankind, that Russia was among the world's leaders in GHG reduction, and that his country was ready to take the initiative in increasing international efforts in researching this and other related environmental problems. However, again what seemed to be signals of a readiness to take a much more active role in international climate change mitigation efforts were soon contradicted by the Russian president himself stipulating that it was unclear if climate change was anthropogenic at all and that it in fact opened up significant opportunities in the Arctic – for example, by rendering the Northern Sea Route navigable and fossil resources there thus accessible. To summarize, since the break-up of the Soviet Union, Russia has been largely underrepresented in the international climate change regime, first numerically and then when it shied away from taking the recognizably lead role that might be expected of the largest country on earth which still has great power ambitions. Short periods of an apparent change of tone in this regard have been frustrated by inaction and seeming inconsistency.

The reasons for this outcome are manifold and range from the structural to the personal. In the economically difficult 1990s, not only was Russia shorn of its former superpower status and the accompanying incentive, emanating from the Cold War, to keep up with the United States in scientific matters affecting the whole world but budgetary constraints made it difficult to send large delegations abroad as well. At the same time, social and economic considerations relegated any environmental concerns to secondary importance. In fact, it was the fossil fuel sector that kept Russia more or less afloat in the 1990s, a circumstance that was put at risk by calls for climate change mitigation. Up to the present, it could be argued that there is a certain logic in Russian decision makers' reticence to engage fully in international efforts to slow climate change, a hesitation rooted notably in Russia's richness in fossil resources and the dependence of its state budget and the wider economy on revenues from fossil fuel exports. However, this logic does not mean that the role and position taken by Russian decision makers with regards to international climate change negotiations has been without challenge. There have been voices within the wider Russian leadership who, from the late 2000s onwards, have argued that closer and more consistent engagement in the international fight against climate change would be beneficial for Russia generally and for its environment and economy more specifically, rendering it more energy-efficient and competitive and underlining its status as a 'responsible country'. It appears that before 2019 they rarely had the upper hand. In the end, such matters come down to the political choices of decision makers.

These choices can be traced back to four basic assumptions. First, by considerably reducing its GHG emissions in the wake of the collapse of the Soviet Union, Russia has done already more than enough to protect the world's climate. Indeed, by setting 1990 as a reference year, the international community has de facto recognized part of this claim. Adopted in 1992 at the Rio Conference, having 1990 as the base year means that all emission reduction aims since then have been pronounced in comparison. For example, the Kyoto Protocol stipulated a zero increase in Russian GHG emissions by 2012 in comparison with 1990, but in reality Russia's GHG emissions reached no more than 70 per cent of the 1990 level, even without any significant mitigation efforts. In other words, the adoption of 1990 as a base year meant that Russia had little incentive to step up mitigation efforts. Secondly, unlike many other countries, Russia stands to profit from climate change rather than be damaged by it, as, given its relatively cold climate, rising temperatures might enhance the opportunities for agriculture in the country, for example. Thirdly, it has not been 100-per-cent proven that climate change is anthropogenic. And finally, the decarbonization of Russia's economy (let alone the world's) would be economically and fiscally devastating for Russia.

Today, some of these assumptions are no longer tenable. In particular, the suggestion that Russia could profit from climate change has been increasingly questioned inside the country. In 2019, President Putin stressed on several occasions that Russia was among the countries hardest hit by climate change (cf. his former optimistic speculation cited in the following section), and in autumn of that year, Russia ratified the Paris Agreement. However, at the same time Putin has made it clear that he still does not accept the anthropogenic causes of climate change and that renewable energy sources are anathema to him, postulating that societal welfare and civilization are inconceivable without hydrocarbon energy. This attitude can in turn be explained by the importance of hydrocarbon resources for Russia and for Putin's regime (see the previous section).

There is, of course, another important factor which must be addressed here, which concerns the mood among the Russian population with regard to climate change. For most of the time, pressure from below for action on climate change has been practically absent in Russia. While important and at times influential environmental movements existed not just in the final years of the Soviet Union – sparked by the Chernobyl disaster and palpable problems with air pollution among other things – but also in post-Soviet Russia, they have been largely concerned with environmental problems at a local and regional level – such as pollution caused by industries and waste disposal, or excessive de-forestation and poaching. All are of relevance to climate change, of course, but the focus has been more on their regional impact on health and the environment. Global climate change has not been a matter of major concern for the majority of people engaged in Russian environmentalism, and polls consistently show Russia to be one of the countries where climate change scepticism is most pronounced. This is for the most part not about the factuality of climate change being doubted, but a scepticism as to its reasons and its consequences. Many Russians doubt that climate change is anthropogenic, that Russia has played a major role in it, or that it has had or will have negative consequences for Russia's inhabitants – or else they harbour all three reservations. Consequently, a survey by the French market research firm Ipsos in 2019 revealed that just 7 per cent of Russian respondents ranked climate change among the three most urgent ecological problems. This compared with 26 per cent in China and Saudi Arabia and considerably higher percentages in Western countries such as the United States and Germany.[8] Like all polls, these figures must be treated with caution and are transient snapshots. Nonetheless, the trend is in line with other polls mentioned above. The reasons behind these attitudes are not plain, but it is clear from several studies that since the beginning of the 21st century

- climate change has been underreported by Russian newspapers and mass media compared with its coverage in Western media;

- Russian state-controlled television has more than once broadcast documentaries and statements arguing that the concern about climate change and international calls for engagement in climate change mitigation were part of a Western plot to further its economy and to outstrip the Russian one;

- leading Russian politicians – including the long-term president – have articulated all three doubts mentioned above on various occasions;

- a considerable fragment of the Russian scientific community has been much more cautious than its Western counterparts about supporting conclusions regarding the anthropogenic nature of climate change and its largely negative consequences.

While the last finding has been ascribed partly to Soviet scientific traditions and to a certain scepticism regarding the modelling methods on which Western climate science has been mostly based, it has also been noted that most of the Russian scientists who are still pronounced climate change sceptics are not themselves climatologists, even though their status as natural scientists gives them a certain credibility among the wider public.[9] Climate scepticism, as disseminated through the mass media or directly by leading politicians and other important figures in Russian society, has been explained by researchers like Veli-Pekka Tynkkynen as a consequence of Russia's 'hydrocarbon culture', with influential figures related to the fossil fuel industry actively engaging in the propagation of climate change scepticism in various forms.

It should, however, be noted that media coverage of climate change within Russia has not been (entirely) one-sided. There have been several periods, such as the phase when Russia ratified the Kyoto Protocol in 2004–5 or the first years of Medvedev's presidency in 2008–10, when climate change was reported by many outlets without sceptical undertones.[10] Russian media have also reported regularly on actions such as the Earth Hour organized by the WWF which calls for all lights to be switched off for one hour as a sign of international commitment to the fight to protect the earth's climate. Even more importantly, some significant changes have occurred lately in the inner-Russian discourse on climate change in several respects. To begin with, Fridays for Future Russia came into existence. Launched early in 2019 by the young Moscow-based musician Arshak Makichyan, within a couple of months the movement had spread to many cities throughout Russia. More often than not, the demonstrations have so far involved no more than a couple of activists gathering in public on a weekly basis to demand action on climate change. However, they have received wide media coverage abroad and in some Russian outlets. The movement is one of many signs that Russia is not an island but is in fact very much operating in a media context where international developments such as the global climate movement, with its preliminary climax in 2019, are keenly observed and reverberate widely.

In fact, developments between 2019 and 2021 have signalled a real change in the attitude of important Russian decision makers as well as the place that climate change occupies on the political agenda and in inner-Russian discussions. To name just some important developments, after long hesitation, in October 2019 Russia ratified the Paris Agreement, thereby committing itself to act towards limiting climate change to 1.5–2 °C in comparison with pre-industrial times. Then, in 2020, the Russian government adopted a hydrogen strategy, making clear its ambition to become an important player in this field and referring explicitly to the global decarbonization trend. The same year, Putin signed a decree ordering a reduction in GHG emissions in Russia with, a year later, an accompanying law coming into force. Also in 2021, in the run-up to the Glasgow climate summit, Putin for the first time spoke of Russia aiming for climate neutrality and announced that this would be achieved by 2060 – on par with China. Already in 2020, the Pacific Island of Sakhalin had been put forward by regional and national authorities as a pilot region for various climate policies, including a cap-and-trade system for GHG emissions and the ambitious goal of achieving climate neutrality as early as 2025. A related federal law was debated in 2021 and came into being early in 2022. It is important to note that there are caveats to all of these developments. The year 2020 also saw the passing of a new coal strategy for the period until 2035, stipulating a huge increase in coal extraction and exports – hardly compatible with the goals of the Paris Agreement. The 2060 goal for achieving climate neutrality can hardly be seen as ambitious, and thus is but a first step. And Sakhalin's 2025 goal presumes, via somewhat dubious accounting, that 90 per cent of GHGs have already been offset by the existence of large forests on the island. Nevertheless, all these developments signal a real and serious change: after a long period of hesitation and doubt, the importance of climate change and its mitigation had finally arrived consistently on the agenda of Russian decision makers as well as the Russian public and businesses, before Russia's invasion into Ukraine started. Throughout 2020 and 2021, this importance and the accompanying debates continued to grow in prominence within Russia.

These changes can also be seen as at least an indirect consequence of the dynamic of the international climate movement, which reached a preliminary apogee with the worldwide climate strikes in September 2019. One of the most widely discussed topics in Russia in 2020–1 has concerned the Carbon Border Adjustment Mechanism that the EU plans to introduce as part of its Green New Deal, which could hurt Russia's export industries if the country doesn't adapt to the new realities. At the same time, the new-found importance of climate change in Russian policies is also attributable to the fact that the dramatic effects of climate change have indeed started to be felt within the country on a scale that is now difficult to ignore.

On the surface: Forest and ice

Large parts of Russia are covered by forest and ice, and both have not only played an important role in Russian history but are also of global significance. The country's boreal forests are the largest wooded region in the world, bigger even than the Brazilian Amazon rainforests (cf. Figure 2.2, below).

Figure 2.2 Russia: Forest coverage.

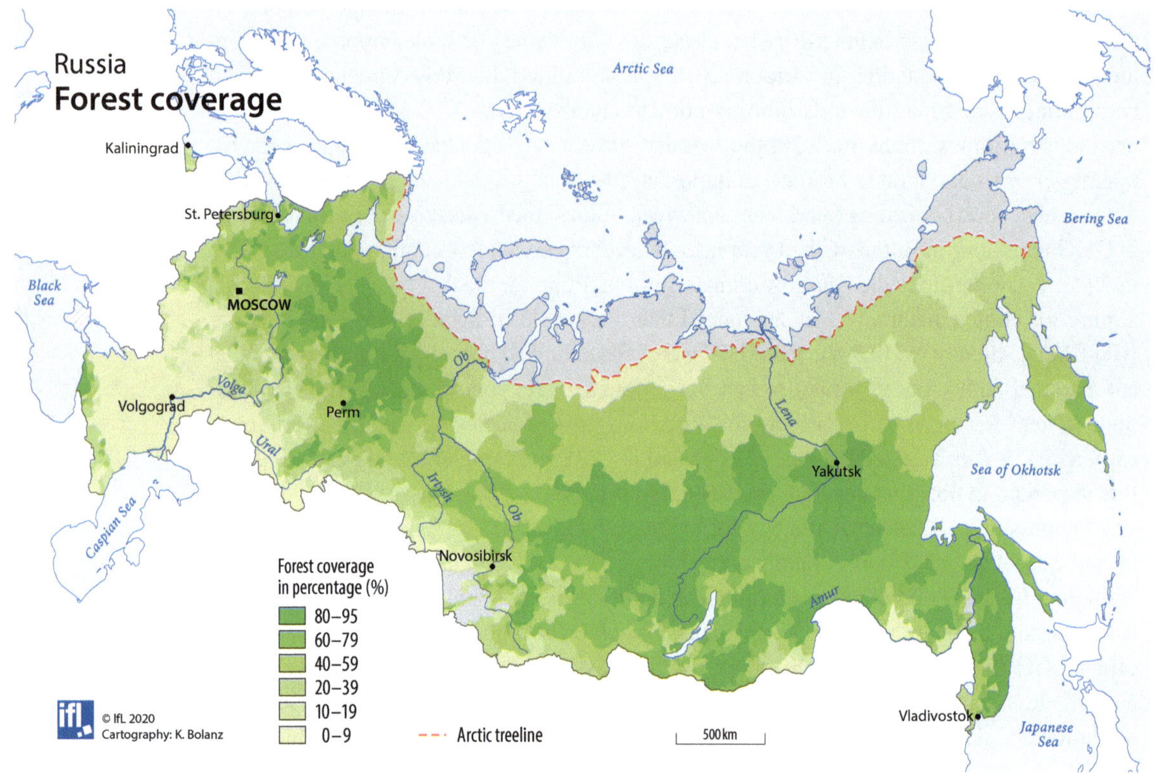

Nonetheless, deforestation was already being debated as a problem in the State Duma before 1917. Russia's relationship with cold and ice has formed the topic of whole conferences. Until recently, almost two thirds of Russia's landmass was covered by permafrost, making it the largest such area on Earth (cf. Map 3, below).

In fact, Russia's vast forests and expansive permafrost zone combine with its abundance of hydrocarbon reserves to link its fortune to climate change and to solutions to this challenge on a global level. Bearing in mind that since the turn of the millennium climate change has been proceeding more than twice as fast in Russia than the world average (cf. Figure 2.4, below) five points must be mentioned here: the melting of permafrost, wildfires, floods, possible agricultural benefits, and the navigability of the Northern Sea Route.

(a) Russia's permafrost has started to melt because of climate change releasing large amounts of methane – which is much more potent as a GHG than CO2. This risks creating a vicious circle with disastrous implications for the global climate. The warmer it gets the more methane is freed from the ground beneath the permafrost and the more climate change is accelerated. In addition, the thawing process itself is a direct hazard to buildings and infrastructure (pipelines, roads, railways) that have been built on permafrost, which is one of the main reasons that climate change has started to be perceived within Russia as a real threat.

Figure 2.3 Permafrost in the northern hemisphere.

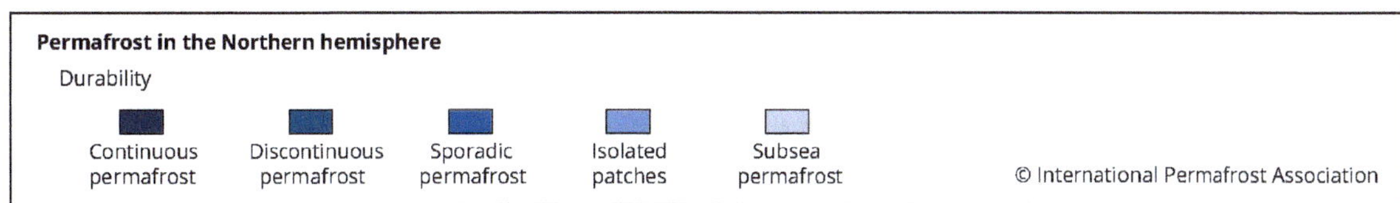

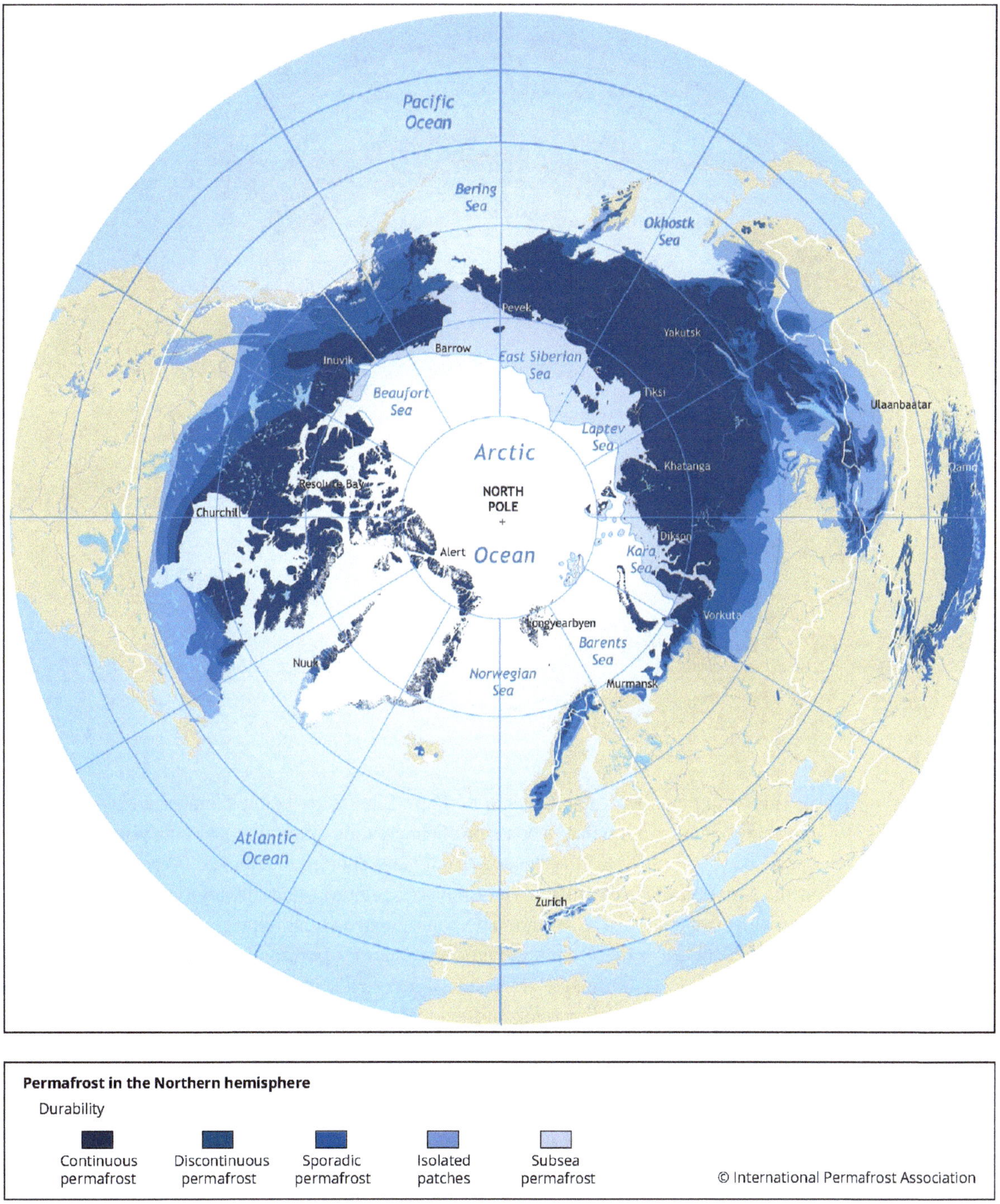

Source: European Environment Agency, The Arctic Environment. European Perspectives on a Changing Arctic (EEA Report 7), Copenhagen 2017, p. 42.

Figure 2.4 Changes of land surface temperatures.
© NASA Earth Observatory 2023

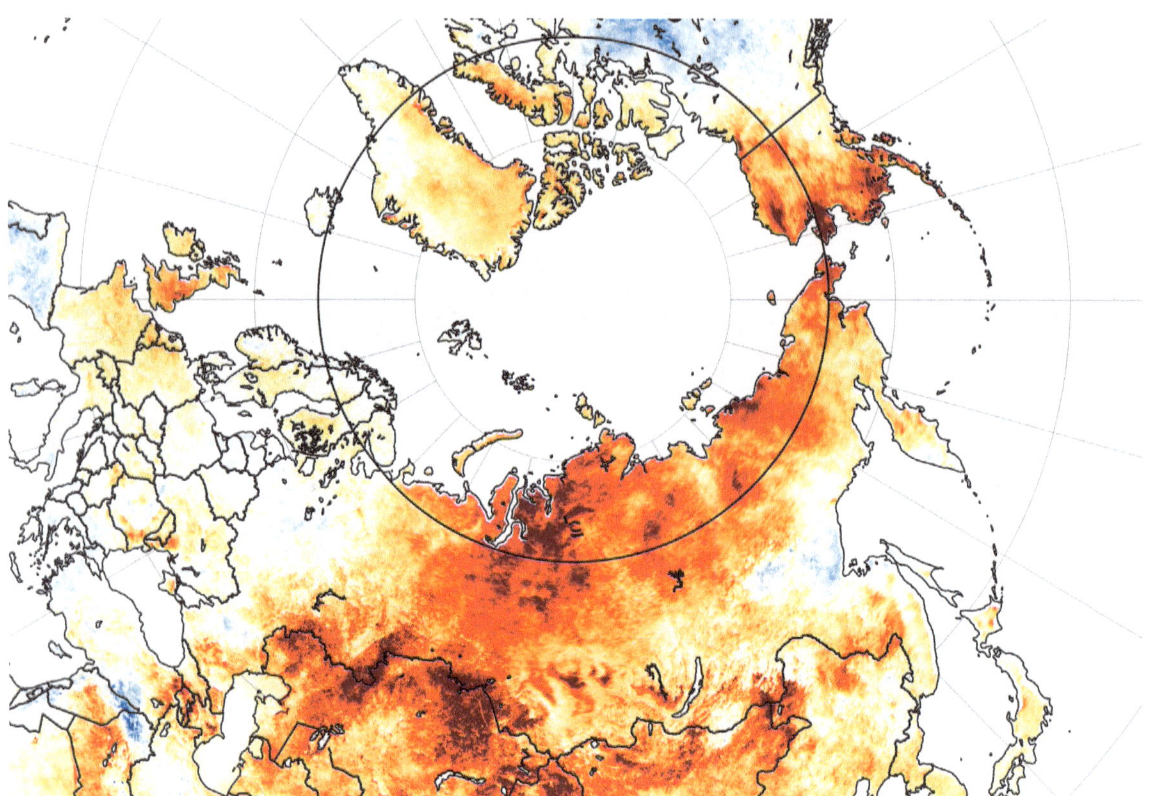

A growing number of buildings in northern Siberia are being damaged by the increasing instability of the ground that they are built on, creating cracks in them with potentially grave consequences for users. As early as 2016, it was reported that almost 60 per cent of houses in the Siberian town of Norilsk (Krasnoyarsk region) were already deformed because of melting permafrost. The most dramatic consequence so far appears to have occurred on 29 May 2020, when a diesel storage tank at a thermal power plant near Norilsk collapsed, releasing some 21,000 tonnes of oil into the region's soil and waters and resulting in the destruction of substantial amounts of the local ecosystem. It was a catastrophe on the same scale as the *Exxon Valdez* disaster in 1989 (37,000 tonnes of oil spilled) and the second biggest oil spill recorded in Russian history. Various experts, the prosecutor's office, and the owner of the diesel storage facility, Norilsk Nickel, all cited subsidence in the ground caused by thawing permafrost as a major reason for the tragedy.[11] While the findings were later denied by a Russian government agency, they were reconfirmed by other experts, and the mere possibility of such a causality is a reminder of the grave danger that climate change poses for Russia's expansive permafrost regions, their ecosystems and their inhabitants – not to mention the vast economic costs resulting from such disasters or the growing damage to numerous buildings, roads, railways and pipelines.

Chukotka: A resource-rich region in the Russian Arctic

Jessica Graybill

Allow me to sketch a portrait of a resource-rich region in the Russian Arctic. Chukotka, in the far north-eastern corner of Russia, is roughly the size of Texas and is the second-least-populated and the least densely populated region in Russia. According to the 1989 Soviet census, ~160,000 people lived in Chukotka; ~50,000 remain today. Chukotka has experienced post-Soviet political, economic and social transformations alongside increasing globalization, requiring the re-imagination of places and economies. Two thirds of the population outmigrated; the remaining post-Soviet and Indigenous populations cope with continued socio-economic and environmental change thousands of kilometres from Moscow.

Enter an oligarch, Roman Abramovich, as Chukotka's governor (2001–8). While Abramovich is credited with investing in Chukotka's infrastructure, schools and housing, such investment stemmed from the desire to develop resources – oil, gas, coal, tungsten and gold. Non-renewable resource development is not new in Chukotka: this began with Gulag labour in the early 1900s and continued with 20th-century Soviet urban-industrial expansion, finally transitioning to post-Soviet oligarchy and transnational investment. For Chukotka's people, this history is one of struggle – with incarceration, collectivization, forced migration, housing and food shortages all played out against a backdrop of extreme Arctic conditions. But, in a country where ~35 per cent of GDP relates to mineral resource production and export, Chukotkans find hope in the extractive industries. Current technologies and politics bolster hope and propel development of, for example, floating nuclear power plants to fuel extraction projects. Chukotka's power is its reservoir of largely untapped resources. As access to resources via new transportation routes becomes viable with new technologies, Chukotkans' hope surges.

What does this have to do with climate change? Everything. And nothing. Regarding 'nothing', climate change is a concept that is part of foreign discourse for most local residents. It has been an abstract concept discussed internationally, and only occasionally nationally by some leaders. For all but some Indigenous groups, it is a topic removed from everyday consideration, in which economic survival based on technological advancement in a newly capitalist economy straddles a still-socialist social infrastructure. Regarding 'everything', the opening of the Northern Sea Route and changing oceanic currents will bring new ships, goods and people into a nuclearized Arctic. Higher sea levels and unstable coastlines will replace melting ice. Coastal erosion will change shorelines, docking capabilities and search-and-rescue operations. Russia has no equivalent of the US Coast Guard, creating possibly hazardous coastal-marine situations.

Five main points follow from this brief sketch. First, ~40 per cent of the Russian economy is industrial (and ~60 per cent and ~5 per cent is in the service sector and agriculture, respectively). It is not surprising that workers and the government consider industrial activity an economic mainstay, especially knowing that nine of Russia's ten main exports in 2012 were of raw minerals and hydrocarbons (wheat being the exception). Thus, federal and, in Chukotka's case, regional economies are biased towards continued resource extraction.

Second, uneven development across Russia's varied physical landscapes continues to influence the type of economic development pursued in different regions. The country's most developed regions are in western Russia, near Europe and the Caucasus. The least developed – and most extracted – regions of Russia have been the same for centuries: the Far East, the Far North, and eastern Siberia.

Third, and related to uneven development, is the lingering importance of legacy structures, both social and physical. The Soviet century of industrialization and urbanization created lasting sites for the production, consumption, mobilization and wastage of energy resources. These nodes of activity (e.g. urban-industrial and military-industrial complexes) and ways to mobilize resources (e.g. railways, pipelines) shape 21st-century geopolitical, environmental and cultural landscapes. Although the legacy landscape remains, where people choose to live and work – and what infrastructure (e.g. fly-in, fly-out camps for resource extraction) the government invests in – has begun to transform it, albeit slowly.

Fourth, the power of individual personalities remains a formidable force for resource development or attention to environmental or climate change concerns. Returning to the sketch above, Chukotka's economic importance was buoyed, nationally, precisely because an oligarch was the governor. A continuing economy of favours meant that Abramovich's ties to other oligarchs and powerful men, including national leaders, put Chukotka and Chukotka's resources 'on the map', economically speaking. Similarly, if Russia's president notes that environmental or climatic changes are or are not important to address, people have largely followed this understanding rather than seeking the information needed to make self-directed decisions.

Finally, Russia's industrial and/or environmental actions matter greatly regarding global climate change. Of critical importance today is the stability of permafrost and boreal forests: if the climate warms dramatically, change to northern landscapes will likely be devastating and permanent. Physical environments in the Russian North will be drastically altered, but change to permafrost regions will affect future climate change globally. How Russia develops into the future – continuing as an exporter of raw resources and consumer of fossil fuels, or investing in and using new energy technologies – will shape the global climate and environment.

(b) Russia's boreal forests, the largest on earth, constitute a vast CO_2 store and thus fulfil a very important role in mitigating climate change. If these forests were lost or severely damaged, it would be a disaster for the world's climate. Russia has consistently lobbied to have these forests taken into account in the international climate change regime. There is some logic to this demand, although if it is fulfilled the consequence would be that demands on Russia for concrete climate action would be even less substantial than they already are by having 1990 as a reference year in the international climate change regime. At the same time, climate change is seriously endangering Russia's forests – as demonstrated by the forest fires that have raged over large tracts of them in recent years. The best known so far occurred in 2010, then the hottest summer on record in Russia. Hundreds of wildfires resulted in smoke blanketing Moscow and other cities for weeks on end and in hundreds of thousands of hectares of burned forests and thousands of destroyed buildings. The estimated death toll from smoke and heat that summer exceeded 55,000, the damage was put at 15 billion dollars. The fact that relatively densely populated western Russia was most heavily afflicted no doubt contributed to the heat wave of 2010 substantially heightening awareness about ongoing climate change in the country. However, subsequent years brought increasing evidence that the exception is starting to become the rule. The years 2012, 2013, 2015, 2016, 2017, 2018, 2019 and 2020 all witnessed record temperatures and devastating wildfires – above all, in Siberia. Climate change is not the only reason for these fires, but it is an important factor. As with melting permafrost, the forest fires are part of a vicious circle: the warmer it gets, the more wildfires there are and the more climate change is accelerated. The wildfires are not only devastating to the local and regional ecosystems, to the people living there – whose health is harmed directly or indirectly – and to nearby buildings and infrastructure; they also contribute to climate change in several ways. The burning of large numbers of trees releases CO2 that has been stored within them for decades. In addition, the wildfires contribute to the reduction of permafrost extent and often affect Russian peatlands, which are also important stores of CO2 and of methane. These repositories have taken thousands of years to form and, once destroyed, will not regenerate soon.

In the summers of 2019 and 2020, wildfires in the Siberian regions of Krasnoyarsk, Irkutsk and Sakha exceeded even those of the previous years. The Russian authorities took the decision not to put out the fires in large areas, explaining that as there were no settlements nearby the expense of extinguishing the fire exceeded the cost of the destruction. However, this led to protests and unease among inhabitants and activists in the region, who were

Figure 2.5 Russia: Effects of climate change.

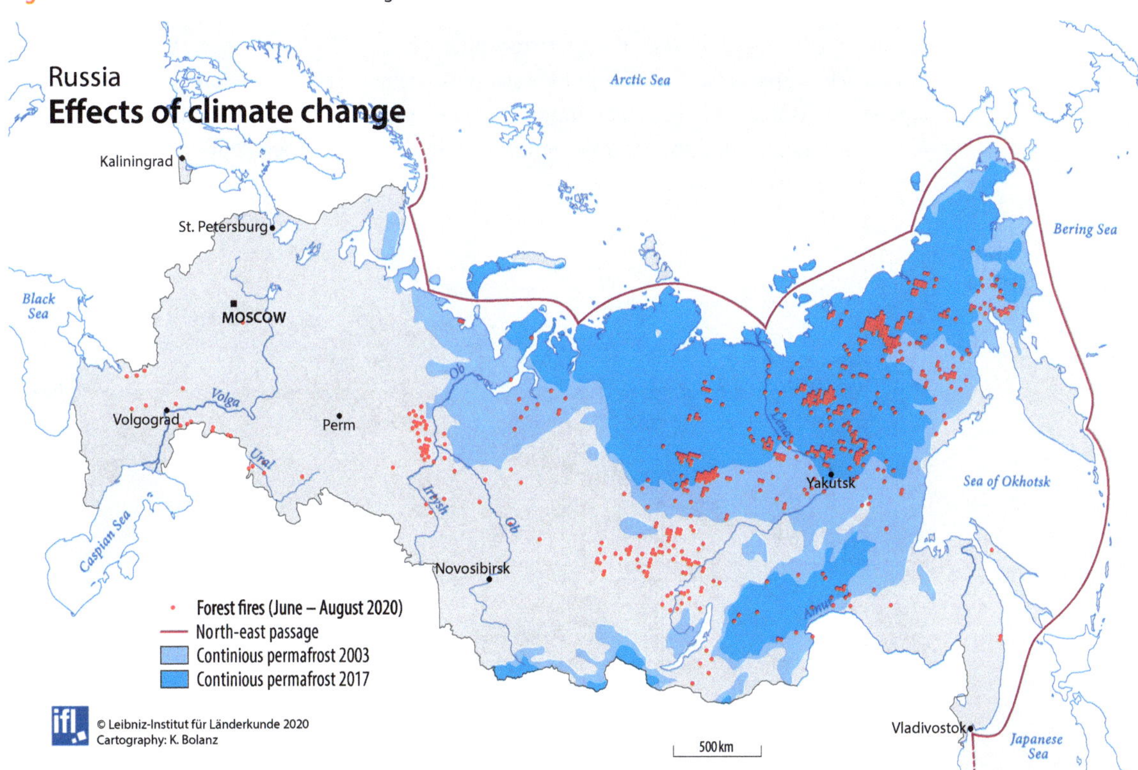

concerned by heavy smoke and an increase in respiratory complaints. In short, the effects of climate change have started to harm social stability. And the effects of climate change in Russia (see Figure 2.5, below) very much reinforce climate change on a global scale.

(c) All experts point to the fact that climate change means more than just a rise in temperature. To no less an extent, it is also about an increase in extreme weather events. With permafrost melting and the frequency of heavy rainfalls rising, floods have been another devastating effect of climate change that is being felt more and more frequently in Russia. For instance, the summer of 2019 witnessed the worst floods in Siberia in a century. Dozens of villages stood under water, tens of thousands of inhabitants were temporarily displaced, livestock was killed and housing damaged, and the number of human lives lost ran into double digits. The floods hit particularly hard in the Irkutsk region, which was also beset by large wildfires in the same year. Elsewhere, Lake Khanka in the far eastern Primorsky Krai has burst its banks for several years in a row, damaging nearby houses and harming inhabitants. Regional scientists cite climate change as the main reason for this phenomenon.[12] On top of events like this comes the growing threat of flooding in Russia's coastal regions (including the long Pacific coast and the densely populated Baltic region). And as sea levels rise, the danger only increases. Fittingly, as far back as 1985 a regional government official in Vladivostok had warned that global warming risked creating a 'second deluge' unless mankind took action to reduce emissions.[13] His warning appears to have been largely forgotten in subsequent decades, but now seems more timely than ever.

(d) The points above concern only the most prominent negative consequences of climate change felt within Russia. Other concerns include a growing lack of fresh water in Russian regions and changes in the maritime biosphere caused by rising temperatures – which particularly impacts on the Indigenous peoples of the Far East region, who traditionally depend on fishing. At the same time, however, climate change has been perceived by various Russian actors also as a potentially positive development. Thus, in the Far East, a

Figure 2.6 Russia: Floods in Orenburg city, 2024.

©Getty Images 2024

number of newspaper articles have mentioned a reduction of heating costs thanks to a shortened winter. Additionally, media reports and comments by Russian politicians and experts have pointed to increased agricultural fertility in the Far East and Siberia as well as in western regions as a consequence of higher average temperatures. In 2020, the debate was enlivened by claims by some foreign and Russian observers that Russia would 'win the climate crisis' and gain both economic and political leverage because its food production would benefit greatly from rising temperatures and receding permafrost, while the same rise in temperatures would lead to a decline in agricultural yields in most Western and many other countries in the coming decades.[14] In fact, Russian agricultural production and exports have multiplied since the turn of the millennium, with wheat exports doubling between 2015 and 2020 alone, making Russia the world's largest wheat exporter by some margin (while the late Soviet Union had to import large amounts of grain to meet its needs – which became a problem when oil prices dropped significantly). However, Russian scientists have shown that much of this astonishing increase in production is due to technological innovations on large farms as well as some government support measures, while climate change is likely to have a negative impact on Russian agricultural production in the medium and long term due to an increasing number of droughts and extreme weather events.[15]

e) Meanwhile, from the perspective of some leading Russian actors, the most important positive results of climate change relate to the successive reduction of ice in the Russian Arctic. Thus, at the Arctic Forum in spring 2017 in Arkhangelsk, while leaders from Finland and Iceland raised concerns about the dramatic negative effects of climate change in the Arctic, Vladimir Putin struck a very different tone, insinuating that it was unclear if human beings could influence climate change in any way and postulating instead that it made sense to grasp the opportunities resulting from it. In the Russian Arctic, these opportunities are twofold: first, global warming promises to render accessible large deposits of fossil fuels and other valuable commodities which have so far been either technically not exploitable or too costly to extract; second, and even more important, the melting of the icepack also renders it more realistic to use the North-east passage to transport goods from East Asia to Europe. In recent years, the amount of cargo shipped this way has indeed started to rise, promising to realize a dream held by generations of Russian governments and visionaries.

The potentials are huge. Since the 19th century, the bulk of goods traded between Europe and Asia has been transported through the Suez Canal. If the Northern Sea Route becomes viable, it will be a considerably shorter – and, by extension, less expensive and less dangerous – alternative. There is thus a perspective that a substantial portion of the huge flow of goods between two hubs of the global economy will be transported through Russian territorial waters. This would lastingly enlarge Russia's geopolitical leverage, provide an additional stable income source and open up prospects for economic development in the country's Arctic region itself. Russia is already building up infrastructure in its Artic ports and energy supply in the region – notably by constructing the world's first floating nuclear power plant, the *Akademik Lomonosov*. It has also substantially reinforced military facilities and other infrastructure in the region and expanded its fleet of nuclear-powered icebreakers. Meanwhile, developing the Russian Arctic region and making it fit to be a major passage for world trade demands both considerable amounts of money and advanced technology. This in turn calls for international partners. From a Russian perspective, it is therefore auspicious that the major Asian-Pacific economies of China, Japan and South Korea have all shown great interest in the Northern Sea Route project. Sino-Russian cooperation in the region promises to be the most pronounced, and a number of Chinese companies are already investing in various infrastructure projects in the Russian Arctic. China has also included the Northern Sea Route in its Belt and Road Initiative (where it is called the Polar Silk Road). At the same time, there is some uneasiness in Russia about China developing its own fleet of icebreakers and about Chinese schemes to circumnavigate the Russian-controlled Northern Sea Route northwards. For the immediate future, however, mutual interests prevail.

Nuclear history

Fabian Lüscher

In 2020, the state corporation Rosatom put a floating nuclear power plant (FNPP) into operation in Pevek, the northernmost town of the Russian Federation. This project, controversial and innovative in equal measure, is an embodiment of Russian nuclear energy policy in the second decade of the 21st century. It heralds Russia's geopolitical ambitions in the Arctic, as a the polar region whose copious deposits of yet-to-be exploited mineral resources will become accessible as the ice melts.

The *Akademik Lomonosov*, as the FNPP is called, is one of several projects which demonstrate the complex interplay of interests and intentions that have characterized the nuclear history of the Soviet Union and its successors. With origins in military use in the 1940s, the civilian Soviet nuclear programme took off in the 1950s accompanied by a broad propaganda campaign featuring slogans like 'Let the atom be a worker, not a soldier.' While the first full-scale nuclear power plants (NPPs) started to feed into the Soviet grid in 1964, the actual breakthrough of the 'atom being a worker' came only in the 1970s, resulting in a construction boom of NPPs on Soviet territory; between 1973 and 1990, at least one reactor went on-line every year.

When information about the 1986 Chernobyl catastrophe became public, an anti-nuclear movement emerged in the Soviet Union and began actively opposing the construction of NPPs and related infrastructure. Although initially successful in the former Soviet Union, the movement fizzled out when construction of nuclear energy capacity slowed down significantly in the wake of Soviet disintegration. Even though nuclear power generation never died completely, the great revival in Russia came in the second decade of the 21st century when expanding the nuclear share became a top priority – a process strongly linked to institutional reforms in the nuclear energy sector under President Vladimir Putin. As of 2020, nuclear contributes almost 20 per cent of Russian electricity production – a figure that is rising.

Several factors determined the development of the Soviet and post-Soviet nuclear industry. In the aftermath of the 1973 oil crisis, several states expanded their nuclear-generating capacities to lessen their dependency on fossil fuels. The oil crisis also intensified integration in the European energy industry, and this affected the Soviet Union: fast-growing markets for Soviet oil could be serviced only if energy demands inside the Soviet state were met in other ways. Expanding the nuclear share was an attractive way of freeing up fossil fuel resources for export. In the wake of *perestroika* and the Chernobyl catastrophe, however, overall conditions for the expansion of nuclear energy in the Soviet Union changed considerably, and the sector was characterized in the Yeltsin years by opaque decision making and shadowy movements of money. Low state capacity remained a problem in Russia's nuclear industry even after the creation of Rosatom in 2004, and was only solved with a far-reaching reform, signed by Putin in December 2007, which turned Rosatom into an extremely powerful state corporation. Rosatom now operated under direct presidential supervision and was, not imperceptibly, directed through informal and personal relations with the Kremlin. Today, it is not only responsible for the world's largest arsenal of nuclear weapons but is also becoming an important factor in Russia's struggle to maintain great power status in an increasingly polycentric world. For example, Rosatom is the only Russian state corporation with the power to negotiate and conclude agreements with other states. It combines this power with aggressive export marketing, offering package solutions covering everything from reactor construction to the management of spent nuclear fuel. Tailored solutions like the small modular reactors aboard the *Akademik Lomonosov* are intended to allow Rosatom to tap into new markets – not least in sub-Saharan Africa, where nuclear energy is yet to gain a foothold.

While the Fukushima Daiichi catastrophe in 2011 led many European states to rethink their nuclear energy policies, Rosatom continues to actively promote nuclear energy as a clean and economical solution to current and future energy and climate challenges. It even used the Fukushima catastrophe to its advantage by profiting from low prices in the uranium market to strengthen its trade business. Whereas Soviet uranium needs were primarily met from mining sites in Czechoslovakia and the GDR, today Rosatom subsidiaries are extracting uranium in Russia, Kazakhstan, the United States, Tanzania and Namibia.

However, Rosatom's power goes far beyond the construction and operation of NPPs in Russia and abroad. As the authorized infrastructure operator of the North-east passage, the corporation is, for example, responsible for preparing Russia for one of the most important competitions for resources in the age of climate change. By developing harbour and coastal infrastructure, modernizing the nuclear icebreaker fleet and operating floating NPPs, Rosatom is likely to shape the future of the Arctic as much as it does the Russian energy sector, whose dependence on fossil fuel is supposed to be further reduced by the use of ever-more powerful NPPs.

All in all, the amount of goods transported along the Northern Sea Route is still minuscule compared with the volumes shipped via the Suez Canal, and some doubt if it will ever be viable. But, from the perspective of the Russian leadership, the potential geopolitical and economic gains available from this route are so great that it is not clear if they are seen as being outweighed by the increasingly obvious and dramatic negative effects of climate change in Russia.

The economic risks of external climate change mitigation

Besides the natural effects of climate change within Russia and their far-reaching repercussions on the local, regional, national and global levels, there is at least one more important consequence of climate change which promises to grow in scale over the coming decades and which will affect Russia's socio-economic structure and development prospects. Tellingly, it is this consequence rather than the natural effects of climate change that was mentioned most prominently as a threat to Russia in various Russian government documents before changes in the official discourse took effect in 2019. It can be best formulated as a question: What if more and more countries engage in decarbonizing their economies to combat climate change, as agreed in the Kyoto Protocol and conspicuously in the Paris Agreement? Remarkably, as of October 2020 not only has the EU pledged to decarbonize its economy by the middle of the 21st century, but Japan, South Korea and China all have also promised to do likewise (China is aiming for 2060). This will inevitably affect Russia's prospects for continuing exports from its abundant fossil resources, and it should be clear from the first part of this chapter that these resources lie at the heart of Russia's current socio-economic structure.[16] Before the Russian full-scale invasion of Ukraine in February 2022, oil and gas prices were arguably already under pressure as a consequence of the worldwide divestment movement and slowing demand growth caused by increases in renewable energy capacities and the adoption of electric vehicles. Confronted with this development, several strategic options are being discussed in Russia. At one end of the spectrum is the option to bet on preserving the current socio-economic model by exporting as much coal and hydrocarbons as possible for as long as there is demand and to hope that demand for natural gas will only increase in the coming decades on the back of its use in China, Germany and other major economies as a cleaner alternative to coal. At the other end of the spectrum is the option to set a course towards investing heavily in renewable energies and other zero-emissions technologies, creating new green jobs, and eventually using the surplus of green energy gained from this to produce green hydrogen that can be exported to energy-hungry EU and Asian-Pacific countries, making the Russian economy fit for a decarbonizing world. The Russian leadership favours the first option so far. The writing on the wall is clear, however: if the Paris Agreement is taken seriously, this socio-economic model will inevitably come to an end within three decades. It will then be much more difficult and costly to adapt to the new realities than if the transition were tackled now.

Conclusion

All in all, Russia's sprawling territory, covering one sixth of the earth's landmass and a vast range of vegetational and climatic zones, holds challenges as well as an abundance of natural resources. In the age of global climate change, Russia's rich natural resources and its vast expanses of permafrost and forests link its fate closely with the world's, and the world's fate with its own. They render Russia both influential and vulnerable. For the country and its inhabitants, this creates tensions that will have to be resolved at some point in the coming years and decades. The solutions chosen will affect the whole world – as the effects of climate change in Russia are already having dramatic implications on the local, the regional and the global level.

At the same time, for better or for worse, climate change mitigation on the global level as stipulated by the Paris Agreement will have far-reaching consequences for Russia's socio-economic structure and future. It remains to be seen if Russian decision makers will set the country on a course to shape this future, or if they will try to prevent such a future becoming reality. The first alternative entails piloting Russia towards a different socio-economic model and structure, a daunting task that lends itself to international cooperation – as does mitigating climate change. Beginning in the 1960s, the country's hydrocarbons had contributed to link the Soviet Union and Russia with countries in Eastern Europe, Western Europe and the Asia-Pacific region. Renewable energies and green hydrocarbon have the potential to do the same.

This chapter has demonstrated the environmental dimension of globality. Russia's global role and transnational connections, together with its economy and environment, will continue to be acted on by its abundant natural resources and by reactions among the international community to the ever-more-acute problem of climate change. At the same time, Russia's own search for the right positioning with regard to these issues is bound to continue for the foreseeable future. The answers that it finds and the effects that climate change has in Russia are of concern to the whole world.

Postscript

With this chapter all but finished, on 24 February 2022 Putin's Russian troops started a full-scale invasion of Ukraine. The longer-term consequences of this war were hardly foreseeable at the moment when the present chapter went to the publisher. It seems clear, however, that this war will have profound impacts on the energy relations between Russia and European countries as well as on various climate policies. Initially, Russian exports of gas, oil and coal were not affected by the swift and harsh sanctions adopted by Western countries in the wake of the invasion. This can be read as a sign of the persistence of the energy entanglements that have connected Western Europe to the fossil fuel riches of Siberia for decades despite all political odds. Western Europe's economies and the welfare of its societies have grown too dependent on hydrocarbons from Russia for these links to be severed instantly without risking major damage to everybody involved.[17] However, it seems clear by now that this extraordinary persistence is reaching its end. If there isn't a dramatic change of course very soon – like an unexpected regime change in Moscow, followed by a swift end to the war in Ukraine – in a very short time Russian oil and coal will stop being imported into Europe. Natural gas from Russia will continue to flow to Europe for some time, due to the infrastructural obstacles standing in the way of a quick replacement. However, in the very best case (for those involved in this business), this will last for another couple of years – after which the whole pipeline net connecting Europe to Russia will lie idle, slowly degenerating into a mere vestige of what had been an extraordinary success story. This will amount to speeding up the change that would have come anyway through robust climate change policies from about two decades to a mere tenth of that timespan, with disastrous consequences for the Russian economy and state budget. To be sure, Russia will strive to replace the European export market with Asian consumers: China and India, in the first instance. But, given a considerable number of contestants – including Australia and Indonesia – and the ever-growing competitiveness of renewables, these Asian players will hardly compensate for the lucrative European export market. Natural gas might be the most attractive Russian export good for Asian countries increasingly concerned about air pollution at home, but these exports will be limited due to infrastructural constraints.

What will the effects be on climate change mitigation efforts? In the short term, Europe will probably rely more heavily on lignite coal, which is available in countries like Germany and Poland but will be disastrous in terms of climate change. China might increase its imports of gas from Russia – possibly available at discount prices once the European export market is closed – which might result, in the best-case scenario, in less coal burned in China, partly offsetting the increased coal burning in Europe. In the medium to long term, strategic-thinking European – and, to a lesser degree, Asian – decision makers will most probably turn to renewables faster and more decisively than they would have without the war, as renewables promise energy autonomy alongside climate change mitigation benefits and tend to become cheaper and more competitive every year, while energy storage technologies continue to develop.

Where does this leave Russia? Climate change will continue and accelerate, bringing with it ever-greater damage to infrastructure built on permafrost and to Russia's huge forests. Rents from oil, gas and coal – the main basis of the country's export economy and state budget thus far – will dwindle much faster and more dramatically than would anyway have been the case with the worldwide decarbonization trend, leaving Russian decision makers with major headaches on how to further finance the state apparatus, at least modest social welfare, and the very investments that would be necessary to lessen dependence on fossil fuels. It is very unclear whether, within such a framework, climate change mitigation and adaptation will remain prominent on the agenda of Russian decision makers – as it was in the years just before February 2022 – and whether projects like the climate experiment on Sakhalin will still be implemented given the growing lack of money and the abundance of other, seemingly more urgent worries. Last but not least, for the foreseeable future there will be no further prospect of a Russian–European climate and energy partnership that would have been possible and suggesting itself. Russia, with its huge territory and consequently huge potential for renewables, could have started large-scale production and a scaling up of green hydrogen and exported it not only to the EU but also to China and other Asian-Pacific countries keen on getting closer to the goal of decarbonizing their economies. This could have turned into the cornerstone of a new energy partnership and into real opportunities for the Russian economy in a world of decarbonization. In autumn 2021, Putin himself spoke for the first time of the possibility of producing green hydrogen for export, thus indicating a pragmatic turn away from his long-standing disdain for renewables. However, for such a new, future-proof partnership and economy to come into being would have required reassurance that Russia was a reliable partner and wasn't ploughing its economic gains into a war machine likely to threaten European peace. Since 24 February 2022, this trust has gone and won't return as long as Putin and his regime are in power. This leaves us with a story of missed chances – tragic for Russia and tragic for a world that needs Russia in the fight against the growing climate crisis.

Is this the end of the story? Hardly so. At some point, Putin (if not removed from office by other means) will die while the climate crisis will go on. No one knows when this moment will come or what changes it will bring about in Russia. However, decision makers in Europe would be well advised to prepare for it and be ready to start new, crucial climate and energy partnerships with Russia as soon as this opportunity occurs. Russia is simply too big and too important a country to be left aside when it comes to fighting the fundamental challenge that climate change poses to humankind. It should not be forgotten that it was Oleg Anisimov, a well-known Russian climatologist and long-standing IPCC delegate, who on 27 February 2022 during a virtual IPCC meeting stated his shame and outrage about the Russian war against Ukraine. It is a reminder to all of us: Putin is not Russia. There is a Russia we can and we should reach out to in the common endeavour to save the world from the climate crisis. And thus, there is hope.

Notes

1   Felix Frey, *Arktischer Heizraum: Das Energiesystem Kola zwischen regionaler Autarkie und gesamtstaatlicher Verflechtung, 1928-1974* (Vienna: Böhlau, 2019).
2   Thane Gustafson, *The Bridge: Natural Gas in a Redivided Europe* (Cambridge, MA: Harvard University Press, 2020).
3   Sergei Ermolaev, 'The Formation and Evolution of the Soviet Union's Oil and Gas Dependence', Carnegie Moscow Center, https://carnegiemoscow.org/2017/03/29/formation-and-evolution-of-soviet-union-s-oil-and-gas-dependence-pub-68443; Boris Egorov, 'Black gold: How the Russian oil industry was born', *Russia Beyond*, https://www.rbth.com/business/326217-black-gold-how-russian-oil.
4   'Crude Oil Prices – 70 Year Historical Chart,' *Macrotrends.net*, https://www.macrotrends.net/1369/crude-oil-price-history-chart.
5   Jonathan Oldfield, 'Imagining Climates Past, Present and Future: Soviet Contributions to the Science of Anthropogenic Climate Change, 1953-1991', *Journal of Historical Geography* 60 (2018), pp. 41–51.
6   Benjamin Beuerle, 'From Continuity to Change: Soviet and Russian Government Attitudes on Climate Change', *Climatic Change* 176 (2023) 6, https://doi.org/10.1007/s10584-023-03488-2.
7   Katja Doose, 'Modelling the Future: Climate Change research in Russia during the late Cold War and Beyond, 1970s – 2010s', *Climatic Change* 171 (2022) 6, https://doi.org/10.1007/s10584-022-03315-0beue.
8   Angelina Davydova, 'Veryat li Rossiyane v Klimaticheskiy krizis?', rrreaktsiia, site inactive, https://climate.greenpeace.ru/veryat-li-rossiyane-v-climaticheskiy/
9   Nikolai Dronin and Alina Bychkova, 'Perceptions of American and Russian Environmental Scientists on Today´s Key Environmental Issues: A Comparative Analysis', *Environment, Development and Sustainability* 20 (2018) 5, pp. 2095–105; Benjamin Beuerle, 'Climate Change in Russia's Far East', in *Climate Change Discourse in Russia*, ed. Marianna Poberezhskaya and Teresa Ashe (Abingdon: Routledge Focus, 2019), pp. 80–96.
10 Marianna Poberezhskaya, *Communicating Climate Change in Russia: State and Propaganda* (Abingdon: Routledge, 2016).
11 Maria Antonova, 'Russia Says Melting Permafrost is Behind the Massive Arctic Fuel Spill', *ScienceAlert*, 5 June 2020, https://www.sciencealert.com/russia-claims-melting-permafrost-is-behind-the-massive-arctic-fuel-spill.

12 Yu. N. Zhuravlev et al., *Transgranichnoe ozero Khanka: Prichiny povyshcheniia urovnia vody i ėkologicheskie ugrozy* (Vladivostok: Dalnauka, 2016).

13 Benjamin Beuerle, 'Urban Air Pollution and Environmental Engagement in the Russian Far East: Developments from late-Soviet to post-Soviet Times (1970s – 2010s)', in *Russia's North Pacific: Centres and Peripheries*, ed. Benjamin Beuerle, Sandra Dahlke and Andreas Renner (Heidelberg: Heidelberg University Publishing, 2023), pp. 65–87.

14 Abraham Lustgarten, 'How Russia Wins the Climate Crisis', *The New York Times Magazine*, 16 December 2020, https://www.nytimes.com/interactive/2020/12/16/magazine/russia-climate-migration-crisis.html.

15 Andrei Kirilenko and Nikolai Dronin, 'Recent Grain Production Boom in Russia in Historical Perspective', *Climatic Change* 171 (2022) 6, https://doi.org/10.1007/s10584-022-03332-z.

16 Thane Gustafson, *The Bridge: Natural Gas in a Redivided Europe* (Cambridge, MA: Harvard University Press, 2020).

17 Katja Bruisch and Benjamin Beuerle, 'Putin´s War in Ukraine and Europe's Carbon Democracies: Paying the Price of Half-Hearted Climate Politics', *Energy Humanities*, https://www.energyhumanities.ca/news/putins-war-in-ukraine-and-europes-carbon-democracies-paying-the-price-of-half-hearted-climate-politics.

Further reading

Bruno, Andy. *The Nature of Soviet Power: An Arctic Environmental History*. New York: Cambridge University Press, 2016.

Goldman, Marshall I. *Petrostate: Putin, Power, and the New Russia*. Oxford: Oxford University Press, 2008.

Henry, Laura A. *Red to Green. Environmental Activism in Post-Soviet Russia*. Ithaca: Cornell University Press, 2010.

Högselius, Per. *Red Gas: Russia and the Origins of European Energy Dependence*. Basingstoke: Palgrave Macmillan, 2013.

Josephson, Paul. *An Environmental History of Russia*. Cambridge: Cambridge University Press, 2013.

Korppoo, Anna and Alexey Kokorin. 'Russia's 2020 GHG Emission Target: Emission Trends and Implemention'. *Climate Policy* (2015). DOI: 10.1080/14693062.2015.1075373.

Oldfield, Jonathan. *The Development of Russian Environmental Thought: Scientific and Geographic Perspectives on the Natural Environment*. Abingdon: Routledge, 2016.

Perović, Jeronim. *Rohstoffmacht Russland: eine globale Energiegeschichte*. Vienna: Böhlau 2022.

Poberezhskaya, Marianna and Teresa Ashe (eds). *Climate Change Discourse in Russia: Past and Present*. Abingdon: Routledge, 2019.

Rindzevičiūtė, Eglė. *The Power of Systems: How Policy Sciences Opened up the Cold War*. Ithaca: Cornell University Press, 2016.

Tynkkynen, Nina. 'A Great Ecological Power in Global Climate Policy? Framing Climate Change as a Policy Problem in Russian Public Discussion'. *Environmental Politics* 19 (2010) 2, pp. 179–95.

Tynkkynen, Veli-Pekka. *The Energy of Russia: Hydrocarbon Culture and Climate Change*. Cheltenham: Edward Elgar, 2019.

Wilson Rowe, Elana. *Russian Climate Politics: When Science Meets Policy*. New York: Palgrave Macmillan.

part I

International Political and Legal Spheres

Editors' Note: Actors of Global Change

'The challenge, for historians like for everyone else, is to envision transnational means to address transnational problems that will not simply create new forms of unaccountable power' (Connelly, 2006). Almost twenty years have passed since Matthew Connelly, a leading scholar in the field of international and global history, made this call, and it has not lost its relevance. To the contrary, when we write these pages, governments and societies around the globe experience a national-istic backlash defying a cosmopolitan world view which had gained momentum since the early 1990s. Growing insecurities, exsacerbated by the COVID-19 pandemic, have accelerated violent conflicts, birthed new wars, and have sharpened power struggles over resources. The plea to make one's own nation-state strong is once again on the rise. Conversely, the need to think transnationally seems stronger than before.

We respond to this need in this part of the book by showcasing people who were concerned with transnational, transregional or global problems, and who found ways of addressing them across borders and dividing lines. Often, they challenged historically rooted power structures by advocating the concerns of vulnerable people, such as children, refugees, or those most heavily affected by epidemics, patriarchal relations, economic inequalities or the nuclear threat. The chapters here offer a journey into international political and legal spheres. During the 20th century, international law and international organizations became increasingly concerned with a remarkable spectrum of topics that were hitherto traditionally regarded as under the strict purview of nation-states. Remarkably, the expansion of this international sphere grew extensively in no small part

thanks to the significant contributions of agents from Eastern
Europe, many of whom acted in their own capacities, or as representatives of civil society (or both). We show their driving role by
tracing the global impacts of their ideas and policies.

In her chapter, Katja Castryck-Naumann, outlines the proactive
and lasting contributions of Eastern Europeans to three core fields
of international politics in the 20th century: health, trade and
disarmament. That today's international health agenda targets
socio-economic causes of diseases, and seeks to provide public
health infrastructures around the world, derives from interventions
made by these actors during the early part of that century.
Likewise, global trade relations that hindered the development of
decolonizing countries were set on the international agenda thanks
to the active advocacy by economists from this region. Innovative
proposals for limiting the nuclear threat, too, had their origins
there. Seeking to make the world more equal and just, Eastern
Europeans have written history – not only their own – but also that
of the international and global spheres.

Azar Aliyev introduces the profound and enduring global impact
of Eastern European socialist law the world over. This marks a shift
from the protection of individual rights to the protection of
specific groups, hitherto disadvantaged or discriminated against by
states. He shows that Soviet law was one of the most advanced,
progressive and liberal legal systems especially in the realm of
family law, which provided, among others, for womens' right to
abortion, divorce, equal lodging and pay rights, and for the equity
of all children – whether born in marriages or out of wedlock.
Family law in the socialist guise was introduced in socialist states
around the world, regardless of their religions and cultural
specifics, from Muslim Asia to Catholic Poland. Freeing marriage in
its legal terms from a centuries-long tradition of serving economic
interests – and serving men's rights in the first place – this vital
contribution by Soviet lawyers is all too often overlooked
nowadays. Yet its reiteration reminds us of the enduring transregional connections that persisted even during the Cold War.
Though partly abolished, Soviet family law remains a powerful

inspiration as to progress in gender relations and age-based equalities.

In her chapter on childhood, Elizabeth White makes a similar argument in view of socialist education concepts that spread globally. The October Revolution of 1917 marked the beginning of a radical socialist project –
the establishment of a comprehensive system of free and compulsory, co-educational education, that was enacted state-wide, and was secular
in its schooling. Its trajectory in the Soviet Union went in parallel to its adaptation in Eastern Europe and in the decolonizing world. While we see in this chapter multiple exchanges in the transregional socialist world, we also understand the competitive constellation that existed with the liberal countries in Western Europe and North America. Interestingly enough, the latter changed their educational policies in light of these socialist influences far more than we tend to assume, wishing as it were not to lag behind the Soviet bloc's educational achievments. As White reveals, children were crucial for the creation of a socialist or postcolonial society, but were also key in the Cold War's international politics . Here, actors from the socialist bloc promoted childrens' rights as part of their own comprehensive vision of human rights during the entire post-1945 period. Their efforts culminated in the adoption of the UN Convention of the Rights of Children (1989) to which every child in the world can refer, which by and large came to fruition as a result of Polish diplomatic efforts.

At the end of our journey Gilad Ben-Nun takes us into the field of international law. Here, too, agents from Eastern Europe played a crucial role, first and foremost in the protection of minorities, in refugee law that compels states to protect uprooted and stateless people (codified in the 1951 Refugee Convention), and in the laws of war. In regard to the latter, Jewish jurists who survived the Second World War were instrumental in the drafting and adoption of the Fourth Geneva Convention for Civilians (1949) which provided the legal basis for all international criminal tribunals set up after the Cold War, and the International Criminal Court's 1998 Rome Statute. In this chapter we also understand the deeper roots of this impact – Eastern Europe's historic vulnerability to external territorial impositions, and the multiethnic, multiconfessional belongings of its peoples. When nations were supposed to be ethnically homogenous, Eastern Europe became a testing ground for international legal experiments in vile ethnic engineering. Yet, in response to such harsh experiments, it was thanks to the work of jurists from this very region that powerful tools to limit the harm of such fatal ideas were created.

Altogether the chapters in this part deal with two international realms, politics and law, which for long remained framed in national and state-centred terms, by historians as much as by other scholars. Yet with every page one turns, one reads how agents from Eastern Europe inscribed common goods like health, children's rights, or the right to economic development, and universal concerns for refugee protection and the world's denuclearization into the agendas of international politics and international law. All this did much to change how our world is governed.

Bibliography

Matthew Connelly. 'Seeing Beyond the State. The Population Control Movement and the Problem of Sovereignty'. *Past & Present* 193 (2006), p. 197–233, here at p. 233.

Making a Difference: Eastern European Experts in International Organizations

Katja Castryck-Naumann

3

For many centuries, states regulated their relations ad hoc and bilaterally or in small alliances. Yet a profound change began in the mid-19th century. Since then, interstate relations and cross-border issues have been gradually ordered though an enduring cooperation within international organizations. In the 1860s, the International Red Cross and the International Telegraph Union were founded as the first institutions of their kind. Just over half a century later, in 1921, the League of Nations' *Handbook of International Organizations* already listed more than three hundred such institutions. Today, there are over 60,000 institutions that operate against the backdrop of 193 sovereign states recognized by the United Nations (UN).

This rapid advance of multilateral institutions was accompanied by two far-reaching shifts. First, states pursued their foreign policies to an ever-larger degree in international institutions, such as the League of Nations (LoN) or the UN – an agenda we call governmental internationalism. However, civil societies around the world have cooperated in this institutional framework as well. The international women's and workers' organizations are among the oldest institutions of this kind. Along with this, doctors formed international professional associations and athletes organized themselves in international interest groups. More recent examples are Greenpeace, Amnesty International and Oxfam – and these are but the tip of an iceberg of so-called non-governmental internationalism. In consequence, international politics is no longer conducted solely by diplomats and state representatives but by a wide range of actors including experts, trade unionists, activists, and officials of various kinds.

Second, in this internationalization of state and society, an increasing number of issues have become of international concern. Initially, issues of war and peace, border-crossing communication and labour conditions were on the agenda, but a wealth of other themes has been swiftly added – from the transportation of goods to the mobility of people, from the circulation of ideas to challenges such as epidemics, human rights or climate change. Currently, almost all aspects of cross-border interdependence are regulated by international organizations, as also are many domestic matters.

This historical development gave birth to the world we now live in. Yet, it stands in contrast to traditional reasoning in some parts of research – predominantly, some schools within political science and international relations theory. Here international organizations are seen in the light of geopolitics and national interest. They are described through the lens of unequal voting powers and as paper tigers when it comes to decision making – or, from another angle, as huge and costly institutions driven by vast bureaucracies that live a 'life of their own', with presumably little understanding, in the words of their critics, of the realities of cross-border problems. Whether seen as weak in a world of nation-states or as disconnected super-institutions, such organizations have often been treated as limited players in international politics despite their high numbers, appeal to states and societies, and the growing list of issues they address.

Without doubt, asymmetrical power relations and national self-interests have continuously impacted on the work of international organizations. However, their past and present is much richer than the conventional national interest-, state- and power-oriented focus has led us to believe. In fact, they have matured into a multifaceted international sphere where trans- and supra-national, regional and transregional, cross-cultural, and even local concerns are voiced alongside great power- and territory-based rationality. International organizations have become networks shaped by social dynamics; they are nodes of entanglements and circulations, places of encounter and learning. Their practices 'transcend the assumption that the political borders of nations determine the nature of experiences, ideas, and politics'[1] in the international sphere.

Among the scholars who paved the way towards such a revision was Ilya V. Gaiduk. His research on relations between the Soviet Union and the United States within the UN in its first decades was published posthumously under the title *Divided Together*. This phrase captures well his core argument. Both sides met as enemies, yet the rivals were alike. Their attitudes and policies towards the UN were strikingly similar, and their tactics often resembled each other's. Moreover, from the mid-1950s, they developed a sort of friendly behaviour towards each other in the public realm of the UN. Their interaction therein went through periods of frost, thaw and crises in a context of ongoing competition. Yet, from the ups and downs of the rivalry arose a sense of togetherness, based on a need and will to get along despite the opposing ideologies and world orders they stood for.[2]

We pick up the image of being 'divided together' in this chapter because it is instructive in a wider sense. It enables us to see that not only the USSR but also all the countries of Eastern Europe were globally connected due to their share in and shaping of the international sphere, and to recognize in turn that the image of the region as having been internationally rather isolated is a distortion.

On the one hand, 'divided together' highlights dissent on how to regulate international relations and how to solve international problems. In the LoN and UN, Eastern Europeans put forward contesting political ideas, policies and concrete proposals that often aimed for decisive change – changes in conventional agendas regarding international policy, changes in global power asymmetries, or changes in debates that had reached a stalemate. This stirred conflict.

On the other hand, the notion of 'divided together' emphasizes the fact that separations, competitions and conflicts took place in a context of togetherness to which all parties remained committed, even in the depths of the Cold War. Consequently, international politics did not follow clear-cut and fixed divisions of power, in which a few superpowers decided courses of action which the 'rest' had to abide by. On the contrary, power constellations shifted with the issues at stake and the tides of global relations. For the involvement of agents from Eastern Europe, this meant that they neither entered the institutions of world government designated as players from a marginal region nor acted as second-rank players. Instead, they positioned themselves in a self-directed manner and as decisive voices. More often than we tend to think, they did so successfully (see the text box, below).

In turn, and as we shall see, the politics of the League of Nations and the UN changed in view of themes and problems either originating in Eastern Europe or supported by East Europeans in transregional alliances with agents from Africa, Asia and Latin America. Understanding international organizations as spaces of divided togetherness allows us to take off the old territorially based and geopolitically focused lenses and to grasp the agency of international actors from Eastern Europe, along with the region's imprint on the expanding world of international governance.[3]

We bring this perspective to the fore with examples from three crucial fields of international politics in the 20th century: health, trade and disarmament. Agents from or based in Eastern Europe shaped the international sphere by initiating with like-minded others a social agenda in international health, the combat against inequalities in world trade, and an alternative concept in nuclear disarmament.

First, we look at the health politics in the LoN and the World Health Organization (WHO). In the 1920s, a group of physicians from East Central and South-east Europe established an innovative and comprehensive agenda based on the concept of social medicine and state intervention (public health). This programme set the course for the development of this field until the present day, and it transformed the oldest domain of international health: the combatting of epidemics. In the second part, we study the quest for a more equal world economic order forwarded by Eastern European economists through the United Nations Conference on Trade and Development (UNCTAD). We will zoom in on how a vital concern, the regulation of international shipping, was made a priority task in international economic politics in the 1960s. Even today, 90 per cent of internationally traded goods are shipped over the oceans. The transportation services offered by shipping companies are thus a core aspect of world trade. Fair(er) access to them and transparent freight rates, among other things, were of crucial concern not only for the decolonizing countries but also for the economies in Eastern Europe. In the final part, we turn to international peace and security matters: disarmament. In the second half of the 20th century, security was under nuclear threat. Among the many Eastern European initiatives to limit the use of nuclear weapons, we look at one undertaken by lawyers and diplomats from the People's Republic of Poland, which aimed to create a nuclear-weapon-free zone in Central Europe. The initial goals of the initiative were not reached, yet the concept of regional disarmament – the idea of zones freed from nuclear weapons – had a lasting impact. It was taken up around the world and became a core tool in international disarmament.

Involvement of Eastern Europeans in international organizations: Some basics

Katja Castryck-Naumann

The comprehensive, manifold and effective involvement of states and societies in international organizations is instructive for recognizing Eastern Europe's participation therein. Yet, until recently, two narratives imbued with a state-centred and geopolitically focused perspective hardly acknowledged international trajectories and impacts from this region.

The first narrative claims that without a sovereign nation-state, work in international organizations is hardly possible. Given the intricate ways of nation-state building in East Central Europe, this large part of Eastern Europe is portrayed as having had little access to international politics until almost the end of the Cold War. Before 1918, societies of this area of the world were part of multiethnic empires that offered them only limited participation in matters of foreign relations. The nation-states that were (re-)established after the First World War were soon confronted with external domination – initially by the German Reich and later by the Soviet Union (officially, the Union of Soviet Socialist Republics). Supposedly only after 1989, when the socialist regimes in East Central Europe were brought down and the 'Eastern bloc' was dissolved, did external domination end and sovereign states come into being.

The second narrative views the international history of the 20th century along the lines of a conflict between old empires – above all, Great Britain and France – and two of the aspiring hegemonic powers – the United States and the USSR. The last-named is depicted as a regional power in Eastern Europe after 1945, but as unable to play at 'eye level' with the old empires in the international sphere before the Second World War or in its rivalry with the United States in the post-1945 period. The USSR was only late and briefly a member (1934–9) of the LoN, set up in 1920 as the first international organization dealing with the entire spectrum of international relations. In the UN, the League's successor, it supposedly remained in the position of a steady contender who could not win out over the United States (Westad, 2017).

Recently, these two narratives have been contested. If we do not limit our view to a state-centric perspective, we can recognize people and movements that 'organized across borders to advance agendas that would not work or even fit within exclusively national frameworks' (Connelly, 2006: 202; Connelly, 2000: 739–69) or even ignored national purposes in the ways they conceived and pursued their interests. International organizations, then, are not only forums where sovereign states negotiate their foreign policies but are also spaces in which all kinds of non-state actors become involved.

Official representation – be it restricted to states or, in the case of non-governmental internationalism, to nationally organized interest groups – is not the only way of partaking. Individuals can enter via routes other than as representatives of their country. Agents from Eastern Europe, just like actors from other parts of the world, found multiple roles and positions through which to engage.

At the same time, a crucial analytical shift revised the role of the USSR in the post-Second World War period. Instead of projecting the outcome of the Cold War rivalry between the USSR and the United States – which, during the 1990s and early 2000s, seemed to present a clear victory for the latter and an 'end of history' – back into the past (Fukuyama, 1992), the power struggle is understood as an open constellation whose ending was not known to the participants in the Cold War. In this line of investigation, the USSR's international politics does not appear as bound to fail but as a real alternative. Its socialist programme contested the liberal internationalism epitomized by the LoN and UN, and this challenge was taken seriously – nowhere more so than in the United States.

Building on these re-evaluations, a new understanding of Eastern Europeans' participation in the world of international organizations has come into view. It is based on three insights:

1 International organizations are complex institutions consisting of a multitude of bodies – the general assemblies of its members, commissions working on specific topics, administrations charged with technical and programmatic work, the leading councils, and a whole spectrum of connected institutions and networks. We speak not of the UN but of at least three 'UNs': the bodies consisting of representatives of its member states; the administrations; and the associated non-governmental organizations (NGOs), independent commissions, academics, experts and consultants (Weiss, Carayannis and Jolly, 2009: 123–42) This complex institutional architecture implies that participation arises from different positions – as, for example, official delegate of one's own country, international officer, expert or consultant. Each position goes along with specific forms of political agency and its limits. We find Eastern Europeans in each of these positions.

2 When we talk about Eastern European actors, we need to keep in mind that the affiliation with the region is only one of the many belongings and loyalties that have shaped people's actions. Territorial affiliations (and representations) are intertwined with social, professional, religious and political identifications, which often run 'over, across, through, beyond, above, under, or in-between polities and societies' (Iriye and Saunier, 2009: xviii). Furthermore 'Eastern Europeans'– a designation that can be both a self-description and an ascription from outside – have entered international organizations from different places in the world; just think of the many people who left the region.

3 Researchers and contemporaries have often depicted the countries of East Central Europe as small states that supposedly had limited space of action in international politics, among others due to underrepresentation. Yet agents often made strategic use of this ascription of having 'minor status' or of being representatives of 'small states'. In an international setting that in principle was based on equality, such characterizations of a community – whether it is bound together by culture, religion, tradition or nationality – can be, and were, used for claiming proactive participation. In addition, in spite of formal representation

and the possession of voting rights, there are many channels to exercise influence in international organizations: from shaping agenda setting to bringing in resolutions, from providing strategic knowledge to conceiving concepts that lead out of blocked negotiations. Therefore, territoriality and geopolitics are best understood as essential conditions, which, however, did not prevent agents from acting in an idiosyncratic manner to deal with conditions on their own terms – including the drive to assert oneself against the superpowers.

Socializing international health politics: From eradicating epidemics to public health

In January 2020, the WHO warned of an outbreak of a flu-like disease in Wuhan (China), which turned out to be COVID-19. Putting to one side for a moment criticism about its belated intervention, no one doubted that the WHO was key in combatting the resulting pandemic. When cholera spread in 19th-century Europe, the situation was entirely different. No international organization for the containment of highly contagious diseases then existed. Contemporaries saw the state as being in charge of protecting its citizens within its territory against border-crossing diseases – above all, through effective border control. The rise of an international health policy that governs epidemics within a broad, permanent programme of improving health conditions around the world originates from an innovative health agenda put forward by medical experts and diplomats from East Central and South-eastern Europe after the First World War. They devised and enforced a concept of international health that was based on three pillars: a socio-economic conceptualization of diseases, technological solutions reflective of local conditions, and centralized state intervention (public health).[4] After the Second World War, this concept was adopted, in particular, by Soviet health diplomats, who changed the WHO's principles of international epidemic control. To understand this process of expanding and transforming international health, largely driven by Eastern Europeans, we need to look at the problems they sought to remedy.

In the mid-19th century, new transportation technologies such as the railway and steam navigation rapidly increased the mobility of people and the trading of goods; yet, alongside this development, viruses and bacteria – not yet known at the time – were now able to spread faster and wider. To safeguard the desirable flows while limiting the unwanted ones, new ways of handling epidemics seemed necessary. From 1851 onwards, a series of international conferences took place that aimed at a collaboration in sanitary matters, especially in view of the cholera then raging in Europe. During the negotiations, cholera and other highly infectious diseases were gradually perceived as problems of international concern: if diseases travelled at a new speed without respecting borders, their prevention could not stop at the borders either. Thus, in 1892, the first international treaty establishing common quarantine measures was brokered – ultimately replacing prevailing, heterogeneous, national quarantine regulations. The unification of the globe *by* diseases was thus accompanied by a unification *against* diseases.[5] These advances in international health politics, however, still perceived epidemics as external threats and their control as a primarily domestic task. Cooperation was limited to defensive measures against their spread, and reinforced the inviolability of state borders. Moreover, restricted in focus to epidemics, health internationalism remained a temporary matter that ended when an emergency faded.

This narrow notion changed with the epidemics that broke out at the end of the First World War, especially in view of the influenza ('Spanish flu') that gripped the entire world. Medical experts, realizing the complex transnational environments of epidemic disease, argued that combatting it must also be a comprehensive endeavour. Governments followed this rationale and approached epidemics from a new angle – as global problems requiring joint action on a worldwide scale. Hence, the LoN had its *raison d'être* not only in the maintenance of international peace and security but also in 'matters of international concern for the prevention and control of disease' (Covenant, Article 23).

An epidemic situation in East Central and South-eastern Europe became a matter of international concern in 1919. The ravages of war had hit this area hard, and Spanish flu, malaria and typhus wreaked havoc in a region that was confronted with overlapping crises – famine, refugees, devasted lands, and profound, conflict-ridden political transformations. The successor states to the Habsburg, Ottoman and German empires as well that of Tsarist Russia were still politically fragile due to revolutionary movements, reactive forces and ongoing military conflicts. In this context, combatting the epidemic emergency became a matter of survival not only for the people but also for their governments. Poland, deeply affected by the typhus epidemic, called for international help in spring 1920. To tackle the worsening health situation, the LoN set up a Health Section in its secretariat and appointed Ludwik W. Rajchman as its head.[6] In this decision, humanitarian and political concerns intersected. East Central Europe had become a *cordon sanitaire* or buffer zone for 'Western' powers after the October Revolution established the USSR as the first socialist state, eager to spread revolution.[7]

Rajchman, a Warsaw-born bacteriologist and director of the Polish National Hygiene Institute, was part of a network of health experts based in Warsaw, Prague and Zagreb. Most of them were in leading positions in state administrations, and together they devised the concept of social medicine. Pioneering at the time, it shifted the predominant under-standing of health as an absence of diseases to a notion of the prevention of diseases. Consequently, it saw the state as being in charge of providing public health care that would eliminate the socio-economic causes of illness. State intervention in health matters was also a novelty. All these ideas answered the needs of the war-ridden and mostly agrarian societies as well as the post-imperial state-building in the region. Remnants of the fragmented health administrations from the dissolved empires were to be replaced, and the nascent nation-states had to prove themselves as efficient political orders. Public-welfare systems were the tool of the day, and health care one of its decisive pillars. Health politics, including epidemic control, became the measuring stick for post-imperial governance.[8]

When Rajchman was called to the Health Section to coordinate international help against the typhus epidemic, he seized the opportunity in its formative phase. The League's statute had left unanswered what the prevention of disease could imply. Supported by his Eastern

European fellows, Rajchman inscribed their concept of social medicine and public health into the League's health agenda. Five permanent programmes were established – epidemiological intelligence, serological and biological standardization, medical demography, data classification and unification, and public health – which were accompanied by smaller programmes on opium, rural hygiene and housing.[9]

The internationalization of ideas developed for Eastern Europe served a double purpose – it fostered nation-building in the region and profiled the League as an effective institution of world government. Within a few years, its Health Section matured into the League of Nations Health Organization, which became one of the League's most successful bodies. Two consequences of this decisive shift stand out. First, international health expanded from the intermittent cooperation of states affected by epidemics to a permanent task of all League members to collaborate in preventing diseases through public health. Second, Eastern Europe became a testing ground and laboratory for a novel approach in international epidemic control. After all, from then on, states were obliged to submit their data to the League Health Organization's epidemiological intelligence programme and integrate their preventive work into public healthcare infrastructures.

The League Health Organization in turn set up an anti-malaria programme for its members in 1924. The coordinative commission included Evgeny Martsinovsky and Petr Sergiev (Moscow), Andrija Sfarčić (Belgrade), Mihail Ciucă (Iași)[10] and Ludwik Anigstein (Warsaw). They pushed for a socio-economic approach that combatted malaria with rural modernization, drainage, quinine distribution and hygienic education.[11] These tools were adjusted to the local conditions of malaria-affected areas, and targeting local ecological, social and economic contexts became the focus of the League Health Organization's anti-malaria programme. This policy reached its limits in areas in Africa and Asia that were under colonial rule since the League did not interfere with the sovereignty of the British and French empires. However, its approach to epidemic control was significant. It enabled, among other things, cooperation with Soviet medical experts at a time when their country was not yet a member of the LoN (joining as late as 1934). They contributed their experiences in fighting typhus and malaria with socially oriented and locally reflective methods, and they, too, conceived health politics as a tool for state-building – just like the experts from other parts of Eastern Europe.[12]

The region's post-imperial situation led to a new stance against epidemics that was carried over after the Second World War. Intervention in the local circumstances of diseases by state-funded national health care systems resonated with the concerns of the postcolonial states in Asia and Africa that emerged in the 1950s and 60s. Initially, however, the WHO, as successor to the League Health Organization, set up a Malaria Expert Committee in 1948 that shifted to a purely technical combatting of malaria. The discovery of DDT (dichlorodiphenyltrichloroethane), as the first synthetic insecticide, promised cheaper and more effective campaigns. For a decade, the WHO focused on spraying DDT, disregarding preventive medicine, context-reflective measures and socio-economic reforms. In fact, this insecticide-based spraying applied worldwide in the early post-war period, only gradually becoming criticized because of its negative environmental effects.

When the USSR and other socialist countries re-entered the WHO[13] in the mid-1950s, they used the waning reputation of insecticide-based technological solutions to push the organization to adopt an integrated approach in epidemic control that combined technological solutions with socio-economic interventions and centralized state coordination. With success, in 1967, the WHO changed its strategy for malaria eradication, now calling for 'the development of basic health services', 'the investigation of the social and economic implications of malaria and of its eradication', and the 'necessary diversification of means of eradication in accordance with the particular requirements of each country'.[14]

In the meantime, the Soviet delegation had initiated a global campaign to eradicate smallpox that was based on their countries' experience in vaccination against this disease since 1919.[15] The Smallpox Eradication Programme (SEP), in full swing from 1967, was a milestone in the development of international health, following the path Eastern European countries had taken. It served as a precedent for all further WHO programmes, including those on tuberculosis, polio and HIV/AIDS. Added to this, the programme rested on a cooperation for which the United States provided much of the funding and the USSR delivered much of the vaccine. This collaboration of the superpowers in the middle of the Cold War was possible because it was conducted by the mid-level technocrat Donald A. Henderson (Atlanta/later Geneva), chief of the Epidemic Surveillance Section of the US Public Health Service's Communicable Disease Center, and the trained surgeon Dmitry Venediktov (Moscow), who, despite his role as Deputy Health Minister in the USSR, prioritized scientific reasoning and technical solutions over ideological issues or geopolitical tensions. The two men, just like Rajchman and his fellow campaigners in the League Health Organization, acted pragmatically in a problem-solving manner and upheld professional medical concerns. The trustful relationship they built in the conduct of the SEP reached beyond the programme itself. It nourished a political atmosphere in the WHO, allowing the Soviet Union to invite all WHO and UNICEF (United Nations Children's Fund) members to a conference devoted to primary health. This took place in 1978 in Alma Ata, the capital of the Kazakh Soviet Socialist Republic, and ended with a declaration in which the WHO committed itself to a comprehensive understanding of international health, not merely the absence of disease.[16] Since then, the so-called horizontal approach has been repeatedly questioned, not least in the context of the neoliberal turn in international health in the 1990s. Yet it persisted, and with it the agenda that Eastern European actors had introduced in the 1920s and which has held on ever since.

Decolonizing world trade: Regulating international shipping

'[O]ver time, developing countries have been the main exporting countries for world trade . . . we clearly had a colonial trade pattern' where these countries 'exported raw materials and imported – as marginal players – mainly consumer goods.'[17] This assessment was not written by scholars studying the history of colonialism. The secretariat of UNCTAD came to this conclusion in 2018. Changing these unequal global trade relations by supporting the so-called developing countries in securing a favourable position in world trade has been the prime task of UNCTAD since its founding in 1964 in response to demands by newly joining countries from the 'Third World'. It was set up as the first international body charged with assisting in economic decolonization through regulations that remove discriminatory global-trading conditions.

This agenda includes action against the vast imbalance in *what* is traded – raw material versus processed goods – but also policies regarding the underpinning transportation infrastructure. International trade remains overwhelmingly seaborne: 90 per cent of it is carried by ships over the world's oceans. Yet the operation of this shipping has been in the hands of companies from very few countries. In the 1960s, these were, above all, European maritime powers – while countries from the so-called Third World had either no or only small trading fleets. At the end of the 1960s, their share in the world fleet was around 7 per cent although they generated about 65 per cent of all cargo transported in ocean trade. They therefore depended largely on foreign shipowners, who determined the terms and conditions of the shipment of their imports and exports.[18]

UNCTAD intervened against this structural imbalance in global transportation from various angles. It helped with the expansion of merchant fleets in Africa and Asia to make decolonizing countries less dependent on foreign transport companies; it worked to make their port facilities more efficient; and it sought to secure their unhindered access to shipping services. The last-named was a daunting task. Liner conferences – associations of a few, large shipping companies – controlled the ocean carriage on the most frequented routes through price agreements. Since access to them was exclusive, a small number of companies determined the freight rates that traders around the world had to pay. In 1974, however, only a decade after its founding, UNCTAD achieved the signing of an international Convention on a Code of Conduct for Liner Conferences that regulated the price policies of these associations (cartels), the access to them and their shares in seaborne transport. In this part, we investigate the history of this Convention in the context of UNCTAD's early work on international shipping and its founding, which has an history of its own, beginning in the 1920s.

While most of the literature depicts UNCTAD through the prism of North–South relations,[19] some Eastern Europeans played a decisive role in its formation. They were instrumental in UNCTAD's political interventions into world trade and maritime transport in its early years, and they helped in larger terms to establish internationally the argument that world trade must be politically regulated to become beneficial for all. We see here agents from Eastern Europe who connected with, plugged into and supported the international political agendas of agents from the newly decolonizing countries.

Yet, these entangled interests had a 'prehistory'. UNCTAD's history goes further back in time, and in the longer trajectory we can also see Eastern Europeans in decisive roles, too, due to shared challenges and goals. Eastern European economies saw themselves in an unfavourable position in terms of global trade. Eastern Europeans had already tried before the Second World War to bring international trading relations, especially shipping services, under political control in view of the dominance of the overseas empires. Branko Lukač (Belgrade), the director of the League of Nations Transport Commission, attempted to set up an international body in which the power asymmetries of the sector could be raised and reduced. Yet resistance was great, and it was lasting. In 1948, the establishment of an International Trade Organization had been agreed in Havana, but it was stillborn as the United States withdrew its support – wanting fewer regulations, not more. In the same year, Lukač – who had moved to the UN, directing its Transportation Commission – was successful in setting up the Inter-Governmental Maritime Consultative Organization (IMCO). Yet IMCO was concerned with technical aspects of maritime trade and transport – and the UN's International Labour Organization, which began to deal with shipping, addressed labour-related issues. Both bodies enforced regulations that improved safety on the seas, i.e. the labour conditions of seafarers, or the technical condition of ships. Overcoming discriminatory structures rooted in colonialism and imperialism remained, however, outside their mandate.

Interest in an international body that would address the political economy of world trade and international shipping grew in Eastern European countries from the mid-1950s. This was related to socialist economic policies that saw the state in charge of economic development, and which at the time began to conceive of foreign trade as an important tool. Because of this view, trading fleets were developed throughout the Eastern bloc and state-owned shipping companies were expanded or founded, even in landlocked countries such as Czechoslovakia, not least because transportation services offered to other countries were recognized as a source of income. Yet in 1960, countries of the Council for Mutual Economic Assistance (without Cuba) had only a 3.5 per cent share of the shipped world tonnage. Even though the amount of their shipped cargo quadrupled in the following decade, their share by 1975 had grown only to 5 per cent.[20] Initially, policymakers and economists in Eastern Europe founded their own liner conference with partners in the decolonizing world, which pursued an aggressive price policy in the international shipping market. Self-directed action was also a goal in their international economic policy. In 1970, Poland initiated the founding of the International Shipowners' Association, which organized the interests of shipping companies in the region and was seen for some time as a counterpart to UNCTAD.

Yet at the same time, agents from the region supported UNCTAD and helped its founding. The Yugoslavian delegation to the UN, in particular, strongly advocated an international body that would enforce international rules for world trade in the context of the non-alignment movement, a coalition of states that remained neutral in the Cold War rivalry between the two superpowers and their 'blocs'. Janez Stanovnik, Yugoslavia's leading representative in the UN, was key in emphasizing the political nature of the structural inequalities between the North and the South, and in pushing towards a restructured world trade that served the needs of all. That plea included socialist countries and, with their support, the call by the decolonizing countries for UNCTAD found majority support in the UN.[21]

Essential for UNCTAD's coming into being in a long-term perspective was the solidarity between African and Asian countries that had gained political independence. It grew in the regional economic commissions that were set up by the UN.[22]

Until the early 1960s, commissions for Europe, Asia, Latin America and Africa had emerged, working on the development of the economies in their parts of the world while also cooperating with one another. The very idea of regional economic commissions had entered the UN through Poland in 1946. The head of the Polish delegation to its first General Assembly, Jan Stańczyk, proposed this idea when the future of international relief and reconstruction of the countries devastated in the Second World War was discussed. Stańczyk argued that neither the existing humanitarian help nor the international economic and financial institutions set up at the 1944 Bretton Woods Conference would suffice. Instead, close and permanent economic cooperation between the countries concerned was needed, organized on a regional basis and through autonomous bodies in the UN. This notion ultimately received support.[23]

Collaboration between the commissions was put into the hands of Władysław Malinowski, a Krakow-born lawyer and economist. He was instrumental in giving shared interests a common aim – namely, targeting the power imbalance in world trade. He drew on the economic analyses of Raúl Prebisch, the head of the Economic Commission for Latin America, and of Hans Singer, a leading economist in the UN administration, which made clear that the division of labour between regions exporting raw materials and regions exporting industrial goods leads to unjust terms of trade, discriminating against the former and handing an advantage to the latter. Malinowski and Prebisch envisaged UNCTAD as a counter force to this trend, and jointly built solidarity between the decolonizing countries, the necessary international political pressure, and support from the USSR and the socialist bloc. Malinowski also looked at the structural trade asymmetry in view of transportation. He was convinced that '[s]hipping was very much an instrument of empire'.[24] In his mission to reverse the existing power dynamics, he drew, among other sources, on the arguments of Kwame Nkrumah, the pioneer of African socialism. Nkrumah had argued in his broadly well-received book *Neo-Colonialism* that the 'so-called "invisible trade" furnishes the Western monopolies with yet another means of economic penetration. Over 90 per cent of world shipping is controlled by imperialist countries.'[25]

Malinowski became head of the Division of Invisibles when UNCTAD was founded, and its headquarters was being staffed. As the name of the division signals, it was devoted to the 'invisible trade', which refers to the costs related to transportation and insurance that made up a large share of the foreign-trade deficits of decolonizing countries.[26] Yet, political resistance from the shipping cartels was massive. At UNCTAD's founding conference, regulations for international shipping were so hard to agree on that only a short 'Common Measure of Understanding on Shipping Questions' was included in the final act. Still, it was decisive. It included the obligation to reform the liner conferences so that shippers from all parts of the world had access to them and could negotiate their terms of operation.

The subsequent process of negotiation, leading to the Convention on a Code of Conduct for Liner Conferences, had – like the founding of UNCTAD itself – an important Eastern European dimension. Malinowski and his team set up a research division dedicated to producing in-depth knowledge about the invisible factors behind international shipping, which at the time were hardly known. A crucial element was the support of an emerging academic field called Maritime Economics. Many of its pioneers approached the subject from the perspective of political economy, which provided the common ground for cooperation with UNCTAD. In this collaboration, shipping experts from the Instytut Morski in Gdansk (Poland) had a crucial contribution to make. The institute was one of the largest shipping-related research-and-policy institutions in Eastern Europe. In the mid-1960s, more than three hundred experts studied and planned the development of Polish harbours, the country's merchant fleet and its state-owned shipping companies. Just like UNCTAD, Polish economic policy was based on the belief that national economies can only prosper when competitive merchant fleets can operate in a transparent and accessible international shipping regime. Foreign trade and trade balances were seen as essential for economic development, which was the same reasoning decolonized countries propagated through UNCTAD. To this end, a division of the Instytut Morski, led by Maciej Krzyżanowski, was devoted to seaborne transportation. It collaborated closely and continuously with Malinowski and his team by sharing Polish experiences and models.

This collaboration included a scheme for a nationally governed system of foreign trade that linked producers, exporters and shippers, and which provided a shared ground from which to regulate the ocean carriage that was much more powerful in negotiations with the cartels than the voice of a single shipper. All these initiatives embodied ideas and goals UNCTAD promoted for the development of the shipping industries in Africa, Asia and Latin America.

This collaboration in knowledge production stirred political action. The jointly prepared, pathbreaking studies and reports were submitted by Malinowski to UNCTAD's political body concerned with maritime issues, the shipping committee. Its recommendations, drawn from the preparatory documents that Malinowski and his collaborators had devised, were later discussed and adopted at the regular conferences of all UNCTAD members. Their resolutions for action were taken up by the UN General Assembly, and led to international treaties such as the Code of Conduct.

The Code of Conduct laid down basic international rules: that all national shipping lines must be granted full membership in the liner conferences; that freight rates must be kept as low as possible; that cartels must make their arrangements transparent; and, finally, that a consultation mechanism should secure for all stakeholders, including shippers, equal rights. Furthermore, the document included a cargo allocation. The shipping lines of each of the two directly trading states received the right to carry up to 40 per cent of the cargo; only the remaining 20 per cent was available to third parties.

In this way, the Code was instrumental in promoting the expansion of the merchant fleets of the developing countries and increasing the participation of their governments, as well as their foreign-trade actors, in maritime trade and transport. More than that, international policy in this area was placed under a new principle: that it was not the economic interests of the shipping companies and cargo enterprises that had priority but the political-economic interests of those involved. The elimination of the unequal terms of trade and the creation of favourable conditions for economic development was of benefit not only for the decolonizing world but also for the socialist world in Eastern Europe.

Although the Code heralded a far-reaching change in world trade, by the time it came into force – in 1983 – the conditions of maritime trade had changed dramatically: the oil crises of the 1970s had raised the price of fuel dramatically; the container revolution – the introduction of standardized containers and corresponding new types of ships – provided for more shipping space than there was cargo to carry; and the high cost of rebuilding ports adapted to this new technology hit countries with small fleets particularly hard. The early 1980s saw the beginning of a long crisis in international shipping, worsened by the trend of the times towards liberalization, which eventually resulted in the Washington Consensus. The New World Economic Order adopted in 1974, and the work of UNCTAD on shipping that was included in it, did not fulfil the hopes it had raised or the promises it had made. Yet from then on, the rationale was established of an international trading policy that saw governments in charge of regulating world trade together in a manner that the gains, and not only the costs, of trade were equally distributed among all participations, and it continues to impact on international-trade governance. It also had its roots in ideas, agendas and political action by Eastern Europeans.

Peace and security under the nuclear threat: Nuclear-weapon-free zones vis-à-vis universal disarmament

On 26 September 2022, UN Secretary General António Guterres opened a special session at the General Assembly devoted to the International Day for the Total Elimination of Nuclear Weapons by saying, 'We come together on this international day to speak with one voice . . . to reject the claim that nuclear disarmament is some impossible utopian dream.'[27] He called for a world liberated from the nuclear threat at a moment when military spending had again reached record levels, when 13,000 nuclear weapons existed around the globe, and when international efforts for their reduction had become most difficult – not least, due to Russia's war against Ukraine.

That nuclear disarmament appears today to many as a utopian dream is a consequence of recent developments since major international treaties have expired and efforts towards their renewal have been lacklustre.[28] Yet even before this juncture, the speed of nuclear armament was much greater than the pace of agreements about its control and limitation. Nuclear warfare began with the atomic bombing of Hiroshima and Nagasaki by the United States at the end of the Second World War in 1945. It soon became part of an escalating arms race between the United States and the USSR in the context of Cold War rivalry, and this antagonism still resonates today. Yet, we should not see the past eight decades of international efforts towards nuclear disarmament only in the light of today's peak of nuclear weaponry.

On the one hand, proposals for what is called 'universal disarmament' were made right from the start. During the negotiations of the '4th Geneva Convention', which provided protection for civilians in times of war and which the International Committee of the Red Cross had initiated in 1949, the Soviet delegation tried hard to include a ban on the use of nuclear weapons in the treaty. It was dismissed, particularly due to the resistance of the United States. A non-binding resolution that would recommend that the Convention's state parties work towards a prohibition of the usage of atomic weapons was rejected, too. In response, the USSR conducted its first nuclear test in Semipalatinsk (near Astana, Kazakhstan) just a few weeks later.[29] In the following years, the USSR and other Eastern European states made numerous proposals in the UN to limit the nuclear threat. Yet, universal disarmament proved to be an elusive goal. In 1952, the United States detonated a hydrogen bomb in the Marshall Islands. In the mid-1950s, NATO (the North Atlantic

Treaty Organization military alliance of the United States and its political allies) equipped its troops with nuclear weapons, while simultaneously accepting West Germany (the Federal Republic of Germany, or FRG) as a member. In response, the USSR and its allies signed a collective-defense treaty that established the Warsaw Pact, which included East Germany (the German Democratic Republic, or GDR). These decisions not only deepened the Cold War divide but also turned the so-called 'Iron Curtain' running through Europe into a military border safeguarded with nuclear power. Any escalation of the ideological conflict would have led to nuclear warfare on the territories of the bordering states, including those in East Central Europe.

Compared with the growing nuclear threat, work to reduce escalation developed only gradually. Initially it was limited to bi- or trilateral agreements between the nuclear powers. In 1963, the United States, the USSR and Great Britain signed the Partial Nuclear Test Ban Treaty, which paved the way for the Strategic Arms Limitation Talks between the USSR and the United States in the 1970s (concluding with the SALT I and SALT II treaties). In parallel, collective efforts within the UN had started that, in 1968, led to the signing of the important Nuclear Non-Proliferation Treaty by over sixty states. This was a landmark in the arena of collective nuclear disarmament. This success notwithstanding, before 1968 and thereafter the dream of what has been called 'universal disarmament' has repeatedly been shattered. The Cold War confrontation often impeded compromises on security issues at the UN, and the hopes for a worldwide system of disarmament spanning around the International Atomic Energy Agency[30] have been crushed again and again.

There is another side to this story, which developed in parallel with the fragile practice of reaching universal nuclear disarmament. It originated in East Central Europe. In 1956, a group of Polish diplomats and lawyers at the Polish Foreign Ministry gave collective nuclear disarmament a new direction. They picked up ideas on moving apart the armed forces of the two atomic powers who faced one another across the Iron Curtain, and devised the concept of Nuclear-Weapon-Free Zones (NWFZ). Compared with the laborious efforts towards worldwide disarmament, this regional approach has been much more successful – not in the zone that was initially at stake (i.e. Central Europe), but in other parts of the world. In the following text, we look at this concept as the last of the three examples in this chapter. It testifies that ideas developed in Eastern Europe circulated widely and impacted lastingly on international politics. It makes us aware that Eastern Europeans not only proactively changed the agendas of international organizations or helped to found new institutions but were also crucial in overcoming political impasses within these institutions.

The idea of NWFZ arose in a double moment of change and chance. The change began after Stalin's death (1953), when Nikita Khrushchev (General Secretary of the Communist Party of the USSR) initiated political reforms in the USSR – so-called de-Stalinization. They resonated in other countries in Eastern Europe and solidified the concept of peaceful co-existence between the 'socialist East' and 'capitalist West'. Although the thaw was brief, it prompted the 'Polish October', a period of internal political liberalization and greater autonomy from Moscow. In this environment, Władysław Gomułka, Poland's leading political figure at that time, tasked the country's pragmatic and liberally oriented foreign minister, Adam Rapacki, to come up with a form of international cooperation that would free Central Europe from nuclear weapons and thereby ensure Poland's and Europe's security in a world of growing military tensions. Rapacki called on Henryk Birecki, Manfred Lachs, Marian Naszkowski, Przemysław Ogrodziński and Józef Winiewicz.[31] Together, they drafted a visionary proposal for the demilitarization of a zone in Central Europe stretching from France and the Benelux countries through the two German states to Poland, Czechoslovakia and Denmark, within which the number of troops and military spending would be reduced. They also envisaged a complete ban on nuclear weapons, with a comprehensive inspection system in a smaller region comprising the German states and bordering areas.

They saw a moment of chance arriving since, from the other side, a nuclear-weapon-free zone in Europe was being considered, too. At the Geneva Summit (1955), the leaders of the United States, Britain, France and the USSR had touched upon the idea of creating a zone between East and West in which military power would be reduced and internationally controlled. The Warsaw Pact came back to earlier proposals for establishing a special zone in Central Europe, which had been included in a comprehensive plan for the disarmament of conventional and nuclear weapons presented to the UN Disarmament Commission in March 1954.

Figure 3.1 Scarf with the wording 'For a nuclear-weapon-free zone in Europe'.

© Sammlung DDR Museum, Berlin

In addition, Adam Rapacki reminded the international public in 1963 why he and his fellow-campaigners took the lead:

> Poland, which has so often been placed by history in the front line of World War battles, is naturally vitally interested in the very idea of even partial disarmament and a reduction of tension along the line of direct confrontation between the Great Powers: the line where the two opposed military groupings confront each other in an area 200–300 kilometers to the west of our frontiers – an area which has a key significance for world peace.[32]

It is not surprising that Poland's own security concerns and a sense of international responsibility in nuclear matters were closely intertwined. When the FRG entered NATO, Polish foreign politicians were fully aware that the FRG had not accepted Poland's western borders drawn at the Yalta Conference in 1945 and still upheld its territorial claims for parts of the sovereign Polish state. This led to tremendous fears about a future revision of the Polish–German border given that the possibility of negotiating neutrality for the two German states had become obsolete due to their integration into the respective military alliances. The pending 'German question', the growing nuclear threat, the fragility within the UN as to universal disarmament, and Polish ambitions to use the moment of change to put forward an effective proposal for international peace – all these came together when the foreign minister and his collaborators worked out what became known as the Rapacki Plan.[33]

In view of this, Adam Rapacki proposed at a UN General Assembly meeting on 2 October 1957 'that if the two German states should consent to enforce the prohibition of the production and stockpiling of nuclear weapons in their respective territories, the People's Republic of Poland is prepared simultaneously to institute the same prohibition in its territory'.[34] His plan met harsh resistance from the United States and NATO.

By autumn 1957, international tension had grown once more: the crushing of the Hungarian Revolution by Soviet troops in autumn 1956 ended the thaw in Eastern Europe; the Suez crisis gripped the world; Britain conducted its first atomic tests; NATO extended its nuclear rearmament; and the USSR tested its interregional ballistic power. Rapacki had made clear, though, that a NWFZ in Central Europe was meant to be a first step, a partial solution that should pave the way towards a systematic demilitarization in Europe based on a supra-national zone of neutrality in the Cold War-ridden region. Within a few months, the proposal was rejected. In addition, two days after Rapacki's speech at the UN, the USSR launched the first artificial satellite, and the 'West' reeled under the 'Sputnik-shock', which, in short order, spurred the so-called space race. In 1958, the Berlin crisis erupted and, all in all, the international military-strategic situation was forced into an arms race with strategic nuclear weapons.

For a period of seven years until 1964, Rapacki continued to campaign for his proposal: twice, he presented revised versions to the UN; he travelled across Europe to seek political support; and he took many opportunities to present its guiding ideas as well as the pacifying potential of a NWFZ in Europe in the international press. In the immediate term, all this was of no use; within the UN, the proposal was off the table. Yet, the idea of a zone freed from nuclear weaponry resonated widely elsewhere – not least since it had been forwarded with the courageous claim that the world's so-called small states had the right to make suggestions for international peace that involved larger states and not only the other way around.

In the following years, schemes for regional nuclear disarmament were devised in many places – most prominently in Finland, with regard to northern Europe, and in Bulgaria and Romania for the Balkans – and Belgian as well as Swedish politicians initiated the first scientific studies of regional disarmament as a most promising alternative to universal disarmament. Localized expressions of the nuclear-free-zone concept surfaced in many places outside of Europe, as well. There were too many of them to be recalled here, but they created a political atmosphere in which it became possible to negotiate international treaties inspired by the ideas and arguments developed in Warsaw in the mid-1950s. First, the Antarctic was denuclearized (1959), then – in loose succession thereafter – land and sea

Table 1. Nuclear arms limitation treaties

Year	Nuclear arms limitation treaties
1959	Antarctic Treaty
1967	Outer Space Treaty (Treaty on Principles Governing the Activities of States in the Exploration and Use of Outer Space, including the Moon and Other Celestial Bodies)
1967	Treaty of Tlateolco (Treaty for the Prohibition of Nuclear Weapons in Latin America and the Caribbean)
1968	Treaty on the Non-Proliferation of Nuclear Weapons
1971	Seabed Treaty (Treaty on the Prohibition of the Emplacement of Nuclear Weapons and Other Weapons of Mass Destruction on the Sea-Bed and the Ocean Floor and in the Subsoil thereof)
1972	SALT I Treaty (Anti-Ballistic Agreement)
1979	Moon Agreement (Agreement Governing the Activities of States on the Moon and Other Celestial Bodies)
	SALT II Treaty (Treaty on the Limitation of Strategic Offensive Arms)
1985	Treaty of Rarotonga (South Pacific Nuclear-Free-Zone Treaty)
1995	Treaty of Bangkok (Treaty on the Southeast Asia Nuclear-Weapon-Free Zone)
1996	Treaty of Pelindaba (African Nuclear-Weapon-Free Zone Treaty)
2006	Treaty on a Nuclear-Weapon-Free Zone in Central Asia
under negotiation	Nuclear-Weapon-Free Zone in the Middle East (first proposed in 1974)

territories around the world, as well as outer space (see table, p. 92). As early as 1963, representatives from Bolivia, Brazil, Chile and Mexico acknowledged their intention to sign a contract in which they would commit themselves not to manufacture, receive, store or test nuclear weapons or nuclear launching devices and to seek to include further states in Latin America in this agreement. Little more than a year later, at its first meeting, the Organization of African Unity in 1964 declared the denuclearization of the African continent and its intention to codify in an international treaty its refusal to manufacture or acquire control of nuclear weapons. From there to today's negotiations about a NWFZ for the Middle East (which began about fifty years ago), we can follow the trajectory of a concept that originated among a group of Warsaw-based lawyers and diplomats. They had seized ideas circulating about a geographical distancing of the superpowers and regional neutralization, turned them into a concrete proposal, and taken them to an international audience. There, these ideas also impacted on debates about universal disarmament, beginning with the Non-Proliferation Treaty of 1968 – itself a result of the debates about regional nuclear disarmament that had been ongoing since the late 1950s, since it included the 'right of any group of States to conclude regional treaties in order to assure the total absence of nuclear weapons in their respective territories' (Article VII). When the UN General Assembly defined a Nuclear-Weapon-Free Zone (Res. 3472 B) in 1975, the concept became an internationally recognized tool for pacifying the world, which is still in practice today.

Conclusion: Eastern Europe in the history of international organizations

In this chapter, we have charted the trajectories of agents from Eastern Europe who strongly shaped the international sphere in the 20th century. We have traced the crucial changes they initiated – a shift in the international health agenda, the challenge of unequal global trade relations in the field of international shipping, and the proposal for an alternative concept in nuclear disarmament. These changes encompass a broad spectrum of interventions – altering programmatic agendas by introducing original concepts, initiating new international organizations, and launching international conventions. Some of them reinvigorated and reframed debates that had reached a stalemate. That led to opposition. Eastern Europeans voiced ideas, policies and concrete proposals that often aimed at transforming asymmetrical international power relations. Efforts to make world trade less unequal met harsh resistance; the concept of regional nuclear disarmament challenged the supremacy of the nuclear powers in preventing a nuclear war; and international health, conceived as the permanent task of a world governance that intervenes in the socio-economic conditions of diseases and epidemics and thus requires public-health measures, contradicted predominant notions of health politics and national sovereignty.

These controversies occurred in international organizations that were impacted on by deep political divides. After the First World War, the League of Nations embodied a liberal notion of internationalism based on international law and multilateralism. The USSR established an alternative concept in the 1920s. Socialist internationalism sought to forge 'socialist' solutions to the pressing international issues of the day. In theory and practice, the two partly intersected – liberal, reformist initiatives overlapped with socialist ideas on how to create peaceful and more cooperative international politics. Yet they were increasingly brought into opposition. After the Second World War, the fierce competition between the two superpowers, the United States and the USSR, strengthened in the context of the global Cold War. Dissent over how to regulate international relations and how to solve international problems was omnipresent. The international sphere was deeply divided.

However, in parallel, we have seen agents from East Central Europe become influential in the international sphere. That became possible to a large extent because international organizations were also sites in which a notion and practice of gradual rapprochement grew, driven by a search to accommodate seemingly incompatible views on how to direct international politics. Within these dynamics, agents from the region, and from other parts of world, could make themselves heard – with lasting impact. Through the processes in which ideological and geopolitical rivalries clashed and were bargained over, a sense of togetherness grew because the confrontations, separations and competitions took place in institutions that had been set up for cooperation – an idea to which all parties remained committed. This provided for polycentric negotiations.

Compromises and ways out of complex situations became possible because of the urgency of global problems such as health and epidemics, unequal trading relations and nuclear threats. In effect, the divided spaces were also continuously held together. During the 20th century, they gradually became the pillars of an international sphere in which the divides were mitigated and international relations could change.

Agents from Eastern Europe seized opportunities for change that arose in the constellation of togetherness, and they responded to the political divides. We have seen lawyers and diplomats, health and economists, who were both visionary and pragmatic, and who made a difference in international politics. Adam Rapacki and his fellow campaigners seized a moment of change to propose a nuclear-weapon-free zone in Europe when disarmament debates in the UN had once again reached a dead end. Rejected in its original version, they continued to promote their idea internationally. That gave inspiration to others and eventually led to the establishment of proposed zones around the world. Ludwik Rajchman and his colleagues wrote an innovative international health agenda for the League of Nations, using the spaces of opportunity during the League's formative phase. Polish and Soviet diplomats and medical experts picked up on their approach when engaged in international epidemic control for the WHO. Władysław Malinowski was instrumental in setting up UNCTAD and in preparing, from within UNCTAD's secretariat, UN resolutions on international shipping that paved the way for an international treaty that regulated the powerful liner conferences. These interventions in international politics were closely linked to concerns in the lands in which these agents had been born or were based, or were connected to agendas of decolonizing countries that they were 'plugged into'.

Whether partaking in the international sphere as representatives of their country or as international officials of the LoN or the UN, their thinking was shaped by the political transformations of post-imperial Eastern Europe after the First World War or by the transformation of the societies and political orders in the region after the Second World War under the aegis of socialism. Some crucial politics of the League and the UN were shaped by themes, problems and concepts originating in Eastern Europe or sustained by agents from that region in alliance with others.

Along the paths of hard negotiation and conflict, Eastern European actors built a multitude of connections and exchanges with agents from other parts of the world because they were all able to meet and interact in the international space that international organizations provided.

Their transformative action shows clearly what we gain when we take off the old territorially based and geopolitically focused lenses – we can better understand international organizations as spaces of 'being divided together', and can make sense of a seemingly contradictory constellation. We can recognize specific political agendas, which often clashed with opposing interests but garnered success because they were forwarded in a multilayered context of togetherness.

In turn, an appreciation of the agency and proactive involvement of Eastern Europeans in the international sphere enables us to better understand the history of international organizations in the 20th century. It shows spaces of manoeuvre at the nexus of rivalry and competition in how to solve international and global problems, and this deepens our knowledge about these institutions. Since the mid-19th century, international politics has increasingly been pursued in the arenas of international organizations. From this crucial dimension of the international history of the last century and a half, we can substantiate a revision of the traditional picture of Eastern Europe as a seemingly internationally isolated or externally dominated region. In fact, Eastern Europe was globally connected through its share in and shaping of the international sphere that arose in the orbit of international organizations.

Notes

1   Sunil Amrith and Glenda Sluga, 'New Histories of the United Nations', *Journal of World History* 19 (2008) 3, here p. 252; Madeleine Herren, *Networking the International System: Global Histories of International Organizations* (Cham: Springer, 2014).

2   Ilya V. Gaiduk, *Divided Together: The United States and the Soviet Union in the United Nations, 1945-1965* (Washington, DC: Woodrow Wilson Center Press, 2012).

3   Sandrine Kott, *A World More Equal: An Internationalist Perspective on the Cold War* (New York: Columbia University Press, 2024); Katja Castryck-Naumann, 'Taking off the Lens of the Cold War—Whose Lenses Do We Use Instead?' H-Diplo Roundtable, XXVI-23, pp. 6–16. For an account of the period until 1918, see Katja [Castryck-]Naumann, 'Verflechtung durch Internationalisierung', in *Handbuch einer transnationalen Geschichte Ostmitteleuropas, vol. I*, ed. Frank Hadler and Matthias Middell (Göttingen: Vandenhoeck & Ruprecht, 2017), pp. 325–402.

4   On the development of international health, see Randall M. Packard, *A History of Global Health: Interventions into the Lives of other Peoples* (Baltimore: Johns Hopkins University Press, 2016).

5   Valeska Huber, 'The Unification of the Globe by Disease? The International Sanitary Conferences on Cholera, 1851–1894', *The Historical Journal* 49 (2006) 2, pp. 453–76.

6   See the chapter by Elizabeth White in this volume.

7   Francesca Piana, 'Humanitaire et politique, in medias res: Le typhus en Pologne et l'Organisation Internationale d'Hygiène (1919–1923)', *Relations internationales* 138 (2009) 2, pp. 23–38.

8   Iris Borowy and Anne Hardy (eds), *Of Medicine and Men: Biographies and Ideas in European Social Medicine between the World Wars* (New York: Peter Lang, 2008); Sara Silverstein,

'Doctors and Diplomats: Health Services in the New Europe, 1918–1923', in *A New Europe, 1918-1923: Instability, Innovation, Recovery*, ed. Bartosz Dziewanowski-Stefańczyk and Jay Winter (London: Routledge, 2022), pp. 142–60.

9   Iris Borowy, *Coming to Terms with Health: The League of Nations Health Organisation, 1921–1946* (Frankfurt: Peter Lang, 2009).

10 A major city in the east of Romania, close to the border to the Republic of Moldova.

11 Here and for the following see the ground-breaking research of Bodgan C. Iacob, 'Malariology and Decolonization: Eastern European Experts from the League of Nations to the World Health Organization', in *Journal of Global History* 17 (2022) 2, pp. 233–53.

12 On Soviet expertise in malaria control in the LoN and the WHO, see the ongoing PhD thesis by Mark Eby, 'Vectors of Socialism: Malaria Control and Soviet Power in Central Asia, 1920-1953' (New York University).

13 After the first General Assembly of the WHO in 1948 had rejected a draft resolution of the Ukrainian SSR that drew on the League's approach, Ukrainian and Byelorussian delegations withdrew from the WHO, followed by other socialist countries.

14 WHA 20.14, Malaria Eradication Program 1967.

15 Erez Manela, 'A Pox on Your Narrative: Writing Disease Control in Cold War History', in *Diplomatic History* 34 (2010) 2, pp. 299–323.

16 World Health Organization Regional Office for Europe, *Declaration of Alma-Ata* (Geneva: WHO Headquarters, 1978). For all its dimensions, see https://www.who.int/publications/i/item/WHO-EURO-1978-3938-43697-61471.

17 UNCTAD, *50 Years of Review of Maritime Transport 1968-2018: Reflecting on the Past, Exploring the Future* (Geneva: United Nations, 2018), p. 5.

18 Niels P. Petersson, Stig Tenold and Nicolas J. White (eds), *Shipping and Globalization in the Post-War Era: Contexts, Companies, Connections* (Basingstoke: Palgrave Macmillan, 2019); Wladyslaw Malinowski, 'Toward a Change in the International Distribution of Shipping', *International Conciliation* 39 (1971), pp. 66–86, here p. 67.

19 John Toye and Richard Toye, *The UN and Global Political Economy. Trade, Finances, and Development* (Bloomington: Indiana University Press, 2004).

20 Hans Böhme and Hartwig Buck, *Die Schiffahrtspolitik der sozialistischen Länder und die Ordnung des internationalen Seeverkehrs* (Kiel: Schiffahrts-Verlag Hansa, 1976), p. 33f.

21 Anne Calori, Anne-Kristin Hartmetz, Bence Kocsev and Jan Zofka, 'Alternative Globalization? Spaces of Economic Interaction between the "Socialist Camp" and the "Global South"', in *Between East and South: Spaces of Interaction in Globalizing Economy of the Cold War*, ed. idem and James Mark (Berlin: de Gruyter, 2019), pp. 1–31.

22 See the chapter by Max Trecker in this volume.

23 Yves Berthelot (ed.), *Unity and Diversity in Development Ideas: Perspectives from the UN Regional Commissions* (Bloomington: Indiana University Press, 2004), p. 56f.

24 Quote from an interview: Michael Zammit Cutajar, 'Oral history interview with Michael Zammit Cutajar, 2000', interview by Thomas G. Weiss, 26 April 2000, (New York, UN Intellectual History Project, City University of New York). See also the commemorative publication for W. Malinowski: Michael Zammit Cutajar, *UNCTAD and the South-North Dialogue: The First Twenty Years* (Oxford: Pergamon, 1985).

25 Kwame Nkrumah, *Neo-Colonialism: The Last Stage of Imperialism* (London: Thomas Nelson & Sons Ltd., 1965), p. 243f. (originally published in 1965).

26 Luda Juda, 'World Shipping, UNCTAD and the New International Economic Order', *International Organization* 35 (1981) 3, pp. 493–516.

27 António Guterres, 'Secretary-General's remarks for the International Day for the Total Elimination of Nuclear Weapons', transcript of speech delivered at United Nations Headquarters, New York, NY, 26 September 2022, https://www.un.org/sg/en/content/sg/speeches/2022-09-26/secretary-generals-remarks-for-the-international-day-for-the-total-elimination-of-nuclear-weapons.

28 William Walker, *A Perpetual Menace. Nuclear Weapons and International Order* (London: Routledge, 2012).

29 Had the United States agreed to a ban on nuclear weapons in the summer of 1949, the USSR might have not detonated its bomb. 'In hindsight, then, it seems as if the credit for the escalation of the nuclear arms post 1949 ought to rightfully belong to the US and UK', in Gilad Ben-Nun, *The Fourth Geneva Convention for Civilians: The History of International Humanitarian Law*, (London: I.B. Tauris, 2020), p. 240.

30 Elisabeth Röhrlich, *Inspectors of Peace. A History of the International Atomic Energy Agency* (Baltimore: Johns Hopkins University Press, 2022).

31 Piotr Wandycz, 'Adam Rapacki and the Search for European Security', in *The Diplomats, 1939-1979*, ed. Gordon A. Craig / Francis L. Loewenheim (Princeton: Princeton University Press, 1994), pp. 289–318. On Lachs, see also the chapter by Gilad Ben-Nun in this volume.

32 Adam Rapacki, 'The Polish Plan for a Nuclear-Free Zone Today', *International Affairs* 39 (1963) 1, pp. 1–12, here p. 2.

33 James R. Ozinga, *The Rapacki Plan. The 1957 Proposal to Denuclearize Central Europe, and an Analysis of its Rejection* (Jefferson, NC: McFarland & Co., 1989).

34 Records of the 12th General Assembly UN, 697th Meeting, 2 October 1957. Rapacki's speech is documented in: Official records of the General Assembly, plenary meetings. Verbatim records of meetings, 17.09.-14.12.1957, UNA(01)/R3, pp. 225–38, quote p. 237; URL: https://digitallibrary.un.org/record/730458?ln=en. Rapacki gave his speech in French; for the recording, see https://www.unmultimedia.org/avlibrary/asset/2232/2232383/.

Bibliography

Connelly, Matthew. 'Taking Off the Cold War Lens: Visions of North-South Conflict during the Algerian War for Independence'. *American Historical Review* 105 (2000) 3, pp. 739–69.

Connelly, Matthew. 'Seeing Beyond the State. The Population Control Movement and the Problem of Sovereignty'. *Past and Present* 193 (2006) 1, pp. 197–233, here at p. 202.

Fukuyama, Francis. *The End of History and the Last Man*. New York: Simon & Schuster, 1992.

Iriye, Akira and Pierre-Yves Saunier (eds). *The Palgrave Dictionary of Transnational History From the Mid-19th Century to the Present Day*. Basingstoke: Palgrave, 2009, p. xviii.

Weiss, Thomas G., Tatiana Carayannis, and Richard Jolly. 'The "Third" United Nations'. *Global Governance* 15 (2009) 1, pp. 123–42.

Westad, Odd Arne. *The Cold War. A World History*. London: Allen Lane, 2017.

Further reading

Castryck-Naumann, Katja. 'Polycentric International Participation after the First World War. Experts from East Central Europe in and around the League of Nation's Secretariat'. In *Remaking Central Europe: The League of Nations and the Former Habsburg Lands*, edited by P. Becker and Natasha Wheatley, Oxford: Oxford University Press, 2020, pp. 99–125.

Castryck-Naumann, Katja. *Transregional Connections in the History of East-Central Europe*. Berlin: de Gruyter, 2021.

Herren, Madeleine. *Networking the International System: Global History of International Organizations*. Cham: Springer, 2014.

Kott, Sandrine, Eva-Maria Muschik and Elisabeth Roehrlich, eds. *International Organizations and the Cold War. Competition, Cooperation and Convergence*. London: Bloomsbury, 2025.

Beyond 'Western' Standards: Global Imprints on Domestic Law

Azar Aliyev

4

Introduction: Eastern Europe as birthplace of Marxist-socialist law

Lasting as it did just over a century from the 1917 October Revolution, one can safely claim that the development and later wide dissemination of the Marxist-socialist legal ethos has had a profound and enduring global impact. The rise of the Soviet Union in 1922 followed by the expansion of socialism from East Germany to Vietnam, and even across the seas to places such as Cuba and Angola, brought with it the broad dissemination of socialist law. This development was nothing less than dramatic. Within four decades, from the early 1920s to the mid-60s, socialist law effectively and rapidly replaced dozens of domestic legal systems the world over.[1]

Within Eastern Europe, socialist law rapidly superseded some of the leading and most deep-rooted continental legal systems – especially those of the successor states to the Austro-Hungarian and Russian empires. It supplanted religious legal systems such as Muslim Sharia and Catholic canon law. In central Asia, it replaced well-established and long-standing nomadic law and corresponding legal custom. Yet it did not stop there. In some cases, it succeeded the colonial legal systems of former European powers within newly emerging now-decolonized states. Seeing as socialism's core geographic area and ideological centre were both located in Eastern Europe, socialist law has often been referred to as 'East European Law'. Yet what exactly is meant by this term? What were the major changes which this so-called Eastern European socialist law brought about? Most importantly, after its precipitate collapse post-1989, what has remained of its legacy today?

The legal revolution of the 1920s–30s

A signal trait of any legal system concerns its sense of *continuity*. Habitually, even profound changes such as those to territorial sovereignty (as in cases of the conquest of a territory and its transfer to another ruler) usually retain *continuity* in a multitude of legal spheres. From family law to the rights of private property, and even to basic taxation, the arc of many legal histories concerns their continuation and retention of long-standing legal structures.

In this sense, the rapid rise of the socialist legal system during the 1920s and 30s – and its complete uprooting and supplanting of the systems hitherto present in the areas where socialist-Marxist rule prevailed – was simply exceptional. The imposition of legal systems by empires in colonized territories and the reception of foreign legal models in the framework of national reforms had been common throughout history. However, never had legal systems been so radically transformed – and on such a global scale – as after the Bolshevik Revolution.

Within several months of the 1917 Revolution, the Bolshevik regime issued numerous decrees which effectively amounted to a general legal revolution, as it overturned Russian society's fundamentals and its entire legal order. Land ownership across the entirety of Soviet Russia – and, later, the Soviet Union – was abolished. The court system of the Russian empire was reset. Foreign trade was nationalized. Aristocratic titles and civil service ranks were eradicated, and family and inheritance rules overturned.

Three features contributed critically to the notion that the new system was seen as a complete severance with the concept of liberal democracy. First, according to the interpretation of Karl Marx's theories by Bolshevism's early legal thinker Evgeny Pashukanis, the state's separation of powers could not protect the oppressed classes since power was already concentrated exclusively in the hands of the ruling classes. A socialist state should regard a unitary, pyramidical governance structure – and law itself – as a mere tool to enforce the dictatorship of the proletariat and achieve the goals of the revolution.

From this stemmed the second aspect – namely, the denial of the concept of 'rule of law'. The principle of the rule of law, which ensures a non-arbitrary form of government, was seen as inherently contradictory to the socialist-Marxist ethos of the state. Logically seen, with full equality among all its members, the state should have no grounds to mishandle, discriminate or act arbitrarily against one of its compatriots. Correspondingly, in Marxist eyes, the individual required no protection from the state. Hence, the part of public law which entitles the individual to hold the state to account in its own court of law (i.e. administrative courts) was rejected.

The third aspect had to do with the inherent equality of all humans – a feature which remains as *the* epistemological bedrock of all Marxist social structures. The concept of socialist de facto equality was fundamentally different to the liberal concept of de jure equality.

From these general principles, actions followed. First among these was a much-needed change to tsarist Russia's legal culture, the rigidity of which dictated the degree of violent change required of the new legal regime in order for it to prevail and not remain solely law in books. Correspondingly, socialist Russia took the most radical of paths: the former court system was completely dissolved. All of the long-standing university law faculties and law schools were closed down – their vestiges included as secondary departments on law and politics within larger faculties for social sciences. Almost all judges and law professors lost their positions, as did most lawyers and legal civil servants, and the majority of them emigrated or were killed during the war on communism.

Yet following the end of the Civil War during the mid-1920s, as life became relatively stable again and reconstruction emerged, the young Soviet state faced the immense legal crisis brought about by its own wholesale destruction of the previous tsarist legal system. From the mid-1920s onwards, the state's own demand for lawyers, judges, prosecutors and investigators skyrocketed. The initial idea of abandoning the law and integrating legal sciences as a minor field within the social sciences had failed. As the state came to recognize that it could not really function without substantial legal echelons in its midst, secondary departments of law within the faculties for social sciences were re-transformed back into new or re-established law faculties. In order to plug the gap, special schools for socialist law were established in areas such as Irkutsk (later moved to Sverdlovsk – today's Ekaterinburg) or Saratov, with secondary and distance-learning legal education also being enabled. By the 1930s, a new generation of socialist lawyers had been educated and entered practice.

East European law as a legal system

Azar Aliyev

Before delving into details, a few words on the basic idea of 'socialist law' are merited. Socialist doctrine regarded law as a tool to enforce the dictatorship of the proletariat and achieve the goals of the revolution. In contrast to the rule-of-law concept, socialist law subordinates individual interests and rights to those of a ruling class consisting of workers and peasants.

The concept of law thus shifted from the protection of individual rights to the protection of the rights of specific groups, usually those hitherto disadvantaged or discriminated against – e.g. women, the destitute and illegitimate children. The law was implemented as an effective tool to enforce political programmes, and the majority of legal norms were programmatic and general – mainly without any connection to personal rights or remedies.

At the same time, for various reasons, the law became a very limited tool of social regulation. On the one hand, legal relations became much more straightforward in a socialist society. Concentrating the means of production and assets – including land, property and industry – under state ownership led to the de facto elimination of any commercial and corporate law. Large-scale succession or divorce cases, for instance, were no longer possible.

Relations between socialist state entities (e.g. factories, collective farms and authorities) were relations between branches of the state, and therefore primarily regulated by non-legal means (e.g. disciplinary measures against management for breach of contract). Disputes between socialist entities did not fall within the competence of the judiciary. New quasi-judicial institutions – state arbitration – were in charge of settling these disputes. State arbitration fell outside the judicial system, and instead formed an integral part of the executive authority. Legal reasoning in decision making had a mere supportive character. The main goal of state arbitration was to maintain the state's economic interest.

At the same time, another goal was to make socialist law accessible and understandable for a layperson. Hence, the legal technique of the legislation was quite low – especially in the first few years after the revolution.

Although socialist law had numerous unique characteristics, a closer examination shows that it developed within the paradigms of the continental legal family – especially its Germanic subgroup, a codified legal system based on strict differentiation between public and private law. It is no coincidence that, before the October Revolution, Russian law was an integral and essential part of this subgroup. Leading socialist lawyers, including Pyotr Stuchka und Evgeny Pashukanis, had enjoyed an excellent legal education in Russia and Germany. Although the elaborations of Pashukanis on nature are construed as a discourse with Hegel, Kant, Kelsen, Jhering, Pokrovskiy and others, he remains within the paradigm of continental law – e.g. by strictly differentiating between public and private law.

Notably, the impact of the continental law system increased in the Stalin era, as the General State Prosecutor of the Soviet Union and the architect of the Stalin Purge Andrey Vyshinsky, in his function as the director of the Institute for State and Law of the Academy of Sciences of the Soviet Union, partly reinstated the professors of the tsarist law faculties. However, those scholars were restricted in their works to 'conceptual jurisprudence' (*Begriffsjurisprudenz*), which was detached from legal reality (Ioffe, 1985; Kelsen, 2021).

The role of courts in the socialist system

Konstantin Branovitskii

The court system's development during the Soviet period began with the Bolsheviks coming to power in October 1917. A judicial system independent from the acts of the executive did not suit the Soviet government at all. In place of the centuries-old judicial system that had been completely destroyed during the Legal Revolution (Decree No. 1, Council of Peoples' Commissars 1917; Decree No. 2, All-Russian Central Executive Committee, 1918), a new one was established. Some of its elements are still to be found in Eastern Europe today. It should be emphasized that during the entire Soviet period there was no independent judiciary as such. The courts were 'organically' built into the system of law enforcement organs – that is, executive authorities (police, prosecutor's office) of which the primary task is the fight against crime and the protection of the socialist system and socialist property – of the USSR and other socialist states. Judicial competence was severely limited. Cases resolved in courts (especially political ones) were supposed to serve the purposes of strengthening 'socialist' legality. The functioning of this judicial system was ensured by many years of selecting people not by their professional qualifications but by their loyalty and party affiliation. Their legal knowledge and dedication to the idea of justice were secondary criteria.

One of the consequences of treating the courts as being among the law enforcement/ executive bodies was the introduction of time limits for the consideration of civil cases and strict control over observance of those limits. Judges were perceived by both state and society as ordinary officials obliged to perform the tasks assigned to them in a short time. Tight deadlines for the consideration of civil cases in fact remain a feature of civil procedure in most of the former socialist jurisdictions.

It is surely no accident that the most prestigious legal profession in socialist states was that of the prosecutor – who, as part of the central executive power, had the competence to supervise compliance with socialist legality. Correspondingly, court judges were also subject to prosecutors' supervisions, which meant the effective and total control of the judiciary by the state's executive power.

The classic system for verifying judicial acts (appeal followed by cassation) was also completely revised. The liquidated appeal was replaced by cassation. The vacated place of the cassation review was filled by supervision procedure (*nadzor*), a legal construct unfamiliar to any other legal system in the world. Its main peculiarity was that this stage of proceedings could not be initiated by the will of the parties to the proceeding. The right to bring an appeal of supervision was vested only in 'privileged' officials – among whom were the presidents and deputy presidents of the respective courts, as well as prosecutors. The inclusion of the last-named increased the role of the prosecutor's office in society, which still persists.

After the Soviet-communist era, former socialist countries gained their independence and embarked on the path of democratization and fundamental reforms. Challenges to the strength of judicial systems began almost immediately. The roads of Eastern European countries began to diverge in terms of approaches to the organization of the judiciary.

Poland, Hungary and the Baltic states joined the EU after undergoing a process of 'decommunization'. The ethical, cultural and territorial proximity of these states to those of the EU, as well as the example of the economic success enjoyed by the countries of democratic Europe, led to a complete renewal of their judiciaries. Joint educational projects have significantly influenced the perception of common European legal values for a new generation of lawyers. From the point of view of the development of national legal systems, there was a direct reception of the existing German and French institutions – which, in fact, meant a return to the 'historical' foundations of the law.

At the same time, some of these countries (even after joining the EU) continue to face the desire of their political elites to play out conservative scenarios and offer their own 'unique path' forward. These aspirations are manifested in a disdainful attitude towards European legal and judicial institutions and values. In a number of cases, this has led to public protests – a massive crisis in Bulgaria in 2020, for example, in protest at corruption in the judiciary and its inefficiency. In other cases, it has spawned politically motivated decisions on the non-execution of the judgements of the Court of Justice of the European Union (CJEU) – for instance, conflict between the EU and Poland over judicial reform, as Poland introduced the Disciplinary Chamber of the Supreme Court of Poland. Such examples show that even in these countries the processes of transformation of judicial and legal systems are not yet complete.

Most of the former Soviet republics (those that have not become EU member states) find themselves in a very difficult situation. On the one hand, there are the prospects of joining the world/European community on a fully-fledged basis (which remain illusory, except perhaps for Ukraine after the events of 2022); on the other, there is the impossibility of ignoring the presence of a huge neighbour, in the form of the Russian Federation, which continues to preserve its hegemony in the post-Soviet space. One needs to be aware that the impact of the Russian Federation and Russian law differs substantively from country to country. The impact had been decreasing over recent decades, and in fact vanished after the new wave of relentless aggression against Ukraine in February 2022. However, even in the early 1990s (a period when Russia itself was striving to be a part of the broader European community), a significant number of these states could not find a solid foundation for creating democratic, efficient and independent judiciaries.

One factor that should be held responsible for this situation is the ideologization of the concept of the sovereignty of these countries. Having 'for ever' broken with the socialist past, the newly formed states began to search for ideas of national statehood in their own history. This search soon ran up against a 'new wall' because most post-Soviet states before inclusion into the Soviet Union were part of the Russian empire and had lost their independent legal systems and traditions about two hundred years before.

Lack of integration in 'Western legal systems', i.e. the European Union, and absence of deep 'historical roots' led, albeit with minimal differences, to the inertial development of court systems and procedures in these states. For example, Kazakhstan and Kyrgyzstan abandoned the Soviet institution of *nadzor* (the above-mentioned extraordinary supervision procedure) only in 2015 and 2017, respectively. One of the reasons for the continued closeness of the post-Soviet countries is the slow process of creating national scientific schools of procedural law. Many states, partly involuntarily, continue the traditions of the Soviet procedural school.

Another distinctive feature of the judicial systems of Eastern European countries (not including those now in the EU) is the atypical role of the highest courts. These are engaged in a 'very broad range', and not 'selective', consideration of cases (the most complex, high-profile, etc.). There are two main reasons for such a phenomenon: first, existing procedural features such as the lack of procedural and substantive filters for filing complaints, i.e. a special admission procedure for filing a case to the Supreme Court; second, the extremely poor quality of the work of the lower courts. Higher courts are unable/not entitled to ignore severe errors in criminal and civil proceedings, which, given the number of such violations, turns the consideration of cases into a 'flow'. In turn, the quality of the work of lower courts is directly related to the poor quality of legal education.

After the Second World War: Eastern European socialist law goes global and diversifies

None of these changes would have had such profound global impacts had it not been for the sheer spatial scale within which they transpired. Indeed, one vital element in the success of this Marxist-socialist legal transformation was its effective imposition right across the vast territory of the entire Soviet bloc – from Vladivostok to East Berlin, and from the northern end of the Eurasian continent to Iran's and Afghanistan's northern borders. Already in 1940, in the midst of war, the Baltic states of Latvia, Lithuania and Estonia were occupied and integrated into the Soviet Union's body politic as the last of the Soviet Republics. Thus, within the vast space of the Soviet Union alone (roughly one sixth of the world's surface), socialist governmental structures and their corresponding legal orders were now effectively imposed, including in even the most remote territories such as the Caucasus, Central Asia and the Far East – areas in which the former Russian empire had never managed to exert any effective or meaningful legal control, let alone integration into the legal system of the metropole.

By the end of the Second World War, socialist law had become the legal system not just of the Soviet Union but also of numerous states in Eastern and South-eastern Europe as well as Asia. This substantial global expansion, however, also demanded the Soviet Union give up the idea that socialist law could exist only within a singular socialist state (as originally envisaged by Lenin). The new socialist states of Eastern Europe, which now formed part of the 1955 military Warsaw Pact, remained sovereign and, at least formally, independent of the Soviet Union. And while the central tenets of socialist law were imposed within them quite rigidly, along with a major replacement of most lawyers connected with their previous regimes, there remained considerable leeway for national specifics within many of these countries. Indeed, sporadic legal traditions such as administrative law and property law in Poland or the civil code in Romania survived the transition to socialist law.

To this development, one must add the rise of parallel socialist legal systems that, while adhering to Marxist-socialist principles, did not come under Moscow's direct control. The

Figure 4.1 The historical advent of socialist law 1917–50s.

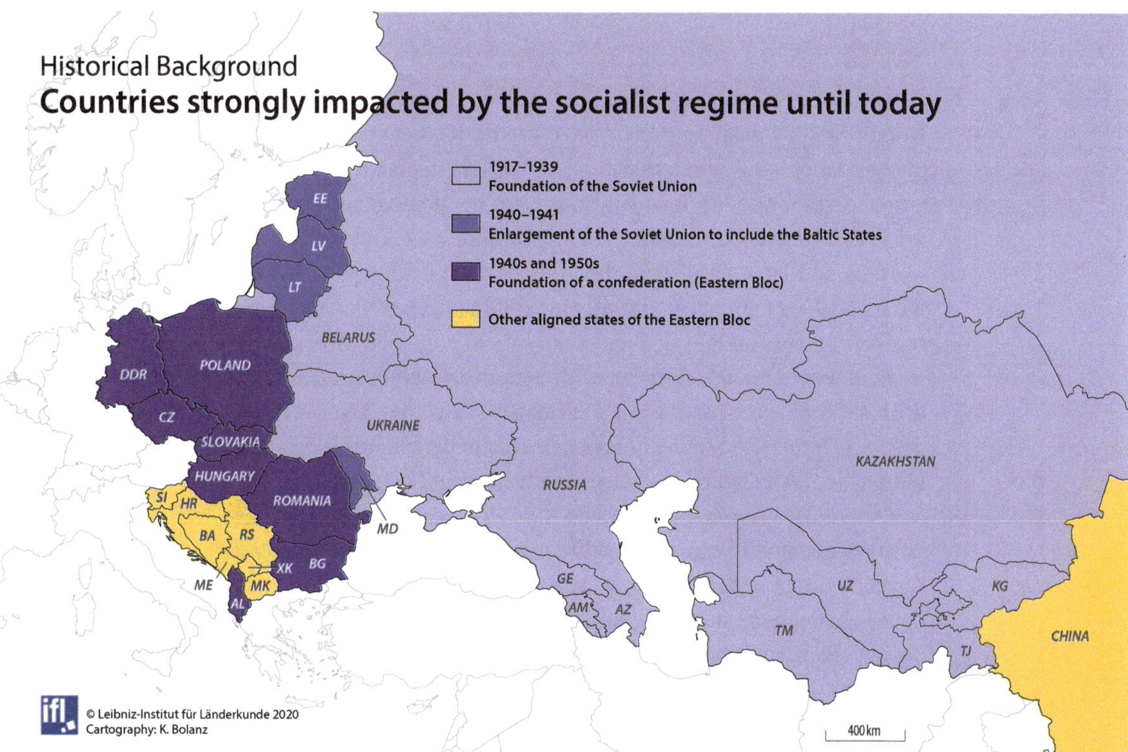

most direct and notable examples of this were Mao Zedong's China and Josip Broz Tito's Yugoslavia. While both countries certainly adhered to socialist legal principles (complete redistribution of property, abolition of previous bourgeois and noble social classes, at least formal declaration of general human equality, full state control, etc.), their radical departure from any alignment with the Soviet Union and their varying regional focuses came to further set Eastern European socialist law as a category apart. China, with its long-standing Confucian regional hegemonic vision of itself, would certainly help impose socialist law in North Korea and North Vietnam.

Nevertheless, from the 1970s onwards, as China's material and economic cooperation with the United States and other capitalist countries (notably Germany) grew following President Richard Nixon's 1974 visit to Beijing, its strict application of a non-capitalist ethos as the central ideological anchor of socialist law gradually subsided. And while Tito's Yugoslavia remained formally socialist, its regional affinities, from the 1960s onwards, were far more attuned towards the non-aligned movement headed by the likes of Ethiopia, India and, more generally, the Global South. By the 1970s, the international expansion of socialism had decayed to a formality. While many African, Asian and Latin American states claimed to have joined the socialist way of development, being formally allied as they were with the Soviet Union, none of them, except for Cuba, followed a path of deep socialist social and corresponding legal reforms.

The twilight of Eastern European socialist law: From the late 1960s to 1989

Joseph Stalin's death and the rise of Nikita Khrushchev gave an essential impetus to the humanization and modernization of Soviet legislation and socialist law in general. Granted, the rule of law continued to be denied and political dissidents were still imprisoned or sent into exile. Yet the Stalin-era executions or imprisonments without trial were by and large abolished; the Gulag prison camps in Siberia, closed. In tandem, from the mid-1950s to the 60s, virtually all codifications of law and fundamental legal acts were revised. As such, this was a major important step away from Stalin-era legislation.

In essence, the developmental direction of Stalinist socialist law, which had tended to drift towards ever-harsher totalitarianism, was de facto reversed. Elements of private property, hitherto completely unacceptable under Stalinist legislation, were reinstated even within the Soviet Union, and also at times within Eastern Europe's Soviet-controlled sphere.

One of the prominent examples is private property. During these years, the majority of families eventually came to acquire apartments and plots of land for dachas. These, while formally not private property, were nevertheless to be used exclusively by the family. They could also now be inherited, and even informally sold. In short, property rights gradually began creeping back into a system whose very genesis had been premised on their abolition.

In a gradual process, Eastern European socialist law thus began to lose more and more of its weight in society. Even legally binding state documents of the highest priority, such as five-year plans for economic development – the very basis of the economy and distribution of resources during the earlier Stalinist era – were disregarded. Falsification of documentation and corruption gradually became the norm. The rigour associated with socialist law during its 1930s heyday was diluted thanks to its subsequent lax and arbitrary application. Broadly speaking, then, the relaxing of socialist law's epistemic *rigour* led to what might be termed a 'legal nihilism' of sorts, which in turn resulted in social apathy and society's wider detachment from that law.

To this outcome, one must add developments within socialist courts. Initially an essential tool of the socialist government in achieving its revolutionary goals, these were gradually degraded to the level of mere bureaucratic authorities which, to varying degrees, came to apply a sort of 'mechanical jurisprudence' – albeit one which was widely seen to have gradually departed from the most basic notions of justice as fairness.[2]

Notwithstanding severe setbacks such as the Soviet invasions of Hungary (1956) and Czechoslovakia (1968), the decentralization of socialist law, which had begun following the Second World War and gathered pace during the 1950s, further accelerated from the 70s to the 80s. The rise of the international humanist agenda as championed by the Helsinki Accord's Final Act of 1975 (itself a Soviet initiative), with its provisions on fundamental human rights, was an important cornerstone of the gradual democratization of the Eastern bloc. Yet the decisive role in the decay of the socialist system and socialist law was first and foremost attributable to the economic crisis which began during the 1970s.

Poland's shrinking economy along with a huge foreign debt of 18 billion US dollars, coupled with an ensuing food crisis (rising meat prices and the prohibition of private trade in meat and meat products), triggered the social movement embodied by the trade union 'Solidarity' in the early 1980s. Yet in contrast to the Prague Spring of 1968, this time around the Soviet Union chose not to intervene in the domestic affairs of its socialist neighbour. And while Solidarity was banned in 1981 and thousands of its supporters detained as Poland became the first declared socialist military dictatorship, the government could not avoid the socio-economic pressures facing it. These finally triggered negotiations with the opposition, which eventually led towards the path of liberalization. Interestingly enough, the initial target of both the 1968 Prague Spring and the 1981 Solidarity movement were notably similar in their moderation: to achieve 'socialism with a human face' while modernizing the Czechoslovak and Polish economies, respectively.

The collapse of global socialist law

The endgame for socialism and its corresponding legal ethos started with Mikhail Gorbachev's attempted reforms of the Soviet Union, which rapidly resulted in a deep economic crisis, social apathy and eventual lawlessness. *Perestroika* and *glasnost* ('restructuring' and 'openness', respectively), the key words of the Gorbachev reforms, initially pursued the modest goal of modernization of the socialist economy. The envisaged reform gave rise to numerous other catchwords such as *uskoreniye* ('acceleration') and *khozraschyot* ('commercialization').

A closer examination, however, yields a view of these reforms as being mostly of a populist character – albeit devoid of any coherent overarching strategy. Fear of far-reaching transformation resulted in the so-called 'salami slicing' of reforms, coupled with huge bureaucratic procedures accompanying each liberal innovation, which further undermined their already limited effects. Gorbachev's scant success in implementation was not coincidental since the Soviet Union had long been virtually unable to carry out any meaningful reform effectively. A crude manifestation of this handicap could be observed in its incapacity to draft and enforce legal norms successfully. The effect of decades of legal nihilism and declaratory norms, exacerbated by an overt lack of objective court control and oversight, severely undermined the capacity and trustworthiness of the state's regulatory potency. *Perestroika* thus became a new ideology, albeit not a master plan for economic and legal reforms. Three notable examples of the idiosyncrasies of the later Soviet Union's legal system under the influence of *perestroika* and *glasnost* can be observed in measures against alcoholism, contradictory permissions for entrepreneurship, and the ultimately backfiring debates concerning freedom of speech.

The production of alcohol, as with every other commercial activity in the USSR, was a state monopoly. The wine industry was quite successful – especially in the Caucasus, Crimea and southern Russia. Yet by the early 1980s, as the state's general potencies dwindled, alcoholism had evolved into a distinct social disaster in the Soviet Union. In one of his first legislative moves as soon as he was elected General Secretary of the Communist Party of the Soviet Union in 1985, Gorbachev set out to pass a wide-ranging prohibition on the consumption of all alcohol – wine and hard sprits alike. By the end of this law's tenure in 1987, valuable vineyards and much of the country's long-standing wine industry had been destroyed. At the same time, the production of adulterated alcohol had risen to unprecedented levels.

Another example is the Law 'On Individual working activity', which enabled commercial productive activity for the sake of profit for the first time since 1928. However, commercial activities were limited to the production of consumer goods and services. The purchase of raw materials and industrial goods was de facto impossible because of numerous limitations: the employment of other persons remained prohibited and the bureaucratic burdens on embarking on commercial activity were extremely high. As a result, private commercial activity became de facto legal only after the collapse of the Soviet Union.

The last example of the adverse application of reforms relates to the policy of *glasnost*, which translates literally as 'transparency and openness', and concerns the social component of freedom of speech. Liberalization in this field quickly triggered debates on the various problems within the Soviet Union, including the historical legacies of Stalin's 'Great Purge' and the high price of its enforcement, which saw millions of people executed, sentenced to prison camps, or displaced to Siberia. In 1990, towards the end of his presidency, Gorbachev enacted the law of free speech. On the one hand, and for the first time, hundreds of thousands of victims were rehabilitated and thousands of dissidents could recover their citizenship. On the other hand, broader Soviet society lacked any immunity against populism and hate speech. Soon enough, public debates inflamed by nationalists began to heat up ethnic conflicts in an all-too-susceptible Soviet Union which was multiethnic, multiconfessional and, indeed, multilingual beneath the apparently unifying veneer of spoken Russian. Within less than a year, ethno-national pressures drove politics ultimately out of control, provoking numerous armed conflicts, from Karabakh to Abkhazia and from Transnistria to the Uzbek region of Fergana.[3] The continuing deterioration of the economic situation and growing social instability led to chaotic reactions by the government and internal conflicts. The Communist Party lost its monopoly over power as it became severed from governmental structures, pursuant to the establishment of a multiparty political system. The process of dissolution of the Soviet Union, triggered by the economic crisis and personal conflict between Mikhail Gorbachev and Boris Yeltsin, was inexorable.

Family law: Soviet law's utmost liberalization beyond 'Western' legal standards

This section discusses what was probably one of the most advanced and liberal aspects of Soviet law – family law – namely, its vision and application throughout the roughly seven decades between 1917 and 1989. Seen retrospectively, Soviet family law far outstripped much of its 'Western' equivalent in its striving for equality and its securing of fundamental rights for all groups in society. As shall be discussed below, the contemporaneous curtailment of women's right to obtain abortions in 'Western' societies (the United States, Poland, Malta, etc.) lies in the starkest of contrasts to Soviet law's consistent guarantee of this right of women throughout the Soviet legal space. Notably, family law was one of the few areas of Soviet law which was de facto functioning. The majority of cases in the Soviet courts dealt with family law – especially divorces and custody issues.

Historically, the Communist Manifesto proclaimed the abolition or cancellation ('*Aufhebung*') of the family as a legal institution, as one of socialism's main priorities. To Marx, the family was based on capital and private gain; in his eyes, wives in the bourgeois family were regarded as a mere means of production. Consequently, as the Bolsheviks came to power, they declared a new model of the family – which was now to be seen as a union of equal partners, free of economic interests. Indeed, this shift in the family's ontological nature was seen by the Bolsheviks as one of the main goals of their revolution.

Several weeks after the October Revolution in 1917, the Soviet government issued the Decree on Civil Marriage, on Children and on Keeping of Civil Registries. In its four concise paragraphs, the Decree basically erased existing tsarist family law in its entirety. Religious marriage was henceforth abolished; formal civil marriage became the sole possible form of family union. Substantively, the Decree significantly strengthened the de facto stature of women, since it now required their written confirmation stipulating that the couple's marriage was indeed voluntary. As such, the centuries-old custom of forced marriage (especially among Russian agricultural serfs) was critically curtailed. In 1918, the Code of Laws concerning Civil Registration of Deaths, Births and Marriages was enacted, with its Part II dealing with matrimony. Part III covered family issues in greater detail and further developed this Decree's revolutionary approach to family institutions.

One can safely claim that, at the time, this Code was by far the most liberal family legislation worldwide. It established legal equality between all humans, thus equalizing men and woman (albeit without stating this explicitly). Voluntary civil union was confirmed as the only recognized form of marriage. Forced marriage was null and void *ab initio*. Many kinds of religious marriage restrictions, such as the prohibition of marriage between persons of different faiths and the celibacy of the priesthood, were annulled. Polygamy was henceforth prohibited for all confessions. The Code established unified and exceptionless rules for all ethnic and religious groups. It unified and universalized the accepted age for marriage at 16 years for females and 18 for males, doing away with discriminatory provisions such as the tsarist rules for the aboriginal population, which had hitherto lowered these marriage ages for certain portions of society to 13 and 15 years, respectively.

Probably the most striking breakthrough in Soviet family law was embedded in its proclamation of freedom of marriage and divorce. Marriage could now be dissolved at the state's registry office or by the local court upon agreement of the spouses. Moreover, and far more critically for the equality of women, marriage could now be immediately dissolved upon the request of either one of the spouses – male or female. Religious marriages made before the Revolution remained valid, yet their termination had now become a universal right. In 1918, this liberal vision of marriage as championed by the Soviet state was virtually unparalleled in its progressiveness in comparison with that of most Western states, let alone less-developed areas.

The idea of freeing marriage from economic interests, and of equating the rights of men and women, necessitated a fundamental revision of the concept of matrimonial property. Marriage ceased to have any implications on the spousal property regime. Upon marriage, the property of each spouse remained separate and their own. Marriage contracts ceased to have any legal power. A spouse could claim maintenance from each other only to cover minimal living expenses. This claim also remained after divorce, so long as the requesting spouse could demonstrate insufficient income for basic living conditions.

The ascent of Soviet women's rights and the drive for equality

The next major revision of Soviet family law took place under the enactment of the 1926 new Code on Marriage, the Family, and Guardianship. This law came in large part in answer to the acute social realities that prevailed in the Soviet Union after the long and harsh years of the Civil War (1918–20).

One of the most important amendments of the 1926 Code was the introduction of the state's recognition of spousal companionship, and its de facto legal equation with the long-standing formal category of marriage. Under the 1926 Code, spousal couples were considered married irrespective of whether or not such a formal act had indeed been recorded by the state. The immediate legal consequences of this implied a loss of legal significance for the formal act of marriage. From 1926 onwards, formal marriage was no longer important for the securing of any rights within the practicality of family life. From now on, what really mattered was the actual condition of longer-term companionship.

This reform implied a substantive retreat by the state from the domain of its citizens' family lives. And such a retreat had far-reaching and important practical implications. After the 1917 Revolution and the years of civil war – with its horrific human, economic and social consequences – multitudes of suffering people found solace in renewed human companionships. By equating these companionships with formal marriage, the state in fact furnished people with the legal framework for the rapid establishment of family households – albeit without the hassle and red tape implied by state registration of companionship, as with formal marriage. This de facto family concept also enabled flexible solutions by the courts.

Returning to the economic aspects of marriage, the 1926 Code drifted away from the initial 1918 Soviet liberal economic model, which had stipulated the strict separation and non-unification of property between husband and wife. Under the new Code of 1926, this separation was abandoned and replaced by joint property formations for assets acquired within the time frame of any companionship union. This shift was pro-female par excellence. The former strict separation of property, which had emerged from Marxism's *theoretical* attempt to undermine marriage's alleged bourgeois economic nature, resulted in *practical* discrimination against and abuse of women. As it turned out, in cases of divorce (especially in rural areas) women were simply expelled and rendered destitute and propertyless after years of family life and childcare. At the peak of absurdity, in some cases men could even enter into companionship (which, as we have seen, was tantamount to marriage) purely for the sake of gaining income during work-intensive summer months, only to expel the woman in the autumn and remain with their accrued income. The amalgamation of property rights between both spouses within the 1926 Code should be seen for what it was: a compromise on one of Marxism's theoretical premises (the capitalist aspects of marriage), in favour of a certain social group (women) due to this premise's practical implications in the real world. Declaratively, marriage was officially termed a 'voluntary matrimonial union of man and woman based on sentiment – free of materialistic calculations'. Yet despite this declared freedom from materialistic considerations, the Code of 1926 did introduce some rather clear regulations on alimony and division of matrimonial property in case of divorce. As such, the people who most benefited from the Code here were women.

The last critical aspect by which women's rights were clearly in the ascendency within the 1926 Code concerned its stipulation in favour of a wide prerogative for the freedom to divorce. Courts of first instance henceforth approved the divorce of spouses upon an application by either of them, if and when a joint life and preservation of the family became impossible (Art. 14). This standard (impossibility of family life) was applied liberally. A statement of the impossibility of joint life by any one of the partners, man or woman, had become a sufficient legal ground for divorce. In the case of a joint application, spouses without underaged children could be divorced in regular proceedings by the state's Registration Authority, in a direct and out-of-court manner. The divorce was automatically valid three months after application, with this 90-day span to be used as a 'cooling-off' period. To put it simply, back in 1926, few countries (if any) could boast women's direct, free, swift and wholeheartedly autonomous ability to divorce their male companions to the liberal extent existent in the Soviet Union.

Soviet law's achievement of equating all children's rights

The 1926 Code also revised the legal status of children. Of foremost importance was its stipulation of equality of all children, those legitimate and those hitherto considered illegitimate (i.e. born outside recognized wedlock) alike. To begin with, the Code henceforth allowed all interested persons to apply for a correction of the state's registration of parenthood, if they could prove the inaccuracy of their parental data. New legislation abandoned the principle '*la recherché de la paternité est interdite*' ('the search for true fatherhood is forbidden') prevalent in many European legal systems. The highly contested principle forbade an illegitimate child to bring action against their alleged father for recognition of paternity or for the granting of maintenance. Gone were the days when the pregnancies of women from the lower classes from relations with male partners of a higher social class – who habitually denied those women's claims of their fatherhood – were accepted at face value, in favour of the men and to the women's disadvantage. The state's rebuttable presumption (i.e. the initial assumption made by the state, which is taken to be true unless someone proves otherwise) rested upon the assumption of accuracy of the State Register. The biological father was from now on obliged to participate in costs associated with the pregnancy, birth, and maintenance of the child. If several persons were held to be the possible biological father of a child, they had to share these costs. Both father and mother received equal parental rights until the 16th birthday of a female child, and the 18th birthday of a male child.

Stalin's 1930s backlash and Khrushchev's revised liberalization of the 50s

Much has been written about the harsh consequences of Stalin's advent and rise to power. From the establishment of the Gulags to mass murder, to engineered famine in Ukraine (*Holodomor*), the price of Stalin's enforcement measures was unimaginable. Millions of people were executed and millions more were sentenced to life in prison camps, while multitudes of others were displaced to Siberia. Following his final victory in taking over from Lenin, and having subdued Leon Trotsky's opposition, the roughly 20-year period from the 1930s to Stalin's death and Khrushchev's ascent in 1953 also coincided with substantial regression in comparison with the overt progressiveness of the 1926 Family Code. Yet seen within the *longue durée* perspective of Soviet rule, these two decades could well be viewed as a single step back after the 1926 Code's many steps forward and before the ultimate liberalization of Soviet law from the 1950s until the fall of communism. This last period under Khrushchev could certainly be viewed as the peak of Soviet family progressiveness, which by the early 1960s significantly dwarfed any comparable liberalization in the 'West'. Female quotas, broadly used in recent decades in 'Western democracies', were the norm in the Soviet Union: female cosmonauts, female engineers, female professors, and so on. Another important element of gender equality was legal anchoring of freedom of marriage and divorce, which evolved alongside the equality of parental rights between men and women, and economic and social guarantees for motherhood – as in paid maternity leave, free kindergarten places, and state grants for unmarried mothers or larger family households.

During the 1930s, the Soviet state retreated from its initial idea of completely withdrawing from family issues. Stalin's new concept of the socialist family sought to develop the family as a basic unit of socialist society. Consequently, the state's regulation of all issues concerning the family became much tighter. Freedom of divorce was limited in comparison with the stipulations of the 1926 Code, and was made possible only on certain specific grounds. Divorce proceedings became substantially more difficult. Courts of first instance carried out only conciliation proceedings. This implied that full divorce could only be secured via the ruling of courts of second instance, which were now the lowest state organ competent to pronounce a divorce. Applicants had to pay substantial monetary penalties for divorce, and these increased for each subsequent divorce. All divorces were immediately noted within the divorcee's passport – and careers could be strongly impeded upon a family's break-up.

Unsurprisingly, within one year of these amendments to the Family Code, the number of divorces decreased by a factor of 31. To Stalin, this tightening of divorce measures was seen not as an ideological, retrograde step back but rather as an alleged practical means to avoid a demographic crisis. Such arguments were further employed in the face of the catastrophic Soviet casualty rate in the Second World War. Men should be encouraged, so it was assumed, to have sexual intercourse without fear of future responsibility for the children that might result therefrom. In line with this thinking, the 1926 Code's initial right to identify the biological father and claim maintenance for children born out of wedlock was revoked in 1944, and during the hardest stages of the war the heavily criticised rule '*la recherché de la paternité est interdite*' was reintroduced into Soviet family law. The only minor solace was to be found in the state's support for single mothers, who now received modest grants to partly compensate for their previous rights for maintenance claims against the fathers according to the 1926 Code – now de facto lost.

Khrushchev's thaw saw the USSR reverse the numerous restrictions of the Stalin era, and revamp Soviet family law's progressive leap forward. Yet this time around, the state's return to progressiveness did not mean its retreat from family regulation as had been the case during the 1920s. The Stalinist concept of the family as the 'basic unit of socialist society' officially remained intact, and the state's role in the regulation of family relations was no longer called into question.

Yet the cumulative effect of the individual reforms of the late 1950s and early 60s amounted to a major liberal leap forward. From the reinstatement of women's full right to abortion to the significant simplification of divorce proceedings, pro-humane, pro-women and pro-children legal thinking had regained the upper hand. In 1968, Soviet family-law liberalization reached its apogee as the Union enacted the Principles of Soviet Family Law that year. These Principles were broadly used throughout the USSR so as to harmonize legislation across all of the Union's Republics. Since family issues were within the competence of the Republics, the 1968 Principles framed Soviet family law within a tight 'corset' for legal application, over and above all local legislation. Only in rare cases, and with regard to very specific issues, did individual Family Codes of Union Republics deviate from the 1968 Principles (e.g. matrimonial age could vary between 16 and 18). This legislative liberal ethos basically remained in force, with minor amendments, until the collapse of the Soviet Union and the socialist system in 1989.

Women's right to abortion: Soviet law's crowning liberal achievement?

Azar Aliyev

The idea that women possess the right to abort their pregnancies is relatively new. Historically, the artificial termination of a pregnancy via an elective medical procedure was widely considered as negative – certainly, from a religious point of view. Within the pre-secular world, and up until the 20th century, human procreation was widely regarded as God-given. Its voluntary termination was seen, and is still seen today by many religious groups, as an infringement against God's intention.

Soviet thinking – being anti-religious to its core, pursuant to Marx's exhortation that 'religion is the opiate of the masses' – was as far removed as possible from any such God-dependent notions. Its coupling with a distinct sense of human equality of race, age and, especially, gender – and its clear objective of freeing the oppressed wherever and whomever they were – meant that those restrictive, religious-based moral considerations were henceforth null and void.

Socialism's first affirmative reference to women's right of abortion came as a reaction to the medical consequences of illegal abortion practices. The administering of these procedures was clearly against tsarist law, and hence they were carried out in secrecy – thus severely risking the lives of the women undergoing them. November 1920 saw the first Decree on Abortion by the People's Commissariat of Health (Order of Commissariat for Health and Justice, No. 471, 1920). Initially, Soviet reasoning in favour of abortion was based upon the desire of pursuing the lesser evil. If women were aborting illegally, and this was causing their death due to infections and false medical procedures, then both the state and its women would be better off legalizing abortion – albeit while still controlling its execution. Under the 1920 Decree, although it was only doctors in hospitals who were allowed to perform abortions, the *choice* to undergo this procedure was now transferred to the pregnant women themselves.

By 1921, this initial right to abortion, as based upon its 'narrow utilitarian' logic of protecting women's health from secretly executed and dangerous medical procedures, was applied throughout the Soviet Union and Ukraine (Avdeev, Blum and Troitskaya, 1995). Abortion was now to be administered by the state, free of charge, at state-run hospitals across the Soviet Union. As such, the Soviet law was the first in any 'Western' country to legalize abortion based upon the sole criteria of women's free choice. The concomitant progressive ideas of the 1926 new Code on Marriage, the Family, and Guardianship, along with its revision of the status of the Soviet family and its liberalization of divorce, significantly strengthened the general feature of freedom in family affairs – especially, and most notably, for women.

Pursuant to the more general retrograde ethos of Stalin's regime, in 1936 abortion was once again prohibited across the Soviet realm and was made prosecutable under criminal law. The sole exception to this was abortion mandated for medical reasons, in the case of risk to the carrying mother's life. Yet even Stalin's retrograde vision did not hold for long. No sooner had Khrushchev assumed control than, in early 1954, Stalin's criminalization of abortion was repealed. By 1955, a full retraction of the prohibition on abortion, in favour of its full legalization as based upon women's free choice, was reinstated. In 1968, it was enshrined in the Principles of Soviet Family Law that remained in force until 1989.

Seen retrospectively, then, the right of abortion's progressive march forward that began in 1921, and which suffered a backlash during the 30s, had come full circle. From the mid-1950s, it had become established across the legislation of all socialist states regardless of their religious and cultural specifics – from Muslim Central Asia to Catholic Poland.

As explained below, the collapse of the Soviet Union and its satellites saw its former states take diverging subsequent legal paths. Yet concerning women's right to abortion, a rather clear pattern has emerged from the early 1990s until today. Figure 4.2, below, charts the current status of rights to abortion cross the former socialist space.

The pentagon within each country signifies both the rights and obligations of women there who choose to undergo an abortion. In general, abortion is a right upon request in all post-Soviet countries. The first nation to completely deny this right, as of 2021, was Poland. The *brown* triangles within the pentagon represent accepted immediate grounds for abortion, beyond a women's mere declaration of her choice. These include: pregnancy due to rape; socio-economic hardships which curtail the prospects of normative child upbringing; and, especially, medical reasons – as in the pregnancy posing a threat to the mother's life. Hence, all these reasons are *conducive* to a women's general choice in favour of abortion.

The bluish and green triangles represent measures *curtailing* or adding an additional factor aimed at *dissuading* the prospective mother from her choice to abort her unborn child. These include: the state's demand for mandatory psychological and medical counselling (without which the state shall not approve the abortive procedure), in olive green, and (in turquoise) the state's demand for the woman to undergo a mandatory waiting period in the hope that she might change her mind and avoid abortion, respectively. One simplified way of reading this map would be to look for turquoise triangles – or simply for blue colour patches (complete prohibition, as in Poland). Countries that show these colours are distinctly more conservative, and more attuned to curtailing women's free choice for abortion, than countries in which these colours are absent. Such a reading yields a rather astonishing insight: the further 'West' one goes, and the more Christian the country, the more conservative and anti-women's choice the situation becomes. With the exception of the Czech Republic, since 1989 the shift towards an anti-abortion stance and the curtailment of women's free choice thereof has taken place mostly within the Soviet satellite countries of East Central Europe – all of whom are current EU member states (Poland, Slovakia, Hungary and the eastern half of Germany). Notably, other predominantly Christian countries of the former Soviet realm – such as Russia itself, Georgia and Armenia – have followed suit in this regression on women's right to abortion. In contrast, virtually all Central Asian countries (which are predominantly Muslim), the Baltic states and the Balkans (with the exception of Albania) have by and large maintained their Soviet-era freedoms with regard to abortion.

Paradoxically, then, with regard to women's right to abortion, the advent of EU law in East Central Europe has unfortunately not coincided with progress in women's rights but rather with their regression. In September 2022, Hungary legislated a mandatory prerequisite proof that requires women requesting an abortion to demonstrate that they have seen and heard their foetus's vital signs. As with the US Supreme Court's recent overturning of *Roe* v. *Wade*, so in East Central Europe, in 2022, the tightening of anti-abortion legislation continues.

Figure 4.2 Women's right to abortion in post-Soviet countries.

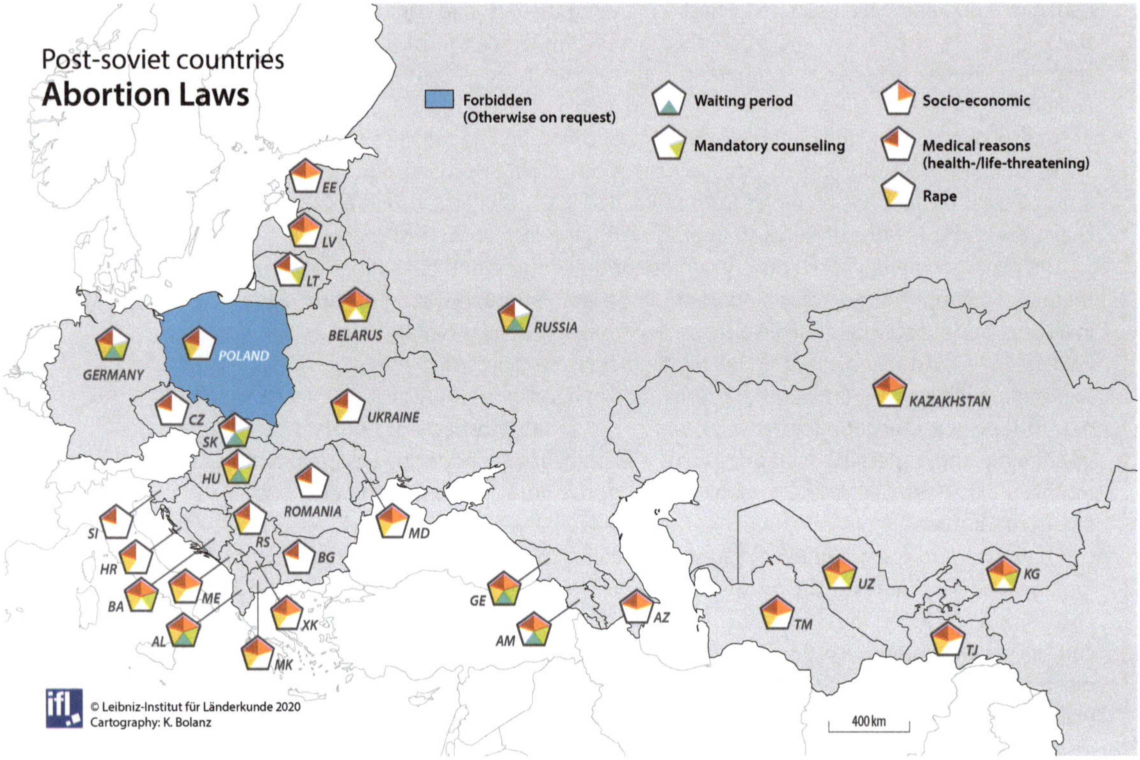

Divergent legal paths after 1989

Perestroika had the effect of strengthening several diverse tendencies in the Eastern European satellite states. On the one hand, countries such as Poland and Hungary further developed their efforts towards democratization. On the other hand, dictatorial regimes such as those in Romania and Bulgaria abstrusely denied these new trends of democratization and broke away towards a policy of resentment which underscored tenets of their ethnic nationalism, in a paradoxical attempt to combine the obviously mutually exclusive ideas of communism and nationalism. Still further, Czechoslovakia and the GDR went down an even more radical path of change, as they came to distinctly question, and eventually fully alter, their state formations. Czechoslovakia split up peacefully into two separate countries (Slovakia and the Czech Republic); the GDR was eventually united peacefully with its western German counterpart.

Notwithstanding the prevailing political and social signals, neither the socialist states nor their Western counterparts were ready for such dramatic developments; both demonstrated a distinct lack of strategy for the subsequent transitions to market economies and democratic political and social systems. If they were to meet with success, these transitions needed to be predicated upon securing some form of national consensus on the key questions of democratization and the re-enactment of market economies, which for many Eastern European countries remained but a remote recollection from the interwar period. Lacking any formal democratic institutions, these societies in transition developed alternative formats for kickstarting these transformations. Bulgaria, the GDR, Hungary and Poland opted for the concept of 'round tables', meeting points for all social groups on an equal footing, as starting points for their shift towards democracy and economic reconstruction.

Seen from a global perspective, the collapse of the Soviet bloc appeared simultaneously both hopeful and alarming. Looking to mitigate the negative consequences of such a tectonic shift in world affairs, OSCE (Organization for Security and Co-operation in Europe) member states, the United States, Canada, New Zealand, Australia, Japan and Turkey quickly joined

Table 1. EU accession processes for Eastern European states

Year of launch of negotiations towards EU Association Agreement	EU economic assistance via membership of PHARE	Year of accession to EU membership
1990	Poland	2004
1990	Hungary	2004
1990	Bulgaria	2007
1990	Czechoslovakia	dissolved into Czech Republic and Slovakia
1991	Estonia, Latvia, Lithuania	2004
1991	Albania	Candidate
1992	Slovenia	2004
1993	Czech Republic	2004
1993	Slovakia	2004
1993	Romania	2007
1993	Yugoslavia (from 1995, Croatia; from 1996, the Former Yugoslavian Republics of Macedonia and Bosnia & Herzegovina)	2013 Croatia; current advanced membership negotiations with Macedonia, Serbia, and Bosnia & Herzegovina

Source: European Union, https://european-union.europa.eu/principles-countries-history_en

their European Economic Community (EEC) counterparts in their support for the many round-table consultation processes that emerged in the now-defunct former socialist bloc. Owing to its geographical proximity and long historical ties, the European Union (as the EEC became in 1993) took the leading and coordinating role in this process. The EEC's first step, with help from allies from abroad, was the PHARE (Poland and Hungary Aid for Reconstruction of the Economy) programme. As its name suggests, the EEC chose for its immediate focus those two states which seemed most progressive in their democratic development, to which concentrated economic aid was delivered so as to prevent their economic collapse. And yet, as far as legal transformations were concerned, these were neither set immediately on the agenda nor were they intimately tied to the EEC's delivered economic aid.

The initial goal of PHARE, which saw its own objective as economic stabilization, was achieved relatively quickly. As early as 1990, one could see the growing rapprochement between the EU and Hungary, Poland and Czechoslovakia – now collectively termed the 'Central and Eastern European States' (CEES). That same year, negotiations were launched between them and the EU towards official Association Agreements. Other states soon followed. In 1993, at its Copenhagen summit, the European Council decided that these Association Agreements could subsequently provide for accession to the EU in their long-term prospective. PHARE thus became the key financial instrument of the EU's pre-accession strategy, providing financing for numerous activities from infrastructure projects to academic and student exchanges. Free elections, functional democratic institutions and the protection of human rights were all prerequisites of association and, later, accession. Much of the framing of these new activities was driven via the vehicle of legal approximation, as in the changing of these state's legislation so as to coincide with EU law – especially in the areas of economic regulations and technical standards.

Differentiating future prospective: CEES countries and the Newly Independent States (NIS)

The decision to open accession prospects to the post-socialist Central and Eastern European States (CEES) was highly contested within the EEC, and later in the EU. The absorption capacity of the EEC was the key point around which these debates revolved, and the EEC decided at a very early stage to differentiate between two groups of states. On the one hand, there was the Europe Agreement which covered those states already under PHARE, several of whom (but excluding the Baltic states) were already receiving its aid. On the other hand, in 1991, the EEC established a programme for Technical Assistance to the Commonwealth of Independent States (TACIS) as a parallel programme to PHARE for the Newly Independent States (NIS) of the former Soviet Union[4] and Mongolia. The treaty framework for cooperation with the NIS comprised the Partnership and Cooperation Agreements (PCAs) concluded by the EEC and later the EU with all NIS with the exception of Turkmenistan. The Europe Agreement was reserved for those states which the EU was eyeing for eventual membership.

The EU's goal for the states under PHARE and Europe Agreement was thus 'return to Europe', whereas the PCAs and TACIS aimed at the establishment of 'special, privileged links'. The fundamental differences between these goals were reflected in the depth and intensity of EU–CEES as opposed to EU–NIS cooperation. Democracy, rule of law and the protection of human rights were cornerstones of both cooperation projects. However, the PCAs did not provide for integration of the NIS into the EU's single market. Hence, they did not contain any direct obligations on adoption of the European *acquis communautaire* (the collection of common rights and obligations that constitute the body of EU law, and is incorporated into the legal systems of EU member states). The only reference to legal approximation between EU law and that of the NIS was a mere 'best endeavours' clause included in the PCAs. Notably, the majority of post-Soviet states were at this stage eager to establish closer relations with the EU. Some of them, especially Ukraine, even insisted on deeper cooperation with accession prospects and indicated their readiness to comply with the EU's requirements. The EU, however, rejected these aspirations.

Nevertheless, the formal approximation of the legal framework of former Soviet states to the legal standards of the European Union's *acquis* and its standards gradually succeeded.[5] Both CEES and NIS countries implemented many amendments to this effect within their legislations relatively quickly. In CEES countries, this process was to some

Figure 4.3 Different regional organisations' state memberships in the post-Soviet space.

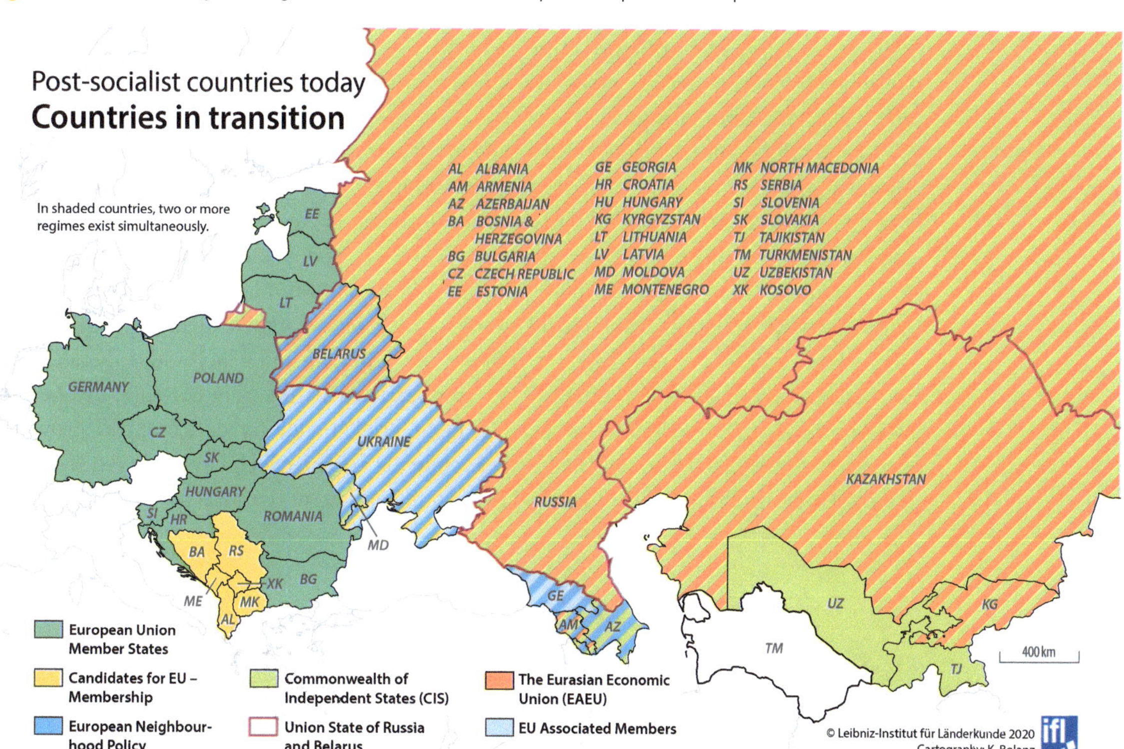

extent easier because the majority of them simply re-introduced much of their pre-socialist legislation, which already contained many aspects and even the basic legal institutions of a market economy. The main difference this time round, however, was the much deeper involvement that EU institutions had in member states' reform processes within the CEES. From the EU's perspective, securing the implementation of reform in the practice of the courts and executive organs of the CEES candidate states was of the utmost importance.

The NIS countries also enjoyed technical aid from the EU, as well as the European member states' individual aid organizations (especially the German Development Corporation GtZ, nowadays known as GIZ, the German Agency for International Cooperation) in the field of legal reform. That said, such support was not linked to any genuine or observable EU interest, and the results of these efforts speak for themselves. At the end of the day, the new legislation within the NIS that emerged thanks to the support of these European bodies has remained in large parts unimplemented. In turn, such non-implementation seems to have posed no major risk for the EU. Alas, numerous amendments have remained on the statute books and have not seen any concrete, 'on-the-ground' application. The EU-backed NIS-implemented legal reforms were in many cases buttressed by short-term capacity-building seminars that addressed specific groups of legal professionals – especially judges. In contrast, broader academic legal education and research were not these reforms' primary focus.[6] In hindsight, the EU and its member states failed to produce a new generation of law professors with the deep understanding required for the new legal institutes and their principles to be better embedded within societies. Academic-education scholarships and professional exchange programmes, as well as academic infrastructure projects of the EU and its member states within the NIS, were barely coordinated alongside the much-required legal reform processes necessary to effectuate long-term change.

Nevertheless, three decades later, one notices some very interesting developments. Gradually, and incrementally, positive law has begun to find its way from the law books into concrete action on the ground in NIS societies. Progress in economic development gradually influences social structures. The onset of economic and social crisis, in turn, triggers a re-emergence of legal discussions. This usually leads to a reinvention, revitalization, or simple reawakening of 'dormant legal norms', which had been there all along within the law books since the early to mid-1990s, had never been applied, and which suddenly underwent amendment and application. Often, a key partner in this triggering of 'legal awakening', serving as a crucial impetus towards de facto implementation of European provisions already existent within NIS legislation, are academic circles which have enjoyed significant developments in their legal education in the course of recent decades.

Conclusion

When one ponders whether or not socialist law has had any enduring influence after 1989, one need to look no further than Eastern Europe and the former Soviet realm today in order to see its lasting impact. From the retention of many aspects of Soviet family law to the ongoing problematics of reinstating property law in many post-Soviet countries, to their divergent paths for regional integration (see Figure 4.3, p. 119), today's Eastern European states continue to be heavily impacted on by the legacy of the socialist legal system which governed their existence for much of the 20th century.

In all probability, the strongest impact of Eastern European socialist law has resulted from the Soviet Union's family law, which was highly influential in all other socialist states. Its main goal was to 'eradicate the harmful survival of customs of the past within family relations'. In other words, its overt objective was to free the socialist person from the burdens of previous tsarist or imperial legal heritage, and equalize all members of society. Correspondingly, its main principles and privileges – such as equality of men and women, equality of children born in and out of wedlock, the right to paid maternity leave, and the right to abortion – were all provided for in the legislation of all the socialist states regardless of religious and cultural specifics – as we have seen, in Muslim Central Asia as well as in strictly Catholic Poland.

Even more interesting has been the development of family law in post-socialist states following the dissolution of the socialist system after 1989. To date, no comprehensive comparative research exists on this issue. Nevertheless, a prima facie analysis of several randomly selected legal orders around specific issues shows that socialist family law has been able to retain much of its basic structure to this day. Civil marriage is still the only possible form of marriage in the majority of Eastern European and former Soviet jurisdictions. Remarkably, while several Christian-majority states have (since 1989) partly reinstated their acceptance of religious marriages, none of the post-socialist states with a Muslim majority have done so. Add to this the overt difference in attitudes towards abortion between former Soviet Muslim states' continuing liberal approach and Christian (now European) states' increasingly reticent attitudes, and one begins to ponder the extent to which EU membership really renders its new members more progressive (see Figure 4.2, p. 116). Sure enough, even within the only post-socialist state to completely prohibit abortion (Poland), this decision has faced massive waves of protest. These point to the simple fact that the unrestricted right to abortion remains associated in Eastern European peoples' mind with deeper and more fundamental notions of human freedoms for women. And this association first emerged within the Soviet legal sphere in 1921. It would take Western democracies roughly half a century before they would catch up with this Eastern European Soviet progressiveness, *Roe* v. *Wade* being ruled upon only in 1973. Readers will naturally be reminded of that ruling's 2022 overturning by the US Supreme Court, rendering the right to abortion non-existent for women in many US states today.

Thus, seen with the benefit of hindsight, Eastern European socialist family law was one of the most progressive worldwide and has remained somewhat avant-garde. The rise of conservative religious and cultural influences in the 1990s and 2000s had no substantive influence on family law. Some revised rules were even reversed back to Soviet standards within just a few years. Azerbaijan, which decreased the minimum marriage age for females to 17 during this period, reversed this rule in 2011 and has returned to the Soviet standard of 18 years of age.

Even the changes to Eastern European family law – which has partly moved away from Soviet notions of the family as divorced from economic interests, and which has shifted back to the economic modalities of family ties – have still retained some of their old 'socialist flavours'. Nowadays, the majority of jurisdictions in Eastern Europe have added arrangements that were prohibited under socialist family law, such as marriage contracts and inheritance contracts. Yet numerous aspects of socialist approaches to the family have remained intact. Formal gender equality in the family has remained unquestioned in most post-Soviet countries. The idea of 'child welfare', as an ever-present vital component of legislation, and of the state's responsibility for oversight in cases of parental neglect has remained firm.

Throughout this chapter, we have engaged with the enduring impacts of Eastern European socialist laws upon the historical legal trajectories of states in the former Soviet realm. Yet, many of the attitudes exhibited *within* this sphere were eventually spread *beyond* this sphere by the Soviet world, as it opted to press for the application of tenets it saw as universal the world over. Readers perusing other chapters in this volume will notice such influences.[7]

The often harsh and inhumane circumstances via which Eastern European socialist law gradually came to be applied from Vladivostok to East Berlin should not be forgotten: Gulags, summary executions, and general states' oppressive mechanisms such as the Soviet KGB, the East German STASI, and the like. Yet on balance, there are certain liberal aspects of this law which did indeed surpass the legal ethos of many, if not all, Western democracies.

From women's right to abortion to gender equality within family relations, up until women's independent right for divorce – and even the state's own responsibility in providing kindergartens and maternal-care facilities so as to enable women's employment – Eastern European socialist law could be, and indeed was, more progressive than any other legal system in the world during its time. At the end of the day, this progressiveness stemmed from deeply rooted seeds embedded in 'classical' Marxist theory. The fruit borne by these seeds, such as children's rights and women's equality, were first applied domestically within the Soviet Union's system of law. They later spread regionally to the entire Soviet-influenced sphere, finally 'going global' in international treaties such as the 1989 UN Convention on the Rights of the Child. Much of this legacy is still with us today.

Notes

1 For a comprehensive and authoritative overview of Eastern Europe's legal history, see Herbert Küpper, *Einführung in die Rechtsgeschichte Osteuropas* (Frankfurt am Main: Peter Lang, 2005).

2 Zdenek Kühn, *The Judiciary in Central and Eastern Europe: Mechanical Jurisprudence in Transformation?* (Leiden: Brill, 2011).

3 Elena Sherstoboeva, 'The Evolution of a Russian Concept of Free Speech', in *Speech and Society in Turbulent Times: Freedom of Expression in Comparative Perspective*, ed. Monroe Price and Nicole Stremlau (Cambridge: Cambridge University Press, 2017), pp. 213–34.

4 Armenia, Azerbaijan, Belarus, Georgia, Kazakhstan, Kyrgyzstan, Moldova, Russia, Tajikistan, Turkmenistan, Ukraine and Uzbekistan.

5 For numerous examples in the field of private law, see Christa Jessel-Holst, Rainer Kulms and Alexander Trunk (eds), *Private Law in Eastern Europe* (Tübingen: Mohr Siebeck, 2010).

6   An interesting example of the different levels of institutional involvement can be observed by examining the European Court of Justice for the CEEU and the NIS, whereby vis-à-vis the CEEU the court shows very high degrees of involvement, as part of these countries' EU accession process, versus almost no involvement in the legal aid projects in the NIS. For analysis of the various NIS jurisdictions, see Arie Reich, Hans-W. Micklitz (eds), *The Impact of the European Court of Justice in Neighbouring Countries* (Oxford: Oxford University Press, 2020).

7   See the chapters by Elizabeth White, Max Trecker, Katja-Castryck-Naumann and Gilad Ben-Nun in this volume.

Bibliography

Avdeev, Alexandre, Alain Blum and Irina Troitskaya. 'The History of Abortion Statistics in Russia and the USSR from 1900 to 1991'. In *Population: An English Selection Vol. 7.* Paris: Institut National d'Études Démographiques, 1995, pp. 39–66.

Ioffe, Olimpiad. 'Decree of the Council of People's Commissars of November 24, 1917, No. 1: "On the Court"'. In *Soviet Law and Soviet Reality.* Leiden: Brill, 1985.

Kelsen, Hans. *The Communist Theory of Law.* 2nd Printing. London: Hassell Street Press, 2021.

The All-Russian Central Executive Committee. *The Decree on the Court № 2 of March 7, 1918.* № 26, Art. 347, 420. N.P.: Collection of laws and regulations of the Workers' and Peasants' Government, 1918. In English available online at: https://archive.org/details/firstdecreesofsovietpower/page/99/mode/2up.

The People's Commissariats of Health and Justice. *The Order on the Protection of Women's Health № 471 of November 18, 1920.* № 90, Art. 471. N.P.: Collection of laws and regulations of the Workers' and Peasants' Government, 1920. In English available online at: https://soviethistory.msu.edu/1917-2/the-new-woman/the-new-woman-texts/on-the-protection-of-womens-health.

Socialist Childhoods: Internationalizing Education and Children's Rights

Elizabeth White

5

Introduction

Education in the European socialist bloc states has been viewed as totalitarian indoctrination and a way of keeping childhood, as adulthood, behind the Iron Curtain. Human rights have been seen as emanating from the Western tradition and deployed successfully against Eastern bloc regimes to bring their end in the late 1980s. This chapter challenges these paradigms by looking afresh at the socialist radical project of initiating universal, compulsory, co-educational schooling systems to produce 'modern' citizens with a 'scientific' and cosmopolitan world view. From the late 1950s the Soviet Union (SU) and the other European socialist states supported decolonization processes, national liberation movements and newly independent states, as part of a strategy of competitive co-existence with the Western bloc. Educational models and concepts of childhood was part of this strategic competition and were arenas to demonstrate solidarity with anti-imperialism. Circulations of educational models and concepts of childhood were part of the network of global entanglements between European socialism and postcolonial states and part of Cold War rivalries.

Children were so important in the Global Cold War as the material for the creation of the socialist or postcolonial 'new person' (*novyi chelovek*) and they were linked with development and modernization. The Soviet educational model[1] and socialist state care for children was promoted by the socialist bloc during the Cold War as one of socialism's greatest achievements, deployed for soft power and cultural diplomacy and as a tool in international relations through bodies such as the UN and UNESCO. Children's rights, as with women's rights, was an area in which socialist states could demonstrate superiority over the West. It was Poland in 1978, trying to prove its human rights credentials in response to US monopolization of the discourse on human rights in the late 70s that initiated the drafting of the UN Convention of the Rights of the Child (1989). This chapter will therefore also look at how Eastern bloc actors – jurists and legal scholars, political figures, and socialist women activists in transnational networks, such as Adam Łopatka and Zofia Dembínska – drove the internationalization of children's rights in the postwar period.

The Soviet educational model: Polytechnical education

When the Bolshevik Party took power in 1917, the revolutionary transformation of childhood and education was an essential part of their programme. They identified children as a key social group and created a network of childcare institutions, scientific research centres and welfare services and sought to revolutionize education. The 'Soviet school' was to produce a generation capable of working for the transition to communism and the modernization and industrialization of the Soviet Union.

The Bolsheviks oversaw the radical transformation and expansion of primary and secondary education in just over two decades. In October 1918 the Soviet government issued the Decree on the Unified Labour School. This created a comprehensive system of free, compulsory, co-educational, state-wide and secular schooling for children aged 8–13 at primary level and 14–17 at secondary level. The Soviet state initially supported experimental approaches and employed pre-revolutionary progressive educational theorists to draw up the new system. At the end of the 1920s, however, during the 'Revolution from Above', Stalin ordered that education become more closely linked to economic modernization and the needs of the new command economy. He also ordered that traditional pedagogical methods be reintroduced such as a centralized curriculum, uniforms, year grades, exams, discipline and a high level of teacher authority.

The expansion of compulsory education is part of the process of state formation and the extension of state power. Stalin oversaw a dramatic expansion of primary and secondary education in the 1930s, particularly into rural areas and the National Republics. By 1940, in comparison to 1922, enrolment in secondary schools in the Russian Republic had quadrupled and it had multiplied even further in all the other Republics apart from Georgia. Between 1927/8 and 1938/9 enrolment in the Soviet school system grew by 19 million; 11 million more in primary schools and 8 million in secondary schools. Overall numbers of children in education rose from 11.3 million to 31.4 million. By the 1950s, 57 million children were enrolled in Soviet schools, compared to 8.1 million just before 1917.[2] In just several decades, the Soviet state had initiated and overseen a historically unprecedented expansion of primary and secondary education in a vast and underdeveloped state. In this time the educational system shifted from one which prioritized experimentation and the autonomy of the child to a more traditional educational system with total party and state control and a centralized curriculum.

After the Second World War, the Soviet model was both imposed on and imitated by the new People's Democracies in Europe as part of the 'modernizing revolution' created by Stalinism and postwar reconstruction. The state-supported infrastructure of children's culture and leisure which saturated the Soviet public sphere was also transferred there.

Before the Second World War, access to education had varied widely across the region as a whole and within individual states, but in general rural schooling was sparse and under-funded and there was little access to secondary education. The new socialist states began to transform their education systems in the second half of the 1940s and early 50s. As had happened in the Soviet Union, all schools and kindergartens were nationalized, and private and church schools closed to eradicate class-based educational inequalities. The communist parties and educational theorists drew up and implemented a co-educational, secular, universal schooling system. State educational planning and the introduction of comprehensive schooling were part of the Soviet-inspired socialist modernization model. The new regimes intended the education system to play a decisive role in transmitting ideology and creating a socialist culture. They wanted to gain support and legitimacy through the creation of a new socialist intelligentsia and increasing social mobility. Party control over education was enforced by a single national curriculum and centrally imposed and officially approved textbooks for each subject and year grade. Positive discrimination in higher education was introduced to benefit peasant and working-class students. In line with the Soviet model, the new socialist states focused on the extension of primary education into rural areas. One sometimes overlooked aspect of the socialist educational revolution was the commitment to eliminating sex-based differences in educational access. The expansion of female education was prioritized.

The reiteration of the Soviet polytechnical principle as the basis for education was now transferred across the socialist bloc. The educational revolution there was an integral element of plans for industrialization, urbanization and modernization. Vocational and technical education was prioritized to meet the demands of modernization and industrialization and to develop a new social structure. At secondary level, students were driven by the state into specific career paths. The socialist education system would create citizens with a 'modern' or 'scientific' world view.

During the crises and stagnation of late socialism and since the end of the Cold War, the socialist bloc educational systems were criticized as undemocratic and hyper-centralized. Their main function was seen as indoctrination and, rather than being a form of modernity, they are viewed as a contributing factor to the decay and disintegration of the socialist regimes in the 1980 as the modernization of education was accompanied by the imposition of an ideology that restricted creativity and innovation. The borrowing from the Soviet model and the negative features of the socialist bloc educational systems have been explained as a result of a 'modernization lag' or 'cultural gap' between East and West. Alternatively, educational developments between 1948 and 1989 are presented as a break in the educational traditions of the region. Post-socialist education systems are seen as 'catching up' with or returning to Europe.

A 'multiple modernities' approach alternatively suggests that the socialist bloc states were on a different modernity path, rather than lagging behind one. In the 1940s and 50s, the adoption of the Soviet educational model was motivated by the desire to close the perceived gap between Eastern and Western Europe and by a specific vision of modernization. The elimination of class and sex-based educational inequality and the expansion of rural schooling were a radical break with the past and in advance of what was happening in the West. Monica Mincu has described the Soviet influence on education in Central and Eastern Europe as both an 'imperialist force and a voluntary borrowing'.[3] Postwar education developed in the European socialist bloc in accordance with a range of factors: the Soviet model and its local adaptation; pre-existing cultural legacies; and from the 1970s an increasing interaction with Western ideas and global models. While educational modernization was initially fuelled by the transmission and translation of Soviet ideas, the Soviet model was not ultimately imposed in its entirety or in a sustained way across Central and Eastern Europe. From the 1960s strict party control was weakened by the inclusion of 'secular' experts in educational planning and some reassertion of national educational traditions. The Catholic Church in Poland sustained an alternative educational vision, while a mixed model of school autonomy was reintroduced in Hungary from the late 1970s supported by UNESCO and the World Bank. To a greater degree than in the Soviet Union, comprehensive primary schooling was combined with highly selective higher secondary school in European socialist bloc states and family social, political and cultural capital also played a role. In most socialist states at the age of 14, pupils transitioned into variants of either vocational training or academic-focused secondary schools which prepared them for university. This was different to the Soviet model, which remained comprehensive, albeit with a range of specialist secondary schools for gifted children.

It can be argued that the Soviet model was not only focused on producing a technical intelligentsia through polytechnical education. It was also based on classical European humanistic values and was a carrier of globalization in the 20th century. The entire socialist educational model has been described as part of the Enlightenment 'cosmopolitan project', whose aim was to produce modern global citizens who could transcend their own environment with a belief in human reason and progress.[4] Emphasis on scientific thinking and reasoning was part of the cosmopolitan project. Socialist education systems also encouraged an outward-looking socialist participatory citizenship.

During the Global Cold War from the 1950s, children in the socialist bloc were encouraged to be cosmopolitan citizens. In the Soviet model, childhood was political and revolutionary, and children were taken seriously as social actors. They were encouraged to engage with the international world and integrate solidarity practices as part of their everyday world. Soviet children participated in the mass state-supported Soviet peace movement and showed solidarity with global anti-colonial struggles. Pioneer rallies included a 'Day for the Defence of Peace'. In the 1960s, a showcase international Pioneer camp, Artek, was set up on the shores of the Black Sea. 'Camp is full of colour but race is one colour we do not see' were the words of a Pioneer in a radio broadcast to Angola in 1961.[5] Pioneer groups from other socialist countries were invited to the Soviet Union and a socialist bloc pen-pal system was established in practices of transnational solidarity. The Soviet state and socialist bloc states offered refuge to children from leftist or anti-colonial political wars, in a tradition dating back to the Spanish Civil War when thousands of Republican children went to live in the Soviet Union after the Franco-ist victory. In the 1940s and 50s, Greek refugee children were taken to East Germany, Czechoslovakia and

Hungary in a show of socialist solidarity and Vietnamese children came to East Germany to be educated.

Pionerskaya Pravda, the leading Soviet children's newspaper, regularly carried reports on international affairs: Churchill's 'Iron Curtain' speech, the Greek Civil War, the division of Germany, and anti-colonial struggles in the Dutch East Indies, for example, in the 1940s. In 1970, *Pionerskaya Pravda* covered incursions by Israel into Egypt, labour unrest and strikes in Italy during the 'years of lead' (*Anni di piombo*), and the extension of the Vietnam War into Cambodia. Children were encouraged to express their opposition to America's war in Vietnam. Pioneer groups across the Eastern bloc learnt Vietnamese, organized 'Aid Vietnam' campaigns, and sent gifts to children in North Vietnam. They collected medicinal herbs for Hanoi's Children's Hospital and created 'Vietnam Corners' in their classrooms. Meanwhile children and adolescents across the Global South read Soviet children's literature, classic Russian literature, science fiction and school textbooks, which were distributed widely and very cheaply by the Soviet Union, 'eliminating emotional, political, social and physical geographies'.[6]

The polytechnical global Soviet educational model: Competitive co-existence

The new Soviet school was always closely linked with the social world and with the wider aims of the state. Practical or vocational work was an integral part of primary and secondary education. The Soviet educational model was based on the principle of polytechnical education. Soviet polytechnical education would prepare the required labour forces for modernization and industrialization. However, it meant not only the acquisition of practical skills and an understanding of the processes of production, but also mastering the materialist conception of the scientific bases of natural and social phenomena. The aim of education was to produce a 'science-based world outlook' and to create the Marxist ideal of a fully emancipated rounded human personality, who would be prepared for all intellectual and practical tasks. The 1959 Theses of the Central Committee declared that Soviet education would produce 'the new person, in whom spiritual wealth, moral purity, and physical perfection will be harmoniously combined'.

In the 1950s, as part of his efforts to rejuvenate social enthusiasm in the post-Stalin years and mobilize society for the impending future transition to communism, Nikita Khrushchev called for even greater emphasis on vocational education. In 1954, lessons in basic manual skills were introduced in primary schools, and in 1955 vocational work outside the classroom was made mandatory in the final years of secondary school. In 1958, after some controlled public debate, the Soviet state issued the decree 'On Strengthening the Link between School and Life and Further Developing the System of Public Education'. The Decree stated that 'the most important task in education is that all children should be ready for useful work, ready to take part in the building up of Communist society'. All 15- to 16-year-olds had to participate in 'socially useful work' and further education combined with productive work in the national economy.

Having dismissed the Soviet education system as producing unthinking and obedient automatons, the successful launch of Sputnik, the first artificial earth satellite, in 1957 prompted alarm and then educational reforms in the United States. It altered the approach to funding educational projects in international bodies such as UNESCO and the World Bank, prompting research into the causal relationship between education and development.[7] The socialist bloc then pushed its educational model to the attention of the decolonizing world, trying to win support in its strategy of competitive co-existence.

Educational policies became part of the Global Cold War from the 1950s as tensions and rivalries crystalized around development aid through education. Khrushchev promoted the Soviet polytechnical educational system as a global vision in education. Under his premiership, the renewed emphasis on polytechnical education and the link between education and labour became fused with the concept of development and made visible in UN bodies and international organizations. The European socialist bloc hoped to create a global socialist intelligentsia and used educational aid as cultural soft power. From 1968, in response to Soviet actions, the World Bank under the presidency of Robert McNamara began massive funding of primary education in postcolonial states as part of its 'redistribution with growth' policy to combat the appeal of communism.[8]

The successful launch of Sputnik in October 1957 prompted global admiration for Soviet education. In 1958, the US Commissioner of Education, Lawrence Derthick, visited the Soviet Union. He reported back that 'we were simply not prepared for the degree to which the U.S.S.R., as a nation, is committed to education as a means of national advancement. [It is] a total commitment. We witnessed an education-centred economy. The privileged class in Russia is the children.'[9] In 1958, the US government passed the National Defence Education Act (NDEA), dramatically increasing federal funding for further and higher education. Eisenhower was worried that America was losing the race for leadership in science and technology. They began to take the education of girls more seriously, realizing the United States needed to fully utilize all its human capital. Kristen Ghodsee has argued that the socialist bloc's commitment to sexual equality in education directly influenced the US government's support for female education and for the liberal second-wave feminism in the 1960s.[10]

Postcolonial states needed to create new national elites and introduce state-wide educational systems. As in the European socialist bloc, new education systems were part of ambitious modernization schemes for economic development, social mobility and cultural transformation. Work has been done on socialist bloc support for higher education and less on support for primary and secondary education, suggesting new lines of research in the future. Students (overwhelmingly male) from postcolonial states or members of national liberation movements came to study in an array of tertiary educational institutions in the Eastern bloc as part of the creation of a new elite and a technical intelligentsia. Education in medicine, engineering, nursing, mechanics and economic planning was prioritized. In 1960, the People's Friendship University (*Druzhba narodov*), renamed a year later after the murdered Congolese independence leader Patrice Lumumba, was founded in Moscow specifically for students from the so-called Third World. Khrushchev announced this while on a state visit to Indonesia, declaring that the Soviet government wanted to help postcolonial states train a national workforce of engineers, agronomists, doctors, teachers and economists.

From the second half of the 1950s, tens of thousands of students from sub-Saharan Africa, the Middle East, Asia and Latin America studied in the socialist bloc states. Some 43,500 African students received higher education in the Soviet Union.[11] This prompted the United States and other Western countries to increase scholarships to students from the Third World as well as educational aid. By the 1980s, the USSR was the third top donor of educational aid in Africa, after France and the United States. As well as offering scholarships, the socialist bloc played an important role in the expansion of education in the postcolonial world. From the late 1950s, the Soviet Union began to set up higher education institutions across Africa and the Middle East, first in Egypt in 1957. Between 1960 and 1966, it created the Polytechnical Institute of Conakry, Guinea, and the Higher Administrative School of Bamako in Mali, both of which were the first higher education institutions in those countries. In 1964, it set up the African Centre for Hydrocarbons and Textiles in Algeria. It also established the National Engineering School of Tunisia and the Bahir Dir Technical Institute in Ethiopia. Workers' Faculties on the Soviet model (*rabfaky*) were established in Vietnam, Cuba and Mozambique, and the Soviet Union provided educational advice to Tanzania.

Meanwhile, the GDR provided educational aid to Mozambique. GDR activists had earlier helped with education in FRELIMO (Mozambique Liberation Front) refugee camps when they were based in Tanzania. The GDR delivered 'solidarity services' to Mozambique in the 1970s and 80s, ranging from printing school textbooks to training Mozambican teachers in the GDR.[12] In turn, GDR cadres went to Mozambique as advisors, teachers, curriculum planners and lecturers. Piepiorka concludes that practices of socialist solidarity through educational aid helped with broader processes of decolonization in Mozambique. The GDR had a School of Friendship in Stassfurt for educating children from postcolonial states. Social Democratic party officials wanted to assert the GDR's leading role in the international arena. These acts of socialist and anti-imperialist solidarity had an internal purpose: they were meant to create support among their own citizens as the GDR was helping to create a just postcolonial order and staying true to its anti-fascist origins.

Children's rights and socialism during the Global Cold War

The traditional historical interpretation is that human rights linked with Cold War geopolitics in the second half of the 1970s, driven by Western states to support the delegitimization of the socialist bloc. After the socialist bloc states signed the Third Basket of the Helsinki Final Accords at the Conference on Security and Cooperation in Europe in 1975, internal oppositions used human rights against their own states. Recent research, however, challenges this interpretation, arguing that throughout the Cold War the socialist bloc promoted – often successfully – its own versions of human rights and also made substantial and significant contributions to the drafting of major UN human rights instruments, particularly those concerning sexual and racial equality and self-determination, and with an emphasis on social and economic rights. Rights activists – jurists, academics, social activists from the Soviet Union in particular, but also Poland and the GDR, distributed and circulated ideas, organized state-sponsored festivals, participated in transnational networks as part of a self-promotion as leaders in human rights. In the GDR, the *Sozialistische Einheitspartei Deutschlands* (SED) adopted the language of human rights in its propaganda and self-presentation and constructed a conception of socialist human rights to legitimize its rule. This lasted until the very end; in 1985, Kurt Hager, the long-time Chief Ideologue of the SED, called for international experts to draft a socialist declaration of rights that could challenge the West's assumption of hegemony in this field.[13]

From the 1940s, socialist bloc women from state women's organizations, sports, the transnational advocacy group 'Women's International Democratic Federation' and academics were successful in internationalizing women's rights in the UN. Elizaveta Popova was the Soviet representative on the UN Commission on the Status of Women (CSW) and had been a member of the Commission on Human Rights during the drafting of the UDHR. Along with feminists from the Global South she campaigned women to have equal pay, which was opposed by Western feminists, and argued for the importance of gender equality to human rights in the aftermath of war. Other Soviet representatives included Zoya Mironova, who was a speed skater, sports surgeon and head surgeon for the USSR Olympic team, and the cosmonaut and political activist Valentina Tereshkova. Representing Poland in the CWS and long-standing Chair was Zofia Dembínska, who had been Deputy Minister for Education in 1951–60 and was an expert in children's education and welfare. In 1963, representatives from Czechoslovakia, Poland and Mongolia in the CSW joined twenty-two developing states and pushed the General Assembly to call for a Declaration on the Elimination of Discrimination against Women (DEDAW) finalized in 1967. Zofia Dembínska was Chair of the drafting committee along with women from the USSR and Hungary. Socialist bloc women also led the UN global campaign for women's rights in the 1970s, resulting in the 1979 Convention on the Elimination of All Forms of Discrimination against Women. The Soviet representative in the CSW, Tatiana Nikolayeva, submitted the first resolution to develop the Declaration into a Convention and drafted the first text.[14]

Although these rights were not specifically for children, child welfare was deeply embedded in them. The Soviet Union put draft clauses in the Declaration on non-discrimination against illegitimate children and argued for the protection of the children of single mothers. For socialist bloc women, women's equality was predicated on economic liberation and the right to work, earn equally to men and support children. Their successful internationalization of social benefits and equal pay for working mothers were key parts for the internationalization of children's rights. They also helped raise the marriage age and outlaw harmful cultural practices against children. Then in the 1970s, the socialist bloc states also took the initiative in internationalizing specifically the rights of children, another area in which they felt they could demonstrate an advantage over the West. Poland asked for the drafting of a Convention on the Rights of the Child, replacing the 1959 Declaration of the Rights of the Child.

Children's rights in the 'Century of the Child'

Civilian suffering in the First World War, and its greater visibility, caused a new commitment to an international ideal for defining the rights of children. Even greater civilian atrocities in the Second World War increased this commitment. The role of humanitarian organizations such as Save the Children International also played a part and this is widely acknowledged, but the role of the socialist bloc has been overlooked.

The first international declaration was the Geneva Declaration of the Rights of the Child, which was adopted by the General Assembly of the League of Nations in 1924. By 1929, the Geneva Declaration had been unanimously adopted by all League member states. The Geneva Declaration had been drafted by the International Save the Children Union (ISCU), an umbrella organization which was developed out of the English Save the Children Union. Save the Children had been founded in 1919 by the social reformers Eglantyne Jebb and Dorothy Buxton to provide urgent disaster relief to children in Central and Eastern Europe and the Balkans in the aftermath of the First World War. The 1924 Declaration consisted of five broad principles. It 'recognized that mankind owes the Child the best that it has to give'. It stated that children must be given the means for spiritual and material development and should be protected and prioritized for humanitarian relief:

> The child that is hungry must be fed; the child that is sick must be nursed; the child that is backward must be helped; the delinquent child must be reclaimed; and the orphan and the waif must be sheltered and succored.[15]

The ISCU acknowledged that this was not a declaration of rights but an assertion of vulnerability and of the responsibilities of adults towards children. It did though declare that children should have economic freedom (training and education) and the right to an upbringing in the values of the League. The Geneva Declaration was not binding, although the League and the ISCU widely publicized it, including in Central and Eastern Europe, and states were encouraged to incorporate its spirit into national legislations.

Around the same time east of Geneva, the new Soviet state was instigating its own revolution in children's rights. In 1918, the new Soviet government declared that 'concern for the child is the direct responsibility of the state'. The Soviet state undertook to provide free paediatric health care, create a child-focused welfare state, state subsided childcare and maternity benefits, universal and compulsory education as well as reforming the juvenile criminal system and establishing an array of state institutions for abandoned or orphaned children. Institutional bodies representing the needs of children as a social group were embedded at the highest levels of the Soviet state. In January 1919, the Soviet government created the Council for the Defence of Children (*Sovet zashchity detei*), soon renamed as the Extraordinary Commission for the Improvement of Children's Life (*Chrezvychainaya kommissiya po uluchsheniyu zhizni detei pri VTsiK*). This body, which lasted until 1935, was known as the *Detkommisiya*, the Children's Commission. From the 1930s, the expansion of the education system was accompanied by the creation of a state-supported infrastructure for children's culture and leisure; publishing houses, cinema studios, theatres and Pioneer palaces and summer camps. The establishment of a universal compulsory educational and the provision of a 'happy childhood' for Soviet children was part of the Soviet Union's projected global image before the Second World War.

After the war, the Soviet state continued to promote its treatment of children as one of the elements of its superiority to the West. Just as foreign visitors to the Soviet Union had been taken to see model Soviet schools in Moscow in the 1930s, now purpose-built Pioneer Palaces were added to Inturist itineraries. In 1961, the Soviet Communist Party adopted the 'Moral Code for the Builders of Communism' at the XXII Party Conference. One of the twelve tenets was 'mutual respect in the family, concern for the upbringing of children'. Soviet parents were meant to raise a child as 'a true patriot, an honest labourer, a good collectivist, a worthy successor and continuer of our great Revolutionary task'. One of the obligations of a Soviet citizen outlined in the 1977 Constitution was 'to bring up children, train them for work and raise them as worthy members of society'. The Soviet Communist Party programme declared: 'To ensure that every child will have a happy childhood – that is one of the most important and noble tasks of the building of a communist society.' By the second half of the 1950s, the Soviet state had implemented universal schooling and a childcare network, created a welfare state and paediatric medical services, overseen a genuine advance in standards of living for children as well as supporting an infrastructure for children's culture and leisure. By 1980, there were around 60,000 Summer Pioneer camps, 6,473 Sports Schools, 4,844 Palaces of Culture for children, and 7,691 art, music and choreography schools in the Soviet Union. Membership in the Pioneers was almost universal in the age cohort. In 1984, 19.5 million Soviet children were members of Pioneer groups. These measures were replicated across the socialist bloc, whose states described children as 'the only privileged class'.[16]

Attempts to draft new international legislation for children's rights began again after the Second World War. The International Union of Child Welfare (IUCW), the successor of the ISCU, tried to get the UN to reaffirm the Geneva Declaration. In 1946, the UN Social Commission began to discuss the possibility of a Declaration or Charter of the Rights of the Child and, in 1948, it began preparations to update the 1924 Declaration. Socialist bloc states led the call for a binding international instrument that would emphasize the importance of legislation and role of the state in safeguarding children's rights to protection and welfare. In 1959, a new Declaration was ratified. The socialist bloc states helped draft the 1959 Declaration and wanted to demonstrate superiority with constitutional rights to education and medical care.[17] The Soviet, Polish and Ukrainian representatives requested that maternity leave and rights for working nursing mothers be added into the draft; and they proposed that 'the child should have the right to proper nutrition, housing, recreation, and free medical services. The state should assure free medical care to all children and expectant and nursing mothers … and provide sports and leisure facilities.'[18] Other suggestions included state institutions for children, family allowances, free and universal primary and secondary education, access to culture, the prohibition of child labour and corporal punishment, and a ban on the dissemination of war propaganda and racial and national hatred. Soviet attempts to insert the word 'State' liberally throughout the draft were unsuccessful as was an attempt to get provision of state support for children outside families and family maintenance payments. Meanwhile, the Polish representative tried unsuccessfully to introduce the principle that 'the child has the right to live in peace'. The

Soviet amendment that 'States should prohibit the dissemination of war propaganda and racial and national hatred in school' was rejected, but a further amendment that children should be bought up 'in a spirit of peace, friendship and brotherhood among nations' was accepted.[19] The resulting 1959 Declaration of the Rights of the Child still foregrounded children's vulnerability and need of protection. Zoya Mironova complained that the Declaration neither saw mothers as economically active nor protected their rights, which would also support their children's rights.

In the mid-1970s, the Polish government took the initiative in a new effort to internationalize children's rights. The Polish economy was stagnating, and Poland was increasingly reliant on economic cooperation with the West. Western loans and economic aid were linked to its human rights record. The internal opposition had also begun framing its criticisms of the regime in the language of human rights. Its leaders were concerned about the country's reputation and wanted to promote a 'progressive, cosmopolitan image' for Poland.[20]

In 1978, Poland submitted its own draft Declaration to the UN Human Rights Commission. This was largely based on the 1959 Declaration, to which Poland had contributed. Adam Łopatka, the Polish jurist who became Chair of the Working Group, recalled that the government's view was that this 'was a good opportunity to show that this type of initiative did not have to be the monopoly of the Western States'.[21]

Poland could present social, economic and cultural rights for children as the socialist bloc's heritage and achievement. In asserting Poland's legitimacy to lead on the internationalization of children's rights, Łopatka also drew on the moral capital of a specifically Polish legacy. He cited the legacy of Janusz Korczak, who accompanied the children and staff of his Jewish orphanage from the Warsaw Ghetto to Treblinka in August 1942. He also referred to the founder of UNICEF, the scientist Ludwik W. Rajchman, and to the suffering of Polish children in both world wars. Janusz Korczak (1879–1942) was a pediatrician, educational theorist and social activist in interwar Poland, who remained a significant figure posthumously in the socialist bloc as a pioneer of children's rights. He was nominated to be UNESCO Educator of the Year for the 1979 International Year of the Child. Korczak was born Henryk Goldszmit in 1879 into an assimilated Jewish family in Warsaw. He adopted his Polish name as a literary pseudonym at the age of 17.[22] He studied medicine at Warsaw University where he was influenced by the thought of the liberal-socialist and positivist Polish intelligentsia in late imperial Russia, who rejected the revolutionary romanticism of the past choosing to focus on constructive daily action and social activism to improve Polish life. At this point, he discovered what he called the 'unknown half of humanity – children'. Korzcak served as an army doctor in three wars (the Russo-Japanese War in 1904, the First World War, and the Polish-Russian War in 1919) where he saw children's suffering at first hand. Much like Konstantin Ventsel, Korczak saw children as an oppressed social group (the 'first proletariat') and he devoted his professional life to working with children and campaigning for children's rights. He began carrying out research on diet and nutrition in working-class children. In Warsaw, he worked at Bersohn and Bauman Children's Hospital (1905–12). He ran orphanages and summer camps for working-class Jewish and Catholic children. He wrote books on children's rights and their education, including *How to Love a Child* and *The Child's Right to Respect*. He published widely in the popular Polish press and had his own radio show, in which he was known as the Old Doctor (*Stary Doktor*). He was a well-known figure in interwar Poland, but his life and work became increasingly constrained in the late 1930s due to growing official and unofficial anti-Semitism. After the Germans occupied Poland, Korczak ran an orphanage in the Warsaw Ghetto. Although he was offered chances to leave the Ghetto, he chose to remain and finally accompanied the two hundred orphans and the staff in his care to Treblinka, where they were all murdered.

Korczak argued that children should have the rights that adults have, including the rights that allow full participation and not only the right to be protected from violence and suffering (as in the 1924 Geneva Declaration: 'the child must be the first to be offered relief').

In his orphanages, Korzcak set up a system of children's courts and councils to involve children in their own lives. The orphanages also had newspapers and publications so the children could express their opinions. He saw himself as a 'constitutional educator', protecting children against the arbitrary actions of adults. He rejected the dominant Western views of children as 'blank slates' and as innocent and weak. He argued that children should have the rights to privacy, freedom of expression and conscience, to education, to love and respect and to their own identity. He argued that children have the right to keep secrets, to own personal belongings, to take risks (controversially, he claimed children should have 'the right to die') and to be considered a full person, recognized, understood and valued for themselves now in their human actuality not as future adults. In the words of modern debates on children's rights, Korzcak prioritized the 'being child', rather than the 'becoming child' and saw the child as having the 'rights of individual personality'. He wrote:

> The child is entitled to be taken seriously, that his affairs be considered fairly. Thus far, everything has depended upon the educator's goodwill, or his good or bad mood. The child has been given no right to protest. We must end despotism.[23]

Korzcak participated in the 1924 Geneva Conference and signed the Geneva Declaration, but criticized it for its lack of any legally binding obligations.

While the First Polish Draft was mainly a reaffirmation of the 1959 Declaration, the Second Polish Draft contained a radically new article: Article 7, guaranteeing the child's right to freedom of expression. This has been described as 'the first step towards recognition in positive law that children have rights of "individual personality"'.[24] Adam Łopatka wrote that the UNCRC 'affirmed Korzcak's vision that children are *human beings*, and as such, are entitled to recognition of their human dignity' and not the '*germ of a human being*' but a 'personality, with their own dignity and individuality'.[25]

Simultaneously to Korczak's work in Warsaw, another emancipatory version of children's rights was circulating in Moscow, again drawing on the legacy of the progressive intelligentsia in late imperial Russia. The Russian educational theorist Konstantin Ventsel had published a draft *Declaration of the Rights of the Child*, which he hoped to put before the Constituent Assembly, the newly elected All-Russian parliament, in January 1918. He also presented the Declaration at the Moscow *Proletkul't* Conference in February 1918. Ventsel hoped that the new Soviet Union would be the first state to issue a declaration of children's rights.[26] He proposed ideas on a child's right to material support and free development, as well as the right to be heard. In his declaration, he wrote that the state and the family should provide children with the right conditions for living and learning and should guarantee them equality with adults. Children should have the freedom of choice in their education and religion, freedom of expression and organization, and the right to be heard in all matters that affect them. They should also have the right to take part in 'public productive work', to have economic rights, meaning and agency, and to create citizenship. Before the Revolution, Ventsel was a teacher in Moscow promoting theories of 'free education' (*svobodnoe vospitanie*) and children's self-governance. In late imperial Russia there was a strong anti-authoritarianism tone in concepts of children's education, drawing on the contributions of radical thinkers such as Mikhail Bakunin, Petr Kropotkin, Nikolai Dobrolyubov and Lev Tolstoy. Ventsel and others established summer colonies, clubs and schools for children along these principles and called for the liberation of children as a social group. Soviet schooling in the 1920s drew on the legacy of some of these experimental and progressive principles. In 1918, however, Ventsel's draft Declaration was rejected by *Proletkult* as insufficiently Marxist, anti-collective and 'speaking with the voice of natural law'.[27]

When initiating the drafting, the Polish government also referred to the legacy of Ludwik Rajchman (1881–1965), the Polish bacteriologist, public health expert and epidemiologist who had been the Director of the League of Nation's Health Organization. He had led the League's campaigns against epidemics in Europe and Asia in the interwar period and was appointed the Polish representative to the United Nations Relief and Rehabilitation Agency in 1945.[28] In 1946, he initiated the creation of UNICEF as a UN emergency medical fund for children to provide nutrition and vaccinations for children suffering from the effects of the Second World War. He served as the first Chair of UNICEF until 1950.

Ludwik Witold Rajchman and the founding of UNICEF

Elizabeth White

In 1943, the Allied powers established the United Nations Relief and Rehabilitation Administration (UNRRA) for the planning and delivery of relief supplies to civilian victims of the war across Europe and Asia. In 1946, the United States, which had been by far the most significant donor, decided to stop funding UNRRA due to increasing Cold War tensions. At UNRRA's final session in Geneva that year, Dr Ludwik Rajchman, who was the Polish government's representative on the Committee, successfully argued that UNRRA's existing funds (around 35 million dollars) should be given over to a new temporary relief agency specifically to help children in all affected countries. On 11 December 1946, the United Nations General Assembly agreed to the creation of the International Children's Emergency Fund. The ICEF was meant to last for three years only to cope with the postwar emergency, but, in 1953, it became a permanent agency of the UN due to the lobbying of developing countries who wanted permanent support for child health. In these early years, UNICEF focused on mass immunization and nutrition programmes in Eastern and Western Europe and Asia, later becoming an agency concerned more with long-term development rather than emergency relief.

Ludwik Rajchman (1881–1965) was an internationally recognized Polish bacteriologist, public health expert and epidemiologist. He had been the Director of the Health Organization of the League of Nations in the interwar period, the forerunner to the World Health Organization (WHO), leading campaigns against epidemics in Europe and Asia. Rajchman had been born into an elite Polish Jewish family in Warsaw and had studied medicine in Krakow, before undertaking postdoctoral training in bacteriology at the Royal Institute for Public Health in London and at the Pasteur Institute in Paris. Part of the progressive Polish intelligentsia, he joined the Polish Socialist Party and campaigned for Polish independence. He set up an Institute of Epidemiology in Warsaw in 1919. In 1921, as a result of his work dealing with the postwar typhus epidemic in Eastern Europe, he was appointed as the Director of the Health Organization. As well as the working on the development of vaccines and the standardization of pharmaceuticals, he promoted preventative work and social medicine and was interested in maternal and child health and industrial diseases. He worked for the expansion of the Health Organization into Asia and eventually moved to China to coordinate the League of Nations' assistance there and worked as an advisor to the Chinese government of Chiang Kai Shek.

By the late 1930s, Rajchman had become isolated within the leadership of the League of Nations due to his openly anti-Fascist and anti-militaristic stance and his socialist past. He resigned from the Health Organization in 1938. He spent the war years as a representative to the United States of the Chinese and the Polish government in exile and promoting policies of postwar universal public health schemes. He was appointed by the new Soviet-orientated Polish government as its representative to UNRRA in 1945 after having undertaken some surveys for UNRRA. Possibly due to his complicated past and Polish citizenship, he was excluded from the planning for the new World Health Organization. This, however, left him free to set up UNICEF, in many ways then a rival agency to the WHO as its focus was on health. He served as the first chair of UNICEF from 1946 to 1950, resigning in protest at UNICEF's refusal to recognize the Chinese Communist government and extend aid to China. The socialist bloc states asked UNICEF to leave at that time, also ending his role as Polish representative. Under suspicion from McCarthyism, he left the United States and moved back to France, frequently visiting Poland until his death in 1963.

Returning to 1978, the First Polish Draft of what would become the Convention on the Rights of the Child was presented in January for inclusion on the agenda of the UN Commission on Human Rights in Geneva. The Draft had been drawn up by the Polish Ministry of Foreign Affairs with input from Polish jurists, specializing in family law. In March that year, the UN forwarded the Second Polish Draft to member states, NGOs, intergovernmental agencies and other interested bodies and specialist agencies. The Polish government wanted the UN General Assembly to ratify the Convention in 1979, which had been designated International Year of the Child. The year 1979 would also be the 30th anniversary of the 1959 Declaration, so this concurrence would give maximum publicity for Poland and its contribution to human rights. However, despite the support of the socialist bloc, it eventually took ten years until a draft was ready for ratification. In 1978, the Soviet representative to the Working Group criticized those states trying to delay the quick adoption of the draft by the Commission as 'all coming from the same geographical region'.[29] At the same time the Soviet representative took the opportunity to emphasize how the long-term goals in the framework of the International Year of the Child were already a reality in the Soviet Union.

During the discussion in the Commission for Human Rights in March 1978 Łopatka hoped member states would support the drafting of the Convention, 'to demonstrate that all countries were prepared to cooperate in the domain of human rights'.[30] However, many issues were looked at in the geopolitical framework of the Cold War. Socialist bloc states, particularly the GDR, allied with postcolonial states in demonstrations of solidarity and internationalism and tried to link the internationalization of children's rights with peace, development and anti-imperialism. This had been a common policy of the socialist bloc from the 1950s. The GDR representative asserted in 1978 that the principal task of the United Nations should be 'to support the peoples in their struggle against colonialism, neocolonialism, racial discrimination and apartheid' and that the protection of children was inseparable from the pursuit of 'peace and détente'.[31] Throughout the years of drafting, the GDR regularly brought up the status of children in South Africa under apartheid and in Palestine under Israeli occupation.[32] The GDR representative told the Working Group that 'children are still the innocent victims of acts of aggression, colonialism, racism and fascism' and that 'centuries of colonial oppression and imperialist exploitation' meant that 350 million children in 'developing' countries lacked the basic necessities of life. In 1989, when the draft was finally complete, the GDR representative regretted that the banning of racist and fascist material had not been added in the articles on the right to information.[33]

At other times though, the postcolonial countries rejected the tutelage of the socialist bloc and their internationalization of children's rights. In 1985, the Senegalese representative to the Working Group argued that more attention should be given in the drafting to the situation of children in the Third World, asking, 'what was the significance of the right to leisure to a sick and starving child?' She questioned what developing countries could adhere to contractually in terms of universal education and medical care, both of which were strongly pushed as universal rights by socialist states.[34] Similarly, in 1986, the Bangladeshi representative said that the UN must ensure that 'the standards imposed for the treatment of children are not so onerous that even their attempted application becomes meaningless and even absurd. Standards developed in market economies or command economies cannot apply.'[35] The Egyptian and Moroccan representatives also complained that the drafting was not taking the needs of developing countries into account.[36]

Many of the debates concerned the balance of civil, political, social, economic and cultural rights. Issues regarding the role of the state, freedom of expression, thought, religion, association and movement were all controversial in the context of the Cold War. One example was the right to family reunification. In 1982, the US representative introduced a draft article that children and their parents should be guaranteed 'liberty of movement and freedom to choose a residence' within a state and 'the right to leave any State and enter any State'.[37] This became Article 10 and was aimed at the socialist bloc limitations on freedom of movement. Poland, the Soviet Union and the GDR all opposed its inclusion into the Convention. Finland and France opposed the inclusion of the rights of parents (as adults) to leave and return to a state in a Convention on the rights of a child.[38]

From 1983, the US representatives submitted suggestions for what became Article 13 on Freedom of Expression and Thought: 'The child shall enjoy civil and political rights and freedoms in public life to the fullest extent commensurate with his age, including in particular, freedom from arbitrary government interference with privacy, family, home or correspondence.'[39] They also asked for freedom of association and the right to peaceful assembly and the right to privacy to be considered in the Convention from the middle of the 1980s. During the discussion on Article 13 in 1987, the US representative declared that 'the protection of children's civil and political rights was of fundamental importance to his country', particularly as the concept of 'child' in the Convention included adolescents and concerned the evolving capacity of the child.[40] The inclusion of this draft was opposed by the Soviet Union, which argued that civil and political rights were covered by other International Conventions which were applied to children by virtue of their humanity. It was also opposed by China, Poland, Algeria and Iraq.[41]

Some of the most controversial areas which preoccupied the drafting did not easily fit in the Cold War framework. Whether childhood began at the point of conception, or at the point of feasible life or birth, was one of the main points of contention. Another was adapting the sections on adoption to the needs of Islamic states, which had their own practice of *Kafala*, in which an orphan was cared for but remained legally outside the new family. The issue of international familial child abduction also took up much time. From 1983, NGOs pushed for the prioritizing of stopping the participation of under-18s in armed conflicts and ending the practice of female genital mutilation. In 1989, then, the United Nations Convention on the Rights of the Child was adopted by the General Assembly. It is the most widely ratified human rights treaty in history.

Conclusion

By the time of the final reading of the Convention of the Rights of the Child in 1989, the Cold War was over. The US representative congratulated the Working Group for having

> corrected the systematic bias in the original draft in favor of assuming centralized government control over matters concerning children and the corresponding disregard of the private sector. In that connection, it had ensured that the draft convention recognized parents' rights vis à vis government intervention as well as the civil and political rights of the children themselves.[42]

The Algerian representative, on the other hand, commented that the draft did not go far enough in social, cultural and economic rights and also failed to address rights of children living under foreign occupation and apartheid.[43] By the late stage in the Cold War, the initiative was with the West. However, it seems this competitive co-existence and the agency of individuals in the Global East drove the adoption of a radical Convention, where in many cases positive law was created without previous demand.

This chapter has explored the global models and global entanglements and transfers of ideas and concepts of education and childhood between the Soviet Union, the socialist bloc, the West and the postcolonial world in the postwar era. The socialist bloc strove to present an alternative modernity and role for education and children's rights during the Cold War. The socialist bloc states pushed educational development, mass literacy and a concept of a cosmopolitan childhood into the global sphere. They internationalized this through diplomacy, participation in international organizations, publishing and propaganda, and practices of postcolonial solidarity and internationalism. Human rights were a state discourse and used to gain international legitimacy and support from postcolonial states. As well as the social and economic rights which were written into socialist states' constitutions, the socialist bloc linked human rights with self-determination, gender equality, peace, development and anti-imperialism. They believed that the interlinking of rights with development, world peace and anti-imperialism in alliance with postcolonial states would enable them to dominate UN bodies. As other historians are beginning to show, the European socialist bloc did not just react to the human rights discourses of the West, but were key to shaping the international arena of human rights, and especially in the case of children's rights.[44] Socialist bloc women in the UN system began to introduce children's rights in their campaigns for women's rights and this was continued into the 1970s and 80s with the drafting and final ratification of the UNCRC.

Notes

1 On the Soviet model of economic development, see the chapter by Max Trecker in this volume.

2 For details on Soviet education and childhood, see Elizabeth White, *A History of Modern Russian Childhood: From Late Imperial Russia to the Collapse of the Soviet Union* (London: Bloomsbury, 2020).

3 Monica Mincu, 'Communist education as modernization strategy? The swings of the globalization pendulum in Eastern Europe (1947–1989)', *History of Education* 45 (2016) 3, pp. 319–34, here at p. 324.

4 Zsuzsa Millei and Robert Imre, 'The "cosmopolitan" project and Hungarian kindergarten education: Re-reading socialism', *Prospects* 43 (2013), pp. 13–149, here at p. 138.

5 Margaret Peacock, *Innocent Weapons: The Soviet and American Politics of Childhood in the Cold War* (Chapel Hill: University of North Carolina Press, 2014), p. 97.

6 Deepa Baasti, 'My Thamnaiah, His Soviet Books, and the Time to Read', in *The East was Read: Socialist Culture in the Third World,* ed. Vijay Prashad (New Delhi: Left Word Books, 2019), p. 98.

7 Charles Doran and Kristen Ghodsee, 'The Cold War Politicization of Literacy: Communism, UNESCO, and the World Bank', *Diplomatic History* 36 (2012) 2, pp. 373–98.

8 Between 1964 and 1977 World Bank investment in primary education rose from 0 to 14%. See Doran and Ghodsee, 'The Cold War Politicization of Literacy', p. 394.

9 Peacock, *Innocent Weapons*, p. 158.

10 Kristen Ghodsee, *Why Women Have Better Sex Under Socialism. And Other Arguments for Economic Independence* (London: Vintage, 2019), p. 5.

11 Constantin Katsakioris, 'Creating a Socialist Intelligentsia: Soviet Educational Aid and its Impact on Africa, 1960-1991', *Cahiers d'Études africaines* 226 (2017), p. 260.

12 Alexandra Piepiorka, 'Exploring "Socialist Solidarity" in Higher Education. East German Advisors in Post-Independence Mozambique, 1975-1992', in *Education and Development in Colonial and Post-Colonial Africa. Policies, Paradigms and Entanglements,* ed. Damiano Matasaci (Cham: Springer Nature, 2020), pp. 291–321.

13 Ned Richardson-Little, 'Dictatorship and Dissent: Human Rights in East Germany in the 1970s', in *The Breakthrough: Human Rights in the 1970s*, ed. Jan Eckel and Samuel Moyn (Philadelphia: University of Pennsylvania Press, 2014), pp. 49–67, here at p. 66.

14 For socialist bloc women and the UN, see Francesca De Haan, 'The Global Left Feminist 1960s: From Copenhagen to Moscow and New York', in *The Routledge Handbook of the Global Sixties. Between Protest and Nation Building*, ed. Chen Jian et al. (London: Routledge, 2018), pp. 230–44.

15 United Nations, *Geneva Declaration of the Rights of the Child* (New York: United Nations, 1924). For the Geneva Declaration of 1924, see http://www.un-documents.net/gdrc1924.htm.

16 White, *History of Modern Russian Childhood.*

17 UN. Office of the High Commissioner for Human Rights, *Legislative History of the Convention on the Rights of the Child*, Volume 1, (New York; Geneva: United Nations, 2007), p. 59. Available online at: https://digitallibrary.un.org/record/602462?ln=en.

18 UN. Office of the High Commissioner for Human Rights, *Legislative History of the CRC,* p. 63.

19 Ibid., p. 68.

20 Gunter Dehnert, 'The Polish Opposition, the Crisis of the Gierak Era, and the Helsinki Process', in *The Breakthrough: Human Rights in the 1970s*, ed. Jan Eckel and Samuel Moyn (Philadelphia: University of Pennsylvania Press, 2014), pp. 163–6.

21 Lopatka, 'Introduction', in *Legislative History of the CRC,* Vol. 1, (New York; Geneva: United Nations, 2007), p. xxxviii.

22 For details of Janusz Korczak, see Marc Silverman, *A Pedagogy of Humanist Moral Education. The Educational Thought of Janusz Korczak* (London: Palgrave, 2017).

23 Silverman, *A Pedagogy of Humanist Moral Education,* p. 152.

24 Cynthia Price Cohen, 'The Relevance of Theories of Natural Law and Legal Positivism', in *The Ideologies of Children's Rights*, ed. Michael Freeman and Philip Veerman (Leiden: Kluwer Academic Publishers, 1992), p. 61.

25 Adam Lopatka, 'An Introduction to the United Nations Convention on the Rights of the Child', *Transnational Law . . . Contemporary Problems* 6 (1996) 2, p. 254 n. 15, and p. 255.

26 Manfred Liebel, 'The Moscow Declaration on the Rights of the Child (1918)', in *International Journal of Children's Rights* 5 (2016), pp. 3–28, here at p. 10.

27 Liebel, 'The Moscow Declaration on the Rights of the Child (1918)', p. 3.

28 See the chapter by Katja Castryck-Naumann in this volume.

29 UN. Office of the High Commissioner for Human Rights, *Legislative History of the CRC*, p. 93.

30 Ibid., p. 88.

31 Ibid., p. 109.

32 Ibid., p. 92.

33 Ibid., p. 266.

34 Ibid., p. 182.

35 Ibid., p. 193.

36 Ibid., pp. 220 and 228.

37 Ibid., p. 463.

38 Ibid., p. 468.

39 Ibid., p. 497.

40 Ibid., p. 497.

41 Ibid., p. 518.

42 Ibid., p. 284.

43 Ibid., p. 313.

44 Ned Richardson-Little, Hella Dietz and James Mark (eds), 'New Perspectives on Socialism and Human Rights in East Central Europe since 1945', *East Central Europe* 46 (2019), pp. 2–3 (November), pp. 169–87.

Bibliography

Balinksa, Marta. *For the Good of Humanity. Ludwik Rajchman, Medical Statesman.* Budapest: CEU Press, 1998.

Black, Maggie. *Children First. The Story of UNICEF, Past and Present.* Oxford: Oxford University Press, 1996.

Brown, Theodore and Elizabeth Fee. 'Ludwik Rajchman (1881–1965). World Leader in Social Medicine and Director of the League of Nations Health Organisation'. *American Journal of Public Health* 104 (2014) 9, pp. 1638–9.

Further reading

White, Elizabeth. *A History of Modern Russian Childhood: From Late Imperial Russia to the Collapse of the Soviet Union.* London: Bloomsbury, 2020.

Eastern Europe's Impact on Modern International Law

Gilad Ben-Nun

6

Introduction

If one were to use a time machine to catapult diplomats from the 18th century into today's diplomatic reality, they would encounter a fundamentally unfamiliar world of international relations. National diplomats' contemporary work, both within international organizations and in their bilateral diplomatic engagements between states, has been revolutionized between then and now. In 1815, when Habsburg statesman Klemens von Metternich negotiated the Congress of Vienna following the Napoleonic upheavals in Europe, the most salient factor determining the power of states was the size of their armies. Trade, which was mostly bilateral and recurring between pairs of countries, was infinitely less important to national security than it is today. Fast-forward some two centuries, and trade has become a fundamental determinant of global power. China's emergence as a rival to the United States could only have come about after 1991, when it was offered membership in an international body – the World Trade Organization (WTO) – which has its own international appellate body to settle disputes between its members. To Metternich, for whom state sovereignty reigned supreme, the very idea that states could sue each other in a globally recognized international court would have seemed absurd. Back in 1815, a case such as that currently being brought by Ukraine against Russia at the International Court of Justice (ICJ), for example, would have been unthinkable.[1]

At the heart of the difference between our world today and that of Metternich lies the existence of so-called 'international space'. Raymond Aron's emphasis on the 'unification of the field of diplomacy', in which 'all states now belong to a single unique system' as symbolized by their membership in today's United Nations (UN), is both

This hand-sketched map (Image 8) opened the book written by East-European Jewish jurists Jacob Robinson, Oscar Karbach, Max Lerson, Nehemiah Robinson and Marc Vichniak, which evaluated the achievements and misgivings of the League of Nations' minorities treaties system. The book, published in 1943, foresaw the inherent dangers to people of difference should ethnic engineering for the sake of demographic homogeneity prevail. By the end of the Second World War, the authors' worst fears had materialized. Remarkably, as this hand-drawn map clearly shows, these authors extrapolated similar observations to those initially stemming from their Eastern European experiences to the Middle East, Turkey and Iraq – thus demonstrating a clearly global mindset.

recent and historically unique. In short, our contemporary reality – whereby international organizations interact with nation-states, regional organizations and non-governmental organizations (NGOs) across one and the same level international playing field – is unprecedented in human history.[2] One pertinent example of the emergence of this single-levelled playing field can be seen in the history of the International Commission of the Danube.

The European Commission of the Danube (1856–1940)

Dietmar Müller

In October 1835, the English *Morning Chronicle* opined, 'The free navigation of the Danube becomes a European question … We can, in fact … see at present the consequences, both political and commercial, to which steam navigation of the Danube is calculated to give rise' (Hajnal, 1920: 55–6). A decade later, in March 1854, as the diplomats of the European powers met in Paris to sign the treaty that ended the Crimean War, these consequences became clear. In order to facilitate and secure the freedom of navigation on the Maritime Danube, this treaty established what would later be known as the European Commission of the Danube (ECD). Initially devised as a temporary, single-issue organ, the ECD quickly developed into a permanent international organization with quasi-state-like features. Correspondingly, South-eastern Europe's Maritime Danube region, as the contact zone of empires, saw significant innovation in terms of international law and transnational governance.

In the two decades between the 1829 Treaty of Adrianople and the 1850s, the Lower and especially the Maritime Danube had turned from regions of periphery to ones of importance for Europe's economy. With the repeal of Britain's Corn Laws in the 1840s, which abolished protectionism for agrarian products, the supply of wheat and maize from the Danubian principalities gradually grew in importance for North-western European markets. To this, one must add the growing pertinence of the 'Eastern Question' whereby the Crimean War prefigured Europe's drive to secure further influence over the Ottoman empire's territories. By establishing the ECD as part of traditional modes of conflict resolution, European powers demonstrated their ability to organize a system of peace and security in a region of vital interests, while opening new paths to increase their global governance – also via their ever-growing encroachment on Ottoman lands.

Freedom of navigation on international rivers was first enshrined as a fundamental principle in international law at the Vienna Congress of 1814–15. A river is considered international when it is navigable from the sea through or along at least two states (Johnson, 1964: 465–84). To include the Danube in this regime of navigational freedom, the ECD's signatory states decided to incorporate the Ottoman empire into the European state system of international legal spheres – thereby changing the criteria for belonging to this legal system from being 'Christian' to being 'civilized'. In comparison with the Central Commission for the Navigation on the Rhine, the ECD created a legal novelty due both to its composition and its jurisdiction. While the Rhine Commission was composed solely of states with immediate rights to the water's edge (so-called riparian states), the ECD had four non-riparian states (Great Britain, France, Prussia and Sardinia) with no direct relation to the river's waters, alongside three riparian states (the Habsburg, Russian and Ottoman empires).

However, the revolution of incorporating the Ottomans into the European state system by accepting their membership in the ECD remained piecemeal. In fact, the further development of the ECD later became a powerful measure for Europe's denial of the Ottoman empire's participation in the continent's international legal system. While both Romania (independent after 1878) and the Ottomans formally remained members of the ECD, western European powers, motivated as it were by 'orientalist' sentiments, gradually began to limit these states' navigational freedom on the Danube. To secure this limitation of 'non-Westerns', European powers used the ECD, whose jurisdiction was expanded both territorially and substantively for that very purpose. Combining state features with those of an international organization, the ECD was charged to execute the works necessary, below Isatcha [Isaccea], to clear the mouths of the Danube, as well as the neighbouring parts of the sea, from the sands and other impediments which obstructed them, in order to put that part of the river and the said parts of the sea in the best possible condition for navigation. (For the English version of pertinent articles of the Treaty of Paris, see Kaeckenbeeck, 1919: 97–100.)

To fulfil this engineering task, the ECD was granted a two-year mandate, after which its competencies would be transferred to a Riverine Commission for the Danube. The Ottoman empire declared that it 'would willingly make the necessary advances for the execution of the works planned by the European commission'. When the Riverain Commission fell apart and was dissolved after a few years, and when the Ottoman empire did not meet its pledge for funding the works, significant steps towards greater ECD autonomy emerged. This competency spill-over, from Ottoman to European powers, was facilitated through a spectacular hydro-engineering success in the Sulina mouth of the Danube: the erection of two piers from the harbour of Sulina into the open sea that helped clear the sand bar by increasing the power of the stream, which, in effect, stabilized the depth of the channel at a navigable scale for seagoing steamships (Gătejel, 2018: 925–53).

In order to secure the ECD's objectives, a quasi-constitutional Public Act was enacted in November 1865. The Act placed the ECD's works under the protection and guarantee of international law and reserved its power to design and carry out all other hydraulic and regulatory works required for navigation along the Danube's waters. Administrative control of the navigation was firmly placed under the ECD's jurisdiction. Local navigation was governed by the 'Regulation of Navigation and Police', enacted by the Commission, and was supervised by two Ottoman officials – the Inspector General of the Lower Danube, and the Captain of the Port of Sulina – who acted in accordance with the ECD's regulations. Besides creating binding law, the ECD also had the power to judge cases of civil procedure arising from navigational exercise, and was granted the power to define the tariff of navigation and how tolls were to be collected by the Sulina Cash Office. Finally, all works and buildings of the ECD, its administrative structures and large parts of its personnel were granted the status of neutrality. From that point in time, the ECD featured significant attributes of a state in terms of legislation, executive enforcement, and the adjudication of legal cases. However, since its competencies and prerogatives derived from an international treaty – which could be withdrawn by its founding states at any time – the ECD also resembled an international organization.

Another special feature of the ECD concerned its financial history. With Ottoman advances for the works in Sulina harbour coming in late and insufficiently, the ECD secured short-duration high-yielding loans from local banks. Once the problems at Sulina had been resolved, and the ECD's day-to-day expenses could be covered by rising income from tolls, its financing changed drastically. Over time, loans became larger in sum, with longer durations and decreasing yields. This drive towards financial independence reached its zenith during the 1880s, when the ECD independently issued bonds across the world's financial markets. Notwithstanding this financial success story, the role of states in the ECD remained cardinal – as Britain, France and Germany continued to serve as the collateral-providing entities behind its bonds.

At the core of the ECD's dynamic development lay its ability to provide for the common good of navigational freedom. Characteristically for the shift from colonialism to imperialism during the second half of the 19th century, navigational freedom was considered a goal to be reached best via collaboration – especially in and around Europe's peripheries.

The ECD's history cannot be told as an endless virtuous circle, whereby the common good of navigational freedom provided economic gains for its Russian, Ottoman and Romanian inferior members. In times of intense conflict such as the First World War, the restriction of navigation suddenly emerged as a tool of economic warfare. Following the collapse of Europe's Continental empires during that war, the ECD's membership was reduced to Britain, France, Italy and Romania. It was formally dissolved in 1940, as economic nationalism triumphed over the quintessentially imperial 19th-century ideals of transnational cooperation.

Underpinning this global political reality is a vast legal apparatus commonly referred to as 'modern international law', which, as explained below, differs from the previous 'law of nations' (*jus gentium*) which was in place roughly until the end of the 18th century. This huge corpus of international treaties, legal norms, agreed customs and collective state practice continues to serve as the fundamental foundation of this international system. From the fight against pandemics such as COVID-19 at the World Health Organization (WHO) to the allocation of Internet IP addresses by the International Telecommunications Union (ITU), to ceasefire talks and peace negotiations by the United Nations Security Council (UNSC), the daily ticking of our global reality takes place through an endless series of actions and transactions – all governed by international legal treaties.

Herein lies the distinct place of Eastern Europe in the historical progression from Metternich's world to our own. For it was in this region, and thanks to its actors, that so much of what we now term 'modern international law' was developed. From the Hague Peace Conferences of 1899–1907, convened and chaired by the Russian tsar's delegate Feodor Martens, to the emergence of minority protection under the League of Nations – and from international refugee law to our contemporary laws of war, international criminal justice, and even international children's rights – few areas have played such a cardinal role in shaping modern international law as has Eastern Europe.

Regional specificities, duress and human agency

The region's vulnerability to external impositions upon its territory and peoples has had much to do with its geopolitical and social characteristics. Strategically located between Europe's powers to the west, Russia to the east, and Mediterranean forces to the south, its political borders were routinely subject to externally imposed demarcations. As both a geographical gateway and a welcoming zone for migrations, Eastern Europe's human landscape emerged as one of the most ethnically diverse, multilingual and multiconfessional in the world. Accordingly, and prior to nationalism's massively violent 'mixing of peoples' during the 19th and 20th centuries, the region's longest periods of peace and prosperity often unfolded under the aegis of overarching empires (Holy Roman, Habsburg, Ottoman, Tsarist) and, more recently, under the multilingual, supranational structure of the European Union (EU).

At a crossroad between competing empires, Eastern Europe has often also been the site of historically significant peace treaties. As early as the 10th century, a series of peace accords (907, 911, 944 and 971 ce) were signed between the rulers of Kievan Rus and the Byzantine empire in the region that is now Ukraine.[3] The Peace of Zsitvatorok in present-day Slovakia, signed in November 1606, marked the cessation of decades of warfare between the Ottomans and the Habsburgs, as well as the end of Ottoman incursions into East Central Europe.[4] Further east and south, Ottoman raids into what is now Romania, Ukraine and Moldova were finally halted by the Russian empire's seizure of these regions from Turkish hands in the 18th century. The Treaty of Küçük Kaynarca (now the town of Kaynardzha on the Bulgarian–Romanian border), signed on 21 July 1774 between Empress Catherine the Great's representatives and those of Sultan Abdul Hamid I of the Ottoman empire, put an end to the Russo-Turkish War of 1768–74.

One pertinent example that demonstrates how Eastern Europeans drew on experiences from their region's history and subsequently changed the global nature of international law concerns the invalidating nature of duress under our contemporary international treaty law. Nowadays, the threat of or resort to force or coercion by any party to an international treaty over another party, for the sake of that treaty's conclusion or in pursuit of its tilting in the usurper's favour, is seen as a solid ground for that accord's invalidation. By and large, a treaty struck under duress is considered null and void – and is seen as non-binding under international law.

However, this understanding of international law, and the view of duress as a negative aspect strong enough to invalidate treaties, is relatively new. It only fully came about after the Second World War and the adoption of the 1969 Vienna Convention on the Law of Treaties. Before that, and at least up until the turn of the 20th century, duress was seen as a broadly legitimate means to secure treaty-based rights. As demonstrated below, the overt prohibition of duress under international law was realized in no small part thanks to the efforts of 20th-century Polish-born jurists such as Hersch Lauterpacht and Manfred Lachs, who framed its prohibition in a clear and distinct relationship to Poland's own experiences over the previous two hundred years.

It was in the context of the inter-imperial scramble for Eastern European territory that Poland's subjugation, and the resort to duress in its treaties, became routine. Nowhere was this more evident than in the three successive, violent partitions of Poland between the Russian, Prussian and Austro-Hungarian empires between 1772 and 1795. With their completion, Polish self-government ceased – only to be renewed in 1918, after the First World War. But even this self-government was short-lived, as the country was again forcibly partitioned by imperial forces – this time, of a Nazi and Soviet nature, under the Molotov-Ribbentrop Pact of 1939. In October 1992, after a further five decades of Nazi and then Soviet subjugation, the last Russian combat troops left Polish soil. This withdrawal ended a presence that had intermittently consolidated foreign political and military domination over that country for two centuries.

Of paramount importance here are the instruments formally used to implement Poland's subjugations. Over the past two hundred and fifty years, the country's repeated partitions have invariably been underpinned by international legal treaties that both sanctioned them and provided them with a pseudo-legitimate mantle of legality. Both the first (1772) and the second (1793) partition of the country required ratification by the Polish Sejm. It was not until the third partition – in 1795, when the state ceased to exist – that such ratification was no longer required.

To enhance the perceived legitimacy of changes brought about by force, Poland's usurpers habitually coerced its national legislatures into ratifying, often at gunpoint, their acceptance of the very treaties that proclaimed their own subjugation. During both the first and, especially, the second partition of Poland, Russian troops effectively held the delegates of the Polish Sejm (parliament) hostage, and at gunpoint, demanding their signature on the territorial division of their own country and leaving those representatives with the choice of either signing that treaty or dying. Upon its signing, and regardless of how this was achieved, the partition of Poland was considered to be internationally legal for all intents and purposes.

Today, such a scenario as occurred in Poland in 1793 would most likely not be considered internationally legal. In fact, today's wholesale revocation of coercion as a legitimate means of securing ratification of international treaty law is directly derived from Poland's experience in 1793. In 1953, when the International Law Commission sat down to consider the grounds on which a treaty could be invalidated, the Commission's first rapporteur, the Polish-Jewish-born Hersch Lauterpacht (1897–1960) argued that duress invalidated a concluded treaty precisely because it contradicted 'the general principle of law that consensual transactions brought about by duress should be avoided'.[5] When Lauterpacht ascended to his judicial chair on the ICJ bench, his successor as Law Commission Rapporteur, Gerald Fitzmaurice, further interpreted the legal meaning of the term 'duress' used by his predecessor. Fitzmaurice's reference to the experience of Polish delegates who had been threatened at gunpoint by Russian forces to ratify their country's second partition in 1793 was even more overt:

> [T]he conclusion of a treaty brought about by duress or coercion, whether physical or mental, actual or threatened, employed directly and specifically against the persons, of *the individual agents, plenipotentiaries, authorities or members of organs engaged in negotiating or signing* [!], or ratifying or acceding to, or any other act of participation in a treaty, vitiates the consent apparently given, and invalidates the act concerned, and consequently the treaty.[6]

The 20th-century context of these words could not be more 'Polish'. Fitzmaurice's open reference in 1958 to the coercion of the Polish Sejm by Russian troops in 1793 was reminiscent of contemporary events in Eastern Europe between 1955 and 1956. The Soviet coercion of Poland and other 'Warsaw Pact' members to sign up to this military alliance by force could hardly be reconciled with that alliance's invasion and mass killing of civilians in other Pact countries, such as in East Germany in 1953 and Hungary in 1956. Nor could the Pact's military prerequisite of stationing Russian troops on the soil of East Central European countries be fully reconciled with the fact that it was the same Russians who, some fifteen years earlier, had orchestrated the mass execution of large sections of the Polish officer corps at Katyn in 1940. For the Poles, then, the hand that pointed a Russian gun at the Sejm delegates in 1793, and pulled the same trigger in 1940 to wipe out any possible military resistance to the Soviet seizure of eastern Poland, was now forcing them to officially sign up to their country's military subordination to Russia in the form of an international legal treaty – the Warsaw Pact of 1955.

In 1969, the prohibition of duress became a universally accepted standard for treaty-making. Article 52 of the Vienna Convention on the Law of Treaties adopted that year stipulated that '[a] treaty is void if its conclusion has been procured by the threat or use of force'. What began with the East Galician-born Lauterpacht in 1953 ended in 1969 – not least, thanks to the work of another Polish-Galician lawyer, who shared his predecessor's ethno-religious Jewish background, Manfred Lachs (1914–93).

Both were East Central European lawyers, first educated on the Continent. Both came to the United Kingdom before the outbreak of the Second World War. Both attended the London School of Economics and completed their doctoral training under the leading expert on the law of treaties of their time – Arnold McNair. Both lost their families in the Holocaust of European Jewry in Poland. Both participated in the Nuremberg Trials as members of different prosecution teams. Both played important roles in the formulation of the 1948 UN Genocide Convention, alongside their Polish-Jewish colleague who was that treaty's principal author – Raphael Lemkin. Both went on to play key roles in the UN Legal Committee and the International Law Commission. A respected representative of both Poland and the Soviet bloc, yet widely admired by the Western powers, Manfred Lachs chaired the UN General Assembly's Legal Committee no less than three times, during some of the Cold War's most contentious periods: in 1949 (in the midst of the Soviet-led 'Berlin Blockade'); in 1952 (at the height of the Korean War); and in 1955 (the year the Warsaw Pact was signed).[7] In 1960, following Hersch Lauterpacht's sudden death, his seat on the ICJ bench was taken over by Gerald Fitzmaurice – who, as mentioned above, had two years earlier articulated duress's incompatibility with international law. In 1967, when Fitzmaurice was reappointed to the ICJ's bench, he was joined there by Lachs, whose election had been secured by an unprecedented consensus majority of both the UN General Assembly and the UN Security Council.

The contrast between Manfred Lachs's achievements in transforming the world of international law, alongside his Eastern European colleagues, and the monumental forces of history against which they struggled is astonishing. Any consideration of Eastern Europe's legal and political realities during his era should normally have pointed to complete paralysis for Lachs's goals. In a life that spanned two world wars, in the second of which his family was annihilated because of their race, and a third (Cold War) conflict, the very idea that he would consider the possibility of making a difference to the world might seem outlandish.

At its core, 'agency' is the conscious behaviour of a human being towards action, coupled with her or his capacity to think and act within given constraints – albeit without necessarily fully complying with them – all the while maintaining their mental autonomy of thought and action. When people act as agents, they direct their behaviour towards a goal. This is preceded by processes of deliberation and decision making. Unlike his colleagues such as Lauterpacht and Lemkin, who opted for the United Kingdom and the United States after 1945, Manfred Lachs chose to remain firmly behind the Iron Curtain, within the Soviet bloc, as Poland's delegate and diplomat, and as a professor of law at the University of Warsaw. Eastern Europe's realities of the curtailment of freedoms, of show trials and purges, and of Soviet violent incursions into neighbouring states (East Germany in 1953 and Hungary in 1956 – followed, by now, by Czechoslovakia in 1968) are well worth remembering; they form the backdrop to Lachs's long ascent to international law's highest global echelons.[8]

In recent years, much debate has centred on the appropriateness or otherwise of author Timothy Snyder's controversial 'Bloodlands' metaphor. The idea that during the 20th century Eastern Europe, between East Berlin and Moscow, was drenched in the blood of the region's peoples – shed, as his book's subtitle implies, by both Hitler and Stalin – has been difficult to fathom for some. And rightly so, for the metaphor is, in and of itself, gruesome. But the fact remains that few areas of the world, with the arguable exception of East Asia between Manila and Hiroshima, suffered as much as 'Europe's periphery', where, for example, almost half of Belarus's population was either killed or displaced by the end of the Second World War – something which 'cannot be said of any other country'.[9] And yet, despite all the odds stacked against them, Lachs, Lauterpacht and their colleagues, through their sheer intellectual ability and willpower, succeeded in transforming the relationship between international law and the abuses of political and military power. Before them, a tacit acceptance of the quasi-legitimate functioning of power prevailed in international law. By the time of Lachs's death, the rejection of the legitimacy of duress to effect change in international law had, at least in theory, become the regularly accepted norm. If one is not prepared to call this human agency, one had better find another name for it.

Nationalism, homogeneity and expulsion

The existence of discernible polities with distinct regional and linguistic characteristics has long been acknowledged. But as Benedict Anderson famously observed, a 'nation' is clearly not a physical object. Rather, it is an imagined concept, which is dependent upon the social construction of an entity's own national consciousness for its emergence. Scholars of nationalism have long debated when exactly such a consciousness first emerged, and whether it was initially conceived in the English-speaking world of the late 17th century or during the French Revolution. In any event, the English word 'international' was first coined by the British liberal philosopher Jeremy Bentham as late as 1775.[10]

By the middle of the 19th century, the idea that there was indeed a strong connection between certain groups of people and certain territories, particularly in Europe, had become widely accepted. The first people to be granted statehood on an international, collective basis were the Greeks. The emergence of modern Greece followed its war of independence against the Ottoman empire (1821–30) in which the Greeks were supported by, and which they won largely thanks to the heavy military intervention of, the European powers Britain, Prussia and Russia. Hard on the heels of Greece, Belgium won its independence from the Dutch crown in 1830 – albeit thanks to a much shorter ten-day skirmish, as opposed to the ten years it took the Greeks to throw off the Ottoman yoke. As in Greece so in Belgium, it was at the behest of the major European powers (in this instance, notably France) that independence was secured. In short, in the early 19th century, nationalisms were celebrated, but only thanks to massive military intervention by the great powers on the side of their emergent European liberation movements.

The emergence of the nation triggered the question of human belonging to it, since nations were initially supposed to be ethnically and linguistically homogeneous. As Eric Weitz so aptly observed, the sharp turn in international law towards 'population politics', as orchestrated by the European powers, did not come about with the revolutions of 1848 but rather in the twenty-five years between 1860 and 1885. The context here is one of a double imposition of Western European territorialization – over Eastern Europe and, simultaneously, over colonial Africa:

> [T]he Berlin Congress of 1878, the Berlin West Africa Conference of 1884– 1885, and bilateral treaties involving population exchanges … laid out the contours of a system that defined majorities and minorities in ethnic and national terms. Depending on the category to which they were assigned, populations could be protected, deported, or civilized.[11]

It was during this period that Eastern Europe's role as a testing ground for international legal experiments in ethnic engineering began to emerge, in stark contrast to the situation in Western Europe. As Stefan Troebst has pointed out, of some twenty-seven international and global congresses held between 1815 and 1914, about half were devoted exclusively to Eastern Europe. Over roughly the past two centuries, from 1830 to the present, while Western Europe has seen the creation of seven new states, the same period has seen the creation of some twenty-five new states in Europe's eastern parts.[12] The birth of the Eastern European state system, especially after the Treaty of San Stefano in 1878, also coincided with the emergence of a definition of who should be considered a 'minority'. As Weitz noted, it was primarily Armenians and Jews, who were clearly not seen as an integral part of Europe's indigenous peoples, who became the epitome of 'minorities'. Unsurprisingly, it was also they who were slaughtered on a massive scale once the demands of national-ethnic homogeneity came to the fore. Between 1882 and 1946, most of Europe's Jewry was to be exterminated. In parallel, during the first part of this period, between 1894 and 1924, some two million Armenians and other Christians (Chaldeans, Nestorians and other sects) were killed in Turkey and Asia Minor, thus ending some two thousand years of Christian presence there.[13]

While Jews and Armenians epitomized stateless minorities per se, many other people in South-eastern Europe found themselves as minorities on the 'wrong side', so to speak, of newly formed, hitherto non-existent national borders: Bulgarians in Greece, Turks in Greece, Greeks and Armenians in Muslim Turkey, Serbs in Albania. Towards the end of the 19th century, the popular notion that the 'crazy quilt of peoples' of South-eastern Europe needed to be undone, with each ethnic group organized within its own territory so as to ensure peace and stability, gradually gained ground. At the turn of the 20th century, the use of forced population transfers as a legitimate measure to bring about ethnic homogeneity in south-eastern Europe's newly emerging states took shape. The roots of such thinking were firmly established in Germany and France. But their application was not directed against such supposedly culturally superior Western Europeans. Instead, these ideas were to be applied to the multiethnic and multiconfessional human mosaic of South-eastern Europe and the Balkans.[14]

Hatching a theoretical idea of forced expulsion for the sake of ethnic homogeneity was one thing. But to give this idea a concrete international legal meaning and, above all, to put it into practice within an internationally acceptable legal framework was another matter altogether. Therein lies the methodological point of emphasizing causality. When talking about the impact of Eastern Europe on international law, one must be careful to distinguish between the general incubation of ideas and their concrete and specific implementation. After all, the wealth of ideas that have been hatched and discussed in the long history of international law is ten times greater than the actual wealth of ideas that have ever seen the light of day in terms of their implementation through a signed treaty. And even then, one is left with the task of assessing whether and to what extent a signed treaty was ever implemented in reality. Sadly, 'copyright' on the development and implementation of the ideas of internationally legalized forced expulsions and forced population exchanges belongs first and foremost to the Greek prime minister and statesman Eleftherios Venizelos. The initial territory on which he sought to apply his ideas was that of South-eastern Europe between the Balkans, Greece and the Mediterranean.

In recent years, much research has been devoted to the impact of Venizelos's invention of this new international legal instrument of internationally sanctioned, forced population exchange. As early as 1923, the Treaty of Lausanne, which provided for the forced exchange of some two million Greeks and Turks, was the last of several treaties in a tripartite population exchange between Greece, Turkey and Bulgaria. The most acute problem with this new South-eastern European practice was that it had become internationally accepted, not to say desired, as a solution to ethnic tensions, with the League of Nations' full stamp of international legality. Once that had happened – once expulsion had been made internationally legal – many more, similar atrocities were bound to follow.

Horrible as it may seem, many of the population exchanges carried out during the Second World War between Nazi Germany and the Soviet Union drew their quasi-legitimate international veneer precisely from this original Greek–Turkish precedent. As if that were not enough, after the Second World War, once the norm of expulsion had been firmly established, some 18 million Hindu and Muslim Punjabis suffered a similar fate during the partition of the British Raj in India in 1947.[15] In the Middle East, where the idea of forced population exchange had been mooted as early as the mid-1930s, the expulsion of Arabs from Palestine and the expulsion of Jews from Arab lands were officially carried out on a reciprocal basis between 1948 and the late 50s.

But perhaps nowhere was the impact of Venizelos's instrument more dramatic than in the aftermath of the 1945 Potsdam Conference, with the expulsion of some 12 million

Germans at the official insistence of dignitaries such as Edvard Beneš, the Czechoslovak president. Within ten years of that conference, when the Soviets invaded Hungary in 1956, more than 20 million Europeans had been forcibly expelled or exchanged. Thus, Venizelos's international legal innovation, originally developed for the Balkans and South-east Europe, would punish Eastern Europeans with a vengeance, almost fifty years later.

In a way, the impact of Venizelos's international legal instrument has never really dissipated. Like a 'genie out of the bottle' that, once released, can never be returned to its safe haven, internationally monitored forced expulsions and internationally accepted forced population exchanges have continued well into the 21st century. From Northern Ireland in the 1960s to Turkey's 1974 invasion of Northern Cyprus, which was broadly accepted as a forced population exchange, to the redrawing of the ethnic map of Bosnia in the 1990s, expulsion, legally sanctioned *post eventum*, has remained with us for the better part of the last century. In 2009, Sinhalese Buddhists effectively wiped out the majority of Sri Lanka's Tamil minority in a partial genocide coupled with expulsions – all under the watchful eyes of the UN. Between 2016 and 2017, the Burmese Buddhist majority in Myanmar used many of the same tactics against the country's Muslim Rohingya minority.

In July 2022, for the first time in its history, the ICJ ruled in favour of the admissibility of Gambia's case against Myanmar for allegedly violating the 1948 Genocide Convention in relation to the latter's targeting of the Rohingya. By an unprecedented majority of the court's judges – with a single dissenting vote from the Chinese judge, and even with the concurrence of Myanmar's own ad hoc judge (Judge Kress) – the court ruled in favour of the right of the African Muslim country to accuse its South Asian counterpart of genocide against its defenceless and targeted Muslims. And so, in a bizarre twist of events, a hundred years after the enshrining of South-east Europeans' forced expulsion into international law in 1923, it was Africans who successfully implemented Polish-born Raphael Lemkin's juxtaposing legal norm of the 1948 Genocide Convention, to the benefit of people in South East Asia. By 2022, then, Eastern Europe's influence on modern international law had come of age.

The protection of minorities and international refugee law

The last two centuries have seen the emergence of a dual approach by European nation-states to people of difference. On the one hand, the rise of the nation-state coincided with a tendency to expel people who were, or were perceived to be, different from the dominant demographic majority in a state in terms of their faith, language or cultural background. On the other hand, it was also nation-states that were the first to seek legal protection for people who belonged to non-hegemonic groups, and to protect those who had already been expelled by other states because of their perceived difference. Often, the same nation-state could both act as an expeller of one group of people and at the same time protect other groups from expulsion on the basis of other human differences within that same territory. In both cases, legal definitions were established to regulate both types of state practice.

The tradition of minority protection long precedes that of the nation-state. As Jacob Robinson, the Jewish-Lithuanian lawyer who was largely responsible for the drafting of the 1951 Refugee Convention, noted towards the end of his life, from the early modern period – beginning with the Edict of Nantes of 1598 which guaranteed freedom of worship and state protection for the Huguenots in France – until 1918, European treaties gradually increased their safeguards for religious freedoms. For almost three hundred years, from the Peace of Vienna (1606) to the establishment of the League of Nations, the overwhelming majority of international peace treaties included special clauses to protect ethno-religious minorities and ensure their social integration into the majority societies in which they lived.[16] It is probably safe to say that few regions of the world have been more closely associated with the concept and issues of ethno-religious minorities over the last century than Eastern and South-eastern Europe.

With the establishment of the League of Nations in 1920 the long-standing tradition of minority protection underwent a major shift, related to the changing nature of international law during this period. A defining criterion of international law concerns its relationship with supranational structures and, in particular, with international organizations, which have their own international legal personality distinct from that of the member states that create and then participate in them. As explained below in the section on the laws of war, an embryonic concept of international law had already begun to emerge during the Hague Peace Conferences of 1899–1907. In reality, however, it was not until the League of Nations was established, in the aftermath of the First World War, that an international legal system really came into being. Mirroring the two-sided duality of states' approaches to ethnic difference between minority protection and expulsion, the League of Nations was, from its inception, caught in a similar duality in its approach to human difference beyond the spheres of the Western European and American victorious powers.

On the one hand, the League represented the emergence of the new idea of national self-determination.[17] On the other hand, colonialism remained firmly entrenched thanks to the League's own structures of domination, manifested in its Mandates and Protectorates Commission, which to all intents and purposes was little more than a justifiable euphemism and an elegant surrogate for the earlier heinous practices of 19th-century colonialism.[18] During the negotiations at Versailles in 1918, a clear distinction emerged between the so-called civilized nations of Eastern, Central and Southern Europe and those of the Middle East, Africa and Asia. The former would emerge as new states – provided they made commitments to secure the rights of minorities within their territories. The latter would be subject to mandates and colonial supervision.

Both the idea of minority protection and its implementation through the instigation of minority treaties – whereby ethnic minorities in Eastern Europe would enjoy direct standing before the League of Nations Minorities Commission, 'over the heads' of their national sovereignties – was largely linked to securing rights and protection for Jews in the region. Advocated by Jewish non-governmental groups in the United States before President Woodrow Wilson, and by the Jewish intellectual Lucien Wolfe in the United Kingdom before Prime Minister David Lloyd George, the very blueprint of global minority protection was realized in the first treaty between the League of Nations and Poland, which was directly premised on the Jewish categories requiring such protection.[19]

The targeting of Europe's minorities in the run-up to and during the Second World War need hardly be mentioned here. By the time the Allies decided to establish the UN Charter in 1945, the whole question of minority protection seemed moot. Those who had not been expelled or exterminated during the war were to be expelled from 1946 until the 60s. Nevertheless, the need to protect minorities around the world would not go away and would remain an ongoing issue, only to return to haunt the world during the wars of Yugoslavia's disintegration in the 1990s. As Mark Mazower aptly observed,

> The awkward truth was that the UN had abandoned the League's commitment, however faltering, to protecting minorities, without willing an effective alternative. It would take Cambodia, Bosnia, and Rwanda, to drive the point home.[20]

The historical 'conjoined twin' of minority protection was international refugee law, which compelled states to protect uprooted and stateless people. If minority rights had largely been introduced in relation to the rights of Jews and Armenians, the emergence of international refugee law was fundamentally linked to two developments in Eastern and South-eastern Europe: the Bolshevik Revolution in Tsarist Russia in 1917, and the Greek–Turkish forced population exchange that was enshrined in the Treaty of Lausanne in 1923. Both events led to a westward flow of refugees from the borders of the now-dissolved eastern empires – Tsarist and Ottoman – to countries in Central or Western Europe. Both events took place after the creation of the League of Nations, which meant that Western European states looked to the League for guidance and leadership in dealing with this transnational challenge. Today, a similar tendency can be observed as European states look to the EU Commission in Brussels for guidance on how to deal with the current flows of refugees from Turkey and across the Mediterranean.

The first refugees to be recognized as such were Russians who, fearing for their lives, could not return east to the Soviet Union.[21] Fridtjof Nansen – the Norwegian diplomat, scientist and explorer who was appointed High Commissioner for Russian refugees in 1921 – initially hoped that the League of Nations would arrange for their repatriation. When it became clear that such repatriation had no chance under Stalin, the work we know so well today of finding asylum for refugees in third countries began.[22] Similarly, it was Nansen who began to worry about, and later was officially charged with ameliorating, the humanitarian chaos that was bound to ensue as a result of the 1923 Lausanne Treaty in the forced exchange of populations between Greece and Turkey. In 1933, the world's first treaty for the protection of refugees, known as the Convention on the International Status of Refugees, was signed. Although significant as the first international treaty to codify the rights of refugees, it was limited in its scope to the benefit of Russian and Armenian refugees.

The major shift in international refugee law came after the atrocities of the Second World War. The mass persecution, expulsion and annihilation of many of Europe's minorities – chief among them Jews, Sinti and Roma – led to a complete overhaul of international thinking on refugees. During the interwar period, the League of Nations' approach to them was characterized by ad hoc thinking: a new international treaty or agreement was sought for each new group of refugees. By contrast, when UN member states came together to legislate what would become the 1951 Refugee Convention, their thinking was decidedly global. Coinciding with the establishment of the UN High Commissioner for Refugees (UNHCR), whose jurisdiction and mandate were clearly global in scope, the drafters of the new Refugee Convention continued to push, against considerable diplomatic resistance, for a treaty that would be also 'global' in its legal scope rather than remaining an ad hoc instrument for the solution solely to Europe's postwar refugee crisis.[23]

If ever there was a distinctly Eastern European international legal treaty that has had a fundamental impact on improving the lives of vulnerable people around the world, it is surely the 1951 Refugee Convention. Drafted in large part by Jacob Robinson, who fled Lithuania in 1940 and made it to the United States, its articulation saw the involvement of many other Eastern Europeans – who, either as diplomats or representatives of NGOs, assisted Robinson in securing most of the 1951 Refugee Convention's protective provisions. These were directly derived from the harsh experiences of Eastern European refugees during the preceding war. Robinson himself single-handedly drafted this treaty's non-discrimination clause (Article 3).[24] The Polish rabbi Isaac Lewin was responsible for drafting the treaty's non-refoulement clause (Article 33), which remains the cornerstone of the entire global international refugee regime today.[25] Much the same can be said of the drafting of the 1954 UN Convention on Statelessness, which grew out of the 1951 Refugee Convention into a separate treaty and which also saw a similar, cardinal involvement of these same Eastern Europeans in its drafting.

Laws of war and international criminal justice

Historically, the field of international law of war and armed conflict is most closely associated with Eastern Europe and, in particular, with the lawyers of that region who developed it. It is well known that the Hague Peace Conferences, which produced the Conventions of 1899 and 1907 that established the first international court (the Permanent Court of Arbitration in The Hague, which still operates today) and which laid down for the first time the basic laws of ground warfare, were convened on the initiative of the Russian Tsar. Feodor Martens, the Tsar's plenipotentiary at The Hague, although originally Estonian, presided over the conferences as the Russian empire's official representative. As Stefan Troebst has aptly noted, there is 'more than a grain of truth' in Russian president Vladimir Putin's claim that the original idea for a global international court was 'born in Russia', referring directly to Martens's leadership on this issue at The Hague.[26]

The interwar period, which coincided with the rise of communism in the Soviet Union, was marked by that entity's general hostility to international law – which, as the late ICJ judge James Crawford noted, was 'the only serious attempt by a state since the 19th century to reject and abandon international law altogether'.[27] On the pretext that international law was an invention of bourgeois society, the Soviet Union chose neither to participate in nor to sign the Third Geneva Convention for the Protection of Prisoners of

War of 1929. Little could the Soviets have imagined that their abstention would have disastrous consequences a few years later, when Nazi Germany used this very abstention to justify the execution of some one million Soviet prisoners of war between 1941 and 1945.[28] The Soviet decision to participate in the International Military Tribunal at Nuremberg in 1945–6 – and the important, substantive contributions made to that tribunal by its Russian-Jewish judge, Aron Trainin, stemmed primarily from a sincere Soviet desire to try to establish international measures that might prevent such atrocities in the future.[29] While the Nuremberg Tribunal, as an important historical benchmark in the history of trying war criminals, was certainly a 'Western' idea, conceived by the United States and the United Kingdom, the influence of Eastern Europe on its Statute, as drafted by Hersch Lauterpacht, brought much of the spirit of his old alma mater, the Lviv Law Faculty, into the courtroom of that historically significant tribunal.

Undoubtedly, Eastern Europeans' most dramatic impact on the development and articulation of the international law of war came about thanks to their support for the drafting of the Fourth Geneva Convention for Civilians, which was adopted in August 1949. As the only treaty in the entire history of modern international law to be signed and ratified by all UN member states, the Fourth Geneva Convention forms, to this day, the substantive bedrock of all our common laws of war. This treaty has also provided the legal basis for all international criminal tribunals trying war crimes since the end of the Cold War, including the International Criminal Tribunal for the former Yugoslavia (ICTY), the International Criminal Tribunal for Rwanda (ICTR), and now the International Criminal Court (ICC).

The Fourth Geneva Convention's drafting, between 1946 and August 1949, was initially undertaken by the International Committee of the Red Cross (ICRC), with later contributions from member states' delegates. On the side of the member states, France emerged as the main drafter as it had articulated this Convention's first draft back in 1947. Its Holocaust-surviving delegate, Georges Cahen-Salvador, also served as this Convention's chair between 1948 and its final adoption in 1949.

The Eastern European states, already firmly behind the Soviet Union's 'Iron Curtain', were largely absent from the first two years of the treaty's drafting. However, events in the region during the recently concluded Second World War were certainly high on their agenda. The treaty's most important achievement – as in its now famous Common Article 3, which extends a minimum set of humanitarian standards to all people, everywhere and under all circumstances, from which no derogation is possible – was certainly influenced by Nazi practices during the war. These included the routine execution of civilians, both Jews and millions of others, as well as the summary executions of Russian prisoners of war, together with the taking of hostages and the virtually unlimited use of torture. Common Article 3 sought to legally prohibit such practices against any human being. As new military occupiers in Germany and Japan after 1945, both the United States and the United Kingdom were reluctant to legislate the Fourth Geneva Convention – a treaty that would revolutionize the laws of military occupation and subject occupiers to many more legal requirements than those originally set out in the Hague Regulations of 1899–1907. In the run-up to the Fourth Geneva Conference of Plenipotentiaries, the central diplomatic venue where ambassadors of states gathered to conclude this international treaty, it became clear that without the support of the Soviet bloc the Convention had no chance of being adopted in its currently pervasive humanitarian form.

In a remarkable turn of history, it was largely thanks to the coming on board of the entire Soviet bloc, led by Eastern European diplomats, some two weeks before the opening of the Geneva Conference of Plenipotentiaries in April 1949, that the legislation of this landmark treaty became possible. In addition to Cahen-Salvador, the Conference appointed the gifted Jewish-Bulgarian diplomat Nissim Mevorah, a Holocaust survivor, as its Soviet vice president. Working closely with the French chairman, Mevorah proved instrumental in securing the voting majorities needed to overturn the wording of many clauses that would have been gutted had the US-/UK-driven wording prevailed. By the end of the Plenipotentiaries' Conference, when the Fourth Geneva Convention was signed in August 1949, the ICRC was reporting internally and confidentially how vital the Soviet contribution to this treaty had really been:

> [T]he delegation of the U.S.S.R took … the most general humanitarian attitude … This frequently resulted in the accord between this delegation and the ICRC, and I had the occasion of coordinating many times with one or the other of the Russian delegates, in order to reach the best result possible … this delegation's role in the Conference was one of the most helpful ones, and I dare not think what would have become of the 'Civilians' Convention had it not been for [the] presence of the Russian delegation.[30]

Moreover, what could not be achieved in Geneva – namely, a call for nuclear arms control, which the Soviets demanded in July 1949, and which the US-/UK-led group in Geneva refused to concede – was later achieved in no small part thanks to Eastern European diplomatic pressures in favour of the 1968 Nuclear Non-Proliferation Treaty (NPT).[31] Back in 1949, the last positive repercussion of Soviet participation in and support for the Fourth Geneva Convention related to the re-emergence of international criminal justice, which resurfaced after the end of the Cold War following the UN Security Council's establishment of the ICTY in its 1993 unanimously adopted Resolution number 827, which Russia and Hungary also supported. Stemming again from events in South-eastern Europe, the ICTY's jurisprudence, and especially its revolutionary ruling in the Tadic case, managed to lay down both the jurisdictional validity of such ad hoc criminal tribunals to judge war criminals and the application of many of the Geneva Convention's provisions also to civil wars and armed conflicts taking place within the domestic boundaries of states. In this sense, one can reasonably claim that Eastern Europe's influence towards judging war criminals – which began in Nuremberg in 1945, and which followed through in the ICTY's proceedings during the 1990s and the 2000s – has recently been invoked in Germany's trial of Syrian war criminals in Koblenz in 2022.

Concluding remarks

Any honest assessment of the origins of modern international law will inevitably give a prominent place to the influence of Eastern Europe – especially in the areas of minority protection, refugee law and the laws of war.[32] The region's important role can also be said for the prohibition of coercion in the drafting and adoption of international treaties. In retrospect, this influence has always been intimately linked to the territory of Eastern Europe, which has showcased a mosaic of peoples, religions, cultures and languages.

In history, more often than not, a signal characteristic associated with pioneering thinking concerns its prophetic abilities. People who have commented on their contemporary events in the past in a way that clearly foresaw the future deserve our special, scholarly attention. As early as 1922, when the forced population exchange of Greeks and Turks was being negotiated in Lausanne, the then British foreign secretary, Lord Curzon, warned that giving an international stamp of legality to this atrocity was bound to subsequently emerge as 'a thoroughly bad and vicious solution for which the world would pay a heavy penalty for a hundred years to come'.

It has taken a hundred years for the ICJ to seriously consider the illegality of similar actions now being taken by Myanmar to expel its own Muslim Rohingya minority. Yet the seeds of Myanmar's current actions were sown internationally in the South-eastern European context of the 1923 Treaty of Lausanne.

The reverse reality, of positive learning from prophetic thinking, is equally relevant. As Jacob Robinson noted in 1971, 'the United Nations has no programme for the international protection of minorities'. Just four years later, in 1975, the Helsinki Conference on Security and Co-operation in Europe would officially reinstate the international status of minority protection. In 1992, the Organization for Security and Co-operation in Europe (OSCE) formally established its High Commissioner on National Minorities. As Robinson so aptly foresaw, in the field of international law 'ideas do not die; they revive in the least expected places'. Little could he have imagined that the region where minority protection began, Eastern Europe in the 1880s, would be the very same region where, after so much turmoil, it would re-emerge internationally some one hundred years later – further testimony to the influence of Eastern Europe on treaties and treaty making.

Writing in 1861, shortly after the rise of European nationalist sentiment and the revolutions of 1848, Lord Acton, initiator and editor-in-chief of the *Cambridge Modern History*, sought to warn readers of nationalism's most obvious deficiency:

> A state which is incompetent to satisfy different races condemns itself; a state which labours to neutralise, to absorb, or to expel them, destroys its own vitality. A state which does not include them is destitute of the chief basis of self government. The theory of nationality, therefore, is a retrograde step in history.[33]

Despite the countless times this passage has been quoted, scholars have far too often overlooked the context in which Acton chose to place this important observation of his. Some twenty pages earlier, in the same essay, Acton had set the stage for his argument about the detriment of exclusive nationalism to humanity. The context was, of course, entirely Eastern European:

> The partition of Poland was an act of wanton violence, committed in open defiance not only of public feeling, but of public law. For the first time in history, a great state was suppressed, and a whole nation divided among its enemies.[34]

How relevant is Acton's reference to the hideous partition and oppression of Poland when one thinks today of the autocratic and non-democratic ideological currents currently engulfing that country? How relevant is his observation that the partition of Poland was carried out in blatant violation of 'public law' (for which, read: international law) to Russia's blatant violation of the same international law in its current war in Ukraine?

It is here that one should point to the role of human agency in Eastern Europe's impact on international law. Jacob Robinson's prophetic 1971 observation on the perennial need for international minority protection underscores this fundamental point. In the era of his predecessors, from the Partition of Poland to the Hague Conventions of 1899–1907, it was states such as Tsarist Russia, Prussia and the like that were the sole arbiters in the affairs of peoples and borders. With the advent of the League of Nations and self-determination, the voice of the peoples of Eastern Europe began to be heard. The fact that the minority treaties were included in the League's work, thanks to the lobbying of non-governmental organizations such as Jewish and Armenian groups, testifies to this rise in the importance of peoples in their attempts to curb statist tendencies when these are clearly responsible for peoples' suffering. This rise of the human agency of Eastern Europeans became even more pronounced after the Second World War, when Holocaust survivors like Robinson suddenly found themselves in the driving seat as drafters of treaties such as the 1951 Refugee Convention: a treaty made by Eastern European refugees for the benefit of refugees the world over.

Finally, there is the concept of 'international law'. Jeremy Bentham, who invented it in 1775, noted that he hoped this new term would replace 'that branch of law which is commonly called the law of nations'. In his subtle sensibility, Bentham was alluding to the fact that the old *jus gentium* explicitly accepted the harsh, naturalistic Hobbesian view that 'might is right'. It was precisely this tendency that Bentham's replacement sought to change through the terminological shift to 'international law'. By the time Immanuel Kant was drafting his vision for perpetual peace, the rise of nationalism in France – and, especially, the violent partition of Poland by its neighbours – had taken place. As Mazower noted, this shattering event more than any other

> suggested that the natural law theorists of the eighteenth century had been much too complacent about the pacific (read 'peaceful') nature of European civilization. It was against this background that Kant produced his famous outline of the path to perpetual peace.[35]

Little surprise, then, that Kant's fifth preliminary principle for world peace stipulated: 'No state shall by force interfere with the constitution or government of another state.' And even less surprising is Kant's call for the establishment of a 'League of Nations' (German: *Völkerbund*) exactly within that same Eastern European attempt to prevent future violent partitioning of states, such as was forcefully wrought upon Poland. It is here that thoughts as to Russia's war in Ukraine – and its overt call for the forceful ripping apart of the east of that country, along with its coercive joining to Russia of Crimea, Donetsk and Luhansk via forceful annexation – resurface.

Borders in Eastern Europe: Historical entanglements and *uti possidetis*

Bettina Bruns and Kristine Beurskens

Looking at borders in Eastern Europe from a historical perspective can be rewarding and confusing at the same time. It is rewarding because in no other region of the world have borders (and with them, states) shifted, appeared and disappeared as intensively as in the region we call 'Eastern Europe' (von Hirschhausen et al., 2019: 368–89). As such, European border studies serve as a rich empirical source for research on statehood, sovereignty and the role of state borders over time. For that same reason, the historical dimension of borders in Eastern Europe can also be confusing. From Poland's partitions to the breakdown of the Soviet Union, and from the emergence of the Czech Republic and Slovakia to the disintegration of Yugoslavia, old and new borders have been drawn and redrawn. With them, newly created states were territorially reconfigured.

When putting these observations under scrutiny, two reverse processes emerge. On the one hand, the historical dimensions of borders play a role in the creation of new borders when applying the concept of *uti possidetis*, as in the cases of the dissolutions of both Yugoslavia and the Soviet Union. One refers to this international legal concept when a new border is established on the grounds of a former one, following exactly the same line inherited by the historical, former border demarcation: '*uti possidetis* implies the application of territorial attribution and sovereign title to the longstanding possessor of a territory, and the demarcation of the territorial boundaries according to the previously recognized boundaries' (Troebst, 2019: 29).

As is evident from the example of Kosovo's emergence from the former Yugoslavia, international insistence on the application of *uti possidetis* can result in a war. As Kosovo was not an independent republic during Yugoslavia's existence, but only an autonomous province therein, upon the country's dissolution it became part of Serbia. As such, the international community, represented by the Badinter Commission of the early 1990s, accordingly ruled that Kosovo had no right to gain independence since it did not pertain to any former state's borders (Hilpold, 2008: 782). In 2008, however, Kosovo unilaterally announced its independence from Serbia, with a majority of the world's states subsequently acknowledging its declared sovereignty.

On the other hand, there exist examples of the non-application of *uti possidetis* – albeit with the now-vanished border remaining firmly in the minds of people despite the fact that it has disappeared completely in any political or material sense. This so-called phantom border phenomenon refers to the effects that earlier territorial divisions continue to have upon contemporary social practices. Contemporary election results in Poland routinely validate this 'phantom border' phenomenon. Poland's former boundaries under its third partition between Prussia, Russia and Austria, which were in place between 1795 and 1918, remain mirrored in the electoral geographies of the most recent rounds of elections there.

These examples of *uti possidetis* show the fragility and simultaneous power of ever-shifting borders in and around Eastern Europe, where borders have repeatedly been invented and contested, reproduced and imagined. While bordering processes can be observed at all scales and in all kinds of social contexts, recent measures taken by states due to the COVID-19 pandemic remind us of the enduring relevance of national borders even within our so-called globalized world.

Eastern Europe's impact on the future of international law? Neighbouring Military Occupations (NMOs)

Gilad Ben-Nun

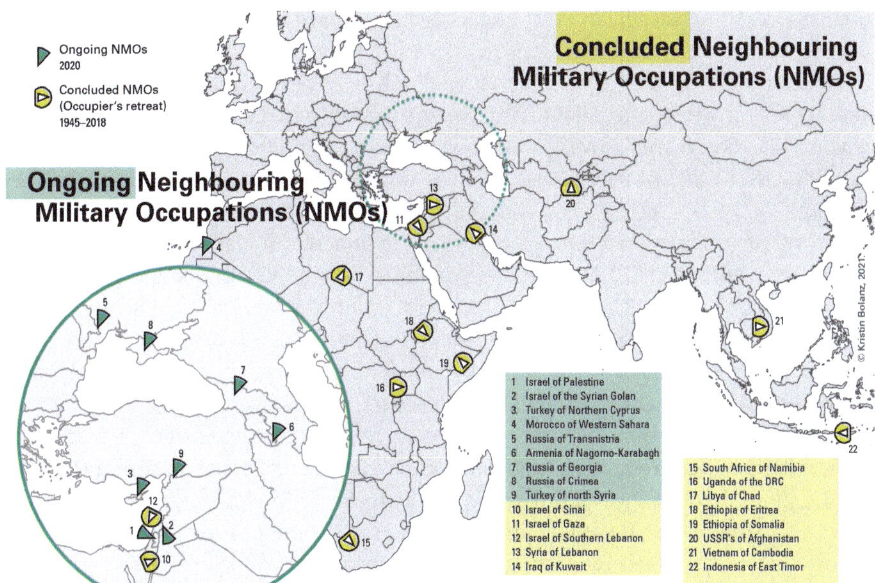

Figure 6.2 Concluded and ongoing Neighbouring Military Occupations (NMOs) since 1945.

Neighbouring Military Occupations (NMOs) are territories occupied by geographically adjacent powers that are internationally considered devoid of recognized legal titles to the lands they have militarily invaded. Since the adoption of the prohibition over the use of force in international affairs in 1945, under the UN Charter's Article 2 (4), there have been twenty-three documented NMO cases worldwide. Of these, fourteen cases have ended with the occupiers' retreat from the territory they had previously forcefully invaded. As of 2023, nine NMOs continue. With the exception of one case in Africa (Morocco in Western Sahara), the majority of remaining NMOs (five cases out of nine) are located in Eastern or South-eastern Europe, with the rest ongoing in West-central Asia.

NMOs differ strongly from 'classic' remote occupations from afar, as in the case of the United States' recently concluded occupations of Iraq and Afghanistan, or in its military occupation of Germany after 1945. Under remote occupations, occupiers habitually avoid voicing any territorial claims towards the lands they have militarily invaded. In stark contrast, the overwhelming majority of neighbouring occupiers habitually do voice claims of ownership towards the forcefully usurped, adjacent territories they have invaded. Importantly, in contrast to remote occupiers – whose eventual retreat is, by and large, a foregone conclusion given their avoidance of voicing territorial claims to the lands they have invaded – NMOs run the long-term risk of irreversibility since occupiers tend to forcefully hold on to territories they consider themselves to have been previously unjustly deprived of, and which they see as having been duly regained.

NMOs also differ from 'classic' occupation from afar in terms of their impacts upon the occupied, native, civilian populations. While remote occupiers largely avoid instigating demographic changes within territories they have occupied, most neighbouring occupiers do in fact forcefully instigate such demographic changes via the transferal of their own nationals into the territories they have usurped, or via the expulsion of local natives from them. In some cases – as in Russia's recent occupation of Eastern Ukraine, and in Israel's occupation of the Palestinian West Bank – occupiers have resorted to a combination of both measures.

Following the United States' internationally illegal invasion of Iraq in 2003, a steady and consistent growth of NMOs has emerged in Eastern Europe and its immediate regional environs. Russia's invasion and occupation of two different provinces of Georgia in 2008 (Ossetia and Abkhazia) was followed by that country's invasion and occupation of Crimea in 2014, Turkey's invasion and occupation of Northern Syria in 2016 (with Russia's tacit consent), and Russia's own invasion and all-out war against Ukraine since 2022. Seen historically, the emergence of these new NMOs under the Russian and Turkish aegis since 2008 correlates with these countries' resurgent imperial visions as harboured by both Russian president Vladimir Putin and Turkish president Recep Tayyip Erdoğan. Both leaders have explicitly drawn references to their countries' imperial pasts, under the Tsarist and Ottoman empires, respectively, as the overt legal pretexts for their countries' territorial claims over the areas Russia has occupied in Eastern and Southern Europe (Ukraine, Georgia, Moldovan Transnistria); and Turkey's occupation of Northern Cyprus (since 1974) and, more recently, Northern Syria. Moreover, both leaders have been adamantly vocal regarding their intentions to continue pressure for executing further such NMOs in territories they consider as belonging to their countries – as based upon their territorial, imperial pasts. While Putin has made clear reference to his views on Russia's alleged claims on the Baltic states and Moldova, Erdoğan has reiterated what he sees as his country's legitimate claim to Northern Iraq's oil-rich region of Mosul (forcefully detached from Turkey by the League of Nations and incorporated into the British Mandate over Iraq in 1926). Time will tell which long-term legal precedents these Russian and Turkish NMOs lay down for international law's future. Yet, be these precedents as they may (and as they may well become), their regional connotations will be inextricably associated with the events that shall transpire in Eastern Europe and its immediate regional environs.

Notes

1   Harold Nicolson, 'Diplomacy Then and Now', *Foreign Affairs*, 1 October 1961.
2   Raymond Aron, quoted in Gilad Ben-Nun, 'The Expansion of International Space: UNHCR's Establishment of its Executive Committee ('ExCom')', *Refugee Survey Quarterly* 36 (2017) 3, pp. 1–19, here at p. 3 n. 4. See also the chapter by Katja Castryck-Naumann in this volume.
3   Lauri Mälksoo, 'Russia Europe Connections', in *The Oxford Handbook of the History of International Law*, ed. Bardo Fassbender and Anne Peters (Oxford: Oxford University Press, 2012), pp. 766–7.
4   Karl-Heinz Ziegler, 'The Peace Treaties of the Ottoman Empire', in *Peace Treaties and International Law in European History*, ed. Randall Lesaffer (Cambridge: Cambridge University Press, 2004), pp. 345–7.

5   ICJ President Robert Jennings, *The Acquisition of Territory in International Law* (Manchester: Manchester University Press 1963, Ch. IV 'Title and Unlawful Force'), p. 58.

6   Gerald Fitzmaurice, 'Special Rapporteur's Third Report on the Law of Treaties' [at the link below, the precise article title is: 'Third report by G. G. Fitzmaurice, Special Rapporteur'], in *Yearbook of the International Law Commission of the United Nations 1958* Vol. II, UN. Doc. A/CN.4/115, Article 14 'Duress', pp. 20–46, here at p. 26. Available online at: https://legal.un.org/ilc/publications/yearbooks/english/ilc_1958_v2.pdf. Italics and exclamation mark added by current author.

7   Oskar Schachter, 'In memoriam: Judge Manfred Lachs (1914–1993), The UN years: Lachs the diplomat', *The American Journal of International Law* 87 (1993) 3, pp. 414–16.

8   Lachs was also key among Polish jurists who developed the concept of 'Nuclear-Weapon-Free Zones'. On this, see the chapter by Katja Castryck-Naumann in this volume.

9   Quoted in Gilad Ben-Nun, *The Fourth Geneva Convention for Civilians: The History of International Humanitarian Law* (London: Bloomsbury 2020), p. 89 n. 15.

10 Mark Mazower, *Governing the World: The History of an Idea, 1815 to the Present* (London: Penguin, 2012), pp. 19–21.

11 Eric D. Weitz, 'From the Vienna to the Paris System: International Politics and the Entangled Histories of Human Rights, Forced Deportations, and Civilizing Missions', *American Historical Review* 113 (December 2008) 5, pp. 1313–43, here at p. 1317.

12 Stefan Troebst, 'Eastern Europe's imprint on modern international law', in *History and International Law: An Intertwined Relationship*, ed. Annalisa Ciampi (Cheltenham: Edward Elgar, 2019), pp. 22–42, here at p. 25.

13 Benny Morris and Dror Ze'evi, *The Thirty-Year Genocide: Turkey's Destruction of Its Christian Minorities, 1894–1924* (Cambridge, MA: Harvard University Press, 2019).

14 Matthew Frank, *Making Minorities History: Population Transfer in Twentieth-Century Europe* (Oxford: Oxford University Press 2017), pp. 11–48.

15 Onur Yildirim, *Diplomacy and Displacement Reconsidering the Turco-Greek Exchange of Populations, 1922–1934* (London: Routledge, 2006), pp. 20–55.

16 Jacob Robinson, 'International Protection of Minorities: A Global View', *Israel Yearbook on Human Rights* 1 (1971), pp. 61–91, here at p. 90.

17 Erez Manela, *The Wilsonian Moment: Self-Determination and the International Origins of Anticolonial Nationalism* (Oxford: Oxford University Press, 2007).

18 Susan Pedersen, *The Guardians: The League of Nations and the Crisis of Empire* (Oxford: Oxford University Press, 2015).

19 Larry Wolf, *Woodrow Wilson and the Reimagining of Eastern Europe* (Redwood City: Stanford University Press, 2020), pp. 190–2.

20 Mark Mazower, *No Enchanted Palace: The End of Empire and the Ideological Origins of the United Nations* (Princeton: Princeton University Press, 2009), p. 148.

21 See the chapter by Michael G. Esch in this volume.

22 Elizabeth White, 'The Legal Status of Russian Refugees, 1921–1936', *Modern Refugees as Challengers of Nation-State Sovereignty: From the Historical to the Contemporary – COMPARATIV* 27 (2017) 1, , pp. 18–38.

23 Gilad Ben-Nun, 'From ad-hoc to universal: The international refugee regime from fragmentation to unity', *Refugee Survey Quarterly* 34 (2015) 2, pp. 23–44.

24 Gilad Ben-Nun, 'The Israeli Roots of Article 3 and Article 6 of the 1951 Refugee Convention', *Journal of Refugee Studies* 27 (2014) 1, pp. 101–26.

25 Gilad Ben-Nun, 'The British-Jewish roots of Non-Refoulement and its true meaning for the drafters of the 1951 Refugee Convention', *Journal of Refugee Studies* 28 (2015) 1, pp. 93–117.

26 Troebst, *Eastern Europe's Imprint*, p. 41 n. 83.

27 Quoted in Rolf Einar Fife, 'Creative forces and institution building in international law', in *History and International Law*, ed. Annalisa Ciampi, (Cheltenham: Edward Elgar, 2019), pp. 12–13 n. 44.

28 Gilad Ben-Nun, *The Fourth Geneva Convention for Civilians*: *The History of International Humanitarian Law* (London: Bloomsbury, 2020), p. 35.

29 Francine Hirsch, *Soviet Judgment at Nuremberg: A New History of the International Military Tribunal after World War II* (Oxford: Oxford University Press, 2020).

30 Quoted in Gilad Ben-Nun, *The Fourth Geneva Convention*, pp. 21–2.

31 See the chapter by Katja Castryck-Naumann in this volume.

32 The same can be said of the region's important role in securing the UN Convention on the Rights of the Child. See the chapter by Elizabeth White in this volume.

33 Lord Acton, 'Nationality', in *Essays on Freedom and Power* (New York: Meridian Books, 1955), p. 168; originally published in July 1862 in *The Home and Foreign Review* 1 (1862), pp. 146–74.

34 Acton, 'Nationality', p. 146.

35 Mazower, *Governing the World*, p. 20.

Bibliography

Ardeleanu, Constantin. *The European Commission of the Danube, 1856-1948. An Experiment in International Administration*. Leiden: Brill, 2020.

Ben-Nun, Gilad. 'How Jewish is International law?' *The Journal of the History of International Law* 23 (2021), pp. 249–81.

Ben-Nun, Gilad. 'Neighbouring Military Occupation (NMO): Modern Surrogate To Conquest'. In *The Palgrave Handbook on Diplomatic Thought and Practice in the Digital Age*, edited by Francis Onditi, Katharina McLarren, Gilad Ben-Nun, Yannis Stivachtis and Pontian Okoth. London: Palgrave, 2023, pp. 421–39.

Best, Geoffrey. *Humanity in Warfare: The Modern History of the International Law of Armed Conflicts*. New York: Columbia University Press, 1980.

Găt,ejel, Luminit,a. 'Building a Better Passage to the Sea: Engineering and River Management at the Mouth of the Danube, 1829–61'. *Technology and Culture* 59 (2018) 4, pp. 925–53.

Hilpold, Peter. 'Das Kosovo-Problem–ein Testfall für das Völkerrecht'. *Zeitschrift für ausländisches öffentliches Recht und Völkerrecht: Heidelberg Journal of International Law (ZaöRV/HJIL)* 68 (2008), pp. 779–801.

Johnson, Ralph W. 'Freedom of Navigation for International Rivers: What does it mean?' *Michigan Law Review* 62 (1964) 3, pp. 465–84.

Troebst, Stefan. 'Eastern Europe's imprint on modern international law'. In *History and International Law: An Intertwined Relationship*, edited by Annalisa Ciampi. Cheltenham: Edward Elgar, 2019, pp. 22–42.

von Hirschhausen, Béatrice, Hannes Grandits, Claudia Kraft, Dietmar Müller and Thomas Serrier. 'Phantom Borders in Eastern Europe: A New Concept for Regional Research'. *Slavic Review* 78 (2019) 2, pp. 368–89.

Weitz, Eric. *A World Divided – The Global Struggle for Human Rights in the Age of Nation-States*. Princeton: Princeton University Press, 2019.

Further reading

Ben-Nun, Gilad. 'How Jewish is International law?' *The Journal of the History of International Law* 23 (2021), pp. 249–81.

Ben-Nun, Gilad. 'The Polyglot Background of Eastern Europe's Jewish International Jurists and Its Talmudic Legal Origins'. In *Transregional Connections in the History of East Central Europe*, edited by Katja Castryck-Naumann. Berlin: de Gruyter 2021, pp. 191–214.
Ben-Nun, Gilad. *The Fourth Geneva Convention for Civilians: The History of International Humanitarian Law*. London: Bloomsbury, 2020.
Hirsch, Francine. *Soviet Judgment at Nuremberg: A New History of the International Military Tribunal after World War II*. Oxford: Oxford University Press, 2020.

part II

Impacts on Cultures and Societies

Editors' Note: Mobility and Transfer

The chapters that follow advertently go beyond the legal, political and economic spheres, as the arenas which all too often remain at the centre of scholarly attention. They focus on Eastern Europe's transregional impacts on cultures and societies. As such, this part of the textbook turns its sites towards migration from and to the region, and its worldwide impacts. It engages with literature and its global entanglements, and guides the reader into the transnational and global aspects of music history composed in the region we are dealing with. In these topics of art and literature in society, in cultural exchange, and in the encounter between worlds, we find themes that bring together everything in and beyond the human being. The world which surrounds us – as the planet that houses us with its resources and the physical movements we perform on it – and the inner worlds we encompass, with all their spiritual aspects and aesthetic sensibilities, and the ways in which these in turn can be transmitted to the outside, all these are explored here. Guiding the chapters in this part are questions of authenticity, of responsibility, identifications and belongings, and, above all, of change. Taken together, they demonstrate how the region's radical social, political and economic changes, in their interplay with global trends and dynamics, affected cultural and social histories. Cross-cutting themes such as 'identities' are being picked up from a variety of disciplines, that interweave with aspects of mobility, movement and transfer. The contributions here depict the multitude of inter-twinements and circulations, from the 19th to the 21st century. In doing so, they illustrate developments in what we defined in the introduction as a phase of globalization that is qualitatively different in its intensity of exchanges when compared with previous eras.

Part II begins with Mónika Dánél and Stephan Krause's analysis of Eastern European literature and films in regard to their global meaningfulness. This chapter, with its focus on the autonomy of the aesthetics of texts (not only of literature), on the region's multilingualism, and on the mobility of motifs and ideas, ultimately offers readers of all disciplines the opportunity to change perspectives, beyond actors and historical trajectories, and to train their attentiveness through aesthetics. Literatures and films invariably have a surplus to various other discourses, as a poetic counterbalance and alternative; they provide us with diverse (re-)understandings of the world, in order to reshape and contrast our world view, while offering a new, nuanced and polyphone knowledge of it. Encounters between worlds happen in the translation and transformation of names and places. In turn, it is concrete actors, in Dánél and Krause's showcased authors, writers and filmmakers, who create those worlds of encounters. Migration is not only an effect of globalization, but an intrinsic part and a key component of its making and remaking.

Looking to better grasp global changes and their impact on cultures and societies in Eastern Europe and the other way around, Michael Esch's enquiry provides an overview of migrations in and out of Eastern Europe. When people are on the move, motives for migration become as diverse and complex as migrants' own itineraries, which as Esch shows, eventually challenge existing knowledge orders, and often create new ones. Transnationally active members of European and North Atlantic intellectual circles, such as Tadeusz Kościuszko, find a place here, as much as workers whose names we do not know anymore, people made stateless, or the many displaced and deported. Migrants often become objects of political agendas, with some even actively participating in their construction. Through these agents, borders and boundaries are put to self-question, as is the idea that migrations were solely unidirectional or transatlantic. Migration, in Esch's sense of this term, is not a mere encounter of worlds, but – as he teaches us

– emerges as an entangled history of a multiplicity of movements and exchanges.

Deepening further our journey into the arts, Stefan Keym singles out areas of cultural production where Eastern European actors had a considerable imprint upon global artistic patterns, from the late 19th century to the present. He brings the vibrant realm of music and the manifold cultural transfers and interconnections in and beyond the region to the reader's attention. In his chapter, the actor-centred approach, a key feature of this textbook, is illustrated through musicians, and, above all, composers, who adapt, reinterpret or relabel styles and materials, such as folkloristic material, for example, to make it suit their needs and agendas.

Each of the chapters allows for a glimpse of encounters between worlds, between the local, national, regional and the international, and depicts the variety of the individuals' reactions to what they either perceive as a clash, threat, or as an opportunity for change. The mobility and global integrations set forth in the introduction, the global interconnections between Eastern Europe and other world regions, is illuminated through those who travelled, organized and regulated their journeys, who create multilingual and fluid worlds in literature and film, of people and borders that come to light through those texts. Global interrelations and particular (one might say peculiar) frictions shine up, especially, when international fame and national music movements dovetail.

The reader is thus called upon to understand the chapters in their interplay, although each has a different geographical focus. Through the multiplicity of the spaces that the authors address, the diversity of Eastern Europes (in the plural), and its potentialities in the ideas and life-worlds of individuals, comes to the fore once more.

Literature and Film: Aesthetics of a Region

Mónika Dánél and
Stephan Krause

7

*We speak of the cities we lived in—
that went into night like ships into the winter sea,
we speak of the cities that suddenly lost their ability to resist—
in front of our eyes,
like a circus show where every
acrobat dies, and so does each laughing clown; enchanted,
you watch, never turning away
(and inconspicuously on the circus set you grow up).*
Serhiy Zhadan, *Stones*, 2012

Introduction

What if we thought about East Central Europe in terms of literature and film. In other words, how do we literarily (and literally!) comprehend a particular region? There's an interesting, possibly unexpected, and non-stereotyped response in the following film dialogue:

Englishman: Sir, you are German, aren't you?
Z: No, I am Hungarian.
E.:   Hungarian?
Z: Hungarian.
E.:   What is that? Is that a nation? Or are you just joking?
Z: By no means! Honestly, a nation.
E.:   And where do the Hungarians live?

Z: In Hungary.

E.:   Where is that?

Z: Between Austria, Czechoslovakia, Romania and Serbia.

E.:   Oh come on! These countries were invented by Shakespeare!

This chat between the male protagonist Z and the Englishman on a boat in Hamburg in Ildikó Enyedi's (*1955, Hungarian film director) first film, *My 20th Century* (Hungary 1989; *Az én XX. századom*), refers to several aspects treated in this chapter: knowledge and the (global) lack of knowledge about 'these countries', the inventedness and reality of the region, and the fictionality (as the state of being invented is called in a literary-science context).

Enyedi's film plot is fictitious, likewise both characters. This frame is host to both an almost typical misunderstanding between West and East and a punchline declaring the inventedness of the whole region. However, beyond that pun, the dialogue raises the question of the very existence of East Central Europe in reality, and yet it also says those countries do exist as literature – as fictitious as conceived in William Shakespeare's (1564–1616) lines 'our ship hath touched upon / The deserts of Bohemia?'[1] alluded to here.

Similarly, Société Réaliste, a French-Hungarian artists' group formed by Ferenc Gróf and Jean-Baptiste Naudy, sketches the characteristics of the region in their artwork *Culture States – Superimposition of political frontiers at the turn of each century between year 0 and year 2000 on the European peninsula and its surroundings* (2007).[2]

It is a digital print that shows real and former geopolitical borders as a cartographic device, and nevertheless it seems completely unreal because it considers the layers of maps from different historical periods on a single imaginary map. However, through graphic superimposition the artwork makes visible the dense veining of borders, contact lines and

Figure 7.1

Superimposition …

conflict zones. It brings up a feature of East Central Europe described as 'the movement of borders over people', on the one hand, pointing to the displacement and the reframing of static spaces and 'the movement of people over borders', on the other.[3] Therefore in East Central Europe many cities, mountains, lakes, rivers, villages, places in general, have more than one name. That parallel existence of multiple names in different languages (allonymy) keeps up the strong traces of history, (often ethnic) identification, and the accent of one or another language, leaving even parts of the local population with an accented pronunciation of a toponym. Thus, a feeling of inventedness could even occur to a local. However, the superimposition (i.e. the stratification) of borders and of political–historical orders, manifests itself in the multilingualism of East Central Europe, its literatures and cinemas. That multilingualism is understood as 'written in many languages'[4] – e.g. Ukrainian, Polish, Lithuanian, Yiddish, Estonian, Sorbian, Armenian, Rusyn, Albanian, Croatian, Bulgarian, Hungarian, Montenegrin, German, Czech, Slovakian, Latvian, Slovenian, Romanian, Macedonian, Bosnian, Kashubian . . . All languages exist in parallel and are neither (necessarily) national languages nor would one language nationally, politically, socially or historically dominate the whole region. By contrast, its highly differentiated and diverse linguistic multidimensionality – of course, including regional languages, dialects, accents and the languages of ethnic groups – belongs to the (not only cultural) treasures of the region.[5]

So, a first draft to answer our initial question says that East Central Europe merely exists in literature, film and in visual art. This provisional conclusion, nonetheless, demands further remarks concerning general features of the analysis of literature and film, also because it differs from the use of fictional texts that historical approaches usually (and mostly) make.

Literature, film and other arts relate with history, the society, people's lives, or more generally with reality in particular ways. In a contemporary perspective, these domains are strongly interconnected, whereas art does *not* represent reality (as the Enyedian-Shakespearian example evidently demonstrates). Rather, literature and arts create possible and diverse (re-)understandings of the world in order to reshape and contrast with our world view, or to offer a new, nuanced, polyphonic knowledge – e.g. about a region: 'In East-Central Europe, a region poised at the crossroads of its history, not only literature, but the political culture itself will benefit from a rethinking that emphasises transnational interactions.'[6]

Texts (to be exact, *all* texts) have a narrator or a lyrical speaker, which is not to be confused with the author as an empirical person. Consequently, the text creates its own reality which may contain similarities, parallels with and references to the reality outside the text. Literary texts and films fabricate possible worlds in which almost everything is conceivable. We thus have to draw a distinction between reference and significance: to read a text referentially means to analyse it as a mere representation of something real by saying that things said in the text or in the film can be compared with real matters, persons or events. To analyse the significance of a text aims at focusing on its meaning regarding content *and* form. Form basically shapes meaning, and it has a meaning – often its own – too. Meaning may differ in relation to the reader, the language, the political-historical situation, the cultural context and so on and so forth – accepting that polysemy is a basic principle in the study of literature and film. Both problems, however – reference and significance – in most cases will appear as entangled features of a concrete reading of a text or a film. Texts and films, therefore, are not being perceived as vehicles transporting the representation of a reality that, by means of an analysis, might be found 'behind' them, or should be tracked down as their factual basics or their very source – nor are they to be taken as documents.

Subsequently, the world – not conceived as a globe, but as the place where humans live – is a matter of literature. Its colourfulness as well as its stylistic and medial differentiation are described as entities (things) of the literary text or the film and of the (possible) world created therein. A text's content is looked at together with its linguistic shape; its mode of saying; and, above all, its very existence *as* language and *in* language.

We consider the global entanglements of East Central European literature and film as matters of analysed (filmic, literary) fiction. The point of departure is that texts and films are capable of conceiving a possible world and of imagining it in fiction. So convergencies and divergencies of the 'local' and the 'global' as well are understood as matters of texts and films, features of the fictional worlds. That approach draws the readers' attention to both the aesthetic shape (often: the form of a text or the way a film scene is shot) and adds its fictional content bearing several cultural, social and historical implications. It is worth interpreting and highlighting the autonomy of the aesthetical, because it helps to understand why and for what purpose literature and film are a surplus to various other discourses, a poetic counter-balance and alternative, the other of language and autonomous discourses themselves that respond to the world in their own way – also due to their global and local implications.

To think of East Central Europe in terms of literature and film, we suggest three main analytical perspectives exemplarily chosen for the overview of literature and film in this text book: first, the multilingualism of the region and of its literatures and films – a principal feature of the region concerning the linguistic and aesthetic shape of literary texts; secondly, the poetics of myths – presenting a form of thought that interconnects the literature of the region and literature in general through (supratemporal) resources of human thought; thirdly, migration and mobility as *sujets* of films – a thematical aspect, traced in filmic narration. These perspectives each concentrate on literary or film examples – the first on prose texts, i.e. novels; the second on poetry about Prometheus as a mythical hero; and the third on filmic depictions of multidirectional migration and mobility between Western Europe and East Central Europe.

Multilingualism: East Central Europe as an accented geopolitical space

East Central Europe geopolitically is positioned between Western Europe and imperialist Russia, a historical 'in-between territory' where dislocating maps resulted in the reframing of static spaces and their inhabitants over the turbulent 20th century. National and ethnic memories co-exist here. They are different from but saturated with each other, layered onto one another together with their changing power hierarchies and asymmetries.

Consequently, a key feature of East Central European literature as representative of its region's culture is its multilingual character, as evidenced in the different languages spoken and written by its varied peoples. A fortiori, East Central European writing rather carries forth this quality of multilingualism via its harnessing of the regions' different languages, many of which can exist in parallel in a single text.

Contemporary authors connected to the region, such as Terézia Mora, Johanna Domokos, Nicol Ljubić, Melinda Nadj Abonji, Kapka Kassabova, Agota Kristof, Dubravka Ugrešić, Ilma Rakusa, Alexandar Hemon, Saša Stanišić and Ismet Pricić, or such Nobel Prize-winning writers as Olga Tokarczuk, Svetlana Alexievich, Herta Müller, Elfriede Jelinek and Imre Kertész are bi- or trilingual and multiethnic authors whose poetic languages create specific 'commuting grammars'[7] between different languages – transferring, juxtaposing cultural worlds and social experiences. They could be analysed within multiple and transnational category systems because they dislocate the traditional descriptive categories of national literary history, as well as that of national literary canons: 'The cultural homogeneity is counterbalanced by becoming multi-faceted, and the national literary horizons and hierarchy are replaced by a non-centred, networked, transcultural relationship system.'[8] Consequently, this literature is not related to one single language, but rather comes into being thanks to its highly differentiated and diverse linguistic multi-dimensionality. As such, this literature provides a continuous reflection of the region, its shapes, its cultures and its multifaceted history.

In this chapter, we will present different text fragments and artistic statements, through which East Central European locales can be experienced as a diversity of multilingual perspectives. The plurality of languages forms a fertile ground for intercultural connections *and* also preserves the restless tensions and conflicts of/in the region's history. Hence, the ruin as the 'silent sign language of history' serves as a key term.[9]

Danilo Kiš (1935–89) is our first example of East Central Europe's literary multilingualism. A Hungarian-Jewish-Serbo-Croatian writer, Kiš was born in the multilingual city Szabadka/Cubotice in Vojvodina (today Serbia) as Dániel Kiss, son of Ede/Eduard Kiss (originally Kohn) and Milica Dragićević. Different names and spellings lay bare Kiš's layered biography almost as an archival record of testimony to the multiple cultural and historical backgrounds from which his family emerged. It distinctly captures how his personal life interwove with East Central Europe's historical events in the 20th century:

> My father came into the world in western Hungary […] in 1944 my father and all our relatives were taken away to Auschwitz, whence almost none returned.
>
> Among my ancestors on my mother's side is a legendary Montenegrin hero who learned to read and write at the age of fifty, adding the glory of the pen to the glory of his sword, as well as an 'Amazon' who took revenge on a Turkish brute by cutting off his head. The ethnographic rarity I represent will, therefore, die out with me.
>
> In 1939, in my fourth year, when anti-Jewish laws were being promulgated in Hungary, my parents had me baptised in the Orthodox faith at the Church of the Assumption in Novi Sad. This saved my life. I lived until my thirteenth year in my father's native region of Hungary, to which we fled in 1942 after the Novi Sad massacre. I worked as a servant for rich peasants, and in school I listened to the catechism and Catholic Bible study […]

> In 1947 we were repatriated by the Red Cross to Cetinje where lived my uncle, a well-known historian [...]
>
> Immediately after we arrived, I took the art-school entrance examination.[10]

Kiš was native to at least two mother tongues: Hungarian and Serbo-Croatian. He started his elementary school in Hungarian, and until the age of 12 spoke better Hungarian than Serbo-Croatian, which only later became his chosen literary language. In *Birth Certificate* (1983), an autobiographical text, Kiš seems provocative, mentioning 'Serbo-Croatian literature in the singular', because he believed it to 'form [...] a whole'.[11] Because of the violent break-up of Yugoslavia, Serbo-Croatian began its gradual turn into a linguistic battlefield of nationalistic tendencies that made 'Kiš's mother tongue' disappear by the end of the 1990s.[12]

His most famous book is *A Tomb for Boris Davidovich* (1976, *Grobnica za Borisa Davidoviča*), which was written in response to the silenced gulag topic in former Yugoslavia – much in line with Aleksandr Solzhenitsyn's (1918–2008) three-volume *Gulag Archipelago* (1973). Yet in contrast to Solzhenitsyn's Russian text, Kiš's gulag account stands out in its multilingualism, which captures the varied nature of languages spoken by the protagonists, pointing towards their natural co-existence as reflected by the book's narrator:

> The story that I am about to tell, a story born in doubt and perplexity, has only the misfortune (some say fortune) of being true: it was recorded by the hands of honourable people and reliable witnesses. But to be true in the way its author dreams of, it would have to be told in Romanian, Hungarian, Ukrainian or Yiddish; or rather, in a mixture of all these languages. Then, by the logic of chance and of murky, profound, unconscious events, a Russian word or two would flash in the consciousness of the story-teller, now something tender like teljatina, now hard like kindjal. If, then, the story-teller could attain the unattainable and terrifying moment of Babylonian confusion, the humble pleading and terrible cursing of Hanna Krzyzewska would be heard in Romanian, Polish and Ukrainian by turns (as if the matter of her death were only the consequence of some great and fatal misunderstanding), and just before the final spasm and stillness her raving would turn into a prayer for the dead, uttered in Hebrew, the language of being and dying.[13]

Tomb and ruins (also of languages) are combined in the prose by Yuri Andrukhovych (*1960), born in Ivano-Frankivs'k, Ukraine. Multilingualism is a key characteristic of this second example, too. He was one of the first writers in post-Soviet Ukraine who 'began to conceptualise the existence of various historical regions within the country'.[14] Andrukhovych endeavours to 'open up Ukrainian collective memory to the previously [in the Soviet period] marginalised and criticised Polish, Jewish, Austrian and Central European history of the region'.[15] Together with Polish writer Andrzej Stasiuk (*1960), Andrukhovych recreates the region's imaginary through the 'floating island' as 'a space of indeterminacy and suspendedness'.[16] They co-authored *My Europe: Two Essays on the Europe called Central*,[17] containing Andrukhovych's autobiographical essay 'The Central-Eastern Revision'. This essay alludes to Kiš and elaborates on how the personal artistic view is determined by regional, or rather textual, world views: 'Since my childhood I've been drawn to ruins, I could repeat after Danilo Kiš.'[18] The term 'ruin' is then connected with several concrete and symbolic meanings based on local cultural geography:

> There are also ruins of cemeteries, especially there where genocide took place, purges, and mass deportations […] I've seen these kinds of ruins – Jewish, Armenian, Lemko. To read the names from the slabs with your hands, you have to tear off the moss […] Besides this, there must be ruins of languages, of words, ruins of letters, of this movable memory.[19]

Following Andrukhovych's 'poetics of ruins and fragments',[20] furthermore, 'an intonation, a gesture, the word order in a sentence, a pause'[21] create a sensual local memory as relics of intimate (father's) languages. Moreover, olfactory memory (smells) together with haptically described ruins combine in an intimate historical location of East Central Europe where this local memory is generated through aesthetical experience – onomatopoetical, olfactorial and haptical at the same time.

Stressing the orality in/of literature, the readers' involvement is further nuanced in Transylvanian-born Hungarian writer Ádám Bodor's *oeuvre*. Hartmut Böhme's idea of the 'silent sign-language of history' (ruins) is also further developed in his works. Born in 1936 in Cluj, Romania (in Hungarian, Kolozsvár), in 1982, following his repeated incarceration by Romania's dictatorial regime, Bodor was forced to emigrate to Hungary.

His novels are set in the borderlands. In their fictitious, reintegrative and intermediate discursive space different cultural, multilinguistic and multiethnic references associate with this region inseparably, organically saturated within each other.

The Sinistra Zone: Chapters of a Novel (1992) displays an indefinite space between the Romanian, Ukrainian, Polish and Moldavian border zones. In this interface between real and imaginary worlds, the characters deliberately wear multiethnic names. For example, Andrei Bodor (Andrej Bodor in the original) is a Romanian-Hungarian mixed name, Béla Bundasian sounds like a Hungarian-Armenian name, Hamza Petrika may be Turkish, Connie Illafeld/Cornelia Illarion is clarified as Carpatho-Rusyn, Toni Waldhütter could be related to Saxon-German origin, Zoltán Marmorstein is a mixed Hungarian-Yiddish/German/Saxon name, and Aron Wargotzki could be a Hebrew/Yiddish-Polish name with possible Germanic spelling. All these names have inherently dispersive pronunciation possibilities, so that the characters' language(s) and nationality/nationalities also remain openly undecided. Consequently, when read aloud, the novel implicitly casts its readership as carriers forth of the region's different linguistic accents. Through diverse pronunciations and accents, the multiethnic memory of the region turns, in the reading, into the audible present.

The region's ruined vernacular is embodied by Connie Illafeld. Similar to Kiš, in Bodor's poetic words the destroyed, ruined multilingualism is also interconnected with violence – especially that wrought upon women. As a consequence of medical torture under the dictatorial regime, Cornelia Illarion (her name designating her Rusyn origin) can speak only in a ruined, multilingual mixture-language:

> She no longer spoke any one single language. Instead, she mixed them left and right, and the only people who could communicate with her somewhat had to know Ukrainian, Swabian German, Romanian, and Hungarian, and it didn't hurt to know Carpathian German and Ruthenian dialects as well. Few such people lived in the

Dobrin forest district, but one of them happened to be the chief bear warden, my friend Doc Oleinek. Connie Illafeld was a sort of pen name. The progeny of the Illarions – landowning, serf-holding Bukovinian boyars – this woman, who lived among simple mountain folk on her family's onetime estate, had originally been named Cornelia Illarion.[22]

While *The Sinistra Zone* focused on ruined Rusyn memory, the imaginary novel world of Bodor's *The Birds of Verhovina. Variations on the End of Days* (2011) is placed somewhere in Transcarpathia. The Verhovina region in Western Ukraine is depicted as a multiethnic one where Jewish, Yiddish and Hungarian heritages and languages appear as cultural ruins. Yet, these peoples do not live there any more. Their former presence appears through architectural traces, which receive a new function with different meaning, following Böhme's idea of the ruin. For example, the disused synagogue 'converted into [a] public wash-house' stands for the disappeared Jewish community in the imaginary world of the novel:

The square, squat building with its ornate façade and oval windows had been built with Isaac Gold's money as a kind of small synagogue, but by the time it was completed both the entire Gold clan and the entire Man clan had converted to Lutheranism. The building stood empty for years, until Anatol Korkodus had it converted into a public wash-house. It was fed by hot water from the slopes of the Paltin's thermal springs. Above the stone troughs set into the walls there ran a conduit with taps carved from oakwood.[23]

The Sinistra Zone, like *The Birds of Verhovina*, is written in Hungarian – albeit that in the depicted novel world the Hungarian language appears as forgotten. It is a cultural ruin that no one comprehends any more. Even the first-person narrator (highly unreliable with a specific humour) does not understand Hungarian, he can just read it:

It's all quite pointless: she doesn't understand a single word, but she listens in awe with her eyelids lowered. Sometimes we make a joint effort to guess what the piece I'd read might be about. But we never get anywhere.[24]

Moreover, *Verhovina* could be seen as a translation without an original. Its Hungarian language works as a medium of the cultural memory of a hitherto-but-no-longer-existing borderland world. We don't know which language(s) the characters speak. Most probably, they talk to each other in different languages as, specific to borderlands, they continue to live in a switching fluidity of multiple languages. The text reveals only that the local written language does not contain vowels:

You're not wrong, I say. What you see are small crosses marking graves. They mean no more than what they say. In these parts we don't use vowels. We write using consonants, the rest everyone adds in their head. STLN – does that mean anything to you? No? Then there's nothing to talk about.[25]

The quasi-explained written language could be deciphered as Hebrew, but a newly arrived person like us can only guess.

The fragmentary and iterative narrations in Bodor's novels are unfinished and variable. These movable forms are also signalled through the subtitles, *Chapters of a Novel* or *Variations on the End of Days*. Bodor's imaginary worlds are saturated by missing cultures, by absent peoples, whose totality could be imagined just through their absence. This phantom-like transformation of Bodor's East Central Europe serves as traces to missing cultures, once inherent to these parts of the region, that seem movable and unfinished according to the novels' poetics.

Similarly, the cultural ruins as transformative signs are interconnected with the floating, mobile imaginary of East Central European literature. Andrukhovych's "river-geographical' discourse'[26] about and around the Dnipro resembles Péter Esterházy's (1950–2016) journey 'down the Danube' conceiving East Central Europe as a geographical, historical, cultural and textual multilingual agency. In his book *The Glance of Countess Hahn-Hahn (down the Danube)* (1992, 1999), East Central Europe is developed as a kind of shared, fluid, imaginary texture bearing a broad variety of interconnections and intertextualities. The last sentence of the novel, as the traveller arrives at the Black Sea, includes Romanian words:

> The Hireling decided that when he woke up he'd find his slip of paper and copy down into his notebook the names of all the ships he'd seen that day, 14 August: Razelm, Istria, Salvator, Bucureni, Polar, Malnaş, Izer, Mîndra, Costila, Tîrnava […] Athanassios D, Tîrgu Jiu, Braşov, Vîrsan, Călimăneşti, Gheorgheni, Voiajor, Leopard, Cardon, Cocora, Dorobanţi, Cormoran, Pontica, Căciulata, Grădina, Amurg, Colina, Zheica, Semnal.[27]

This marks a frontier, just as the meaning of the Romanian *semnal* is 'signal, sign' – indicating that the Hungarian (literary) language, as well as the Hungarian reader, reaches a limit. The listing of Romanian names indirectly signals the lack of Romanian sentences. The limitations of one language mark the space opening up for the other, and, at the same time, they constitute the basis for one's own language to open up. Subsequently, the shared multilingual co-existence of East Central Europe is turned into an accented reading. The accent itself signals the effort to appropriate the foreign, and renders this effort audible. The strangeness of the list, its liminal linguistic experience, is also an impulse for the imagination as these ship names transfer the reader into an imaginary geography of travelling, and it forms a highly poetic image of East Central Europe's multilingual legacy marking a permanent mobile and shared co-existence – a connectivity exposed as a mobile constellation of floating ships. Consequently, the special value of the East Central European multilingual literatures 'is that they convey an inherently *dialogical notion of literacy*, as opposed to the monolingualism of monocultural works'.[28]

Myth and literature

We have seen the intricate and (linguistic-cultural) knowledge of multilingual texts and have discussed the ability of authors such as Danilo Kiš and Ádám Bodor to aesthetically draw upon their plurilingual personal and collective histories. The previous part of this chapter showed the literary manifestation of East Central Europe's linguistic shape.

Literature is a huge apparatus of narratives that are present in different genres – prose (e.g. novels, short stories), poetry and drama, just to point to a major differentiation. Literature picks up narratives; conveys them; distorts, exposes or just (re)tells them – several subjects therefore developing a long tradition of appearances and reappearances in different forms and various contexts (e.g. aesthetical, cultural, linguistic, national, historical). They generate reception (echoes in the literary sciences, in critique, in literature itself). The choice of an example from myth(s) allows to pursue the phenomena and the literary-poetical realizations of a subject that has already aroused a tradition. Following French literary scholar and expert of myths Pierre Brunel (*1939), the word myth 'obstructs today's language, whereas we would rather expect it yesterday, or before, this *mythos* that the Greeks hardly distinguished from the simple *logos*, while having, in the best of cases [...], the feeling that it could be a *different* language, giving access to realities and truths of a different order'.[29] Characteristically, a myth's tradition is independent from an origin, but it gains meaningfulness from the significance it carries by and in itself. German writer Franz Fühmann (1922–84) convincingly states that there is just *no* graspable origin, and that in consequence 'being faithful to a myth demands to be unfaithful to all existing versions of it'.[30]

The example chosen here is Prometheus. According to Greek mythology, he steals fire from the gods and gives it to humankind. Prometheus is therefore punished by Zeus, the king of the gods, and is bound to the rocks of the Caucasus where an eagle (in some versions a vulture) eats his liver, which keeps growing again.

Interpretations of this myth (that is, works picking it up) exist in the visual arts, in music, film, philosophy and (maybe even to the largest extent) in literature. Prometheus' story can likewise be found in literary texts from East Central Europe. The examples here are poems written in Polish, Hungarian and Romanian between 1946 and 1996. In the following text, brief interpretations of the poems also lead to explaining several theoretical approaches to myth that demonstrate its importance as a form of thought and as the basis of a perspective onto literature that is able to integrate a global contextualization precisely by applying it in an even more general sense. The relevance for looking at East Central Europe lies in the use these poems make of both the variability and the constancy of myth – although certainly without essentializing them as 'the' East Central European Prometheus. The accessibility of the texts is, rather, brought in by the significance of the mythical that works regardless of the regional context and is still imbued by the regional itself.

Preliminary examples from literatures outside East Central Europe are considered to underline the fact that the mere mythical subject and its narrative form supply the canonical contexts of this choice: there is *Prometheus*, a poem by Johann W. von Goethe (1749–1832), one of the best-known German writers; *Prometheus Unbound* (1820), a drama by Percy B. Shelley (1792–1822), English writer; *Prométhée mal enchaîné* (1899), a sotie by French romancier André Gide (1869–1951, Nobel Prize in 1947); Prague-born German-language writer Franz Kafka's (1883–1924) prose text *Prometheus* (1918/31); the short story *Prométhée aux enfers* (1946) by Albert Camus (1913–60, Nobel Prize in 1957), French writer and philosopher born in Oran, French North Africa (modern Algeria); or *Prometheus. Die Titanenschlacht* (1974, *Prometheus. The Battle against the Titans*), a novel by German writer Franz Fühmann. The analyses here draw upon the following literary texts that deal with Prometheus: *Strofa o Prometeuszu* (*Stanza about Prometheus*) by Polish poet Kazimierz Wierzyński (1894–1969); *Prometeusz* by his Polish contemporary Leopold Staff (1878–1957); *Stary Prometeusz* (*Old Prometheus*) by Polish canonic poet Zbigniew Herbert (1924–98); *Prométheusz* by Transylvania-born Hungarian poet Sándor Kányádi (1929–2018); *Die Befreiung des Prometheus* (*The Liberation of Prometheus*) by German playwright and poet Heiner Müller (1929–95); and *Ficat locuit* (*Inhabited liver*), which is part of a circle of Prometheus poems written in 1996 by Romanian poet Marin Sorescu (1936–96).

Wierzyński's *Stanza about Prometheus* (1946) depicts Prometheus as a tough and firm man. The title and the form hint at considering this poem as an extract from or a part of something larger, i.e. from the continuous strand of mythical narration. Prometheus does not accept being unfree, and defends himself with strong self-confidence. He upholds his responsibility for having provided humanity with fire, and withstands his punishment head held high. In order to hint at the myth it is sufficient to (casually) name features such as fire, rock, chain, imprisonment, punishment and the vulture in the poem – a list of certain 'malleable elements' of the plot:

Kazimierz Wierzyński
Stanza about Prometheus

You ask who this prisoner is? An impudent convict,
who has not been afraid of his fate and has toiled.
On the mountains chained to a rock,
Punished by the gods, tortured by men,
He did not give up his freedom and stuck to it
And with his eye to his distant hosts,
And whatever happens, whatever else he is guilty of –
He will stand by his fire. And woe to you – vultures![31]

Prometheus is a sufferer here who resists Zeus by enduring his punishment and pain. However, he is aware of the spectators of his torture. Similar to the first line, in the end the speaker turns round to 'you', which the reader may well interpret as an apostrophe to him/her. So 'vultures' also addresses him/her, and raises the question of mankind's responsibility for Prometheus' pains at the same time.

While Wierzyński's poem, with its strictly regular form, focuses on his captivity and protest, *Prometheus* (1958) by Leopold Staff stages – foremost in free verse and dialogue – his liberation. Jupiter's (the Roman version of Zeus) order to Heracles to free Prometheus is presented in direct speech, as if spoken in the very moment the poem is read – in Polish as its original language, neither in Greek nor in English. Jupiter literally speaks Polish with Heracles, a fact that points to the (universal) translatibility of mythical content:

Leopold Staff
Prometheus

Having once got out of bed on the wrong side, Jupiter the stern
He convened the Olympian gods to an assembly

And said: 'I have had enough of this! Let Heracles go
And instantly free Prometheus from his bonds,
Whether you like it or not,
I'm sick of this boaster's liver
And the eagle that forever devours it,
And chains, and wild rocks, et cetera.'
And to unchain him Heracles went with a hammer,
But Prometheus said: 'Not a word of it,
Don't touch the shackles, don't even dream about it!
Can't you see how I face this Caucasus?'[32]

In Staff's poem, Prometheus rejects Heracles' effort to liberate him. He deliberately remains autonomous – almost like in Heiner Müller's short story (1972) which varies the moment of liberation, saying that Prometheus over the centuries has lived in a symbiosis with the eagle and is covered by his excrement, it having become his nourishment as Heracles arrives. The hero is disgusted by the unbearable stench around the rock. Staff's poem shows Prometheus rebelling against nature (the mountain), too. This is an elaborate metaphor of him as the icon of humanity's combat with nature. Humans have learnt to rule the fire and, up until today, have built the industrialized, basically fire-powered high-tech societies – a use that has even led to human-made climate change.

Zbigniew Herbert's Prometheus (1974) has given up his existence as a rebel. He is now living the settled life of an aging bourgeois who keeps the souvenirs of his insurrection as somehow appeased memory objects: the domesticated fire in his household, the stuffed eagle, a trophy alike. Prometheus has made friends with the local parson and the pharmacist. His profound opposition has been transformed into a slight smile:

Zbigniew Herbert
Old Prometheus

He writes his memoirs. He is trying to explain the place of the hero in a system of necessities, to reconcile the notions of existence and fate that contradict each other. Fire is crackling gaily in the fireplace, in the kitchen his wife bustles about – an exalted girl who did not bear him a son, but is convinced she will pass into history anyway. Preparations for supper: the local parson is coming, and the pharmacist, now the closest friend of Prometheus.

The fire blazes up. On the wall, a stuffed eagle and a letter of gratitude from the tyrant of the Caucasus, who successfully burned down a town in revolt because of Prometheus' discovery.

Prometheus laughs quietly. Now it is the only way of expressing his disagreement with the world.[33]

However, as a former rebel he has started to reflect on his own role and on the world. He is finally thinking over the political weight of heroism, while living in economic safety and having given up resistance. A grotesque trace of that opposition reappears in his horribly laconic final comment, though.

Sándor Kányádi's poem is dedicated to Zoltán Latinovits (1931–76), one of the best-known Hungarian actors in films and onstage. It deals with Prometheus the sufferer:

Sándor Kányádi
Prometheus
for Zoltán Latinovits

not the chain
not the beak and claws of the eagle
which with clockwork accuracy
keeps returning

but the smoke of betrayal hurts
the shame of suffocation
why did you have to ignite
the forest about me[34]

This Prometheus denies that his pain would be the eagle or the shackles; rather, it is the fact – metaphorically addressed in the smoke[35] – that others, 'you' in the plural, had been unfaithful. The sharp smoke bothers Prometheus: setting the forest on fire and turning his gift against nature (climate change alluded to here, too) were meant to turn it against Prometheus himself, and to add to his physical pain those of shame and of being betrayed by those he has loved.

Marin Sorescu's *Inhabited liver* (1996) describes the eagle in close-up. It focuses on Prometheus' organ, the liver. Despite the absence of his name, the evocation of ingredients of the myth and the context of the poem series by Sorescu allows an apparent association with Prometheus:

Marin Sorescu
Inhabited liver

I feel the wings of the eagle
Stretch wide the lips of my liver;
I feel its talons,
I feel its iron beak,
I feel the enormity of its hunger for life,
Its thirst for flight
With me in its talons.
And I fly.
Whoever said I was chained?[36]

Again, Prometheus can be identified as the lyrical speaker here (likewise in Kányádi, whereas in Staff he is quoted in direct speech). In Sorescu's poem, he defines himself through his pains and even through the eagle's hunger. The pains are expressed by references to canonic features of the myth, though the most remarkable aspect is that Prometheus is freed by the eagle, taking wing with him in his talons. Prometheus finally even questions having been shackled to the rock. *Inhabited liver* varies the story in an important way similar to Müller's version, wherein Prometheus had arranged and even allied himself with the eagle and tried to resist Heracles' attempts to free him. Sorescu's poem goes beyond that version and shows the eagle as Prometheus' liberator, thus taking over the role of Heracles (who doesn't even appear). As a result, Prometheus doubts his imprisonment – leaving the reader to decipher the strong depiction of liberation as either a political-cultural vision (in East Central Europe, too) or a mythically utopian imagination or as what else …?

It is precisely the openness of that question that goes beyond the poems and demands theoretical contextualization. Subsequently, a brief introduction to the poetics of myth, the literary understanding of it, is provided. 'Poetics'' roots lie in the Greek verb *poiein*, which means 'to make' – so, to regard the poetics of a text is to analyse its 'making of', the principles that it follows. Myth is a form with genuinely poetic and narrative quality, circulating throughout literatures, films and the other arts. It has no original form (no first source). It is precisely this lack of origin that produces the richness of potential meanings, the very significance lying in the story itself. So, apart from being known as a feature of antiquity, to the present day, myth represents an (epistemological) characteristic of literature. Philological and philosophical texts from different traditions are decisive for conceiving myth as the form of thought in which it appears in the aforementioned poetry, too. Further, as the mythical element in literature it produces significance and provides 'models of human experience'[37] contained (i.e. narrated) in the text. Moreover, this element bears its very own matter of truth, its truthfulness, so that its narrative capacity, its (poetical) attractivity and its matter of effect – according to Fühmann, that is precisely the effect of the 'mythical element in literature' – lie in its ability to explain things that are 'scientifically inexplicable' by putting them into words.[38]

French philosopher and literary theorist Roland Barthes' (1915–80) concept of *mythologies* (1957's *Mythologies*) is a more comprehensive approach, though, which stresses the semiological basis of myth as a system of signs in mass culture. Elements of everyday culture are taken as semiotic expressions, Barthes claiming that 'myth is a language[,] […] a mode of signification, a form'.[39]

To the present day, German philosopher Hans Blumenberg's (1920–96) theory of myth counts among the most important. The features observed in the poems can be recognized in his description:

> Iconic constancy is the most characteristic element in the description of myths. The constancy of its core content allows myths to appear embedded as an 'erratic' element even in traditional contexts of different kinds. The descriptive predicate of iconic constancy is only a different way of expressing what impressed the Greeks in myth as its archaic antiquity. Its high level of durability ensures its diffusion in time and space, its independence of circumstances of place and epoch. The Greek *mython mytheistai* [to tell a 'myth'] means to tell a story that is not dated and not datable, so that it cannot be localised in any chronicle, but a story that compensates for this lack by being significant [*bedeutsam*] in itself.[40]

Consequently – again, a feature we have seen with the poetry examples above – there is no first version of a myth:

The fact that its reception is not superadded, that it does not enrich it, but that instead myth is handed down and known to us in no other condition than that of always being already in the process of reception, is the result – in spite of their iconic [constancy] – of its elements' capacity for being deformed, of the fact that […] it is not composed of 'figures of granite' any recourse [*Zugriff*] to which must turn into violation [*Sich-Vergreifen*].[41]

The (maybe not merely literary) significance of myth as a poetical form of thought is a major point for the study of literature. It is based on a long-term conveyed (narrative) configuration and on the essential–productive absence of a primary source. '[I]conic constancy' as defined by Blumenberg proves to be the crucial quality to contextualize and to interconnect literature and mythical subject – understood as both the (lyrical) subject of the text *and* 'subject' in the sense of topic. It vigorously demonstrates the – occasional *and* canonic, disseminated *and* common – ability to entangle with the global conditions in which literature – not only in East Central Europe – has always existed.

Migration and mobility

Attempts to narrate and to depict migration and mobility are not new to art, nor to film or to literary texts; rather, they canonically appear in literature – Homer's *Odysseus*, who wanders about the seas, may be seen as a classical example.

Part III concentrates on two films where migration and mobility are a contemporary plot, *Bolse vita* (*Bolshe vita*, Hungary/Germany 1995) by Hungarian director Ibolya Fekete (*1951) and Hans-Christian Schmid's (*1965) *Lichter* (*Distant Lights*, Germany 2003). The film analyses pay attention to how mobility and migration are construed with global and local effects.

Tourists and vagabonds are typical figurations of mobility. According to Polish philosopher and sociologist Zygmunt Bauman (1925–2017), they are metaphors of contemporary life representing the main split of postmodernity,[42] e.g. between East and West after 1989. After the fall of the Iron Curtain, people from former socialist countries started to explore Western Europe, probing into the freedom to travel after four decades behind the East–West border. With their 'great expectations', they mostly played the part of vagabond as 'tourist's *alter ego*',[43] though.

Fekete's *Bolshe Vita* picks up that historical scene and explores the moment when the division of Europe ended. It is introduced by a voice-over:

It's hard to remember how you felt while things were changing. When the impossible became reality overnight. Ultimately, our story started when Hungary opened its Western borders. Then everything we hadn't even dreamt of happened. It came in a flash and it went just as fast. We had a short but memorable period when Eastern Europe was happy. And on the top of everything the Russians went home. They returned shortly, with many others and a new era began while all of Eastern Europe tried to get to the West via Hungary.

Bolshe Vita is set in Budapest. The plot follows six characters in quest of a future. There are Maggie from Wales and Susan from the United States, who – in Eastern European people's perspectives of that time – seem unimaginably unencumbered and free. Both young women are disillusioned with capitalism, by contrast in Eastern Europe they are searching for 'human contacts'. Furthermore, there are Yura, Vadim and Sergey from the former Soviet Union, and Erzsi, a Hungarian ex-teacher of the Russian language, renting her flat in Budapest out to Russian people. Maggie regularly shows up in her house to teach Erzsi, who is retraining to become an English teacher. Her home is now a meeting point for languages, cultures and even for different (political) systems. The film is exceptional because it depicts the regime change through multidirectional mobility and not exclusively from the perspective of people moving East–West, which is stereotypically associated with that dichotomy.

Stylistically, *Bolshe Vita* combines traits of a road movie with the partly documentary staging of people from postsocialist and post-Soviet countries. It depicts the incessant movement of mingling languages, an iconic place for which is the so-called COMECON market in Budapest, a typical institution of the postsocialist epoch where various (cheaper) new goods are sold on a platform similar to a flea market.

In *Bolshe Vita*, different Eastern European mobile figures interweave different cultures, languages and memories, bringing their very own accents to Budapest, the city becoming a conglomerate of diverse real spaces and of differently imagined futures. Nonetheless, there is a certain tension between the new freedom and individual dispositions – displayed, for example, in Sergey's tragic character. He says, 'They all shout the world opened up. I thought I might become cosmopolitan or something to live the way I want to and where I want to.'

Sergey's attitude resembles the 'expectations in vain' which the Croatian philosopher Boris Buden (*1958) coined as 'false' when trying to catch up with the West.[44] So in Sergey's and Erzsi's temporary-couple relationship, illusionary expectations and realistic continuity are exposed. Though Russian is their common language, their different attitudes towards recent developments become clear. Susan and Vadim do not stay together either, because of linguistic barriers and social and cultural differences. By contrast, Maggie and Jura develop an English–Russian–Hungarian language mixture and create visions for a relationship helping them overcome (cultural–historical) differences between East and West; one of the last frames shows them with their son at the English sea coast. It is only their love that offers an imaginary unification on a personal and singular level.

Budapest is depicted as a contact zone – both real (e.g. Soviet architecture as shards of an existing legacy) and imaginary (e.g. in the travellers' inner images, fantasies, memories and hopes) – it is a place for the articulation of various identities. The Russian characters represent a moving texture of quotes, allusions to (Soviet) Russian culture, literature and music that are difficult to understand for the Western girls. In these intercultural, interlingual interactions they look like oscillating, accented human fragments – and their own lives under state socialism (their past) as well as their imagined future appear to be absent.

The title 'Bolshe Vita' is multilingual, too – *bolshe* in Russian meaning 'more' or 'big', *vita* in Italian meaning 'life'. It refers to Federico Fellini's (1920–93) canonic film *La dolce vita* (1960), which reconceptualizes his metropolis (Rome) in different social and mental circumstances. While quoting Fellini with a similar-sounding word (*bolshe – dolce* (Italian) – 'sweet'), Fekete's title also echoes the word *bolshevik*, denoting a member of the Communist Party in the USSR. The film alludes to this legacy and places its characters in a collage zone between 'bolshe vita' and a classically Italian-sounding idea of 'sweet life' in East Central Europe, in which 'bolshe vita' incorporates 'bolshevik' as an audible allusion and legacy.

The location of Schmid's *Distant Lights* is the Polish–German border region and the banks of the river Oder. It shows the situation, the fears, the materialistic and social problems of its protagonists in parallel. Moreover, it depicts the circumstances of their existence, their feelings and dilemmas, as well as their partly insoluble personal catastrophes. Several narrative strands are interwoven by cross-cutting. Migration appears in manners of local and global mobility.

The film's title hints at this subject by the significance of light for the cinema (a film technically being a work of art 'made with light'). Moreover, 'light' plays a role in all the part-narratives of *Distant Lights*: it is a symbol of the place the migrants want to reach (just as if it was almost logically following the cover version of *Go West!* by the Pet Shop Boys [1993]); it also hints at Berlin as the city they are heading for, illustrated and shaped by its lights – where Kolja, a Ukrainian refugee, once arrived, takes photos of the harshly illuminated construction sites and the radiant buildings on Potsdamer Platz: he records the modern architecture in photographical pictures that are produced with light themselves. The first scene of *Distant Lights* is shot in a forest in the gloomy darkness of dawn. A truck with dimmed front lights slowly approaches on a sandy pathway. About a dozen people jump off the loading space: 30- to 40-year-old men, but a family with a baby, too. They are briefly instructed in Russian spoken with a Polish accent, Berlin being said to be 'next door'. All slowly walk away into the woods. The truck leaves backwards.

This sparsely lit scene depicts 'illegal migration' – as a classification of the action might sound according to law – as it appears in the middle of Europe. However, the compassion expressed towards the migrants neither judges nor betrays them. Schmid's filmic narration of the early 2000s starts precisely here, in the borderlands that can be compared with those at the Romanian–Hungarian border in Marian Crişan's (*1979) movie *Morgen* (Romania 2009) or even with the thick forest area in Kornél Mundruczó's (*1975) long métrage *Jupiter's Moon* (Hungary 2017, *Jupiter holdja*) – films that also depict the contemporary situation of migrants.

The scene discloses the clandestineness of migration. By its concrete pictures, the film cinematographically stages the very process of 'doing migration' – including empathy and hope, repeatedly embittered by failure, betrayal and fear. The film pursues, for example, the destinies of Anna and Dmitro with their baby, and Kolja's way, too. Anna and Dmitro almost drown when attempting to cross the Oder with the help of Antoni, a taxi driver who takes them in until they finally decide to return to Ukraine. Antoni, with qualms, is shown as being unable to refrain from stealing money from Dmitro's pocket. He uses it to buy his daughter a dress for her first Communion. Kolja successfully swims across the river, but gets arrested by the German border guards and is sent back to Poland. At the German police station it is Sonja, an interpreter, who feels solidarity with him and wants to help Kolja to finally make it to Germany. She decides to search him in Słubice (Poland) and smuggles him across the border in the trunk of her car. That action causes a conflict with her boyfriend, a photographer (he leaves his camera in Sonja's car, from which Kolja steals it as she drops him off in the centre of Berlin). Both these narrations display compassion, helpfulness and active support, on the one hand, while showing ethical conflicts and moral defections stimulated by migration as a combination of insurmountable conditions, on the other.

Analogous moral conflicts reoccur in the film's strand about four cigarette smugglers working in the borderlands. Their leader is a man, literally reigning over three teenagers (a girl and two boys). The hierarchy in the group is marked by mental and physical violence, traces of the social decay they are trying to cope with and that leaves no room for feelings. Andreas's love for Katharina is true; nevertheless, he remains too weak to flee together with her even though they accidentally have the whole haul from the smuggling in their hands. The circumstances prove not to leave any room for a happy ending.

Similarly, Ingo, a luckless and clumsy businessman, remains unable to understand that Simone's help is motivated by honest solidarity. He tries to run a mattress shop, goes bankrupt and has to watch his goods being taken away – only to immediately reappear in a new shop round the corner. Ingo attacks the owner and is beaten up. The violence of business tactics results in physical violence, too: the other side of the insecure material conditions in the border region. This narrative strand depicts economic decline and failure in the region, and it mirrors globalized reasons for migration at the same time.

With its unobtrusive camera eye (sometimes a hand-held camera is used) *Distant Lights* pursues the feelings and the existence of the protagonists. The film expresses understanding and sympathy, and replaces the inconceivable shape of figures in statistics, or the debates on border protection and refugees' routes, with conflicts fought out in a woman's or a man's emotions – a drama inside them affecting their individualities, in the region and under the global condition alike.

Both in *Distant Lights* and *Bolshe Vita*, the multidirectional aspects of mobility from Eastern Europe to Western Europe as much as from the West to the East play a major role. The interaction between (post-)socialist and (post-)capitalist personnel is not only staged in both films, but it is also narrated as the main global difficulty and its most successful solution at the same time.

Conclusion

Multilingualism, myth, and migration and mobility – these three dimensions have shaped and guided our approach to a region that the film character in Enyedi's *My 20th Century* declared a Shakespearian invention. Giving a concise insight into East Central Europe through literature(s) and films, these three perspectives open it up literally and not (only) fictionally.

The region covers a historical in-between territory and merges traces of different national and ethnic memories, probably making its multilingualist map one of its most striking characteristics, an everyday experience and even a lifestyle. Such 'multilingual self-awareness'[45] provides – Cristian Mungiu's (*1968) recent feature film *R.M.N.* (Romania 2022) intricately testifying to this, too – an important creative source for literature created upon 'commuting grammars'.[46] Furthermore, it is this transnational shape which transmits and translates the multilingual experience and the polyphonic cultural memory of the region. By juxtaposing (conflicting) historical mnemonic legacies and differences, artworks create localized perspectives – transforming them into a (globally) shared, dispersed and accented contemporary reading experience or/and into an audible vernacular memory.

In addition to this linguistic multidimensionality, myth represents a narrative form of thought. It interconnects the region's (not only) literary production with ideas of generally human shape and it reflects global effects. Moreover, East Central European literature participates in (re)producing and forwarding mythical narration and it is affected by the reception of such narratives. So, as exemplars of human experience – a category that goes fairly beyond any global condition – myths are present in the region's literatures and similarly (re)present the region's contribution to the aesthetic and epistemic reservoir of myths.

The increasingly intensifying mobility of people and the importance of migration as displayed in the two film examples narrates the region – represented by Budapest (*Bolshe Vita*) and the borderlands (*Distant Lights*). It is a crossroads of cultures, biographies, languages and ideas. That multidirectional mobility is even intensified in contemporary films where capitalism is depicted in different facets, such as *First of All, Felicia* (dir. Melissa de Raaf and Răzvan Rădulescu, Romania 2009) about migrating workers returning home or *Toni Erdmann* (dir. Maren Ade, Germany 2016) staging global-capitalist market-extension processes that collide with Eastern European local interests.

Finally, the Englishman's riposte in *My 20th Century* proves to be as true as it is false – since major initial questions raised in this chapter will remain further on: How do we literarily (and literally!) comprehend East Central Europe, and 'where is that'? Any literary text or any film will contribute to new, somewhat differing, and fruitfully surprising responses.

Sándor Petőfi's migrating statues

Stephan Krause and Mónika Dánél

Quito, Buffalo, Szeged, Мукачево, Milano, Tarnów, Херсон, Weimar, Bratislava, Debrecen, Shanghai, Cleveland, Київ, Sighişoara, Beijing, Zagreb, Budapest, Venice (Florida), Wien, Târgu Mureş, Miskolc, Bucureşti, Noto, Ужгород, Pécs – all these cities host at least one statue of Sándor Petőfi (1823–49), a poet, one of the most important authors of Hungarian literature, and an indispensable figure in Hungarian history. There are about two hundred and fifty depictions of Petőfi, an important number of which are placed all over the globe. The score is only exceeded by the even higher number of streets named after him: according to the artists Attila Bujdosó, Zoltán Csík-Kovács and Gábor Papp, Petőfi even beats the statesman and politician Lajos Kossuth (1802–94) in that respect. So, the main street of their Hungarian 'average village' would be named 'Petőfi Sándor utca'.

The first Petőfi statue was sculpted in 1860. The large majority of Petőfi-depictions are placed in Hungarian cities and villages. Petőfi is probably the poet with the most statues of all, possibly even surpassing German playwright and poet Friedrich Schiller (1759–1805) and easily challenging William Shakespeare (1564–1616).

To better understand the extraordinary status of Petőfi, it is important to briefly explain who he was. Sándor Petőfi is perceived as the national poet of Hungary. Major texts of his poetry address the landscape of the Great Hungarian Plain (Hungarian: *Alföld*): they portray its people and its nature, associate feelings with it and substantially coin it as a place of poetry. The depiction of the rural population in harmony with the description of that wide countryside forms a characteristic feature of Petőfi's poems. Verses and language appear as formed with ease and fresh elegance, while the subject and voice of the poems engage with the fictional reality. Petőfi also wrote political poetry which sings of revolution, freedom, Hungarian independence and of the fight for these ideals. *Nemzeti dal* (*National Song*) is one of his best-known poems. The Hungarian Revolution is said to have started with that poem once Petőfi had read it out to his comrades on 15 March 1848 in Pilvax Café in Pest.

Petőfi was born in the little town of Kiskőrös, situated about 120 kilometres south of Budapest. Both his parents, István Petrovics (1791–1849) and Mária Hrúz (1791–1849), were of Slovakian origin; his father came from Upper Hungary. Mária learned Hungarian only as a teenager. István rented a butcher's shop in Petőfi's birthplace. At the age of 19, he published his first poem and still signed as Petrovics, which he changed that same year into Petőfi. His first volume of poetry came out in 1844. Petőfi's most productive period began in 1846, the year he married Júlia Szendrey (1828–68), who was also a poet. In 1848, Petőfi was with the Youths of March and took part in initiating the Hungarian Revolution that led to the War of Independence (Hungarian: *Szabadságharc*) of 1848/9. He died in an encounter on 31 July 1849 in Fehéregyháza (today Albeşti, Romania) near Segesvár (today Sighişoara, Romania). His corpse was never found.

His name and his poetry survived, and there is hardly any Hungarian author after him who did not refer to his literature in one or another way. He keeps living on in that reception as well as in statues and busts.

The statues commemorate Petőfi and his legacy; they partly (re)create and support his canonicity as an iconic poet and establish a powerful reference for Hungarian culture. The best-known and most referenced statue of Petőfi was inaugurated in 1882 in Budapest. It had exclusively been funded by donations, the majority of which were collected by Ede Reményi (1828–98), a prominent Hungarian violin virtuoso. Reményi gave concerts for the benefit of the statue for more than two decades. In 1956, when the Hungarian uprising against Soviet occupation started, the first student demonstration in Budapest gathered in front of the Petőfi statue.

Another example is the statue in Segesvár (Transylvania), erected in 1897. In 1916, during the First World War, the Hungarian administration decided to store it in Budapest because the Romanian Army was about to take Transylvania, which became a part of Romania as a consequence of the First World War and the Treaty of Trianon (1920). In 1922, the statue moved again and was given to Kiskunfélegyháza where Petőfi had gone to school. This migration of the statue draws a parallel with the territorial consequences for Hungary after the First World War. Sighişoara (former Segesvár) set up a 'new' representation of Petőfi, a bust (1959), made by Romanian artist Romulus Ladea (1901–70). This new Petőfi does not replace the other, but it points to the partly Hungarian culture of the region while, by its history, the statue in Kiskunfélegyháza refers to the change of political geography.

Furthermore, in the United States, Petőfi has importance for the Hungarian diaspora that arrived there at the turn of the 20th century, after the Second World War and after 1956, when Cleveland, Ohio, was the biggest Hungarian city in North America. The poet's image had crossed the Atlantic Ocean not only in poetry books on the shelves of the emigrants; his sculptural depiction formed an additional reference to the homeland left behind. Finally, in Noto (Sicily), a Petőfi statue points to the interlingual migration of his poetry via translation, related to a second one in Kiskőrös portraying his Italian translator Giuseppe Cassone (1843–1910). The response to this statue in the same artistic medium is a bust of Cassone in the statue park of Petőfi's translators next to his house of birth in Kiskőrös.

These migrating figurations of Petőfi represent poetry itself, even its multilingual phenomena – though they reference Hungarian culture, too, and they (visually) point to the universal, thus transnational, character of (not only) East Central European literature.

Figure 7.2 Statues of Sándor Petőfi.

© Stephan Krause 2023 (for the collage); © for image Erich Lessing: akg-images / Erich Lessing; © for image Sándor Petőfi at Riverside Park: Buffalo Olmsted Parks Conservancy.

Notes

1. William Shakespeare, *The Winter's Tale* 3.3, lines 1439/40.
2. Digital print on Dibond 47 1/5 × 78 7/10 in | 120 × 200 cm. The artwork is available online at: https://www.artsy.net/artwork/societe-realiste-culture-states-superimposition-of-political-frontiers-at-the-turn-of-each-century-between-year-0-and-year-2000-on-the-european-peninsula-and-its-surroundings.
3. Rogers Brubaker, *Grounds for Difference* (Cambridge, MA: Harvard University Press, 2015), p. 136.

4   For the concept of 'multilingualism' in linguistics, see Anat Stavans and Charlotte Hoffmann, *Multilingualism* (Key Topics in Sociolinguistics) (Cambridge: Cambridge University Press, 2015), esp. pp. 11–58. doi:10.1017/CBO9781316144534.

5   However, Jane Hiddleston and Wen-chin Ouyang (eds), *Multilingual Literature as World Literature* (New York: Bloomsbury, 2021) – for example – lacks any study on the region.

6   Marcel Cornis-Pope and John Neubauer, 'General Introduction', in *History of the Literary Cultures of East-Central Europe. Junctures and Disjunctures in the 19th and 20th Centuries*. 4 vols, here vol. 1. (Amsterdam: John Benjamins, 2004), p. 1.

7   Beáta Thomka, *Regénytapasztalat: Korélmény, hovatartozás, nyelvváltás.* (Budapest: Kijárat Kiadó, 2018), p. 146.

8   Thomka, *Regénytapasztalat*, p. 19.

9   Hartmut Böhme, 'Die Ästhetik der Ruinen' ['the aesthetic of ruins'], in *Der Schein des Schönen* ['The appearance of beauty'], ed. Dietmar Kamper and Christian Wulf (Göttingen: Steidel Verlag, 1989), pp. 287–304.

10   Mark Thompson, *Birth Certificate: The Story of Danilo Kiš* (Ithaca: Cornell University Press, 2013), pp. 1–2.

11   Thompson, *Birth Certificate*, p. 271.

12   Ibid., p. 272.

13   Danilo Kiš, *A Tomb for Boris Davidovich*, trans. Duška Mikić-Mitchell (New York: Penguin, 1978).

14   Olena Dvoretska, 'In search of the other Europe: The city of Ivano-Frankivs'k in the works of Yurii Andrukhovych', *Central Europe* 15 (2017) 1–2, pp. 4–17, here at p. 8.

15   Dvoretska, 'In search of the other Europe', p 8.

16   Jagoda Wierzejska, '(Post-)bordering Galicia in Ukrainian and Polish post-colonial discourse: The cases of Yurii Andrukhovych and Andrzej Stasiuk', *Journal of European Studies* 47 (2017) 2, p. 177.

17   Yuri Andrukhovych, *Moja Europa: Dwa eseje o Europie zwanej środkową* (Wołowiec: Czarne, 2000); Yuri Andrukhovych, *Moja Jevropa* (Lviv: VNTA-Klasika, 2001).

18   Yuri Andrukhovych, *In My Final Territory. Selected Essay*, trans. Mark Andryczyk, Michael M. Naydan and Vitaly Chernetsky (Toronto: University of Toronto Press, 2018), p. 5.

19   Andrukhovych, *In My Final Territory*, p. 9.

20   Dvoretska, 'In search of the other Europe', p. 11.

21   Andrukhovych, *In My Final Territory*, p. 48.

22   Ádám Bodor, *The Sinistra Zone*, trans. Paul Olchváry (Cambridge, MA: New Directions Press, 2013), p. 101.

23   Ádám Bodor, *The Birds of Verhovina*, trans. Peter Sherwood (London: Jantar Publishing, 2023), p. 88.

24   Bodor, *The Birds of Verhovina*, p. 46.

25   Ibid., p. 265.

26   Galyna Spodarets, 'One River, Two Ukraines? Yurii Andrukhovych's Imagined Geography of East-Central Europe', *Central Europe* 15 (2017) 1–2, p. 46.

27   Péter Esterházy, *The Glance of Countess Hahn-Hahn (down the Danube)*, trans. Richard Aczel (Evanston: Northwestern University Press, 1999), p. 244.

28   Beáta Thomka, *Déli témák. Kultúrák között* (Zenta: zEtna Publisher, 2009), pp. 73–4.

29   Pierre Brunel, *Dictionnaire des mythes d'aujourd'hui* (Monaco: Éditions du Rocher, 1999), p. 9.

30   Franz Fühmann, 'Das mythische Element in der Literatur' [1975, The Mythical Element in Literature], in *Essays, Gespräche, Aufsätze 1964-1981*, ed. Franz Fühmann (Rostock: Hinstorff, 1993), p. 105.

31   Original in: Kazimierz Wierzyński, *Poezje zebrane* Vol. 1 (Białystok: Łyk, 1994), p. 469.

32   Original in: Leopold Staff, *Dziewięć Muz* (Warsaw: Państ. Instytut Wydawniczy, 1958), p. 49.

33   Zbigniew Herbert, 'Old Prometheus' [1974, Stary Prometeusz], in *Zbigniew Herbert, Mr. Cogito. Poems*, trans. John Carpenter and Bogdana Carpenter (Hopewell: Ecco Press, 1993), p. 38.

34 Sándor Kányádi, 'Prometheus' [1974, Prométheusz], trans. Leslie A. Kery, available online at: https://www.magyarulbabelben.net/works/hu/K%C3%A1ny%C3%A1di_S%C3%A1ndor-1929/Prom%C3%A9theusz/en/75886-Prometheus.

35 A self-reference, too, quoting his poem *Füst – Smoke* (1965) where Prometheus' gift is mentioned as a 'deed conflicting with law'.

36 Marin Sorescu, 'Inhabited liver' [1996, Ficat locuit], in *The Bridge,* ed. Marin Sorescu, trans. Adam J. Sorkin [and Lidia Vianu] (Bloodaxe: Tarset, 2004), p. 20.

37 Fühmann, 'Das mythische Element', p. 96.

38 Ibid., pp. 90 and 124.

39 Roland Barthes, *Mythologies* [1957, Mythologies], trans. Annette Lavers (London: Jonathan Cape, 1972), p. 109.

40 Hans Blumenberg, *Work on Myth* [1981, Arbeit am Mythos], trans. Robert M. Wallace (Cambridge, MA: MIT Press, 1985), p. 149.

41 Blumenberg, *Work on Myth*, p. 216–17.

42 Zygmunt Bauman, *Tourists and vagabonds: heroes and victims of postmodernity*, Reihe Politikwissenschaft / Institut für Höhere Studien, Abt. Politikwissenschaft, 30 (Vienna: Institut für Höhere Studien (ICHS), 1996), p. 1. Available online at: https://nbn-resolving.org/urn:nbn:de:0168-ssoar-266870.

43 Ibid.

44 See Boris Buden, 'Das Elend des Nachholens', in *Zone des Übergangs: Vom Ende des Postkommunismus*, ed. Boris Buden (Frankfurt am Main: Suhrkamp, 2009), pp. 52–73.

45 Beáta Thomka, *Regénytapasztalat: Korélmény, hovatartozás, nyelvváltás* (Budapest: Kijárat Kiadó, 2018), pp. 34–43.

46 Thomka, *Regénytapasztalat*, p. 146.

Further reading

Apter, Emily. *Against World Literature: On the Politics of Untranslatability*. London and New York: Verso, 2013.

Cornis-Pope, Marcel and John Neubauer (eds). *History of the Literary Cultures of East-Central Europe. Junctures and Disjunctures in the 19th and 20th Centuries*. 4 vols. Amsterdam: John Benjamins, 2004.

Gott, Michael and Todd Herzog (eds). *East, West and Centre: Reframing Post-1989 European Cinema*. Edinburgh: Edinburgh University Press, 2015.

Kányádi, András. *Figures mythiques en Europe centrale: aspects d'un panthéon variable*. Paris: Institut d'Études Slaves, 2010.

Király, Hajnal and Zsolt Győri (eds). *Postsocialist Mobilities: Studies in Eastern European Cinema*. Newcastle upon Tyne: Cambridge Scholars Publishing, 2021.

Migration and Migratory Impacts: Coping Strategies on a Global Scale

Michael G. Esch

8

Over the past two hundred years, migration has been deeply associated with Eastern Europe and with its 'backwardness'. Mass emigration indicated deficient economic development; numerous waves of political refugees leaving the Russian empire and the Prussian East were proof of inherently oppressive political systems. The migration of Jews across the Atlantic was attributed to Slavic and Magyar anti-Semitism; emigration during the Cold War labelled as flight from communist oppression. The historiography on the forced migrations and genocides during and after the 'Second Thirty Years War' (1914–45) added to representations of migrants as merely victims and of migration as an agent of social, cultural and economic loss. A closer look at migratory patterns in Eastern Europe reveals, however, a more layered picture: the causes of emigration were manifold, transfers took multidirectional routes, and effects were diverse.

Undoubtedly, Eastern Europeans often migrated due to poverty or persecution. But first, these circumstances, as well as being coping strategies, were effectuated by and affected changing terms of trade and political concepts on a global scale. Secondly, migrants participated actively in the political, economic and sociocultural contexts they found themselves in and created intricate entanglements between old and new places of residence. Migration from Eastern Europe was not merely a result of globalizing processes, it was an intrinsic part and a key component of them.

In a swift dash through the streams of migration over the past two hundred years, this chapter presents some aspects that a global history of Eastern European migrations has to consider. We start with a very rough outline of pertinent migration waves and phenomena since the Partitions of Poland, followed by some considerations about structures and actors. The third part deals with the contexts in which these migrations happened. Finally, we take a look at how the enlargement of the European Union (EU) eastwards seems to have somehow reversed the role of the region in global migration systems.

Two hundred years of modern migration: An overview

For a long time, Eastern Europe received rather than sent migrants. Since the 12th century, peasants from the West settled in Polish and Czech territories – mostly by invitation of the monarchs there. Privileges like self-administration under the regulations of German municipal law or partial autonomy in the case of Jews and Armenians in the 14th century were decisive for the development of a social and political organization more complex, integrative and at times unstable than the estate-based society of Western Europe. Simultaneously, Tatars settled in certain regions of Poland, Lithuania and Belarus.[1] The Polish-Lithuanian Commonwealth, established in 1569, and parts of the Habsburg and Russian empires welcomed religious dissidents when they possessed skills in crafts, trades or agriculture essential for the development of their respective economies and administrations. Even into the 18th century, Catherine II (most commonly known as Catherine the Great) 'adopted' German Mennonites for the colonization of *Novaja Rossiija*. Conversely, Poles and Czechs participated in the colonization of the Americas and the Global South, while Cossacks from present-day Ukraine were forerunners in the Russian colonization of Northern Asia.

In the early 19th century, the West–East direction of such migration was reversed. The advent of the (republican) nation-state with the American and French Revolutions and the emergence of globalizing capitalism fundamentally changed the reasons for, the conditions under which and the methods how people migrated. This modernization – basically a replacement of corporate belonging with a direct, homogenizing relationship between the individual and the state – proved to be particularly problematic in Eastern Europe with its multitude of ethnicities and autonomous, but entangled and interacting, societies and its subsistence economies. Since the nation-state was conceptualized as a political as well as a cultural entity, the proclamation of ethnically identified titular nations often collided with highly multi-ethnic contexts – to deleterious effect. With regard to migration, the displacement of individuals and groups now followed the dialectics of foreign-workforce exploitation, the individual pursuit of happiness and ethno-social exclusionism, while the introduction of faster ships and railways enlarged the geographical scope of migration. Eastern Europe was in this respect no exception, especially after constitutional reform of the Polish-Lithuanian Commonwealth in 1791 led to its eradication from the political map of Europe in 1795 – which, again, provoked the rise of several nationalist and revolutionary movements.

Just as the French Revolution produced the first modern political refugees (i.e. the émigrés among the nobility and clergy), so the first migrants from the East in this period were politically motivated as well. Waves of repression in the Russian empire after the Decembrist Uprising in 1825 or the rise of revolutionary populism in the 1870s drove growing numbers of democrat and later socialist intellectuals and activists to choose exile – most notably, in France and England. Others intended to complete their studies in the West, where they adopted, and sometimes transformed, radical thinking and practice. After the November Uprising of 1830/1 in Poland, several thousand insurgents – mostly officers and officials in the provisional government – followed an invitation from the French government and settled in France. After the revolutions and revolts of 1848, Poles, Czechs and Hungarians were granted refuge in France, Britain, Belgium and the Ottoman empire. The same was true after the Polish January uprising of 1863, with former insurgents prominently participating in the Paris Commune of 1871.[2]

The year 1881 saw the first massive wave of a new type of migrant – namely, Jews from the Russian empire and Romania. Their migration was surely triggered by anti-Semitic pogroms organized after the assassination of Tsar Aleksandr II by Russian populists, but it was in equal measures motivated by the quest for affluence – a motive shared with other migrants. As a form of betterment, migration, often directed overseas, complemented non-Jewish seasonal migration paths from the western provinces of the Russian empire and Austrian Galicia to the eastern provinces of Prussia and Saxony: since the 1870s, agricultural labourers from the Russian and Habsburg empires had spent the warmer months on the large estates to the east of Labia, where they filled the gaps left by the migration of rural youth to the cities and to the expanding mining and iron smelting regions in Silesia. Even more adventurous, young Jewish and Christian men, women and families chose the industrializing Ruhr valley; northern and western France; or, after the 1880s, North and South America as destinations for temporary or long-term migration. Estimates say that between 1876 and 1910, three million Habsburg subjects (i.e. about 8 per cent of the total population in 1910) and two million subjects of the Tsar (i.e. 2.2 per cent of the 1890 population) crossed the Atlantic to the New World for an extended period of time or for good.

'The emerging emigration state': State responses to overseas migration in East Central Europe before 1914

Ulf Brunnbauer

In 1911, the Diet (*Sabor*) of the kingdom of Croatia and Slavonia, then an autonomous unit of the kingdom of Hungary within the Habsburg empire, discussed the bill for a 'Law on Emigration'. This should create a legislative framework for the intended control of the government over out-migration at a time when each year thousands of citizens of the kingdom left for overseas, mainly the United States. One of the clauses stipulated that the government 'ought to morally and materially support the emigrants, so that their love, sympathy and attachment to their home country survives'. The bill never became law, but it illustrates political concerns concerning the consequences of emigration. For years, Croatian politicians had pushed the provincial government to act against emigration, which had become massive in the 1890s, as a result of the crisis of farming and the job opportunities in America. Policymakers framed emigration as a danger for the nation; they associated the United States with immoral lifestyles and feared that migrants would return with unwarranted ideas, such as socialism. While they acknowledged the economic importance of emigration for the most affected regions, they still criticized the emigrants for their 'unwise' use of savings from America (for an extended discussion of these questions, see Brunnbauer 2016, pp. 145–206).

Already before the First World War, Central European states found themselves in what James Hollifield has called the 'liberal paradox' of migration policy. At that time, the Habsburg empire had become one of the major suppliers of immigrants to the United States, and other South-eastern and Eastern European countries, such as Russia and Greece, as well experienced massive overseas emigration. How should they react to it? Hollifield stresses that 'the economic logic of liberalism is one of openness, but the political and legal logic is one of closure' (Hollifield 2004, p. 887). The question of emigration was made even more acute by the intensive nation-building processes at that time: people (of the right stock) were, of course, the most important resource of nationalism. For example, when Serbia and Bulgaria, two young nation-states aiming at national expansion, registered the first signals of an emerging emigration wave in the early 1900s, their governments enforced strict rules for departure, basically reducing emigration to a trickle.

Political as well as scholarly interest in migration policy concentrates on the side of the immigration state. Yet, governments of countries massively affected by out-migration tend not to ignore this issue either. After all, emigration undermines basic claims at sovereignty and is often associated with fears for a loss of labour vital for economic development. Questions of prestige are also concerned, since strong out-migration is often seen as an indicator for the peripheral position of a country. State bureaucracies are wary of the financial costs of spontaneous actions of their citizens: the only country for which emigration from Cisleithania (the Austrian 'half' of the Dual Monarchy) was ever banned was Brazil because so many Austrian emigrants fell into destitution and had to be repatriated on the account of the Foreign Ministry. Austrian officials, and the media, were also wary of an inversion of racial hierarchies: Brazil massively recruited migrants from the poorer parts of Europe after slavery had been abolished in 1888.

Aristide Zolberg has described the 19th century as the exit revolution, when previous bans on emigration, stimulated by physiocratic ideas about economic development, were lifted in Europe (Zolberg 2007). A closer look into one of Europe's most salient emigration regions before the First World War urges to qualify this notion. Pressed by publics concerned over migration or by special interests – such as of Polish large landowners in Austrian Galicia or Hungarian magnates who feared for their sources of cheap labour – governments sought ways to at least control, or even restrict, the departure of able-bodied men and women. Some went so far as Serbia and Bulgaria. The other extreme was Austria, where the right of emigration was enshrined in the constitution of 1867 – until the Army got its way in 1913, forcing the government to clamp down on emigration of recruits. But across the region, governments tried to impose some form of control, often in the name of protecting emigrants. They also tried to prevent the departure of those who would be barred from entry into the United States – a clear indication of the transnational dimension of immigration rules. The facilitation of emigration was often outlawed or strictly regulated – without much of an affect but emigration (sub-)agents at least provided a useful scapegoat for governments who failed to improve living conditions so that people did leave in the first place. By making these facilitators of emigration responsible for the huge number of emigrants, policymakers and the media denied agency to the migrants (see also Zahra 2016).

One important vector of early emigration policies was nationalization: if emigration could not be stopped, it should at least further the interests of the nation, as defined by the political elite. The Hungarian government, which pursued aggressive Magyarization policies, tried to prevent Magyars from departing but was happy to see so many members of non-Magyar nationalities leaving its kingdom. When it started a repatriation campaign in 1907, the prime minister made clear that only Magyars should feel invited to come back. The government in Budapest unsuccessfully tried to reign in anti-Magyar activities by Slovak émigrés in the United States but at least managed to prohibit the import of their newspapers. In Russia and the Ottoman empire, where emigration was technically illegal, the governments turned a blind eye on the massive emigration of minorities (Jews in the first case, Christians in the second).

Emigration, thus, gave rise to new forms of population and identity policies which (re-)enforced ethnic understandings of nationhood. What else than notions of common descent could link together an increasingly trans-territorial nation (see Torpey 2000, p. 72)? In times of war, this connection would become actualized in the forced expulsion of ethnic minorities, tragically a frequent occurrence in 20th-century Eastern and South-eastern Europe.

These maps show the ethno-religious composition of the population in a Chicago district *c.* 1910 and in the Rue des Rosiers, the centre of the 'Jewish' quarter in Paris in 1927. While the former stems from a contemporary sociological and statistical study, the latter is based on my own work with the *Listes nominatifs du reccensement de 1927* in France. As religious affiliation was not an accepted category in a secularized state like France, Jewish migrants have been provisionally identified by their names and birthplaces. As we see, the formation of immigrant quarters was not a unique feature of North and South American cities, which had themselves basically been created by migrants, but occurred in old cities in Europe as well. They also show that despite common representations, the pertinent immigrant groups constituted maybe the most prominent, visible or suspected segment of the population but not its majority. Far from unitary, they were never as homogeneous, nor as impermeable, as public discourses and moral outrages often depicted them.

The Paris map also indicates that migration of nationals into large cities played as important a role as immigration of foreigners. This did not preclude ethno-religious community-building, but it also indicated a considerable amount of intergroup interaction. This interaction was surely facilitated by the fact that cities were (and are) segmented according to social status. In most cases, ethnicity and/or religion were the primary 'denominations' for these communities; in some cases, however, these were partially transcended either by birthplace or by overarching regional affiliation. Additionally, in everyday encounters as well as in identity formation, class was therefore just as important as – and was entangled with – mother tongue, geographical origin or religion. This seems to have been particularly the case in proletarian quarters like those shown here, where – due to rural traditions and overcrowded accommodation – much of everyday life took place in courtyards and streets.

Figure 8.1 a/b Ethno-religious composition of a district in Chicago (1910) and in Paris (1927).

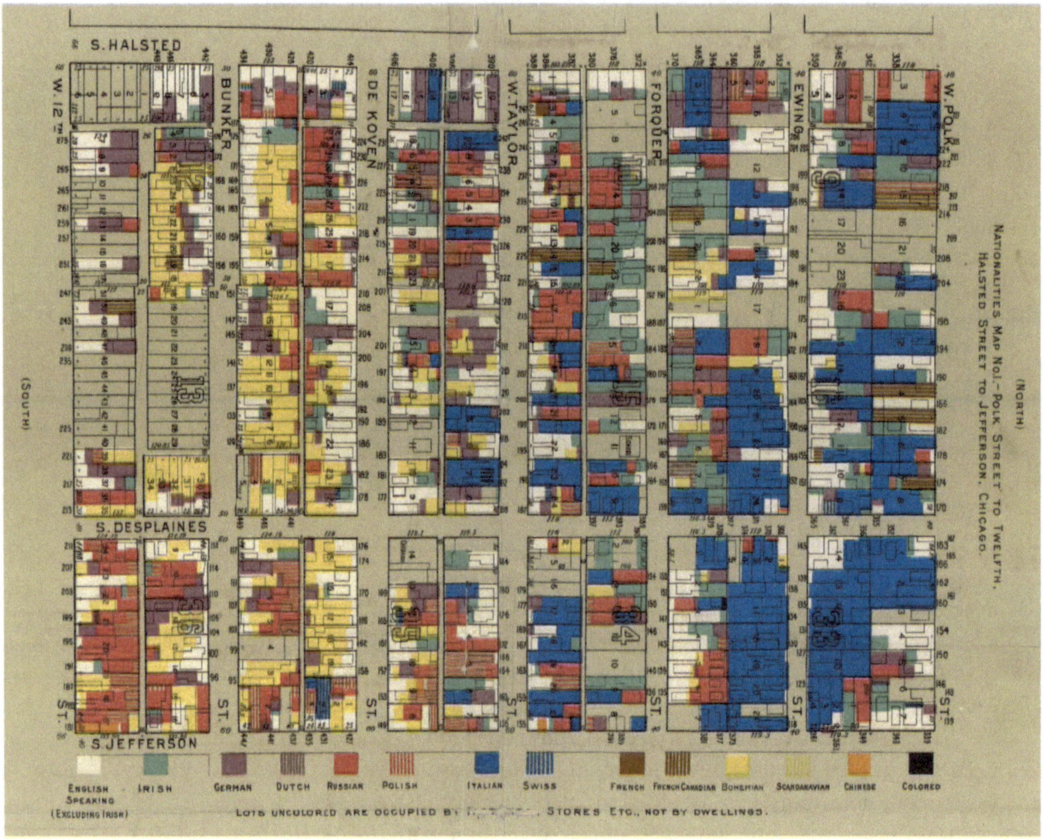

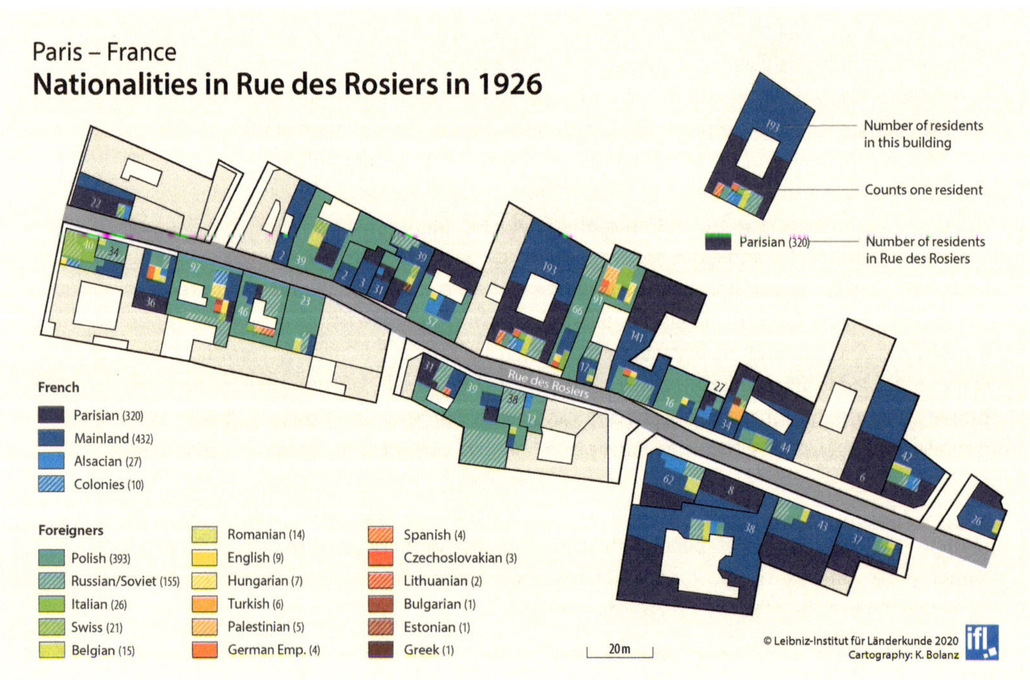

Forced migrations and ethnic cleansing, 1914–50

After the French Revolution, international conflicts became confrontations not between monarchs and their armies but between nations and their systems of social organization. In consequence, warfare increasingly involved and affected the 'civil' population. With the 'nationalization of the masses' in the late 19th century, the loyalty of any segments of the population that were not part of the hegemonic or titular nation(s) was regularly questioned, which in turn motivated forced population movements. While the aftermath of the Franco-Prussian War of 1871 brought about a certain degree of 'ethnic cleansing' in Alsace-Lorraine, the First World War brought population expulsions, deportations and refugee migration on a hitherto unknown scale on all fronts. About one million Belgians fled westwards from German occupation, while Russian authorities displaced several million members of non-Russian 'nationalities' inside the empire's borders. German postwar plans included the gradual removal of Poles, Ukrainians and Jews from large territories in the East and their colonization with German settlers.

One effect of the world war in Russia gave birth to a new conceptualization of refugees: Russian subjects who had fled the country because of the October Revolution of 1917 or during the Civil War. Hoping to return quickly, these refugees first concentrated in neigh-bouring territories such as Poland, Bulgaria, Turkey and Shanghai. The former Wrangel and Denikin armies, constituting a significant part of the tsarist armed faction during the Civil War and numbering several tens of thousands of soldiers and their entourages, were transferred from Turkey to France, where most of them would settle. The 1–2 million refugees from the former Russian empire, who ranged politically from monarchist to anarchist and socially from peasant and worker to high aristocrat, formed several communities all over the world – some of which would remain highly visible culturally and politically, such as at the Russian University in Prague and various associations and publishing houses in Berlin and Paris. Their presence also motivated the first attempts to define an internationally sanctioned legal status for refugees.

Additionally, seasonal and permanent migration from Eastern Europe to the West resumed – particularly, to France and Germany. The economic crisis of the late 1920s, however, encouraged an intensification of measures to prevent unwanted, and to regulate wanted, migration. While receiving countries like Germany and France sought control via binational migration agreements, the United States in 1921 and 1924 installed a quota system that specifically reduced immigration from Southern and Eastern Europe and banned it from East Asia. At the same time, some countries in South America like Argentina and Brazil encouraged the influx of migrants from Eastern Europe, including Jews, in an effort to 'whiten' their populations. Sending countries like Poland and Czechoslovakia, as well as Jewish private organizations, participated in the recruitment, selection and support of such migrants.

The turn to fascism and authoritarianism in several European and American countries – Hungary in 1920, Italy 1925, Argentina 1930s, Germany 1933, Poland 1935, Spain 1936–9 and Brazil 1937 – again tightened the grip on migrants. In Europe, fascism expanded the use of migration as an instrument of positive and negative population policies. It also produced new waves of political and Jewish refugees. But while Russians and Armenians, the recognized and partially protected refugees of the immediate aftermath of the war, had been welcomed in times of economic upswing, refugees now met bleaker conditions – especially after the beginning of the Great Depression in 1929. Political considerations even prevented their international recognition as refugees. Poland and Hungary impeded the re-migration of unwanted citizens like Ukrainians, Germans, Slovaks and particularly Jews during the 1930s. In October 1938, Poland expatriated every Polish citizen who 'had lost ties to Polishness', a measure directed against ethnic Ukrainians, Germans and particularly Jews – who, in retaliation, were then deported from Germany. Even a still-democratic country like Czechoslovakia claimed the right to forbid the emigration of specialists in certain crafts. Nonetheless, migration continued, sometimes along different routes, as an economic necessity for certain industries and for migrants looking for a better life.

The intertwined logics of ethno-social exclusion, valorization and imperial(ist) aspirations culminated during the First World War. In spring 1939, Germany opened its borders to illegal Polish migrants when Poland refused to provide the agreed contingents of seasonal workers. Soon after the attack on Poland in September 1939, Germany prohibited the same workers from going back. In 1941, a system of forced-labour recruitment based on racial hierarchization was established – with Jews and Poles at the bottom, Czechs, French and Belgians at the top. While German Jews had been pushed to emigrate until 1939, Jews in occupied Poland and Czechoslovakia were interned in ghettos – and thus prevented from migrating. The failure of resettlement schemes proposed by right-wing Zionists and anti-Semites alike since the mid-1930s resulted not in the abandonment of such projects but in their radicalization: beginning in late 1941, the German authorities exterminated Jews from Poland and other occupied territories in extermination camps. About six million Jews together with 13 million other civilians – including seven million Soviet citizens and nearly two million non-Jewish Poles – fell victim to the Nazis' utopian plans. Military projects for the occupied Soviet territories involved death by famine for more than three million people, while the Generalplan Ost, a series of concept papers from 1941/2, foresaw the 'Germanization' of large tracts of territory stretching as far as the Crimea and conceptualized the forced displacement of several million people. Some of Germany's allies also pursued plans for ethnic cleansing: Hungary asserted territorial claims against Slovakia that were backed by Germany in exchange for handing over the territory's Jews, who were subsequently deported to the extermination camps and to Auschwitz. By a similar logic, Bulgaria permitted the deportation of Jews from newly acquired Yugoslavian territory while protecting from persecution those possessing Bulgarian citizenship.

German crimes committed during the war, together with the now non-negotiable identification of political and ethnic nationality, legitimized extensive population relocations. As in the foundation of new Eastern European nation-states after 1918, migrants and exiles themselves participated significantly in shaping these plans.

In 1944, Poland, Ukraine, Lithuania and Belarus agreed on population swaps modelled after similar exchanges between Turkey, Bulgaria and Greece in 1923 – which, while theoretically voluntary, had effectively amounted to treaty-based expulsions. From 1945 to 1949, more than ten million supposed Germans were forcibly resettled from Eastern and South-eastern Europe to East and West Germany. This ethnic cleansing, too, had been internationally sanctioned – at the Yalta and Potsdam conferences – albeit without German participation. Western governments partially withdrew their approval for these resettlements because of the emerging Cold War in spring 1946. In Poland, the removal of ethnic Germans allowed for the settlement not only of Polish 'repatriants' from the East but also of indigenous 'surplus population'. The massive replacements of population came to an end when, in 1950, state-socialist countries enacted new citizenship laws that accorded full citizenship to everyone still residing within their borders. The forced removal of Germans had often separated family members, which resulted in a thin yet continuous flow of out-migration by *Spätaussiedler* – people presumed to be ethnic Germans who had chosen or been forced to remain in the East. Between 1950 and 1959 alone, more than 430,000 *Spätaussiedler* migrated to West Germany. What is less widely appreciated is that, even among them, there was a small but continuous flow of return migration.[3]

Forceful removal of populations: The Ottoman empire and the Armenian Genocide

Onur Yildirim

The demise of the Ottoman empire occupies a special place in the long history of migration in South-eastern Europe. Throughout the 19th century, the secession of Ottoman territories by the newly emerging nation-states brought about a significant volatility in the demographics of 'European Turkey' together with a de facto transfer of properties therein among the communities of various ethnic and religious backgrounds. The double-edged process of displacement and dispossession throughout the region gained momentum especially in the last quarter of the century when Russia, in alliance with Bulgaria, Romania, Serbia and Montenegro, defeated the Ottomans in the Balkans and in the Caucasus. The Russo-Ottoman War of 1877–8 caused many Muslims to migrate to the Ottoman empire from territories ceded to Russia and its allies in the Balkans and Caucasus. A rough estimate of half a million people were forced to abandon their homelands during this turbulent period. Towards the end of the century, the migratory movements in the region were further amplified by the violent response of the Ottoman state to the national awakening among its Armenian populations. The Hamidian massacres of Armenians from 1894 to 1896 was the first step on the part of the Ottoman state to uproot and mass-murder ethnic Armenians across the imperial territories. Although the Young Turk Revolution of 1908 would bring an Indian summer for the non-Muslim populations of the empire, the two consecutive Balkan Wars (1912–13) and the ever-growing tension in the Ottoman–Russian borders produced sporadic displacement of populations throughout the Balkans and Anatolia. While Bulgaria, Serbia and Greece forced their Muslim populations to migrate to the Ottoman territories, the Ottoman government systematically shuffled the Greek and Armenian populations in coastal and border areas of its remaining territories out of security reasons. On the eve of the First

World War, the Ottoman government concluded with Bulgaria and Greece two separate agreements for the voluntary exchange of populations, which were intended for the most part to confirm de facto situations. The outbreak of the Great War caused the upsurge of security concerns and the adoption of violent measures on the part of the Ottoman authorities. The arrest and deportation of many Armenian intellectuals and community leaders on 24 April 1915 heralded the total eradication of the Armenian populations across the imperial lands. The massacres of many Armenian able-bodied males coupled with the deaths of numerous women, children, elderly and feeble Armenians during the deportations – conducted according to the newly adopted Ottoman Law of Expulsion – marked the total annihilation of the Armenians in Anatolia, which was later called the Armenian Genocide. Anatolia was nearly completely cleansed of the Armenians before the de jure dissolution of the Ottoman empire in 1923 and between 800,000 to over one million Armenians are estimated to have lost their lives by then. The majority of the survivors ended up in Syria, Armenia and Greece or joined the treks of Armenian refugees who had been migrating to the Americas since the later decades of the 19th century. The most tragic episode of the region's migration history was followed by another massive displacement of populations that was decided by a combination of war and diplomacy. The Greek-Turkish War of 1920–2, fought on the Anatolian terrain, forms the last chapter of the disintegration of the Ottoman empire. It brought about the flight of nearly one million panic-stricken people of Greek Orthodox faith from the war zone and stirred some mobility among the Muslim populations who lived within the borders of the Greek nation-state. Greece and the newly established Turkish state negotiated the terms of peace under the auspices of the League of Nations at a conference held at Lausanne. The first phase of the Conference was concluded (30 January 1923) with the signing of the Convention for the Compulsory Exchange of Populations between Greece and Turkey, which stipulated the forceful removal of remaining Greek populations from Anatolia (exempting the Greeks of Constantinople) and the Muslim populations from northern Greece and the islands (exempting the Muslims of western Thrace). The war and the ensuing Convention affected the fate of nearly two million people on both sides who contributed greatly to the religious if not ethnic and linguistic homogenization of the two states. While the refugees arrived in Turkey were mainly of rural background, the refugees on the Greek side stemmed primarily from the urban areas and comprised a high number of skilled labourers. The Lausanne Convention was registered in world history as the first internationally sanctioned agreement for the forceful removal of populations in the name of peace and security, which made it a precedent to be referred to and emulated to settle ethnic conflicts across the world.

Refugee migration, internationalization and the Cold War

The necessity to again deal with immense numbers of 'displaced persons' – prisoners of war, forced or slave labourers, survivors of the Holocaust, refugees from Eastern and South-eastern Europe – opened the way to the creation of formal international status and a legal framework for refugees – namely, the UN Refugee Convention of 1951.[4] The Convention is considered more successful than the nomination of a High Commissioner

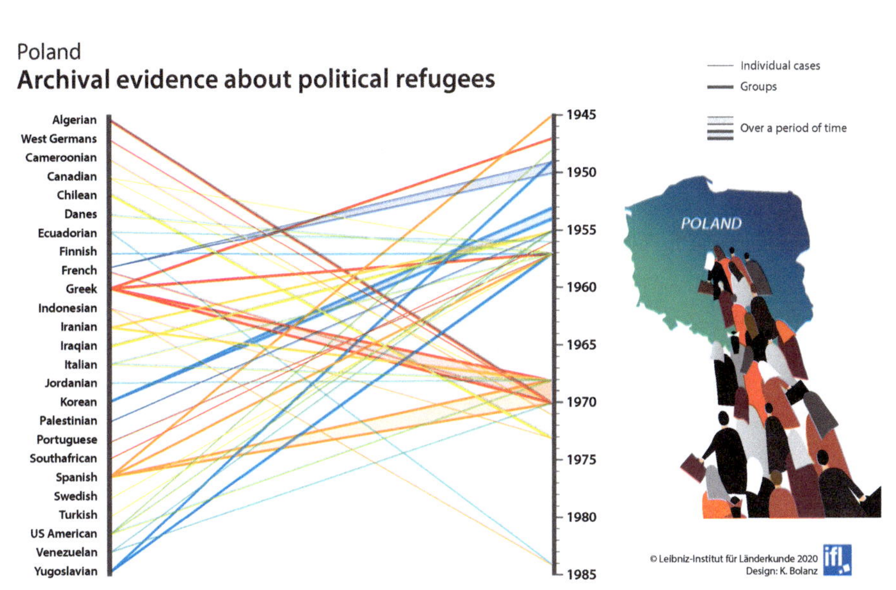

Figure 8.2　Poland: Archival evidence about political refugees.

There is almost no pertinent literature on immigration and flight migration into state-socialist countries. This is all the more deplorable as the ideological structure of the Cold War, with its dichotomy of Western witch-hunt and Eastern repression, indicates that asylum was also sought by persecuted communists. In fact, several state-socialist countries had followed the Soviet example and included quite liberal asylum rights in their constitutions. Unfortunately, published statistics do not exist and archival evidence is scarce. This map can thus only depict mentions of political refugees in archival documentation found during a research residency in Poland in 2017. Nonetheless, we see, particularly when it comes to groups, how proxy wars, US interventions and US-backed regime changes triggered flight migration from certain states into state-socialist countries – sometimes even several times over, and often under particular circumstances. Greek refugees came in considerable numbers after the Civil War of 1946/7 and after military putsches. The Koreans of the early 1950s were not refugees but war orphans sent to the Eastern bloc for safeguarding. Spanish Civil War refugees consisted of several smaller groups declared undesirable by the French authorities. Yugoslavians were a special case, as refugees *from* an officially socialist state. Most of them fled periodic Party cleansings resulting from the reorientation of Titoism to close cooperation with capitalist countries. Although the state-socialist stance on asylum was focused on repatriation, communist refugees were quickly integrated: already in the 1950s, the governments provided approved newspapers and radio programmes in their mother tongues, and they even benefited from augmented pensions for Party members. The accommodation of refugees was thus, in most cases, an act of proletarian solidarity. Nonetheless, their return was intended as soon as the situation and the state of the war between the classes allowed or necessitated.

for Refugees in 1921 or the failed Évian Conference of 1938, although the Soviet Union, whose predecessor – Soviet Russia – had been the first state to include a right to asylum in its constitution (in 1921), and its satellites in Eastern Europe chose to not sign the Convention. In fact, the Convention identified displaced persons and refugees as a result not only of fascism and Nazism but of Stalinism as well. It stressed the integration of refugees rather than the facilitation of their returning home, as the Soviets had wanted. After its expansion in 1967, the Convention grew into a viable if ambiguous and fragile basis for granting asylum in the modern world outside state socialism. It also established refugee migration as a topic under international law.

The Cold War not only produced massive waves of refugees but also increased the political significance of dealing with them. In 1947–9, about 100,000 combatants fled after the defeat of communist forces in the Greek Civil War and were distributed among the socialist states. In 1953, several thousand war orphans from North Korea were accommodated in Poland, Czechoslovakia and other socialist states for several years. Stepping up to the challenge, Western countries such as the United States and Sweden soon organized adoption campaigns for war orphans from South Korea. In 1956, the Soviet invasion of Hungary provoked the flight of about 200,000 people to Austria, Switzerland and West Germany. About the same number followed from Czechoslovakia after its invasion by Warsaw Pact troops in 1968. Although these refugees were welcomed as proof for the superiority of Western society, not all of them were determined anti-communists: a considerable number returned after the stabilization of the regimes at home.

In most European countries, cross-border migration gradually re-established itself. However, neither Europe nor the world returned to a policy of free movement as had been in effect until the late 19th century. Western industrialized nations like France, Germany, Belgium and the Netherlands signed recruitment agreements with some countries that had traditionally supplied workforces and with some new ones. Major labour suppliers were Italy (agreement with France in 1947, Belgium 1946, the Netherlands 1948, Germany 1955); Turkey (Germany 1961, Belgium 1964, France 1965); and Yugoslavia (the Netherlands 1964, France 1965, Germany 1968, Belgium 1970). As in the interwar period, the effect of these agreements was ambiguous: they guaranteed certain standards in work conditions, but they also gave the state the right to select who was allowed to migrate. In the FRG (West Germany) before the 1960s, the regulations even allowed for the social and physical isolation of 'guest workers' (*Gastarbeiter*).

While the resurrection of the capitalist economies in the West led to a rapid renewal of foreign-labour recruitment, the state-socialist countries closed their borders – opting for self-sufficient economies and development. Western governments in turn discouraged migration or even visits to state-socialist countries until the 1960s. Borders in this divided Europe world were, however, not impenetrable: even in Stalinist times, there had been cases of immigration into the Eastern bloc not only by re-migrants but also by visiting young communists and socialists who had fallen in love with locals. There was also a certain amount of exchange of specialists for industrial reconstruction – particularly between the West and Poland. During the 1960s, several socialist states agreed to facilitate local cross-border traffic, which enabled commuting as well as temporary migration. In 1968, Poland renewed an interwar cooperation with Italian car manufacturer Fiat, which included receiving equipment and specialists from Turin. Since 1971, the *Sovet ekonomičeskoj vzaimopomošči* (Council for Mutual Economic Assistance – COMECON) had regulated the exchange of labour between socialist brother states. Numbers are difficult to come by, as no statistics were officially published, and even archival evidence is scarce. However, we know that Czechoslovakia employed Bulgarian farm workers after 1947 and concluded contracts on labour recruitment with Yugoslavia and Turkey in the 1970s. In the GDR (East Germany), which was the main receiving state-socialist country for foreign labour, about 60,000–70,000 workers from Poland, Hungary, Bulgaria and Yugoslavia as well as individually recruited Turks were employed by the end of the 1970s. Since the 1960s, socialist countries had also increasingly invited students and apprentices from the Global South and hosted contract workers from Vietnam and Cuba. According to UN data, the total number of migrants in Eastern Europe including the western parts of the USSR was nearly seven million in 1960, and six million in 1975. In a more informal manner, betterment migration even resumed on East–West routes. Poles entering Yugoslavia on tourist visas, for example, travelled temporarily to Austria and Germany for work.

Détente politics after the late 1960s brought an intensification of economic and cultural exchange and a progressive integration of state-socialist countries into the structures of globalization, which again sparked individual betterment migration. But although borders were crossed in both directions increasingly often, a liberal migration regime such as that within the European Economic Community and the parallel waiving of visa requirements within the COMECON states did not develop between the blocs. The perseverance of ethnic German nationalism, however, facilitated betterment migration for those capable of documenting any kind of ethnic-German heritage. Particularly in Poland under martial law in the early 1980s – which was also a time of severe economic crisis – many Poles eager to leave made use of this loophole.

The fall of European state socialism in 1989–91 also tore down a border regime that had successfully curbed East–West migration – not necessarily to the delight of Western migration agencies, who now feared an unhindered influx of masses of unwanted immigrants. The dissolution of the Soviet Union prolonged the in-flow of ethnic Germans, as descendants of Germans deported by Stalin now had privileged access to residency and citizenship. The same provisions concerned Soviet Jews, who were granted immediate German residency in 1991. But as the Cold War ended, Germany abolished such ethnic privileges in 1993.

Simultaneously, the role of Eastern Europe gradually changed from a region mainly of outmigration into a migration destination. After the ratification of the Schengen Accords by Poland, Czechia, Slovakia and Hungary, migration from them into other Schengen states became completely free. With this, these countries became more attractive for migrants and refugees from the Global South, thus making them immigration countries – a development these governments and societies were not necessarily prepared for. At the same time, the task of strengthening the EU's eastern borders against unwanted immigration was transferred to them. The rise of right-wing populist politics in Poland and Hungary is one of the unbalanced reactions to the role assigned to these countries, as well as to perceived domination by the EU in general. At the same time, the shift of moral panic from

Eastern European to Muslim immigration has transformed the migration of Eastern Europeans to the West into an unquestioned normality.

Structures and actors

Modern migration is produced by demographic, economic and sometimes political imbalances in an increasingly entangled world. Nonetheless, it would be insufficient to explain mass betterment migration solely as a result of push-and-pull factors – poverty and oppression vs. wealth and liberty – or as a secondary effect of globalization. Motives for migration are as diverse and complex as itineraries, with external agencies certainly playing significant roles in these movements; however, migrants themselves have been their constituent agents as well. The North Atlantic migration system of the late 19th century, for example, relied in equal measure on recruitment strategies operated by industrialists and landowners as on communications between migrants and their peers at home: *c.* 1900, most Poles, Slovaks and Hungarians who worked in Pennsylvanian factories were recruited by countrymen/women who had already settled in. Additionally, aggressive, and sometimes misleading, marketing practices engaged in by travel agents incited people to migrate who had hitherto not considered that an option.

With the exodus of workforces into the cities and the exportation of cheaper cash crops from North America, the grand estates of Eastern Prussia increasingly depended on seasonal migration from Eastern Europe. This migration not only facilitated the survival of pre-modern extensive farming but also transformed subsistence economies in Galicia and elsewhere. Coal mining and iron production in Alsace-Lorraine, the Ruhr area and the Americas needed workforces that were not easily found nearby. Migrants from the East thus became an integral part of the proletariat that made the rise of heavy industry possible, in Europe and abroad: Chicago became the second largest 'Polish' city *c.* 1900; in Cleveland and Pittsburgh, Poles (and Slovaks) constituted about one third of the workforce in the iron and steel industries.

Economic contributions by Eastern migrants to national economies did not stop there. In Paris and New York, Jewish migrants worked as low-level labourers in haute couture and ready-made fashion houses like Chanel – sometimes moving between the two cities. They founded the hat-making industry and vastly expanded the fur trade in Paris, London and New York. Russian refugees in the 1920s participated in the rise of the French automotive industry, both as factory workers and as taxi drivers. Bohemian and Moravian glass blowers and glass workers were sought-after specialists in Western Europe and in South America.

Long-term and seasonal migration also transformed areas of origin in multiple ways. It exposed local subsistence economies to the capitalist global market and its goods: remittances from migrants could constitute 80 per cent or more of the overall income in many a Galician village and introduced commodity-based lifestyle options. The return of 'enlightened' migrants endangered traditional, patriarchal structures and opened such villages up to an ambiguous modernity. The resulting social and economic crises in turn affected oppositional thought in the West, be it among Eastern European intellectual exiles or their Western peers such as Karl Marx. Simultaneously, the experience of migration shaped and strengthened an ethno-national identity essential for founding and funding national liberation movements.

Structures were not only filled with individual migrants, they were also created by them. Migrants from Eastern Europe participated in the European expansion, directly and indirectly shaping the settlements, cities and countries they lived in. As the 'lowest' of European migrants, they often became canvasses onto which the shape of the nations into which they integrated could be drawn. Their presence also legitimized the extension of state technologies to regulate migration – particularly during the emergence of the welfare state and the 'nationalization of the masses' in the late 19th century, which inspired the sharpening of categories like resident, seasonal migrant, refugee and undocumented that defined access to rights and protection and the degree of control the individual was subjected to.

This drive for comprehensive categorization and control by state and civil-society actors should not obscure the fact that migrants did not and do not always behave in the way in which they are supposed to. They engaged in the establishment of transnational practices and networks that, in their endeavour to cope with the always difficult status of being a migrant, misused, circumvented, evaded or directly challenged the measures implemented to keep both them and migration in general in check. This included the already-mentioned autonomous recruitment of workers but also the exchange of (not always truthful) information, remittances, and the provision of facilities and services ranging from accommodation or weighted job opportunities, as in the Parisian migrant *Bourse du Travail*, to the procurement of legitimizing papers or spouses – be they indigenous or from the home country.

In fact, this migrant inventiveness was one of the driving motives for the development of increasingly effective instruments of migration control: passports, recruitment agreements, quota systems regulating who could migrate, and integration policies. On the other hand, migrant practices reinforced distinct nationalizing tendencies as much as they contradicted them: Migrants transnationalized their ethnic nations by organizing emigration and return migration, setting up specific facilities and shops, printing newspapers in their language and celebrating national holidays. In most cases, the migrants would shape their identities and behaviour as a contingent mixture of where they came from, where they were and how they positioned themselves socially and spatially. In official contexts, they shaped 'paper identities' corresponding to the administrative exigencies of the situation they found themselves in or the goal they wanted to achieve. In some cases, migrant and official deviations converged: in the 1920s, categorization as a Russian refugee was not only claimed by Russians fleeing the Civil War but also by Jewish and occasionally gentile migrants from the successor states finding it difficult to get new papers from nationalist consulate officials. The Parisian Office des Réfugiés Russes complied, as a greater number of clients enlarged its significance and funding. In the 1960s and 70s, migrants from state-socialist Poland rejected the refugee status imposed on them by Western authorities and instead worked undocumented in order to be able to return home. Obviously, migration from or in Eastern Europe, as any significant social phenomenon, results from and happens in a complex interaction between structures, discourses and practices.

Contexts, representations and effects

We have indicated that migration into and out of Eastern Europe cannot easily be shoehorned into simplistic unidirectional and unambiguous categories. However, categorical simplifications are essential to discourses on migration. Although discourse never translates into reality directly, it coalesces in specifications and variations of regimes – and it exerts influence on practices. Discourses form the ground on which conceptual frameworks are developed that re-affect social phenomena by transforming them into categories destined to identify, control and manage real people. These categories are eventually translated into social realities, but they are also constantly renegotiated, transformed or evaded by the actors and agencies involved. In the period under consideration, discourses shaped the conditions encouraging migration; the creation of a shared, republican European and North American identification; and the expansion of state interference in matters affecting the general population, like mobility control and identification.

From heroes to troublemakers

It is astonishing to see the extent to which discourses about Eastern migrants have changed over the two hundred years we are dealing with. Until the 1860s, these migrants were represented mostly positively. In a predominantly republican and later democratic discourse in the North Atlantic region, Poles after the partitions of 1772–95 as well as dissidents and exiles from the Russian empire were considered comrades in the fight for a reformed if not revolutionized Europe – comrades who had actually suffered the worst of Europe's oppressive regimes. Some emigrants became transnationally active members of European and North Atlantic intellectual circles: in 1776, Tadeusz Kościuszko, a descendant of Polish gentry who had been influenced by the French Enlightenment during his studies, decided to join the North American fight for independence. He later returned to Poland, where he staged an uprising against the Second Partition. The Russian Mikhail Bakunin participated in the Dresden uprising of 1848 together with Richard Wagner and became Karl Marx's main opponent in the First International. The Magyar Lajos Kossúth co-founded a European Democratic Society in London in 1852. The Czechs Tomáš Garrigue Masaryk and his pupil Edvard Beneš, as well as the Poles Roman Dmowski and Józef Piłsudzki, used their intellectual networks (as well as the creation of armed legions against the Central Powers) to successfully promote independence after the First World War.

After the November Uprising of 1830/1, no fewer than 50,000 Polish insurgents left Russian territory and found refuge in Prussia and Austria. Even before the uprising, the designated head of a renewed state, Adam Czartoryski, had secured French and British support in case of failure. So, it came as no surprise that the French government was urged by republican public opinion to invite the insurgents to come to France. In many of the German towns the émigrés passed through, they were celebrated and welcomed as republican comrades and heroes of a common cause; the same was true, at least initially, for the French cities where they were accommodated. The presence of these refugees caused an upswing of national, republican and democratic sentiment, which again was a strong incentive to reforms in Western countries that remained monarchies. Europe as a whole began to represent itself as the superior alternative to apparent Russian despotism. This discourse affected even outspoken critics of Western bourgeois society: around 1848, Friedrich Engels argued that Magyars and Poles had not only the right but were even obliged to be nationalist. Similarly, Russian anarchists and revolutionary populists were courted icons among radical European activists in the 1870s and 80s.

The usual depiction of Polish emigration in 1831 as a triumphal procession of the Polish nation through German territories and into France, however, was at least in part a mythologization. The so-called Great Emigration comprised only about 10,000 individuals who, as insurgent officials and officers, were either not affected by or unwilling to accept an amnesty granted by the tsar. About 40,000 refugees chose to return home; many of them would later participate in the colonization of Siberia and the Caucasus. Prussia and other German states – all monarchies – were well aware that republican aspirations could be kindled by the transit of the refuges, so they split the 10,000 into smaller groups and sent them on mandatory routes to the French border. The French government was far from delighted with their arrival as well: it granted regular pay as for an allied army, but only on condition that the exiles agreed to be accommodated in barrack camps far from the capital. Nonetheless, the elite of the Polish diaspora found their way to Paris and managed to keep the 'Polish question' on the agenda of European political discourse. Czech, Hungarian and Romanian exiles would follow their example. A similar pattern was used after the January uprising in 1863. By then, however, the situation had fundamentally changed.

The Revolutions of 1848; the foundation of the International Workers Association in 1864; the waves of strikes beginning in the 1860s; and the anarchist assaults of the 1880–90s in Italy, Russia, France, Britain and the United States made it abundantly clear that radical change was popular not only in a supposedly backwards East. France and Britain, which had granted subsidies to the arriving Polish insurgents in 1863, thus now suspected them – along with Russian education and economic migrants – to be agents of anarchist and communist subversion. Privileges for Eastern political refugees would be revoked immediately when they became involved with indigenous radical movements. The fact that immigrants participated in these endeavours should have been proof of their successful integration into the national proletariat, but it was often recast so as to identify subversion as the work of foreigners. It was also used to intensify state control over migrants: in 1901, Leon Czolgosz, an anarchist with Polish parents, assassinated US president William McKinley. Although Czolgosz was a born US citizen, the assassination legitimized extensive measures against Eastern European, Italian and poor immigrants in 1905. Eastern immigration also triggered anti-Semitic moral panics. While in 1881, Jewish migrants fleeing from the East were represented as victims in need of help, the rise of

North Atlantic anti-Semitism since the 1890s was occasionally fostered if not inspired by the influx of poor Jewish migrants – who, at the same time, became projection screens for local Jewish intellectuals in debates about renewed Jewish authenticity or complete assimilation.

Moral panics about migration grew to particular proportions in the German Reich, with its specific convergence of out- and in-migration. They centred on a fear of hostile foreigners watering down a national identity and culture already threatened by the emigration of valuable nationals. In 1886, a law on rural settlement aimed to [re]germanize rural territories in the East afflicted by the exodus of German farmworkers to the West. Polish nationalists responded by buying formerly German land and distributing it among Polish peasants. Both measures, together with systematic and informal discrimination against 'Poles', created a national consciousness that most peasants and workers had not yet exhibited. After a school strike against compulsory German lessons in the Poznań region and with an eye on established Polish-speaking communities in the Ruhr valley, the Prussian government became increasingly suspicious of Eastern European migrants in general. Misgivings intensified after the first Russian Revolution in 1905 and the exodus of left-wing activists and Jews following its suppression in 1906/7. Defending Germany against these imagined threats resulted in an innovation: the German Reich and the United States were among the first states to introduce not only the obligation to carry a passport when crossing borders but also, for seasonal workers from the East, to carry standardized identifying documents at all times. Identity papers would become mandatory for foreigners in all warring countries after 1914, and this requirement would soon afterwards be extended to all nationals in the interwar period and again after 1945.

In the 1920s, the stabilization of the Soviet regime offered the opportunity to unleash a repressive wave against the North American Left, including the deportation of 173 Russian anarchists to the Soviet Russian border. Together with a nationalist wave, this 'Red Scare' helped to install the quota system. At the same time, the existence and accommodation of refugees – most notably, the aforementioned 1–2 million Russian refugees in the 1920s – seemed to prove the moral and political superiority of Western Europe's political order. The rejection of the UN Convention on Refugees of 1951 by the state-socialist bloc reinforced this representation, while the depiction of refugees became ambiguous on both sides of the bloc divide. 'Defectors' and refugees legitimized the given domestic social, economic and political order, while the fear of infiltration by covert agents made them a target of suspicion. The right to asylum gradually lost its importance in the years of détente and was called into question when, from the 1980s onwards, it was increasingly used by war, economic and other refugees for whom it had not been designed.

The politicization of asylum during the Cold War also affected migrants who initially were far from embracing Western superiority: with the gradual opening of borders even between the two blocs in the 1960s and 70s, the exchange of education migrants and artists increased between East and West. In 1965, beat poet and underground activist Allen Ginsberg visited Moscow and Prague, where he became *Král Majálesu* ('King of May') during a short-lived student festival but was arrested for homosexual depravity soon after. Some exiles, like Czech jazz musicians Jan Hammer and Miroslav Vitouš, were in the

United States on scholarships in 1968 and preferred to become leading figures in the emerging North American Jazz Rock scene. In the early 1970s, Paul Wilson, a Canadian university drop-out in Prague, participated in the developing musical underground. Ginsberg and Wilson effectively joined the anti-communist cause after their return to the Americas (although with an anti-authoritarian twist), while Welsh hippie John Porter joined the Polish avant-garde rock scene in 1976 and stayed there. On the other hand, illegal seasonal migrants from Poland into Austria or Germany were pressed to apply for asylum even though they explicitly intended to return to their socialist home countries.

In some respects, the virtually impassable fortified borders between the two Germanies, between the Baltic Soviet states and Finland, between Hungary and Austria and in the Balkans reaffirmed the closure of borders and the tightening of border regimes since the 19th century as technological expressions of growing state interference in migration. Taking the view of *longue durée*, the territorial regime in Europe and the North Atlantic world included increasing state control over foreigners and their movements, but also – via the introduction of standardized identity papers – over the general population. The abolition of 'internal' borders was complemented by the solidification of external borders and a sharper differentiation between citizens and aliens, particularly with regard to the expansion of the welfare state to include more and more members of the working classes. In Europe, but to a lesser degree in the Americas, these processes were often catalysed by debates about Eastern European migrants.

Migration and national health

Another panic tied to Eastern immigration was the fear of epidemics, which had been present in European societies at least since the Black Death of the 14th century and was revived in medical discourses in the 19th century.[5] As bacteriology prevailed as the dominant discourse to explain the spread of contagious diseases, the East was quickly diagnosed as a substantial source of pathogens. Interestingly, the isolation of Eastern European migrants in the context of disease control began as a protective measure: when a local outbreak of yellow fever in Buenos Aires in 1851/2 affected Finnish and Russian sailors more severely than the already adapted local population, German and Austrian observers recommended quarantine for the sailors' protection. This quarantine – approved by Swedish, Russian, Austrian and Hamburg authorities – mutated into a compulsory measure applied to all immigrants into Argentina in 1911, when migrants from Eastern Europe were considered to be carriers of typhus and spotted fever. Similar measures were called for by the US Army in the mid-1840s but were not put into practice until fifty years later. Beginning in 1892, the United States converted Ellis Island (New York) into a quarantine station for the medical, psychological and educational inspection of immigrants. In Germany, the identification of disease with Eastern Europe was more direct: Robert Koch, founding father of bacteriology, developed his concepts with special regard to Eastern Europe. He visited the Russian empire several times and established close contacts with local public health officers. Of particular concern were diseases that had been more or less absent in Western Europe such as typhus, cholera and spotted fever. Koch identified specific sections of the population as the main sources of contagion – particularly, poor Jewish communities. Beginning in the early 1880s, Eastern and particularly Jewish migration was thus considered not only a social and political but also a medical problem – especially after a cholera outbreak in Hamburg in 1892 had been triggered by Eastern migrants. After 1910, Germany intensified border controls, systematically screening for infectious diseases. The discourse identifying (Eastern) migration with disease was certainly taken to its extremes in medical discourse in Germany, but it was not a German monopoly: Louis Pasteur followed a very similar path in France; and Russian, Austro-Hungarian and Chinese hygienists were prominent at the International Hygiene Exhibition in Dresden in 1911.

The identification of migrating people as carriers of infectious diseases also played a role in the ghettoization of Jews under the German occupation of Poland after 1939 and the destruction of the Warsaw Ghetto in 1941. Both were driven by arguments of hygiene, indicated by the original designation of the ghetto as a *Seuchensperrgebiet* ('quarantine zone'). Illegal crossings of borders between the ghetto and the 'Aryan' districts were identified as a hygiene problem that ultimately was to be solved by annihilating the ghetto population. After the war, German deportees were screened for infectious diseases.

Transnational nationalization: The reordering of migration and colonization after 1918

The most obvious effect of the end of the First World War was that the fragmentation of East Central and South-eastern Europe into nation-states meant that formerly internal migration routes now crossed borders – while in Poland, with its composition of parts of three empires, former state borders were abolished. As emerging nation-states and national economies, these polities took a keen interest in measures regulating and channelling migration. The scope of the New Order and its being a result of a devastating war stimulated efforts for conflict prevention and peaceful management that included migration politics via the International Labour Organization (ILO). As a branch of the League of Nations and later the UN, the ILO standardized employment contracts and thus prevented overexploitation. It also distributed Russian refugees to countries willing to welcome them as permanent citizens. Together, these intertwining processes of nationalization and internationalization provided for a multilayered process of juridification that affected and was affected by migrants from the East.

The nationalization of societies that began in the late 19th century had affected Eastern Europe to a similar degree to Western European and transatlantic countries, although in sometimes reversed forms. Since the late 19th century, Polish, Hungarian and Czech/Slovak civil society actors had engaged in social and cultural assistance initiatives that helped migrants but were also designed to imbue them with national or ethno-national identities. In other words, they transnationalized the nation by transforming individual migrants into an organized diaspora – which, in turn, played a crucial financial and political role in the formation of nations and the founding of nation-states in East Central Europe in 1918. In a similar manner, Russian revolutionary exiles were essential for the survival of the movement in Russia and for the escalation of the revolt there up until the

October coup of 1917. In this nationalizing process, migrants were identified as sometimes particularly valuable components of the sending nation, i.e. as citizens abroad. This was even the case for Russian refugees whose controlled return was unsuccessfully demanded by the Soviet government before they were denaturalized in December 1921.

But these new polities not only sought to bind their nationals to the finally acquired nation state, they also endeavoured to get a grip on emigration. For the capitalist successor states in East Central Europe, the possible benefits were numerous: out-migration fostered an exchange of students and workers and provided the necessary administrative and technical elites. Emigration could unload parts of the population that were considered an obstacle for socio-economic and national restructuring – the rural surplus population and insufficiently integrated minorities, for example. Members of the titular nations could serve as outposts of their respective states.

After 1919, the new regimes signed bilateral treaties with countries like Germany, Austria and France. Austria's treaties with Hungary and Yugoslavia regulated international movements that until then had been internal, while Poland's agreement with Germany placed formerly spontaneous migration under state tutelage. Since the successor states had no colonies, migration into developing countries – particularly, in South America – seemed tempting. Already, early Zionists had discussed the possibility of erecting a Jewish state in non-civilized parts of Argentina. The new nation-states hoped that emigration to the Global South would not only provide areas for the settlement of rural surplus populations but also access to markets and natural resources. Non-government organizations often played an important part in this. In Poland, the 1924-founded *Liga Morska i Rzeczna* (Maritime and River League; after 1930, the *Liga Morska i Kolonialna* (Maritime and Colonial League)) became one of the largest Polish mass organizations and an important agent in migration overseas. Czechoslovakia also supported seasonal and permanent migration across the ocean, but retained the right to exclude skilled specialists from emigrating at all. Hopes of informally extending national territory through these settlers, however, were soon disappointed: the latter showed no interest in serving the aspirations of distant governments. Shifts to the nationalist right – e.g. in Brazil under Getúlio Vargas – led to the denunciation of Polish settlers' hitherto applauded self-sufficiency. Nonetheless, Eastern European migrants, including Jews, were still welcomed in South America: in 1937, Poland concluded a migration agreement with Bolivia; and at the Évian conference in 1938, only the Dominican Republic and Costa Rica were willing to accept a larger number of Jewish refugees – albeit in an obvious effort to 'whiten' their populations.

The intervention of state and international agencies safeguarded migrants from overex-ploitation or at least granted them consular and sometimes social or moral assistance. However, it also standardized migration procedures, rendering autonomous migration increasingly difficult, and enabled the selection of people entitled to migrate in ways that had not been possible before. In France, migrants had no freedom of movement and were often forbidden to take up residence or even employment in Paris. Similar restrictions were placed on mobility in Germany, where all workers from the East (with the exception of Czechs) had to leave the country for the winter. Also, the safeguard against overex-ploitation was tenuous at best, as state-induced betterment migration also stipulated that the migrant had to remain in the agreed job even if the conditions proved intolerable.

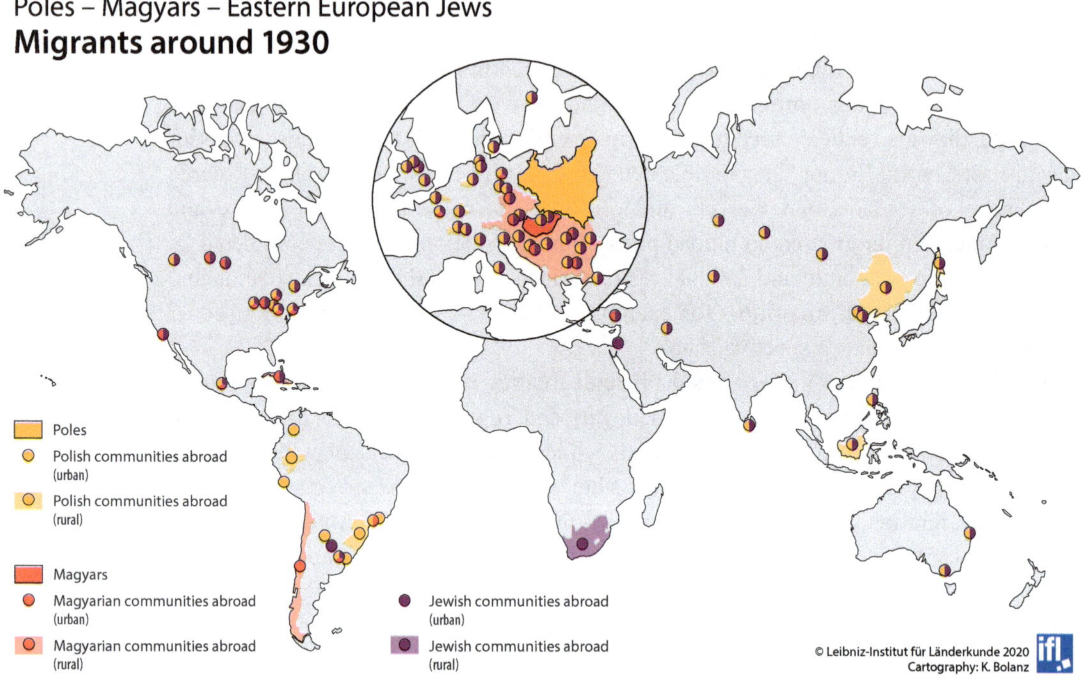

Figure 8.3 Migrants around 1930.

Eastern European migrants formed larger or smaller communities nearly everywhere in the world. In order to ascertain a certain degree of clarity, this map singles out (Catholic) Poles, Magyars and Jews from Eastern Europe, and shows roughly where in the world they settled in significant numbers. It does not show the size of these communities, as data is scarce. As we see, migrants of different denominations often settled in the same regions, where sometimes they interacted quite intensely. There are, however, differences between the various ethno-confessional groups. These were related to chance and opportunities created by non-governmental bodies and/or receiving countries – but also to the external processes of nation building, like early Jewish immigration into Palestine. It is important to remember, however, that these communities were neither completely isolated from their new environments nor cut off from their regions of origin: migrants kept close ties to their former homes, and migrated between communities and between the latter and their birthplaces. The map thus represents a rough sketch of the 'mental maps' that migrants and their fellow countrymen at home, from these three denominations, created in the 19th and early 20th century.

State-induced migration: Refugees, deportees and defectors

As mentioned earlier, Eastern Europeans were among the earliest modern political refugees. The institutionalization of modern refugeedom – with its complex interplay between governments, refugees and their public and social representation – also had strong roots in Eastern Europe: in 1881, the arrival of tens of thousands of Russian and Romanian Jews in border towns like Brody initiated the first modern European refugee crisis and established a new concept of refugees. As Hannah Arendt put it, until that point, a refugee had been a person evading persecution for something he/she had done. From then on, refugees were persons persecuted for something they supposedly *were*. An element of the *ancien régime* remained, however: providing support for these new refugees/migrants was left almost entirely to their peers, who in this case were not political comrades but transnationally active co-religionists. Jewish committees and congregations thus negotiated the distribution of the refugees/migrants with local and national administrations who would not intervene of their own accord. The same was true for the massive displacements that took place during the First World War: in Belgium, France and Russia, expelled and deported persons were taken care of not by official agencies but by private actors, mostly motivated by religious charity. The fact that it was mainly people from the middle and upper classes who took care of deported persons and prisoners of war who were originally from the working classes and peasant families was an additional factor in the nationalization of societies that had begun in the late 19th century. This was even the case in Russia, where the *Zemgor*,[6] a constitutionalist association of townships and rural communities, organized support for the deported and thus gained considerable social and political agency. Unsurprisingly, the *Zemgor* became one of the nuclei of the provisional government after the Russian Revolution of February 1917 – with its head, Prince Lvov, becoming the prime minister of post-imperial Russia.

The situation changed with the already-mentioned massive wave of refugees fleeing Russia after the October Revolution and the ensuing Civil War that raged until 1921. The main attribute of the Russian émigrés was that they were victims of an emerging, radicalizing ideological conflict. As former opponents of Bolshevism and now its apparent victims, these refugees from Russia were of immense political, propagandistic and – in view of French and British aspirations to recruit new forces against the Soviets until 1924 – even military value. Many were administratively, militarily or professionally skilled, and so they were in demand in several national economies including the Soviet one. After the Soviets' attempt to negotiate the controlled return of these refugees failed, the Bolsheviks made good on their threat to expatriate them. Their statelessness was particularly problematic in a world that had adopted the modern concept of state citizenship as the sole basis of access to social and political rights, a concept that had been introduced by the French Revolution in 1789 and had gained momentum as Europe developed modern nation-states with absolute sovereignty over access to citizenship and its associated rights.

As national aspirations and expansionism had led to brutal global war in 1914, the postwar intention was to temper the nationalization of territorial, social and political regimes by integrating nation-states into the League of Nations and its subordinate agencies. One of these agencies was the High Commissioner for Refugees (HCR), an independent office created in 1921 and headed by the renowned Norwegian scientist and explorer Fridtjof Nansen. Nansen's activities were concerned with Eastern Europe on several levels. Immediately after his appointment as High Commissioner, he tried to gain international support for the victims of the 1921–2 famine in Russia. With the de facto expatriation of Russian refugees and the displacement of Armenian survivors of the Turkish genocide of 1915, the HCR had to deal with 1–2 million stateless persons whose return home was inconceivable. As any effort to locate them had to deal with their lack of civil rights, Nansen's office strove to create an internationally accepted legal status for refugees. For this endeavour, it employed a number of French, British and Russian specialists in international law also involved in (mostly religious) humanitarianism. In essence, refugee status was an effort to banish the ghosts produced by modern nation statehood through positive, i.e. man-made and nationally enacted law. Although it proved conceptually impossible to overcome the principle of state sovereignty, the HCR did succeed in creating a travel document that enabled the refugees to look for a new life elsewhere – with the support of the ILO.

The Nazi genocide perpetrated against Jews and 'gypsies' was undeniably unique, but it was nonetheless entangled in global contexts. Ethnic cleansing had already reached unprecedented levels both during and after the First World War. The dissolution of the Ottoman empire and the foundation of Turkey as a modern nation-state had been accompanied by the first modern genocide – against the Armenians – and population exchanges, benign on paper but in fact forced, between Turkey, Bulgaria and Greece. The systematic mass murder of the 'genetically challenged' and later of Jews, Sinti and Roma in the Third Reich had as much do with eugenics, racism and anti-Semitism – which in themselves were transnational concepts – as it did with modern technologies of migration control, social and economic planning. Also, Nazi policies in Eastern Europe mirrored and radicalized colonial policies of the 19th and early 20th centuries in more than one sense. In some ways, German expansionist politics after 1914 and their radicalization after 1939 were a re-creation of an imperial(ist) order with the technological, administrative and discursive means of the modern republican (although not democratic) nation-state. The German project of creating a socio-economically and biologically perfected Europe under German rule and with a supposedly German race at the pinnacle ultimately collapsed irreversibly after the war, as ethnic Germans were deported almost completely from Eastern and South-eastern Europe. The expulsion and forced resettlement of these ethnic Germans was an international undertaking, agreed upon (at least in principle) at the Allied conferences in Yalta and Potsdam. However, it was inscribed in the same discourses of social and economic engineering as the Nazi plan, with the state-socialist governments acting as the consummators of a historical process finally reaching its conclusion in the (socialist) nation-state.

We have already mentioned that the practice of systematic labour recruitment from abroad resumed in Western countries after 1945, while the bloc divide put a provisional end to the Eastern branch of the North Atlantic migration system. The reticence of state socialism vis-à-vis migration was not merely a result of oppressive politics: socialist theory presumed that socialism rendered betterment migration – correctly understood as a product of social and economic inequality – unnecessary. Nonetheless, workers were desperately needed in countries which had suffered German occupation, mass murder and the more or less systematic destruction of infrastructure. Also, particularly in Poland the expulsion of the German population had left gaps that could not always be filled by re-settlers from the western Soviet republics. Instead of promoting emigration, the Polish

People's Republic and, to a lesser degree, the Czechoslovak Socialist Republic thus encouraged the return of earlier betterment migrants who had found work (and acquired skills) in the Ruhr area or eastern France during forced labour in German factories. As mentioned earlier, from the 1960s onwards socialist countries also relied increasingly on transnational or even imported labour. The end of state socialism in the last two decades of the 20th century seemed to reinstate the more liberal migration regime that had existed before the world wars, but with a twist: the United States reformed its quota system, becoming increasingly restrictive towards immigration (now almost exclusively from Asia and, later, the Global South generally). At the same time, Eastern Europe, now divided between an eastern part affiliated with Russia and a western part integrated into an enlarging EU, resumed labour-related and educational migration while simultaneously importing specific segments of labour migrants – for example, in a kind of continuation of the labour-recruitment policy of socialist times, Poland now imports (Catholic) labour migrants from the Philippines. The extension of a new, internally more liberal order through the eastward expansion of the EU and its challenge through the Russian attack against Ukraine have, again, produced a wave of refugees that, as of 2022, substantiates claims of moral superiority of the North Atlantic world – now including East Central Europe. The peculiar Janus head of European migration policies between integrative nation building and external closure, particularly when it comes to the European frontiers in the Mediterranean and the EU's eastern flank, has assisted the rise of right-wing populist movements in Poland, Hungary and now Italy. Although a rejection of right-wing populism appears to be European common sense, such dismissal is just as ambiguous as the European migration regime: on the one hand, its apparent exclusionism seems to challenge European discourses of unity, intercultural openness and a welcoming culture for migrants and refugees; on the other, its rigidity against (Muslim) immigration ensures a much sought-after impermeability required by the eastern borders of 'fortress Europe'.

Concluding remarks

Migration was and is an integral part of Eastern Europe's global entanglement. The complex history of migrations into and from the East of the continent shows that emigration cannot simply be identified as an expression of backwardness, poverty or isolation. Migrants from the East were embedded in and played intrinsic roles in European and North Atlantic – sometimes, even global – political, social and economic developments: the advent of modern nation-states, republicanism and socialism, the colonization of the Global South and the rise of North American industry. The resulting transnationalization of social, cultural and economic practices was in no way restricted to generically transnational actors like intellectuals, artists or other social elites, but encompassed – in socially specific ways – migrants of all social classes and denominations. Migrants served as objects of political, administrative and hygiene agendas; some of them actually participated in their construction. Even forced migrations and genocide during the world wars, which ended in the nearly complete removal of the ethnic German population from Eastern Europe, should not be seen as rooted in this region's incapability to properly modernize. They should, rather, be understood as an incompatibility of its basically integrative multiethnic societies with a concept of ethnic nation that was imported from the West and engendered consequences as murderous as those of colonialism. Migration and migrational aspirations and their political instrumentalization occurred even during the division of Europe, as asylum became firmly established as a politically legitimizing concept on both sides of the 'Iron Curtain'. Labour-related migration from East to West was impeded – soon to be replaced by reoriented, treaty-based migration systems. Since the present victory of Western liberalism and capitalism, the East–West avenues have reopened while the tension between national self-assertion and international respectively intercultural integration has generated right-wing populist responses to migration with results that are not yet clear. The success of right-wing populism in Austria, the United States, the Netherlands and Italy as well as the rise of Islamism seem to make it obvious, however, that a swing to repressive exclusionism is not a peculiarity of the East. Once again, Eastern Europe is showing itself to be every bit as entangled with and integrated into global developments – both migratory and ideological – as other regions of the globe.

Notes

1   See the chapter by Zaur Gasimov in this volume.
2   The term 'refugee' is – as every other denomination of moving people – ambivalent in that it is first and foremost an administrative category constituting a certain legal and discursive status. Yet it also tends to structure migrant behaviour and identity. Cf. Michael G. Esch, 'Refugees and Migrants: Perceptions and Categorisations of Moving People 1789-1938', in *Immigrants and Foreigners in Central and Eastern Europe during the Twentieth Century*, ed. Włodzimierz Borodziej and Joachim von Puttkamer (London: Taylor & Francis, 2000), pp. 7–32.
3   According to a report from 1980, about 362 applications for residency in Poland were received from capitalist countries, most of them from citizens of the Federal Republic of Germany [AIPN BU 1594/446].
4   See the chapter by Gilad Ben-Nun in this volume.
5   This medical discourse was particularly virulent in Germany, where it ultimately contributed to the mass murder of the Jews. Cf. Paul Weindling, *Epidemics and Genocide in Eastern Europe, 1890–1945* (Oxford: Oxford University Press, 2000).
6   *Ob'edinennyj komitet zemskogo sojusa i sojusa gorodov* (the United Committee of the Union of Zemstvos and the Union of Towns) was founded in 1915 as a civil society organization to support the government during the war. It moved to Paris in 1921 as the *Comité des Zemstvos et Municipalités Russes de Secours des Citoyens russes à l'étranger*.

Bibliography

Brunnbauer, Ulf. *Globalizing Southeastern Europe. America, Emigrants and the State since the late 19th Century*. Lanham: Lexington, 2016.

Hollifield, James F. 'The Emerging Migration State', *International Migration Review* 38 (2004) 3, pp. 885–912.

Torpey, John C. *The Invention of the Passport: Surveillance Citizenship and the State.* Cambridge: Cambridge University Press, 2018.

Zahra, Tara. *The Great Departure: Mass Migration and the Making of the Free World*. New York: W. W. Norton & Co., 2016.

Zolberg, Aristide R. 'The Exit Revolution'. In *Citizenship and Those Who Leave: The Politics of Emigration and Repatriation*, edited by Nancy L. Green and François Weil. Urbana: University of Illinois Press, 2007, pp. 33–62.

Further reading

Brandes, Detlef, Holm Sundhaussen and Stefan Troebst (eds). *Lexikon der Vertreibungen. Deportation, Zwangsaussiedlung und ethnische Säuberung im Europa des 20. Jahrhunderts*. Vienna: Boehlau, 2009.

Brunnbauer, Ulf. *Globalizing Southeastern Europe. Emigrants, America, and the State since the Late Nineteenth Century*. Lanham: Lexington Books, 2016.

Cabanes, Bruno. *The Great War and the Origins of Humanitarianism, 1918–1924*. Cambridge: Cambridge University Press, 2014.

Esch, Michael G. 'Migrants from East-Central Europe in South America: Discourses and Structures between Mission, Pogrom Escape, Human Trafficking, and "Whitewashing"'. In *Transregional Connections in the History of East-Central Europe*, edited by Katja Castryck-Naumann. Berlin: de Gruyter, 2021, pp. 259–90.

Gatrell, Peter. *The Making of the Modern Refugee*. Oxford: Oxford University Press, 2013.

Hoerder, Dirk. *Cultures in Contact. World Migrations in the Second Millennium*. Durham, NC: Duke University Press, 2002.

Torpey, John C. *The Invention of the Passport. Surveillance, Citizenship and the State*. 2nd Ed. Cambridge: Cambridge University Press, 2018.

Transnational and Global Aspects of Eastern European Music History

Stefan Keym

9

The status of music from Eastern Europe in international music historiography is rather ambivalent. Although many musicians from the region have played, and continue to play, a prominent role in international musical life – and although many important movements, especially in the 20th century, have received strong impulses from there – the main achievement explicitly attributed to 'Eastern European music' is that it introduced 'national traits' into art music. This narrative is highly problematic insofar as it reduces the great variety of musical trends originating in the region to a very one-sided, distorted sketch. Furthermore, it presumes a value judgement whereby 'national music' is a peripheral, regional phenomenon of far less importance than 'universal music'. Taken to its logical conclusion, the narrative confines 'Eastern European music' to a ghetto and thus suggests to musicians from the region that it is better to hide their cultural roots if they want to be taken seriously on the global stage.

The aim of this chapter is to deconstruct this widespread image by showing that 'national music' was neither a purely Eastern European product nor was it the principal type of music from the region. It will explore the diverse contributions to international music life of Eastern European composers and artists, some of whom were in fact highly innovative in comparison to their equivalents in other regions. In the opening section 1 we will show how the 'national music' narrative worked in 'Western' and 'Eastern' music discourse and why it was nurtured by writers on music, both from the respective country and from outside it. It is, of course, important to avoid veering from one extreme to the other by minimizing or even completely ignoring national aspects, as some avant-garde-oriented publications can be seen to do. Accordingly, in the second section we will look at the common features of the cultural context underlying Eastern European music and consider special local conditions, without falling into the trap of nationalist narratives. We will also outline, in as much detail as possible in this framework, some of the characteristic differences between the nations in question with respect to the role music plays in their self-images. Due attention will also be given – in the third section – to the central and ever-growing contribution to international music life made by Eastern European musicians, especially pianists and violinists, as well as to the changing role which composers from the region played at the crossroads of 20th-century avant-garde concepts, political repression and emigration – examined in the final section. In summary, this chapter will deal with narratives of music historiography, stereotypes of Eastern European music and musicians, the musicians' own strategies towards positioning themselves in the national and international arena, and the impact of intercultural transfers in the field of (mainly classical) music.

Using music to discuss the impact of Eastern Europeans on the global development of the arts seems justified considering the clear narrative of 'Eastern European music', which lacks a counterpart in other art forms. This means that music can form a starting point for shedding light on general problems in international perceptions of artistic phenomena in and from the region.

The universal paradigm in 'Western' music historiography and its attitude towards 'national music'

In contrast to literature and to general history, the history of music – and particularly that of European art music – is usually told as a transnational narrative. Thus, the approach of comparing seemingly homogeneous national units, which was the main object of criticism for pioneers of intercultural transfer theory and transnational history, seems at first glance of less consequence here.[1] However, the conviction that music is a 'universal' art not determined by language (a belief that lies at the basis of the traditional transnational narrative of music history) did not prevent writers on music (music critics, musicologists, etc.) from thinking mainly in national categories or from using nationalist rhetoric. In fact, claiming a worldwide hegemony for one nation's music for a specific historical period of this so-called universal music has been very common since Franz Brendel's ground-breaking 'History of Music in Italy, Germany and France' (1852).[2] A pioneer of music historiography, Brendel adopted the Neo-Hegelian notion that the cultural 'world spirit' (*Weltgeist*) travelled from one (national) area to the other. In this sense, the Renaissance era has often been referred to as the Dutch (or Franco-Flemish) period of music, the Baroque as the Italian age and the 19th century as the German (or Austro-German) epoch. These labels are not completely without foundation, of course. However, they produce an oversimplified, one-sided picture that, by focusing on one area as the most important for a given historical period, leaves aside other regions like Eastern Europe. Furthermore, the diffusionist concept of 'influence' – i.e. the wide-spread conviction that cultural and artistic products 'intrude into' or 'conquer' other countries due either to the efforts of their producers or to their inherent qualities and persuasiveness – is still rather common in musicology.

This means that there is still significant potential for rediscovering the foreign or transnational roots of musical concepts that used to be considered, for example, 'purely' Italian, German or Russian. A careful analysis of the different aspects of such intercultural transfers (see text box, below) can help overcome deep-rooted stereotypes and lead to a better understanding of hidden cultural connections in music history – and this, in turn, might serve as the basis for a new, genuinely transnational narrative of music history.

This is particularly the case when Eastern European music comes into play. According to the logic of the 'universal music' paradigm, the Austro-German era of late-18th- and early-19th-century Classical and Romantic music could have been followed by an Eastern European period (and then by an American one). Such a view did not gain wide acceptance, however, despite the fact that the ever-growing international influence of musicians and composers from the region would have supported it strongly.

Instead, the new trends that Eastern European composers brought to the international art music scene in the 19th century were labelled 'national music' and were thus relegated from the outset to a secondary, peripheral level from which they could not really threaten the supposed hegemony of Germanic music. At the time, there were many reasons, both internal and external, for this tendency in the international reception of Eastern European music, but it is hard to understand why such a one-sided view endured and is still dominant in international music historiography today (from research publications through to school textbooks), with important practical consequences for concert and opera repertoires.

Generally speaking, the arrival of Eastern European music on the international art music scene is a 19th-century phenomenon. What we might call an introductory phase in the first half of the century, spearheaded by the Polish composer Fryderyk (Frédéric) Chopin, was followed in the second half by a much broader wave of 'national musics' in many Eastern European regions, especially Russia and the Czech territories.

Of course, musicians from these regions had provided important contributions to international music history previously. In the 18th century, many German courts awarded important positions to composers with Slavic roots from Bohemia (Jan Dismas Zelenka in Dresden or Johann Stamitz in Mannheim, for instance). However, these composers were not perceived as representatives from a Czech, Slavic or 'Eastern European' cultural area and community at the time but as part of German music. Indeed, one of the first music prints to put forward the label of 'German music' was a collection of symphonies printed under the Italian title *La Melodia Germanica* in Paris in 1760; it consists mainly of compositions by Czech composers such as Stamitz.

In turn, some 'Western' composers occasionally drew upon material from Eastern European folk music: polonaise rhythms and Russian tunes (*airs russes*) provided themes for variation sets and pieces written in a rustic style called 'Hungarian' (*alla ingharese, à la hongroise*), and became popular in the context of a growth in exoticism – itself a by-product of early-19th-century Romanticism. These works brought isolated elements of a seemingly foreign, folkloristic culture into 'Western' art music by dint of their otherness. Regarded as little more than interesting exceptions, they did not change the system in general or lead to an acceptance of the foreign music culture as an independent phenomenon of equal value to the dominant one.[3]

When music critics from other parts of the world first became aware of the growing presence of 'Eastern European' composers on the international music scene, that scene's norms were largely dominated by German instrumental music (centred on Vienna, and later Leipzig) and by Italian and Parisian opera (later also by Richard Wagner's music drama). In order to be taken seriously, composers from Eastern Europe had to prove that they could adapt to and master these norms. However, they also had to distinguish themselves from the international (so-called universal) mainstream in order to attract the attention of critics and the public. It seemed inevitable that they would emphasize those traits of their music which they regarded as stemming from their national or regional culture, and which the international public appreciated as 'exotic', in order to get noticed. Thus, the concept of Eastern European national music was, to a certain degree, a 'Western' product – created by the expectations of music critics and publics in Western Europe, whose interest in Eastern European music was limited to what seemed to be 'national' or based on folklore. This interest in turn strongly influenced the stylistic strategies and choices of composers from the region.[4]

If Eastern European composers profited to a certain degree from this national labelling strategy, it also placed them in a sort of musical ghetto. This dilemma was already apparent in the reception of Fryderyk Chopin's music by Robert Schumann in the 1830s. On the one hand, Schumann wrote an enthusiastic review of Chopin's *Opus 2*, praising the freshness and poetic charm of the work; on the other, only a few years later he advised his Polish colleague to leave the 'small interests' of his native 'soil' and the 'sharp nationality' of his early works behind if he wanted to be taken seriously on the international stage.[5] In fact, Germanic writers on music often expressed such scepticism towards the use of folkloristic traits with national connotations. However, their defence of the supposed superiority of their own music (whether conscious or not) was not only a product of their cultural nationalism; it was also a consequence of the Neo-Hegelian ideology of musical 'progress' propagated by Brendel and others, according to which the integration of folkloristic material (such as ancient modal scales) was a backward, retrograde approach. For example, Hugo Riemann, one of the pioneers of German academic musicology, considered some Czech and Russian composers to be 'dialect composers' who deliberately cultivated an atavistic, primitive musical idiom for political reasons.[6] Composers and musicologists (mostly of Jewish origin) who emigrated from Nazi Germany to the United States in the 1930s took this attitude with them, thus furthering a global distribution which persists until today.[7] One of these émigrés was Arnold Schoenberg, the inventor of the avant-garde technique of dodecaphony. In 1947, he argued against symphonies built on folk tunes, defending the typically Germanic opinion that such material was not appropriate for the thematic development necessary in large forms.[8]

Research on intercultural transfers

Stefan Keym

Research on intercultural transfers has been developing since the 1980s, beginning with the pioneering work of the Parisian historians of culture Michel Espagne and Michael Werner. (Espagne and Werner, 1988; Espagne, 1999; Espagne and Middell, 2020) It investigates processes of international exchange involving people, goods, scientific and artistic concepts, and institutional structures between different cultural areas. The two aforementioned authors refute the basic assumption of the theory of cultural imperialism, according to which such processes usually imply the domination of the receiving area by the giving area and the idea that the latter is the active, driving force (as the terms 'influence' and 'diffusion' presuppose). On the contrary, Espagne and Werner focus attention on the members of the receiving cultural area, claiming that without a real interest and need on this side no intercultural transfer could succeed.

Matthias Middell (2007: 53–8) has distilled a four-step system for analysing intercultural transfers, pointing towards research on: a) the interests and needs of the members of the receiving cultural area, which provoke the appropriation of a foreign object or concept; b) the actors, media and routes of the transfer process; c) conscious or unconscious modification of the adopted object or concept in the course of its appropriation, including 'creative misunderstandings' and mixtures (métissage) with other elements that already exist in the receiving cultural area; and d) debates on the transfer process (mainly within the receiving cultural area), at the time of transfer and afterwards (e.g. strategies for hiding the foreign roots of the adopted object or concept).

Over the long term, the adopted object or concept may even strengthen the cultural identity of the receiving cultural area (as in the case of the appropriation of the ideas of German philosopher Immanuel Kant by French laicism). The principle aims of research on intercultural transfers are to reveal the 'Foreign within the Own' and to deconstruct national stereotypes and an essentialist, homogeneous and diffusionist understanding of culture.

The rise of 'national music': A transnational perspective

There were, of course, also important arguments from the perspective of Eastern European culture that motivated composers to fulfil the expectations of the 'national music' paradigm, and eventually even become a 'national composer'.

At the base of this paradigm was the concept of the 'cultural nation' (*Kulturnation*) which stirred cultural pride and identity as a substitute and compensation for the lack of a national state.[9] While the term '*Kulturnation*' was first coined by historian Friedrich Meinecke at the beginning of the 20th century, the idea itself can be traced back to around

1800, when it played an important role in political and ideological mobilization against Napoleon in the disparate German states. It led to a cult of the nation's 'great classical composers' (complementary to the canonization of Goethe and Schiller as German classical poets), and this process of national canonization contributed greatly to the rise of music and musicians in people's aesthetic and social estimation (particularly purely instrumental music, which had already long been a German speciality).[10]

However, the Romantic ideology of pure or 'absolute music', which claimed that (instrumental) music was a sacred realm beyond this world, did not allow German composers to express their nationality or other political topics explicitly in their compositions. Instead, they always insisted that their music was of universal value. Brendel even coined the term '*Weltmusik*' for this, corresponding with Goethe's claim of writing '*Weltliteratur*' (and in marked contrast to today's signification of the term 'world music', which is global folk music).[11] However, the so-called universal values which German composers excelled at were modelled after German works. This sort of hidden nationalism has been revealed and criticized since the 1920s, mainly by Eastern European musicians and scholars such as Polish composer Karol Szymanowski and musicologist Zofia Lissa.[12]

Eastern European composers were not impacted on by the ideology of absolute music in their own countries. In fact, it was quite the opposite as their compatriots expected them to bear witness to their nation in their works. Their use of elements from folk music was inspired by the ideas of Johann Gottfried Herder, according to whom the soul and the genius of a nation were to be found in the common people and its cultural products, such as folk songs. There were, of course, differences between each Eastern European nation or country when it came to the application of these ideas to their respective cultural traditions; for example, music had a higher status in society and was used more often to express the 'national genius' in the Czech territories than in Poland (where literature was the dominant art form) or in Russia.

The emergence of national music movements began in the first half of the 19th century in Poland (Fryderyk Chopin), Hungary (Ferenc Erkel, Franz Liszt) and Russia (Mikhail Glinka), continued in the Czech territories after the Spring of Nations' Uprising in 1848/9, and reached many other nations and regions in the late 19th and in the 20th century (Norway, Finland, the Baltic and Balkan states, Ukraine), continuing all the way through to the nationalist renaissance in the 1990s. Although the situation in Russia was somewhat different from that of the other Eastern European countries due to the existence of a national state, Russian music had been dominated by foreign models and musicians since the Baroque period (including Italian opera composers at the imperial court, many lesser-known German musicians working as teachers privately or at the St Petersburg and Moscow conservatories founded in the 1860s, as well as some more prominent figures such as François-Adrien Boieldieu or John Field). The aims of the Russian nationalist music movement led by the 'Mighty Five' composers (Mily Balakirev, Alexander Borodin, Cesar Cui, Modest Mussorgsky and Nikolai Rimsky-Korsakov) were to become musically independent and to do away with a cultural inferiority complex.[13] However, this project was also coupled with a political emancipation process led by liberal bourgeois activists such as the art critic Vladimir Stasov, who tried to use cultural nationalism as a weapon in pursuit of political reform in the country. Nonetheless, it is important to note that cultural nationalism was originally a 'Western' concept that spread to Russia with Westernization.[14]

Eastern European composers engaged in nationalist cultural politics in their home country to varying degrees. Some even succeeded in becoming regarded as 'national composers'– in other words, as being among the main cultural and spiritual representatives of their nation in music. In the best-case scenario, this concept of mutual identification between an acknowledged artist and a nation was a win-win situation, as it benefited both the composer's career and the nation which embraced him as a national hero. The process recalled the development of literature, with the Polish poet and politician Adam Mickiewicz as a prototype. Chopin was put forward by his compatriots to play a similar role in music, but it was a mission which he fulfilled only reluctantly and partially by composing impressive sets of Polonaises and Mazurkas, raising these models of Polish dance music to a highly individual and sophisticated level. Others, such as Liszt or Smetana, showed more enthusiasm about being selected as national composers.

The case of Franz (Ferenc) Liszt is of particular interest, since he neither mastered the Hungarian language nor lived continuously in Hungary beyond his childhood. However, his mix of Parisian and (Austro-)German artistic and intellectual socialization finally gave way to his identification with the Hungarian movement for national emancipation and to his supporting it culturally by composing piano rhapsodies and symphonic poems as well as church and other vocal music in honour of the Hungarian nation. In contrast with his fellow Germans (such as Brendel), Liszt did not see any contradiction between cultural nationalism and artistic progress; on the contrary, he was convinced that elements of Eastern European folklore and the unconventional ideas of composers from the region would act as a sort of cure for European art music by refreshing and rejuvenating it. As a result, he encouraged all music movements in the region that tried to link progressive traits with a nationalist agenda.[15]

The Czech Bedřich (Friedrich) Smetana was perhaps the most conspicuous example of a national composer. He became (and still is) regarded as the most typical and successful national composer, earning himself the position of the key figure in Czech national music by virtue of his multiple activities as a conductor, composer and music critic. He achieved this despite having spoken primarily German in the first half of his life, before undergoing his 'national' conversion. A further example of how linguistic shortcomings did not present a decisive obstacle to becoming a national composer is provided by Finnish composer Jean Sibelius, who belonged to the Swedish-speaking minority in the country. Clearly, national composers are not born; they are products of selection, identification and construction.

One important reason these composers were selected as cultural representatives of their nations, despite being rank outsiders in terms of language, was that national composers had to fulfil representative functions not only at home but also abroad. Paradoxically, international fame was deemed necessary to stir national pride. This also leads to the question of which musical genres were the most appropriate for propagating national values. On the one hand, composing operas, cantatas, songs and other vocal music was always a central mission of national music movements. However, the more the contents of these works were charged with ideas rooted in the particular history or literature of a specific nation, the less comprehensible they were to an international public. Thus, Smetana's main serious national operas, *The Brandenburgers in Bohemia* and *Libuše*, are known even today only in the Czech territories, whereas his lighter and less ideologically charged comic opera *The Bartered Bride* is staged worldwide and is understood as a typically national opera. Among Smetana's six symphonic poems grouped together as 'My Fatherland' (*Má vlast*, 1874–9), the idyllic 'landscape painting' *The Moldau* (*Vltava*, the river that flows through Prague) is much better known than the poems referring to events in the Hussite wars (*Tábor, Blaník*). Similarly, the operas by Michail Glinka and Stanisław Moniuszko are still rarely staged outside their respective countries. Only operas combining national elements with progressive stylistic traits and socially engaged plots, such as *Boris Godunov* by Modest Mussorgsky or *Jenůfa* by Leoš Janaček, have enjoyed international success. In general, nationally coloured instrumental music worked better abroad, such as Chopin's Polonaises and Mazurkas, Liszt's Hungarian Rhapsodies, and some symphonic poems and symphonies (particularly those by Antonín Dvořák).

Early musicology also played a role in musical nationalism. Eastern European pioneers of the discipline spent a considerable amount of time collecting the folklore of their country (following the model recommended by Herder), trying to find the roots and the very essence of their nation's music in it. These efforts often led to the invention of traditions and to the construction of myths. For example, the mountain-folk music of the *Górale* (the inhabitants of the Tatra mountains around Zakopane) was considered particularly Polish (and thus inspired many nationalist compositions, from Moniuszko through to Karol Szymanowski) when, in fact, it was of multinational origin.[16]

It is relatively easy to deconstruct the roots of much 'national music'. Most of such works written by Russian or Czech, but also by Norwegian or Spanish, composers in the late 19th and early 20th centuries share similarities. They draw from a common pool of anti-academic stylistic devices (such as augmented fourths, minor or augmented seconds, leaping or missing leading tones, drones and other static harmonic structures), which served as markers of the 'national'.[17] The main function of these markers was to distinguish the works from the Central European musical mainstream, and especially from what was taught in German conservatories. Thus, a dualism existed between a purportedly universal classicist or academic style, on the one hand, and a variety of supposedly national styles, on the other.

This constellation may be illustrated with the help of Dvořák's *Symphony from the New World*. Dvořák was the most famous Czech composer besides Smetana; he was less politically engaged but just as devoted to folklore-based music. In 1892, he became director of the National Conservatory of Music of America in New York and was asked to compose an American national symphony. The fact that he was given this commission demonstrates that Eastern Europeans were considered specialists of national music in general; they represented a sort of avant-garde of global national music. In fact, Dvorak composed the symphony in his typical manner, using material similar to folklore (without quoting directly). Drawing on American spiritual tunes as well as on Czech rhythms, the work became one of the most popular late-19th-century symphonies.

However, Dvořák's contribution to music history goes far beyond the composition of 'national music' imbued with folklore for Czechs or Americans. Many of his works do not fit into the national paradigm, and the same can be said for many other 19th-century composers from Eastern Europe. These composers skilfully shifted between different styles, including the national. A particularly good illustration of this is Peter (Pyotr) Tchaikovsky, who cultivated explicitly national musical traits in only a small part of his creative output (such as his *Second Symphony*).

The objection that Tchaikovsky's music was 'not Russian enough' (or 'too German') was initially raised in Russia by his rivals in the 'Mighty Five' nationalist circle of composers (especially Cui) and their patron Stasov.[18] In the long term, however, this criticism did not prevent Tchaikovsky from being canonized in his home country as the most important Russian composer. Instead, it was in France in particular that Tchaikovsky came under attack, where, beginning in the 1880s, he was accused (in a book on Russian music by Cui)[19] of lacking stylistic patriotism. At the time, French writers on music were thirsting for an alternative to German music models and found an answer to their dilemma (and, in effect, a counterpart to the political and military alliance between France and Russia sealed in 1892) in the nationalist Russian music school centred on Balakirev.[20] In fact, other composers of Tchaikovsky's generation also switched between different styles; for example, Johannes Brahms composed *Hungarian Dances* and Camille Saint-Saëns wrote several works with oriental elements. But unlike Tchaikovsky, they were not accused of betraying their nationality. Indeed, Eastern European composers were part – and even at the forefront – of a broader, international trend towards stylistic pluralism (which included several styles associated with particular areas or epochs). It was Eastern Europeans' affection for drawing upon pre-classic stylistic elements and genres (e.g. the suite), a predilection shared by Tchaikovsky as well as Rimsky-Korsakov, that anticipated a stylistic movement carried on by Igor Stravinsky in the 1920s and later called 'Neo-Classicism'.

Eastern European musicians as actors in international music life

If acceptance of Eastern European composers in international music life was slow (and chiefly as an exotic and peripheral phenomenon), musicians from the region were able to integrate more easily. Eastern European instrumentalists became highly important in this rapidly growing and increasingly international field, interpreting not only works by their compatriots but the entire international classical canon.

The three most famous pianists in the 19th century – Franz Liszt, Anton Rubinstein and Ignacy Jan Paderewski – were all born in Eastern Europe. All three became prototypes of the modern star pianist who tours all over the world, creating passion among a large (often predominantly female) public. Unlike Liszt, who finished his playing career relatively early (in 1848) to become a 'serious composer' in Weimar (in accordance with the German model), both Rubinstein and Paderewski toured the United States, thus playing decisive roles in the intercontinental globalization of Classical music from Western Europe. A large part of the fame, fortune and influence enjoyed by Paderewski in particular derived from his time in America.

The 'national question' played an important role in the lives and careers of all three pianists, though for each in a rather different manner. As already shown, Liszt considered cultural nationalism a means for artistic progress and willingly assumed the role of a representative of the Hungarian nation, even if his national identity was primarily a product of his own cultural and artistic self-positioning. Rubinstein was denied belonging to Russian culture by the nationalist circle around Balakirev on account of his Jewish origins – and this despite his great achievements on its behalf as a founder of the St Petersburg conservatory, the cradle of the Russian instrumental schools to gain global fame. As a result, he primarily followed a cosmopolitan agenda. Paderewski, on the other hand, was an ardent Polish patriot who identified himself more and more with his homeland throughout his life. He even composed a large symphony in B minor (1903–9), in which he musically anticipated the liberation of Poland by quoting the Polish national anthem and employing a tonal dramaturgy leading from a minor to a major key, symbolizing the breakthrough from darkness to light.[21] This sort of dramaturgy was very common in 19th-century German music (from Beethoven through to Mahler). However, by charging it with a contemporary political message Paderewski modified and renewed the symphonic concept – as is often the case in such intercultural transfers. Some years later, Paderewski's musical vision came true when he became a decisive figure in the Polish fight for national independence.[22] He benefited not only from a large fortune but also from international fame and personal contacts with politicians in the United States, Britain and France, which he exploited in his campaign to have the restoration of an independent Polish state put on the agenda of peace negotiations at the end of the First World War. Indeed, he became the first prime minister of the new Polish state in 1919 and so signed the Treaty of Versailles.

This sort of intense political engagement among musicians has remained rather exceptional (probably because it seems incompatible with the Romantic idea that music is a realm not of this world). However, it is conspicuous that of the small group of politically engaged musicians, many are Eastern Europeans (including Soviet cellist and dissident Mstislav Rostropovich as well as musicologist and first Lithuanian president from 1990 Vytautas Landsbergis). Thus, it was also in politics that Eastern European musicians played an avant-garde role.

The strong tradition of major, internationally renowned pianists from Eastern Europe continued throughout the 20th century (Artur Rubinstein, Vladimir Horowitz, Evgeny Kissin, etc.) and persists today. It is reflected in prestigious international piano contests such as the Chopin Competition in Warsaw or the Tchaikovsky Competition in Moscow and St Petersburg. A similarly dominant role has been played by Eastern European violinists, beginning with Polish virtuoso Henryk Wieniawski and continuing with many members of the 'Russian Violin School' (including Igor and David Oistrakh).[23] Eastern European conductors and singers came to international attention somewhat later, but they seem particularly prominent today (for example, Russian conductor Valery Gergiev and Russian soprano Anna Netrebko).

In view of these impressive and widely recognized contributions by Eastern European musicians, the marginalization of Eastern European music culture seems all the more remarkable.

Eastern European composers of the 20th century: Between political repression and 'Western' avant-gardes

If there is a strong continuity in the contribution made by Eastern European musicians to the international art music scene, the relationship between composers from the region and 20th-century avant-garde music is more complex and ambivalent. On the one hand, many prominent figures in the various streams of this 'new' or contemporary music have Eastern European roots. Viewed from that perspective, the global influence of the region has increased significantly in comparison with its impact in the 19th century, and perhaps Liszt's prophecy that the future of music belonged to the East has been fulfilled to a degree. On the other hand, the national and geographical origins of its composers have often been neglected or played down in historiographical narratives.

In the early 20th century, the 'national music' paradigm continued and even reached new peaks. Notably, the triumphs of Russian ballets (*Ballets russes*), organized by the impresario Sergej Diaghilev and presented first in Paris and then in London and other cities in western parts of Europe in the years immediately preceding the First World War, were considered particularly Russian manifestations and owed much of their international appeal to this quality. Their nationally tinged surface apparently made it easier for the ordinary Western European public to accept the shocking musical and choreographic modernity of the three avant-garde ballets by a young Igor Stravinsky: *The Firebird*, *Petrushka* and *The Rite of Spring*. The last-named work, especially – which evokes an archaic, bloody ritual in pre-historic pagan Russia with the help of original but dissonantly transformed folk-music material – seemed an excess of Russian-ness and modernity at the same time.[24]

This sort of modernist folklorism (or folkloristic modernism) was also propagated by the Hungarian composer Béla Bartók, who personally undertook extensive field research in several Balkan regions to collect 'authentic' folksongs. Stravinsky and Bartók became models for many young folkloristic composers in the 1920s (in both parts of Europe, and even in North and South America, e.g. Aaron Copland and Heitor Villa-Lobos), who, in the words of the Polish composer Karol Szymanowski, greeted them as leaders of national 'liberation movements' rising up against the hitherto 'German musical hegemony'.[25] Several composers from the new Eastern European countries (Hungary, Czechoslovakia, Poland) also played a prominent role in international organizations, such as the International Society for Contemporary Music (ISCM), founded in 1922, or the International Institute of Intellectual Cooperation within the League of Nations.

In the long term, however, Stravinsky did not embrace his role as a musical nationalist and a 'young savage'. After his definitive emigration from Russia in consequence of the Bolshevist Revolution, he changed his style and began applying his transformation techniques not to folkloristic material, as before, but to pre-Classical music of Western Europe. The result was the new style of 'Neo-Classicism' that became dominant in the musical avant-garde circles of most countries in the 1920s. This style was also adopted by his younger compatriot Sergej Prokofiev, who spent many years in France as well.

Politically motivated emigration in fact became a decisive factor in the careers of many 20th-century Eastern European musicians and composers: it first affected Russians after 1917 and then artists from many other countries during and after the Second World War.[26] Naturally, the movement fostered the global spread of musical concepts from the region but, at the same time, these intercultural transfers led to a mix with ideas from countries hosting the émigrés. This meant that the Eastern European roots of the concepts involved were often blurred and not internationally acknowledged. For instance, it is not well known that a decisive impulse in the discourse on the relationship between time experience and music, which is crucial for 20th-century music aesthetics in general, came from Stravinsky's philosophical advisor and ghostwriter Pierre (Pyotr) Souvtchinsky.

If the October Revolution was an unintended catalyst for this wave of intercultural transfers and mixing of artistic concepts via emigration, the Stalinist repression of modernist art concepts beginning in the 1930s further weakened the position of Soviet and, after 1945, other Eastern European composers in the global art music scene. Soviet cultural diplomacy never played an important role in the field of music, whether avant-garde or popular. The new international avant-garde, which started to take shape in 1949 at the 'Darmstadt Summer Courses of New Music', was clearly dominated in its early years by young composers from the traditional 'music countries' (France, Germany, Italy). However, some Eastern European composers soon joined this elitist club. György Ligeti, a Hungarian composer (born in Transylvania) who emigrated to West Germany in 1956, became highly influential, introducing a new avant-garde style of '*Klangkomposition*' (sound composition). However, Ligeti chose to hide his Balkan roots in this period. While he had used folkloristic elements up until his emigration (building on the tradition of Bartók), he avoided such material for the next twenty-five years – revisiting it only in the 1980s, when he mixed it with elements from other areas (e.g. Africa).[27]

In contrast, a whole group of Polish avant-garde composers (including Witold Lutosławski and Krzysztof Penderecki) clearly emphasized their national origins. They became internationally known following the 'Warsaw Autumn' festival initiated in 1956, which served as the main meeting point for avant-garde composers from both sides of the Iron Curtain during the Cold War. Western European avant-garde musicians accepted the nationalist rhetoric of the Polish composers because of its drive to resist Soviet cultural unification. The branding of a specifically Polish avant-garde music (called '*sonorism*') and jazz was even encouraged by parts of the Polish communist government. However, the term 'Polish school' of the avant-garde was coined in the West.[28] In fact, the reception of this music was mixed and included critical comments continuing old prejudices against supposedly 'barbaric' Eastern European music.

Nevertheless, Eastern European avant-garde composers in general succeeded in attracting a larger public than most of their colleagues because they often cultivated a style that was less abstract and elitist. One of the main new elements that they contributed to avant-garde music was the emphasis on sound, exemplified by Ligeti's *Klangkompositionen* or Polish *sonorism*. This focus was combined with (and probably caused by) the aim of expressing something: emotions and often also a concrete political, religious or humanistic message. This inclination towards musical expression and meaning obviously fulfilled a certain need in music audiences in Western Europe and beyond – a need that was neglected by most avant-garde composers from those regions, who were devoted to a more hermetic '*l'art pour l'art*' aesthetic.

The fact that Eastern European composers were more inclined than their counterparts in the West to express messages in their music certainly had something to do with the heritage of the 19th-century concept of national music; but it was also connected with the contemporary situation: the influence of socialist cultural policy (even after the official doctrine of socialist realism was rejected) and the difficult political situation in Eastern European countries. This is remarkable since it demonstrates how nationalism and socialism, even though they are usually seen as in opposition to each other, often have similar consequences on the artistic plane – especially in music.

Several of the Eastern European composers who reached a considerable audience in the West were Polish, such as Krzysztof Penderecki (whose *St. Luke Passion*, premiered in Münster in 1966, became a cornerstone in the renewal of sacred music), Henryk M. Górecki (whose *Third Symphony, Symphony of Sorrowful Songs*, 1977, was used in several films and even entered the international charts in 1992) and Wojciech Kilar (who wrote both concert and film music, e.g. *Dracula* and *The Pianist*); but Soviet composers who emigrated to the West in the 1980s or 90s – such as Arvo Pärt, Sofia Gubaidulina or Alfred Schnittke – also gained a degree of popularity. Some embraced elements of minimal music (a style originating in the United States based on extremely repetitive patterns), combining them with religious ideas; others – including Schnittke, who, like Kilar, had considerable experience with film music – cultivated an eclectic 'polystylisic' approach. Dmitri Shostakovich, the most famous Soviet composer, is today a firm fixture in the international concert repertoire as one of the most important symphonists and chamber music composers of the 20th century despite having a very complicated relationship with the official Soviet system and experiencing severe criticism from West European music critics, both for political and aesthetic reasons.

It would also be very interesting to look at the impact of Eastern Europeans on global popular music – for example, their success in the Eurovision Song Contest since the fall of the Iron Curtain. This, however, would be a topic for another chapter.

In sum, it can be concluded that 19th- and 20th-century Eastern European music culture was not only highly important on the international, and even global, level but that it also reveals much about general issues – such as music and meaning, music and politics, music and emigration – and thus deserves more attention from musicologists and other researchers.

Notes

1   Michel Espagne, *Les transferts culturels franco-allemands* (Paris: Presses Universitaires Françaises, 1999); Michel Espagne and Matthias Middell (eds), *Intercultural Transfers and Processes of Spatialization* (Leipzig: Leipzig University Press, 2022).
2   Franz Brendel, *Grundzüge der Geschichte der Musik* (Leipzig: Druckerei Fr. Rückmann, 1848).
3   Ralph Locke, *Musical Exoticism. Images and Reflections* (Cambridge: Cambridge University Press, 2009).

4   This problem has been pointed out in many publications by Richard Taruskin; see Richard Taruskin, *Defining Russia Musically. Historical and Hermeneutical Essays* (Princeton: Princeton University Press, 1997); and Richard Taruskin, 'Non-Nationalists, and Other Nationalists', in *Cursed Questions. On Music and Other Social Practices*, ed. Richard Taruskin (Oakland: University of California Press, 2020), pp. 33–51.

5   Articles by Robert Schumann on Chopin published in 1831 in the *Allgemeine musikalische Zeitung* and 1836 in the *Neue Zeitschrift für Musik*, see Robert Schumann, *The Musical World of Robert Schumann. A Selection from his Own Writings,* trans., ed. and annotated by Henry Pleasants (London: Gollancz, 1965), pp. 5–7 and 91–2.

6   Hugo Riemann, *Geschichte der Musik seit Beethoven (1800-1900)* (Berlin and Stuttgart: Spemann, 1901), p. 520.

7   Taruskin, 'Non-Nationalists, and Other Nationalists', pp. 35–6.

8   Arnold Schoenberg, 'Folkloristic Symphonies' [1947], in *Style and Idea. Selected Writings,* ed. Arnold Schoenberg (New York: Philosophical Library, 1950), pp. 196–203.

9   David Gramit, *Cultivating Music. The Aspirations, Interests, and Limits of German Musical Culture, 1770-1848* (Berkeley: University of California Press, 2002).

10   Stefan Keym, *Symphonie-Kulturtransfer. Untersuchungen zum Studienaufenthalt polnischer Komponisten in Deutschland und zu ihrer Auseinandersetzung mit der symphonischen Tradition 1867-1918* (Hildesheim: Georg Olms Verlag, 2010).

11   Brendel, *Grundzüge der Geschichte der Musik*, p. 40.

12   Karol Szymanowski, *Szymanowski on Music. Selected Writings*, ed. and trans. Alistair Wightman (London: Toccata Press, 1999); Zofia Lissa, 'Über den nationalen Stil', in *Beiträge zur Musikwissenschaft 6* (1964), pp. 187–214.

13   Taruskin, *Defining Russia Musically*; Taruskin, 'Non-Nationalists, and Other Nationalists', pp. 33–51.

14   Taruskin, 'Non-Nationalists, and Other Nationalists', p. 34.

15   Zofia Redepenning, '"Ils valent la peine qu'on s'en occupe sérieusement, dans l'Europe musicale." Franz Liszt als Mediator russischer Musik in Westeuropa', in *Russische Musik in Westeuropa bis 1917. Ideen, Funktionen, Transfers*, ed. Inga Mai Groote and Stefan Keym (Munich: Text & Kritik, 2018), pp. 17–31.

16   Zbigniew Jerzy Przerembski, 'The Multicultural Nature of Mountain-Folk Music in Poland', in *Polish Musical Culture within the European Context*, ed. Zofia Helman (Warsaw: Institute of Musicology, 2004), pp. 116–30.

17   Michael Beckerman, 'In Search of Czechness in Music', *19th-Century Music* 10 (1986) 1, pp. 61–73.

18   Taruskin, 'Non-Nationalists, and Other Nationalists', pp. 40–2. A similar view on Russian music (though with a less negative judgement of Tchaikovsky) was spread in England by Rosa Newmarch.

19   César Cui, *La Musique en Russie* (Paris: Sandoz & Fischbacher, 1880).

20   Inga Mai Groote, *Östliche Ouvertüren. Russische Musik in Paris 1870–1913* (Kassel: Bärenreiter, 2014).

21   Stefan Keym, 'The Tradition of "per aspera ad astra" in Polish Symphonic Music from Zygmunt Noskowski to Karol Szymanowski', *Muzyka* 54 (2009) 3–4, pp. 21–44; Keym, *Symphonie-Kulturtransfer.*

22   Ignacy Jan Paderewski and Mary Lawton, *The Paderewski Memoirs* (London: Collins; New York: Scribner's Sons, 1939).

23   Yuri Yankelevich, *The Russian School of Violin. The Legacy of Yuri Yankelevich*, ed. and trans. Masha Lankovsky (Oxford: Oxford University Press, 2016).

24   Richard Taruskin, *Stravinsky and the Russian Traditions. A Biography of the Works through 'Mavra'* (Oxford: Oxford University Press, 1996).

25   'Szymanowski on Contemporary Music' [1922], in Szymanowski, *Szymanowski on Music*, pp. 199–200.

26 Anna Fortunova, *Russische Kultur im Berlin der Weimarer Republik Eine multiperspektivische Analyse* (Hildesheim: Georg Olms, 2019).

27 Rachel Beckles Willson, *Ligeti, Kurtag, and Hungarian Music During the Cold War* (Cambridge: Cambridge University Press, 2011); Márton Keréfky, 'Verwendung, Verleugnung, Wiederentdeckung. Ligeti und ethnische Musiken', *Studia musicologica* 57 (2016), pp. 35–47.

28 Ruth Seehaber, *Die 'polnische Schule' in der Neuen Musik. Befragung eines musikhistorischen Topos* (Vienna: Böhlau, 2009); Lisa Jakelski, *Making New Music in Cold War: The Warsaw Autumn Festival, 1956–1968*. (Berkeley: University of California Press, 2016).

Bibliography

Espagne, Michel and Matthias Middell (eds). *Intercultural Transfers and Processes of Spatialization*. Leipzig: Leipzig University Press, 2020.

Espagne, Michel. *Les transferts culturels franco-allemands*. Paris: Presses Universitaires Françaises, 1999.

Espagne, Michel and Michael Werner. 'Deutsch-Französischer Kulturtransfer als Forschungsgegenstand. Eine Problemskizze'. in *Transferts. Les relations interculturelles dans l'espace franco-allemand*, edited by Michel Espagne and Michael Werner. Paris: Ed. Recherche sur les Civilisations, 1988, pp. 11–34.

Middell, Matthias. 'Kulturtransfer und transnationale Geschichte'. In *Dimensionen der Kultur- und Gesellschaftsgeschichte. Festschrift für Hannes Siegrist zum 60. Geburtstag*, edited by Matthias Middell. Leipzig: Leipziger Universitätsverlag, 2007, pp. 49–69, here at pp. 53–8.

Further reading

Keym, Stefan and Anna Fortunova (eds). *Eastern European Emigrants and the Internationalisation of 20th-Century Music Concepts*. Hildesheim: Georg Olms Verlag, 2022.

part III

Forays into Global Economic Processes

Editor's Notes: Moments of Global Change

The association of globalization with the rise in flows of economic activity and exchanges between different world regions runs to the very heart of this historical phenomenon. Indeed, even the emergence of globalization as a field of study can be traced back to this discipline's early association with the rise of global mass economic exchanges, as evident in the early seminal works of 1970s, where terms such as 'Modern World System' were associated with capitalist agriculture, and the idea of the existence of a 'capitalist world-system' was first articulated (Wallerstein, 1974). Substantively, two major influences upon this early economic stratum of global thinking could be found in the works of Fernand Braudel, and specifically within geographic works that followed Marxist economic logics (Braudel, 1972; Harvey, 1982).

In his chapter on Eastern Europe's vital role as a global supplier of grain, Uwe Müller alerts us to the need to pay attention to *both* flows and controls, as one delves into the study of economic globalization. A key moment in this process could be seen in Britain's 1846 repeal of its Corn Law, which opened the way for a globalized trade in grain in which Eastern European actors began to play a vital role as securitizers of global food supplies thanks to their grain export.

A second crucial moment in Eastern Europe's global history took place during the October 1917 communist revolution in Russia. As Max Trecker so pertinently demonstrates, the rise of Soviet Bolshevism provided for a single, and most important, ideological challenge to globalization's capitalist underpinnings, ever since its emergence. Arguing against contemporary neoliberal economic currents,

Trecker shows us just how far Soviet developmental models for the decolonizing world in Africa, Latin America and Asia continue to shape our thinking. Ideas such as the debt moratorium to developing countries, that was initially proposed by the Soviet bloc during the early 1970s, was eventually adopted by sternly capitalist institutions such as the World Bank and the IMF during the late 90s. Nowadays, the stringent centralist governmental oversight of markets, via active and heavy-handed interventions such as by national banks, is seen as globally merited, in the perennial struggle to avoid tumultuously destructive 'rise and crash' economic cycles. Yet such centrist economic modes of thought were distinctly alien to the Western neoliberal capitalist economic thinking ethos during the Cold War. Their contemporary ascendance to the degree of consensus as shared between virtually all the world's major central banks demonstrates just how much a bulwark Eastern European Marxist economic thought has proved to be for destructive neoliberal 'disaster capitalism' (Klein 2008).

There can be little doubt that '1989' served as a watershed moment in the history of globalization. And here to, this global caesura is inherently tied to Eastern Europe. Above and beyond its tectonic political implications for the redrawing of borders and military alliances, the collapse of the Soviet bloc spelt first and foremost the collapse of its Marxist-driven economic world vision. While different world regions reacted differently to this major shift in global politics, it was the countries of Eastern Europe who embraced most emphatically the West's economic 'winner ideology' of harsh neoliberal capitalism. As Thilo Lang shows, this embrace of neoliberalism in countries such as Hungary, Poland, Slovakia and Romania has had detrimental effects on their social cohesion, as the gaps between peripheral rural regions and centrist urban ones has dramatically grown.

A last decisive moment in a long history of global entanglements that is deeply connected with Eastern Europe which we survey here concerns China's 2001 ascendance to membership of the World Trade Organization (WTO). China's rise to become the world's second largest economy after the United States, over the past two decades, has been dovetailed by her promotion of a stark alternative to Western-based centuries-old models of globalization. As Lela Rekhviashvili explains, China's foray into Eastern Europe is part of its Belt and Road Initiative (BRI). This new approach to global trade departs considerably from the global trade models which for the past five centuries have been firmly anchored in maritime distribution routes. In contrast, China's BRI vision is premised, first and foremost, on a landed vision of trade routes across the Eurasian landmass, thus demanding strategic partnerships with all the countries through whose territories the BRI actually runs. Relying also on an auxiliary set of maritime port outlets around the Mediterranean and Indian oceans, time will tell whether China's geographically landed modality for global trade has managed to seriously challenge the Western maritime model.

Bibliography

Braudel, Fernand. *The Mediterranean and the Mediterranean World in the Age of Philip II (1550–1650)*. New York: Harper & Row, 1972.
Harvey, David. *The Limits to Capital*. London: Verso Books, 1982.
Klein, Naomi. *The Shock Doctrine: The Rise of Disaster Capitalism*. London: Penguin, 2008.
Wallerstein, Immanuel. *The Modern World-System I: Capitalist Agriculture and the Origins of the European World-Economy in the Sixteenth Century*. Berkeley: University of California Press, 2011 (repr. of the 1974 ed.).

Positioning Strategies in the Global Commodity Market since 1850

Uwe Müller

10

Introduction

Economic globalization has many facets. Its most important indicators are flows of goods, capital and labour. Its intensity and effects change over time and according to its spatial dimension. These processes are influenced by a large number of actors – individuals as well as companies, interest groups and NGOs, nation-states and international organizations. Economic globalization – which is often presented in political discourse as a given, superior, almost natural law process – is, in fact, the sum of the efforts of countless people and the institutions within which they have sought to improve their position in sometimes world-wide or transregional but often also in cross-border competition. An understanding of their intentions and actions, and the results of these, which are interpreted here as 'globalization projects', as well as the interactions between them allows us to grasp how globalization actually develops and changes. This is important since many other approaches are highly normative; they assume that the freest possible movement of production factors, especially free trade, brings about an optimal increase in prosperity (i.e. neoclassical economics). Similarly, approaches related to the dependency theory only insufficiently explain the historical change of transregional relations.

This chapter deals with the role of Eastern Europe in the global economy since the mid-19th century. The temporal focus of the main chapter is on the phase of so-called first globalization from 1850/70 to the First World War and the period of so-called deglobalization and economic nationalism in the first half of the 'short' 20th century marked by the two world wars as well as the Great Depression. The first text box (by Pavel Szobi) deals with the second half of the 'short' 20th century, during which Eastern Europe saw itself as the core of a socialist economic area but nevertheless had interconnections with other parts of the world. The second text box (by Susann Schäfer) analyses the development of the last two decades, during which Eastern Europe struggled to gain an advantageous position in the world economy under the conditions of a renewed push towards globalization.

The chapter focuses on the positioning of Eastern Europe in global commodity markets. However, this focus should not be taken to imply that movements of labour and capital from Eastern Europe to other parts of the world and vice versa have been unimportant. In fact, there were indeed significant migration movements from Eastern Europe to the west of the continent, as well as to the Americas, both between 1880 and 1930 and since 1990. Moreover, Russia was the country with the largest stock of foreign capital before the First World War. Additionally, between 1990 and the world financial crisis of 2008/9, economic development in almost all East Central and South-eastern European countries were shaped by foreign direct investments.

Trade in commodities, however, has been of central importance for the development of the global condition since 1850, and especially for the integration of Eastern Europe into the 'first globalization'. This is particularly true for the trade in grain. It made up more than 20 per cent of world trade before the First World War, with more than 50 per cent of that grain being wheat.[1] The trade in wheat thus constituted one of the first truly 'global markets'. Unlike the global movement of capital, this form of global interdependence affected a large number of people in rural societies on different continents. In Eastern Europe, it was mainly farmers and peasants as well as merchants and forwarders from Russia or the Soviet Union, Romania and Hungary who were involved in the global grain trade. During the Great Depression around 1930, the wheat market again played a pioneering role in the history of economic globalization. Actors from Eastern Europe were active in attempts to stabilize wheat prices through international treaties on quotas and preferential tariffs. Therefore, through the history of the wheat trade and its regulation we can understand how actors from Eastern Europe have participated in and shaped economic globalization.

In the current phase of globalization, the structure of trade has changed. Commodity trade has lost importance within global trade in terms of both value and quantity. This has primarily been due to the increase in so-called intra-industry trade resulting from the much more intensive division of labour and multilayered global value chains. This, however, does not mean that exporters of food and raw materials have automatically begun to occupy a peripheral position within global trade. In fact, in the period around 1900, the three leading industrial countries were also important exporters of cotton and grain (the United States), coal (the United Kingdom) and sugar (Germany). The revenues from these exports often served to build modern industries. In the second half of the 20th century, oil – the 'black gold' – and natural gas were important strategic raw materials. The text box (below) shows how the Soviet Union used its rich deposits of these raw materials and made use of the advantageous terms of trade during the 1970s in order to overcome the obstacle of the Iron Curtain with a massive increase in exports and to generate important foreign exchange earnings. The imports of modern technologies that were financed with this money had less effect than Soviet economic leaders had hoped. The socialist superpower was a technological leader almost only in areas relevant to military strategy. The deterioration of conditions on the global oil markets for producers contributed to the collapse of the Soviet economic system, and thus to the downfall of state socialism. Overdependence on the export of raw materials remains a central problem of the Russian economy even today.

The role of oil in the Soviet entanglement in the global economy

Pavel Szobi

The early Soviet industry was based on coal energy, but that started to change after the end of the Second World War when aside from the Caspian oil wells, the exploration in the Volga-Ural Region led to the extraction of an unprecedented amount of oil. From the mid-1950s, the Soviet Union was producing a surplus of this natural resource. By 1960, the country made more oil than Venezuela and held the second position globally after the United States. The Soviet satellite countries in Eastern Europe were self-sufficient in energy production in the 1950s. Still, a decade later, due to the high expansion rate of heavy industries, their dependency on Soviet oil increased.

Nonetheless, the growing oil production in the Soviet Union created a space for exports across the ideological borders to Western European countries. Those were regarded as potentially important trading partners and sources of hard currency income. In the early days of the Cold War period, the Soviet oil export strategy triggered US fears of Moscow's leverage over the Western European countries, leading NATO to urge its members not to buy Soviet oil. In 1962, the West eventually imposed an embargo on the sale of steel pipes and pipeline technology to the Soviet Union as pipelines could be used for oil transportation. Despite these measures, the first oil pipeline between the Soviet Union and Western Europe called Druzhba was successfully completed in 1964. Western Europe's imports of Soviet oil increased steadily following the completion, and the embargo was lifted in 1966. In 1968, the Soviet Union exported 85.8 million tons of oil – approximately one half of these exports were directed to Western Europe.

The United States eventually accepted the existence of the East–West oil trade and did not perceive the Soviet Union as a rival, but merely a disruptive factor in their global oil interests well into the 1970s. Although some US companies even explored the possibility of participating in energy projects in western Siberia with rich oil and gas reserves, the US observers underestimated the Soviet capacities to use the region's potential. The global energy crises of the 1970s led many Western European countries to perceive energy supplies from the Soviet Union as more reliable than those from the crises-ridden Middle East, allowing the Soviet Union to regain significance as an exporter of oil and gradually gas, too. That triggered the decision in Moscow to expand investments into energy-rich western Siberia. In exchange for Western European credits, pipe steel and technology, some of western Siberia's gas was shipped directly to Europe via a new pipeline, which massively expanded the Soviet–Europe energy relations and made the Soviet Union into Europe's crucial energy supplier. In some smaller European countries, such as Finland, energy exports could serve now as a means of expanding Soviet political influence. But the primary function of Soviet energy exports was to gain access to

Western technology and hard currency. This access enabled the Soviet Union not only to finance its energy projects. It created funds to buy wheat and consumer goods and compensate for the dumping prices of oil and gas sold to the Eastern European allies. The core element of the cooperation between the Soviet Union and Western European countries was that it was not hampered by ideological competition. Quite on the contrary, it was driven by national economic interests and the challenges presented by the regional and global markets. The growing flow of oil and gas through newly constructed pipelines ostentatiously ignored the Iron Curtain's existence. The two partners became more and more interlinked through shared economic ambitions.

In the 1970s, Eastern European countries were becoming more and more dependent on Sovietoil supplies, too – East Germany, Bulgaria and Czechoslovakia for more than 90 per cent. Pressed with the need to boost oil shipments to Western Europe, Moscow was increasingly reluctant to provide its Eastern European allies with cheap natural resources. The Soviets did a radical decision and cut the allies' oil deliveries by approximately one third until the mid-1970s. In addition, the socialist brother states had to pay for parts of the Soviet oil and gas supplies with hard currency and had to contribute to the development of raw material deposits in Siberia and to the construction of pipelines. Thus, the affected countries were faced with the need to start looking for alternative oil sources in Africa and the Middle East. Czechoslovakia negotiated with oil-producing countries like Iran, Poland with Iraq, and East Germany with Angola. All these countries also rediscovered and started to squeeze their aged coal capacities in order to meet the high energy demand at home. Most of these countries were also experiencing a profound debt crisis at the time. The economic problems of the Soviet allies eventually led Moscow to reconsider its hard-line policy and sold more oil deep below the market prices, like in the case of Poland in 1981.

In this period, the Soviet Union obtained 80 per cent of its foreign currency from energy exports. It made the country almost entirely dependent on fossil energy sales in order to acquire foreign currency and fuel the failing economy. In the 1970s, high prices on the world's oil and gas markets allowed the Soviet Union to delay much-needed reforms. But the reliance on a single export commodity did not pay off. The sharp decline of oil prices in the second half of the 1980s was one of the reasons provoking the economic reforms Mikhail Gorbachev tried to implement. Although those attempts failed, the collapse of the Soviet Union in 1991 did not rupture the oil and natural gas trade. It continued to provide energy for European households and industries, and the energy sector has been one of the primary columns of the Russian economy ever since.

However, after the years in which the Soviet Union had to import wheat in the 1970s (mainly from the United States), Russia has recently risen again to become the world's largest wheat exporter – as shown in the text box (below). It is true that agriculture within its national economy and, consequently, the export of agricultural products within foreign trade are no longer as important today as they were 110 years ago. However, the ability to be self-sufficient in grain and the orientation of wheat exports towards Western Europe supported Russia's geostrategic ambitions around 1900. The same applies to today's wheat exports towards leading countries of the Global South like Egypt, Nigeria and Indonesia.

Current dynamics on agricultural commodity markets in Eastern Europe

Susann Schäfer

Wheat is currently one of the most important cereals produced and consumed worldwide. It is grown globally on more land than any other crop and remains the most important cereal for human consumption (Curtis, 2002). For many Eastern European countries, such as Russia, Hungary and Romania, exports are an important pillar of economic value added.

In the 1960s, wheat production increased very sharply due to the 'Green Revolution'. In the decades that followed, wheat production continued to develop a although not to the same extent as it did during the technological change that came with the Green Revolution (Pingali, 2012). As production has grown, so has the volume of traded grain: exports of agricultural goods have grown strongly in Russia, Romania and Hungary over the past decade. All three countries are currently among the top fifteen exporters of wheat in the world (Workman, 2020). With about US$ 6.4 trillion and a global market share of 16.7 per cent of wheat exports in 2019, Russia has been the world's largest wheat exporter since the turn of the millennium. Compared to Russia, the shares of the global grain market of the producer countries Romania and Hungary are much smaller (less than 5 per cent; Workman, 2020). These export goods play an insignificant role in the value added to the respective national economies, as well as to their export statistics. In all three countries, the agricultural sector has decreased in economic importance since industrialization. Today, this sector contributes less than 5 per cent to their national GDP.

Global wheat trade is subject to three main dynamics that influence production volumes, prices and value chains. These include: a) climate change, b) new markets and changing demand for wheat, and c) trade regulatory measures.

Unlike other globally traded commodities, the production and thus global trade dynamics of agricultural commodities are inherently volatile from one growing season to the next, and thus subject to annual fluctuations. In addition to these short-term fluctuations, the global climate is changing, also affecting Russia and these other two Eastern European countries, and will continue to change in the future (Belyaeva and Bokusheva, 2018). While crop losses are expected in southern Russia (e.g. the Volga Valley), wheat growing conditions will improve in northern Russia. It is assumed that wheat yields there will increase, and unused fallow land worked for wheat production (Svanidze et al., 2019). Considering other changes to infrastructure, the volume of wheat in circulation will therefore increase.

In addition to climate issues, from the perspective of these three countries in Eastern Europe, global wheat trade is characterized by shifting supply relationships. Up to now, their main customers have been from Egypt, Nigeria and Indonesia. Increasingly, however, sales markets in Southern Africa and South East Asia are also playing an important role for Russian wheat exports. Although the overall demand for wheat flour for human consumption has remained largely constant since 2000, there has been an increasing demand in some regions, such as Indonesia, due to a shift towards Western consumption practices and growing incomes. The dynamics between supply and demand are regulated to a massive extent by government intervention (e.g. tariffs, export restrictions). The reasons for government regulation are, on the one hand, food security for the country's own population, but also the influence on the world market price for wheat, which results from a complex web of available trade volumes, exchange rates and expected production quantities. Due to the COVID-19 pandemic, for example, the Romanian government temporarily banned wheat exports to third countries in April 2020 with the aim of securing its own food needs (FAS, 2020).

It is to be expected that grain exports from Russia will continue to increase in volume and thus in importance on the global grain market over the coming years. Extensive investments in modern port and storage infrastructure will allow grain to be exported constantly throughout the year. In addition, in July 2019, the Russian government announced plans to invest approximately 60 billion EUR in infrastructure with the aim of increasing production capacity and export volumes (Reuters, 2019). They plan to increase the 79,000 billion tons of wheat produced in 2020 to 90,000 billion tons by 2029 (OECD-FAO, 2020). However, according to Svandize et al. (2019), not only is extensive investment in transportation infrastructure needed, but also the development of commodity futures markets to reduce price risk and the expansion of market information systems to improve market transparency.

The emergence of a global wheat market and Eastern European strategies for positioning (until the First World War)

Foreign trade relations on the European grain market intensified considerably in the middle of the 19th century. The most important structural reason for this development was the increased demand for food in Britain and, a little later, other parts of North-western Europe due to population growth, progressive urbanization and industrialization. The main institutional precondition for the reconstitution of the European cereal market was the strengthening of free trade through the abolition of the British Corn Laws (1846) and the establishment of a system of most-favoured-nation trade agreements between major European states.

European wheat-exporting regions were all located in the eastern part of the continent. Within Eastern Europe, however, there was a shift in the importance of the individual wheat export regions. The Polish lands, which were the most important source of Dutch and British wheat imports between the 15th and 18th centuries, lost this function. In the meantime, Hungary, with its fertile areas along the Danube, became the most important wheat exporter. Since the end of the 19th century, the Romanian lowlands and, above all, the Russian empire – with its black earth region – developed into the quantitatively most significant wheat export regions in Europe.

In the 1870s, the wheat market changed within a few years from a European to a global affair. The expansion of the reach of the market affected mainly the suppliers' side. Canada, Argentina and later Australia and India also entered the market as new 'overseas' participants in addition to the United States. They competed with the Eastern European exporting countries and with the respective local farmers for the sale of grain on the markets in Western and Central Europe and gradually in the Mediterranean region.

The most important structural causes for the creation of the 'global condition' in the wheat trade, which is exemplary for other commodity markets, were the revolutionary changes in transport and communication. The former led to a significant reduction in transport costs in both ocean shipping and rail shipping. The railway made it possible to use the large fertile areas in temperate climates that were well suited for growing grain. This process was often preceded by the displacement or extermination of the indigenous population through the settlement of immigrants. In the case of overseas production, it was possible to transport the cereals to ports by the new land routes, and from there across the oceans to Europe.

The reduction of transport costs created a necessary but not sufficient condition for the globalization of the wheat market. Equally important was a general reduction in transaction costs, the technical prerequisite for which was the establishment of a global telegraph network. Information on prices, grain transports on the world's oceans, and stocks and harvest prospects elsewhere in the world became available within minutes at any location in the world that was connected to the network. In addition, the standardized determination of wheat quality characteristics made the global wheat market more transparent.[2]

Global and economic historians have mostly described the problem of 'grain invasion' and the subsequent protectionist reaction of continental European countries, especially France and Germany, as a North Atlantic entanglement. Meanwhile, actors from Argentina, Australia and Eastern Europe have so far hardly been taken into consideration. Recent studies of the integration of the global wheat market emphasize the fact that the effects of market integration depended mostly on political decisions rather than on technical progress, and indicate a clear negative influence of continental European protectionism on Eastern European grain exports.[3] However, when we look at the shares of the individual world regions and countries in the international wheat trade, a different picture emerges—despite certain uncertainties regarding the accuracy of the data (see Table 1). The data show that both Russia and the Danube countries achieved considerable success in the fight against non-European competitors.

Similar to its overseas competitors, Russia's success on the European grain market had initially been possible thanks to the decline in transport costs and expansion of cultivation areas in the south-eastern part of European Russia (the so-called New Russia) and later also in the North Caucasus and western Siberia. The Russian state pursued an export-oriented globalization project with its railway construction policy and the expansion of ports on the Black and Baltic Seas as well as the promotion of internal colonization. Although labour productivity and incomes in agriculture in Russia also rose between 1870 and 1913, the country's successes on world markets were largely owing to its low labour costs by international standards.

Information about the global wheat market also reached Russian provinces through the parallel expansion of railway and telegraph networks. An American traveller reported from Nikolaev that the

> peasants on arrival at the market with their grain were asking 'What is the price in America according to the latest telegram?' And what is still more surprising: they know how to convert cents per bushel into kopecks per food.[4]

Table 1. Distribution of average annual world wheat exports, 1854–1913 (percentage)

Country/Region	1854–1858	1884–1888	1909–1913
USA	25	36	14
Russia	12	25	22
Danube countries	10	19	16
Canada	6	1	13
India	3	10	7
Argentina	0	1	13
Australia	0	2	7
Others	44	6	8

Source: R. M. Stern, 'A Century of Food Exports', *Kyklos* 13 (1960), p. 58.

The world market price also influenced the price formation on the domestic market in Russia. At the same time, Russian cereal traders were trying to avoid the centralization of trade processing in Chicago and Liverpool. Thus, after the settlement of the Russian-German customs war in 1894, direct trade between these two countries increased. Russia became the most important supplier of wheat, animal feed and many other agricultural products to the German empire.

These export opportunities led to grain continuing to be grown on 75 per cent to 90 per cent of the arable land in the Russian empire. The share of wheat in the grain area had increased to 32 per cent by 1913, exceeding that of rye (29 per cent), oats (19 per cent) and barley (12 per cent). The positive experience with wheat exports from 1880 onwards led to an increase in exports of other cereals, for the cultivation of which the conditions in large parts of Russia were more favourable and the competition on foreign markets was much less intense. In 1913, 40 per cent of all Russian exports consisted of grain. Between 1909 and 1913, the Russian share of world wheat exports was 25 per cent. The shares for rye, oats and barley were 37 per cent, 43 per cent and even 71 per cent, respectively.[5]

In Table 1, the category 'Danube countries' includes both Hungary as part of the Habsburg monarchy and, above all, Romania. Romania's political and economic elites pursued a similar globalization project to that of Russia, and managed to make their country the fourth-largest wheat exporter in the world before the outbreak of the Second World War. The decision to increase export production despite falling world market prices was based on various motives and constraints. Although switching to livestock exports would have been more lucrative in terms of trade, it was, on the one hand, a viable solution only to a very limited extent because of the protectionist policies of the potential target countries – especially of Austria-Hungary. On the other hand, income from the export of raw materials and grain was considered indispensable for the development of Romanian industries in the medium term.

Similar to the Russian case, the success of Romanian wheat exports was based on relatively low labour costs, with large landowners skilfully exploiting the compensation rules that had been enacted in the agrarian reforms of the 1860s. As transport costs fell, this Balkan state went through an intensive economic integration with other parts of the continent. Around 1910, Romania exported about one quarter of its national income and thus had a very high foreign trade quota compared with other countries in Europe or even worldwide. Almost 80 per cent of its exports were grain deliveries. Therefore, Romania was heavily dependent on the development of demand and prices abroad for wheat.[6]

Wheat producers in Hungary, almost all of whom had large estates, reacted to the increasing competition on the European wheat market with two other strategies. The first and most important countermeasure was a protectionist agricultural foreign trade policy that began in the late 1870s, which was in the common interest of the Austrian and Bohemian industrialists as well as the Hungarian landowners. This policy was maintained until the outbreak of the First World War. Although this protectionist turnaround made their wheat exports more difficult, it largely shielded the Habsburg monarchy's sales market from grain imports. As a consequence of this strategy, the share of Hungarian exports of grain and flour that crossed the borders of the Habsburg monarchy, which had still amounted to two thirds in the 1880s, fell to one fifth in the 1890s and to only one tenth after 1900. Over 90 per cent of the grain and flour 'export' thus went to the Austrian half of the Habsburg customs union. It is no coincidence that flour dominated the goods leaving the customs union. Indeed, the second globalization project strategy of the large-scale Hungarian farmers was to develop the milling industry and to export flour instead of unprocessed wheat. The terms of trade here were much more advantageous. Austro-Hungarian foreign trade policy supported this strategy by allowing mills to import duty-free wheat as long as a certain quota of flour was later exported. This was used to import wheat varieties that were not sufficiently available in Hungary from the Balkan states and then to process them into high-quality flour and sell it at some profit in Austria and further abroad.[7]

The First World War and its impact on the global wheat market

The outbreak of the First World War divided the globalized markets for agricultural products along the borders of the military blocs. In Russia, hostile sea blockades in the Black and Baltic Seas prevented the export of grain. Since no income could be generated through exports, grain production declined significantly until 1917 and more drastically than agricultural production as a whole.

Romanian wheat exports almost came to a complete standstill after the outbreak of the war, mainly due to the massive disruption of shipping traffic on the Black Sea. It was only at the beginning of 1916 that the then still neutral state succeeded in selling parts of the good wheat harvest from the previous year to the Central Powers and Great Britain. Romania's entry into the war on the side of the Entente, its rapidly ensuing military defeats, and the subsequent German occupation caused considerable damage to agricultural production – especially to grain cultivation. The production and export of agricultural goods declined in occupied territories such as Romania because no seeds were sown, the rural population passively resisted, and the country's infrastructure was destroyed.

On the Entente side, however, the war also led to a sharp decline in domestic agricultural production – particularly grain production – especially in France and Italy. Large parts of Australia and North and South America increased their agricultural production year after year during the war – in some cases by double-digit rates – in order to supply France, Great Britain and Italy. This growth in production was possible primarily thanks to an expansion of the area under cultivation, which increased by 50 per cent in Canada and doubled in Australia.

The balance of power between the suppliers on the global wheat market thus changed considerably as a result of the war. Experts from the Food Research Institute, which was founded at Stanford University in 1921, noted: 'The decline in Russian, Danubian, and Indian exports [was] much more than offset by increases from Canada, Argentina, and Australia.'[8] The overseas producers naturally wanted to keep or even expand their market shares. Wheat exports were highly important for the economies and national budgets of Argentina, Australia and Canada.

In the whole of Eastern Europe in the early 1920s, agricultural production remained lower than it had been before the war. However, in the second half of the decade, Romania and Hungary had almost completed the reconstruction of their agriculture sectors and were

Table 2. Distribution of average annual world wheat exports, 1909–1938 (percentage)

Country/Region	1909–1913	1924–1928	1934–1938
USA	14	22	8
Russia (Soviet Union)	22	2	4
Danube countries	16	4	8
Canada	13	35	28
India	7	2	2
Argentina	13	17	19
Australia	7	11	16
Others	8	7	15

Source: R. M. Stern, 'A Century of Food Exports', *Kyklos* 13 (1960), p. 58.

trying to finance the import of industrial capital goods with the help of revenues from agricultural exports. Similarly, the Soviet Union also wanted to revive the strategy of Tsarist Russia and increased the export of wheat, while at the same time the leadership under Joseph Stalin expanded heavy industry and infrastructures.

However, the global economic conditions for an increase in Eastern European grain exports were much less favourable at the end of the 1920s than they had been before the First World War. This was, first, due to the previously mentioned strong overseas competition. Secondly, the war had also changed the attitudes of many Western European politicians towards their agricultural sectors. Countries such as Germany, Italy and France were striving for a higher level of, or even complete, self-sufficiency – especially in the field of wheat production. The ultimate goal was now to increase wheat production, even if this required considerable investment in breeding new varieties and improving the soil through fertilization or amelioration. Many grain-importing countries began to subsidize their farmers, increase customs duties and establish other trade barriers even before the outbreak of the global economic crisis. Of course, potential Eastern European agricultural goods exporters suffered as a result of this development. However, the same Eastern European countries that exported agricultural goods reinforced the trend towards protectionism by also pursuing a policy of protective tariffs, mostly in the interest of their young industries.

The wheat market during the Great Depression

As a result of the growing supply from overseas producers, wheat prices in Europe fell below pre-war levels as early as 1920/2 – although the reconstruction of agricultural production at that time was not yet complete in many parts of the continent, and food was still lacking in some regions. Between 1923 and 1925, agricultural prices rose. However, between 1925 and 1929, they fell again while almost all industrial prices rose. This worsened the terms of trade at the expense of agricultural goods exporters. Nevertheless, the size of the 'world wheat area' increased by 13 per cent between 1924 and 1929. This led to a significant drop in wheat prices, whereas, at the same time, stock increased – especially after the good global harvest of 1928.

This analysis of wheat prices shows that the so-called Great Depression – that is, the world economic crisis between 1929 and 1933 – further reinforced an already existing downward trend in the profitability of the grain export industry. In East Central and South-eastern Europe, the relationship between industrial and agricultural commodity prices also changed, to the disadvantage of the rural population.[9] The reason for this development was the confrontation of the grain sector, which was already in a structural crisis, with a general recession that led to the stagnation or even decline of consumption.

In addition to falling demand for wheat on the most important markets, wheat exports from the countries of Central and South-eastern Europe suffered from the Soviet Union's more concerted attempt during the global economic crisis to tie in with the export traditions of the Tsarist empire. In its early years, the Soviet Union had been neither willing nor able to export wheat in the face of wars against external and internal enemies, and under the conditions of 'war communism' and the famine of 1920/1. The resumption of grain exports was first achieved in 1923, with the Soviet leadership accepting supply shortages on the domestic market – similar to the situation in Tsarist Russia. The volume of Soviet wheat exports remained relatively low in the 1920s, as harvests fluctuated widely, and production was mostly below pre-war levels while domestic consumption increased. In addition, farmers had little interest in export production even in the period of the New Economic Policy because the state-fixed prices were not lucrative. It was not until the good harvests of 1930 and 1931 that Soviet wheat exports could reach respectively 2.3 million and 5.2 million metric tonnes. However, due to the low world market prices these brought in considerably less foreign exchange for the state treasury than the leadership around Stalin had hoped for. In the following two years, wheat exports fell as production plummeted due to poor natural conditions and the consequences of forced collectivization. There was a great famine during this period, which claimed several million lives in the wheat-growing Soviet regions – particularly in Ukraine.[10]

The global wheat crisis was mostly interpreted as an overproduction crisis, and is considered one of the causes of the extraordinary severity of the Great Depression. The *wheat-importing countries* reacted to this by strengthening their respective national protectionism; creating incentives to raise domestic prices; and, consequently, increasing their own agricultural production. They adopted a policy of economic nationalism as a means of keeping people on the land or making the nation more self-sufficient in food in the event of another war.

It was much more difficult for *wheat-exporting countries* to find a strategy to protect their farmers from ruin. Farmers in the four overseas states which had dominated the wheat market since the First World War (Argentina, Australia, Canada and the United States) were now faced with a shrinking market. While the wheat trade averaged, with a slight increase, 808 million bushels per year between 1927 and 1931, the amount fell to 572 million bushels between 1932 and 1936.[11] The bad harvest of 1930 outside of Europe made clear how important wheat exports were for foreign trade, and for the entire national economy in the case of Argentina, Australia and Canada.[12] It gradually became evident that a further increase in production would only exacerbate the problem.

At the same time, only political interventions seemed to be able to break the vicious circle of procyclical action. First, it now became blatantly clear that the cereal crisis could not be tackled by national measures alone and instead required global solutions; moreover, the creation of regional alliances was also seen as possibly helpful. Secondly, attempts were made everywhere to regulate the market or even to shut it down completely. Both objectives were related. For example, an international agreement on production quotas or the sharing of markets necessarily presupposed control over production or, at least, over trade in each individual state. In the agricultural sector, which was characterized by a large number of producers, this could not be achieved by cartel agreements but through institutions that were either owned by or acting on behalf of the state. Thirdly, wheat-exporting overseas states tried to support farmers affected by falling prices or production restrictions by means of subsidies. These state interventions not only burdened national budgets, which were already strained during the global economic crisis, but also often failed to meet expectations.

Figure 10.1 Global wheat trade between 1850 and 1940.

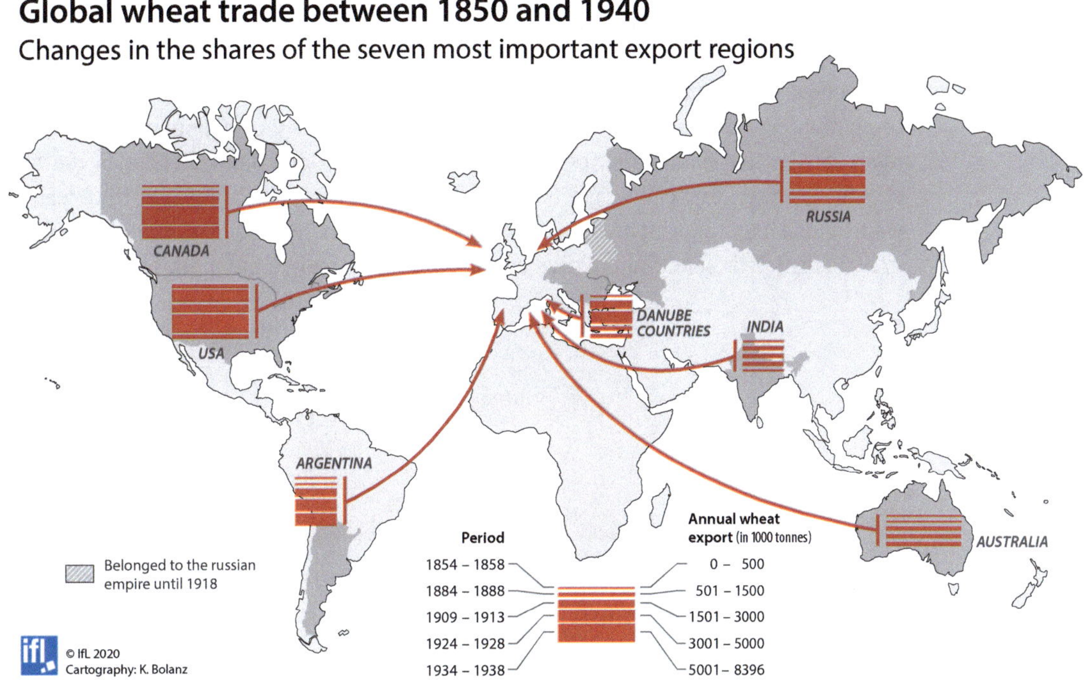

Independently from agrarian policy, Poland, Romania, Hungary and Yugoslavia were, at the beginning of the crisis, already the most heavily indebted countries in Europe. In 1930, the wheat harvest in Eastern Europe – unlike that overseas – was exceptionally good and offered an opportunity to generate much-needed export revenue by increasing volume despite falling prices. In fact, Bulgaria, Hungary, Romania and Yugoslavia tripled the volume of their grain exports from 1928 to 1933. This development was possible thanks to a large number of government measures designed to promote the export of agricultural goods in general and often of wheat in particular. Producers received subsidies intended to enable them to offer wheat on external markets at dumping prices. At the same time, interventions in domestic markets ensured that prices were higher there than they were in world markets.[13]

These measures could only be implemented through the forced cartelization of agricultural trade, the establishment of state monopolistic trade organizations, and the central management of foreign exchange. In Hungary, for example, the export of flour was subsidized by the state and all agricultural trade was controlled by semi-governmental agencies in the form of cooperatives or joint stock companies. In addition to the purchase of products and subsidizing of exports by the state, Romania, Bulgaria and later Poland and Yugoslavia enacted laws cancelling part of the debts of many of their farmers.

All these measures taken by the countries of Central and South-eastern Europe could only dampen the consequences of a structural agricultural crisis exacerbated for farmers and farm workers by the economic slump. These measures were also connected with serious side effects and inefficiencies that created an enormous burden on already-strained national budgets and operated at the expense of domestic consumers. In each case, national measures caused ruinous international competition between the Eastern European states. It became increasingly clear that only internationally coordinated measures could overcome the procyclical vicious circle of Western European protectionism and Eastern European export promotion. The depth of the crisis and obvious unsuitability of nation-state policy instruments meant that national elites were prepared to hand over competences in the field of economic policy, especially agricultural policy, to 'Europe'. If the Eastern European states wanted to achieve a result favourable to them at an international or European level, they had to recognize their common interests and act together despite other political differences.

The Eastern European 'agrarian bloc' and internationalist strategies for regulating the wheat market

On the one hand, the First World War represented a massive setback for all international institutions and projects aimed at economic cooperation and integration. On the other, more intensive cooperation within the Entente, as well as between the Entente and its overseas food suppliers, was established. Numerous networks that were created during the war continued to operate in the postwar period and influenced various bodies of the League of Nations, which was founded in 1919. Both the victorious powers of the war and the League – dominated by the former – pursued an apparently plausible goal in terms of the world economy: a return to free trade and the gold standard.

However, confrontation with the Great Depression and the growing economic nationalism everywhere made it clear to the experts of the Economic and Financial Organization in the League of Nations that these goals did not meet the complex requirements of the postwar situation. During the preparations for the World Financial and Economic Conference held in London in 1933, advisors of the League of Nations, who had previously been strict free traders, developed flexible responses to the protectionism of nation-states. They now advocated a combination of international solutions, regional agreements and bilateral negotiations that would at least reduce customs duties and other trade barriers, as their outright abolition was considered completely illusory. Agreements to regulate global commodity markets by setting quotas for production and trade – for example, for coal, meat and especially wheat – now also seemed to be desirable or, at least, the lesser of two evils.

However, the initiative for this paradigm shift in trade policy did not come from the League of Nations. The fact that the representatives of national agricultural protectionism also took up international cooperation from the prewar period was just as important. The International Commission of Agriculture (Commission Internationale d'Agriculture, CIA), which had been founded in 1889 on the fringes of the first International Congress of Agriculture, played a central role in promoting international cooperation. In 1925, the CIA was re-established at a conference in Bern. It involved representatives of sixty-eight agricultural associations coming from large Western states such as Germany, France, Italy and the United States as well as from Eastern European states – namely, Estonia, Latvia, Poland, Czechoslovakia, Hungary and Yugoslavia. At the first official meeting of the CIA in Paris in March 1927, among the twenty-one states attending, six countries from Eastern Europe were represented. The CIA was soon called the 'Green International' – that is to say, an institutionalized alliance of agricultural interest groups that opposed the liberal orientation of the first World Economic Conference organized by the League of Nations in Geneva in 1927.

In terms of trade policy, the CIA aimed at the creation of European agricultural protectionism – a shielding of national markets through coordinated measures, such as the levying of import duties and the introduction of non-tariff trade barriers – and a global organization of agricultural markets through production and foreign trade planning by means of international commodity agreements. The cartels that were established in some industrial sectors, and which combined protection and intergovernmental cooperation, served as a model. The Eastern European member associations linked these two objectives with their demand for an intra-European system of tariff preferences. Their support for the protection of Western European markets against cheap cereals from overseas was made conditional on the creation of privileged access for their (i.e. Eastern European) exports to these markets. The willingness of the Western European associations to respond to this demand depended on how they assessed the attitudes of domestic farmers and the chances of being able to enforce their own demands against overseas grain exporters.[14]

Between 1930 and 1933, twenty international conferences on the agricultural crisis took place, at which appropriate multilateral solutions were sought and compromises were reached in the face of conflicting interests. When it comes to the role of the Eastern European countries in this process, it must first be pointed out that the Soviet Union was initially excluded. Nevertheless, the other Eastern European countries, which were mostly summarized as the 'Danube countries' in contemporary sources, played an important role from the beginning. No less than seven out of these twenty conferences were used exclusively by representatives of the Eastern European countries for internal communication. The core of this grouping was formed by the four wheat-exporting countries, Hungary, Yugoslavia, Romania and Bulgaria, as well as Poland, which exported very little wheat but instead traded rye and barley and various other agricultural products. However, Polish agricultural policymakers had recognized that the problems of the wheat trade were particularly serious and that regional alliances and international solutions in this area could serve as a model for other commodities.

In March 1930, after numerous failed attempts, the League of Nations used questionnaires to ask its member states for proposals for measures to improve relations between industrial and agricultural states. The Romanian minister of trade and industry, Virgil Madgearu, sought to find a common position among the Eastern European agricultural goods exporting countries, and invited his colleagues from Yugoslavia and Hungary to a meeting in Bucharest. Madgearu aimed at the removal of the most-favoured-nation clause contained in most of the trade contracts for the grain trade. He argued that deleting this clause would pose no harm to Western European farmers and only minimally reduce the sales of the overseas cereal exporters who dominated the market, while greatly helping Eastern European cereal producers. Madgearu's demand was rejected by an overwhelming majority at the Geneva Conference for a Tariff Truce in February 1930, as many saw it as an attack on a fundamental principle of free trade policy. In Bucharest, however, Madgearu managed to persuade his colleagues from Hungary and Yugoslavia to return the questionnaires to Geneva with uniform demands to do away with this clause; however, this did not translate into the elimination of competition between the Eastern European wheat exporters, which Madgearu additionally wanted to achieve.

At the end of August 1930, Poland organized an international conference of agricultural countries in Warsaw, in which almost all Eastern European states took part. Only the Soviet Union and Lithuania were missing due to their strained relations with the host country. The aims of the conference were once again the establishment, first, of cooperation between the states themselves and, secondly, of joint actions at the international level. The states agreed to facilitate mutual trade by amending or abolishing veterinary regulations in particular, which had mainly served as non-tariff barriers to trade. An agreement to abolish export subsidies mainly affected the wheat trade and was a first measure against ruinous competition in the form of mutually outbidding subsidies. In addition, in Warsaw and in the following meetings of the Eastern European agricultural states, measures for mutual information and coordinated action on export markets were agreed on, which helped to ensure a certain regulation of the market and, above all, a stabilization of prices.

The demand that was originally made by Romania and then again by Yugoslavia and Hungary for a general deletion of the most-favoured-nation clause was modified in Warsaw with supporters seeking only a temporary preference to be granted to European agricultural products, especially to cereals, on all European markets. In this form, preferential tariffs were also accepted by conference subjects, such as Czechoslovakia, that had no direct interest in this point. This increased the assertiveness of the Eastern Europeans in the international arena as the members of the 'agrarianist bloc' formed in Warsaw jointly stood up for the demands decided on in the conference.[15]

Subsequently, the CIA leadership took up the idea of preferential tariffs for grain. Through their growing influence in the Agricultural Expert Commission, which had been founded in 1929, the preferential tariffs became an important element of the strategies discussed at the League of Nations to overcome both the agricultural crisis and the world economic crisis. Therefore, in 1931, the League of Nations, which until then had been a major proponent of the principles of free trade and thus also of most-favoured-nation status, founded the Committee to Study the Problem of the Export of Future Harvest Surpluses of Cereals, which promoted the development of a European preference system.

The climax and turning point in the movement initiated by the Eastern European states for a European grain market protected from the outside world was the Stresa Agricultural Conference in September 1932. Delegates from all the major European states except the Scandinavian countries, Spain and the Soviet Union attended the conference, where they were to agree on proposals with which the Study Commission for the European Union – founded in 1930 by the League of Nations – was to represent a common European position at the World Financial and Economic Conference in 1933. The crisis in the Eastern European agricultural states was at the centre of these proposals. In retrospect, the Stresa conference appears an extremely ambivalent event. On the one hand, proposals were made to combat the wheat crisis at an international level – and these had a considerable impact. In addition to a large number of foreign trade agreements which were to constitute an intra-European preference system, there were various credit programmes that were to benefit both indebted agricultural states and their farms as well as the establishment of a fund for the improvement of economic structures in agricultural Eastern Europe, which was to be financed by all participating states. On the other hand, Stresa's internationalism was not global but exclusively European – in other words, regionally oriented. In addition to economic and European policy approaches, power policy objectives played a central role. France, in particular, tried to attract the Eastern European states through generous offers, thereby reducing the influence of Germany and Italy. This French attempt succeeded only to a limited extent, because states like Romania did not want to give up important German and Italian sales markets. Consequently, the French lost interest in the European project.

The International Wheat Conference in London in 1933 is considered 'the first global effort by major wheat producers to manage the world trade in wheat by setting export quotas and reducing the volume of land seeded to wheat'.[16] In fact, all major wheat-exporting and wheat-importing countries participated in this conference. The Soviet Union was also present, although it was not yet a member of the League of Nations and had not yet been recognized by other important participating states under international law.

The wheat-exporting countries agreed on two measures to stabilize wheat prices and to avoid overproduction in the future. First, the volume of wheat trade was to be reduced to 560 million bushels in 1933/4 and to only a slightly larger quantity in 1934/5.[17] To this end, appropriate quotas were set for the individual exporting countries. Canada was allowed to export 200 million bushels, Argentina 110 million, Australia 105 million, the Danube countries 50 million, the United States 47 million, and other states including the Soviet Union 48 million. Secondly, the acreage used for wheat cultivation was to be reduced by 15 per cent within a few years. However, only the four largest overseas producers committed themselves to this target. The Danube countries once again justified their strict refusal to reduce their own wheat cultivation area by even a single acre by referring to their historical rights to Western European markets. In doing so, they referred to the loss of their once very favourable position in the world market caused by the the First World War. In their view, '[a]creage movements in the Danube countries were not of international concern so long as their exports were below the prewar level'. Therefore, 'acreage reductions should be made by countries where the greatest expansion over prewar acreage had taken place'.[18]

Conclusion

We have found that Eastern European wheat exporters were able to hold a notable position until the First World War in one of the first truly global markets. This was possible thanks to extensive production growth, especially observable in Russia and Romania. Yet the Eastern European cereal monoculture naturally represented a structural disadvantage for modern Eastern European agriculture in the medium and long term. On the other hand, it formed an irreplaceable basis for the intense integration of Eastern Europe into the world economy. Particularly in Hungary, there were also attempts to counter the increasing international competition on the wheat market with a mix of protectionism, a higher degree of processing of export goods, and the diversification of agricultural production and exports.

In the 1920s, the tendency towards overproduction on the global wheat market increased significantly. One reason for this was that exporters from overseas had taken over a large part of the wheat supply of Western European countries during the First World War and tried to maintain this position after the war. In this constellation, the structurally induced inability of wheat producers to react to changes in market conditions unfolded. During the Great Depression, the Eastern European states intervened in the grain trade with a previously unimaginable intensity, despite their high level of debt, and tried to prevent a decline in agricultural exports through subsidies. Furthermore, they developed the concept of a European system of tariff preferences. This was transferred to the League of Nations by the International Commission of Agriculture (CIA), where it replaced older liberal market concepts. A decisive prerequisite for this development was the establishment of an Eastern European agricultural bloc, which had a great deal of influence in the CIA.

In conclusion, it should once again be emphasized that the Eastern European grain economy was extraordinarily closely intertwined with the world economy between 1870 and 1939. It is true that as a result of war, revolution and political transformation in the years after the war, Eastern Europe's share of the global wheat market declined dramatically. In the world economic crisis, foreign trade in general and the wheat trade in particular collapsed. However, both the Soviet Union and the Danube countries made various efforts to revitalize and restructure the wheat trade, and increasingly benefited from the actions of international organizations. Thus, we have to depart from the traditional view that Eastern European economies were not successful on the world markets; to the contrary, actors from the region shaped the processes of economic globalization in various ways and often with innovative strategies.

Notes

1   Gema Aparicio and Vicente Pinilla, 'International Trade in Wheat and Other Cereals and the Collapse of the First Wave of Globalization: 1900–38', *Journal of Global History* 14 (2019) 1, pp. 50–2.

2   Jacek Kochanowicz and Bogdan Murgescu, 'Rural and Urban Worlds: Between economic modernization and persistent backwardness', in *The Routledge History of East Central Europe since 1700*, ed. Irina Livezeanu and Árpád von Klimó (London: Routledge, 2017), pp. 89–95; Iván T. Berend, *An Economic History of Nineteenth-Century Europe: Diversity and Industrialization* (Cambridge: Cambridge University Press, 2013), pp. 288–303; Kevin H. O'Rourke, 'The European Grain Invasion, 1870–1913', *Journal of Economic History* 57 (1997), pp. 775–801.

3   David Chilosi and Giovanni Federico, 'The effects of market integration during the first globalization: a multi-market approach', *European Review of Economic History* 25 (2020), pp. 20–58.

4   Barry Goodwin and Thomas Grennes, 'Tsarist Russia and the World Wheat Market', *Explorations in Economic History* 35 (1998) 4, pp. 405–30, here at p. 408.

5   Peter Gatrell, 'Poor Russia, Poor Show: Mobilizing a Backward Economy for War, 1914–1917', in *The Economics of World War I*, ed. S. Broadberry and M. Harrison (Cambridge: Cambridge University Press, 2005), pp. 235–75.

6   John Lampe and Marvin Jackson, *Balkan Economic History, 1550–1950: From Imperial Borderlands to Developing Nations* (Bloomington: Indiana University Press, 1982), pp. 159–64; Peter Gunst, 'Agrarian Developments in East Central Europe at the Turn of the Century', in *Hungarian Agrarian Society from the Emancipation of Serfs (1848) to the Re-privatization of Land*, ed. Peter Gunst (New York: Columbia University Press, 1998), pp. 29–34.

7   Miklós Szuhay, 'The Capitalization of Agriculture', in Gunst, *Hungarian Agrarian Society*, pp. 118–120.

8   Stanford University. Food research Institute. *Wheat Studies of the Food Research Institute* 1 (Stanford University, CA, 1924), p. 26. See also Gatrell, 'Poor Russia', pp. 241 n. and 256–9; Lampe and Jackson, *Balkan Economic History*, pp. 344–6; Avner Offer, *The First World War: An Agrarian Interpretation* (Oxford: Oxford University Press, 1989).

9   Vladimir Timoshenko, *World Agriculture and the Depression* (Ann Arbor: University of Michigan Press, 1933), pp. 553–69; Wilfred Malenbaum, *The World Wheat Economy 1885–1939* (Cambridge, MA: Harvard University Press, 1953), pp. 8–11 and 106; Ivan Berend, 'Agriculture', in *The Economic History of Eastern Europe 1919–1975*, Vol. 1., ed. M. C. Kaser and E. A. Radice (Oxford: Clarendon Press 1985), pp. 171–4; Jari Eloranta, Stefan Nikolić and Flora Macher, 'Between Disintegration and convergence: 1918-1939. Flows of capital, goods, and labor', in *The Economic History of Central, East and South-East Europe. 1800 to the Present*, ed. Matthias Morys (London: Routledge 2021), pp. 225–31.

10   Robert Lewis, 'Foreign Economic Relations', in *The Economic Transformation of the Soviet Union: 1913–1945*, ed. Robert Davies, Mark Harrison and Stephen Wheatcroft (Cambridge: Cambridge University Press 1994), pp. 205–10; Robert Davies and Stephen Wheatcroft, *The Years of Hunger: Soviet Agriculture 1931–1933* (Basingstoke: Palgrave Macmillan, 2003).

11   One bushel corresponds to 27.2 kilogrammes.

12   Gregory Marchildon, 'War, Revolution and the Great Depression in the Global Wheat Trade 1917–1939', in *A Global History of Trade and Conflict since 1500*, ed. Lucia Coppolaro and Francine McKenzie (Basingstoke: Palgrave Macmillan, 2013), pp. 142–62, here at p. 145 n.

13   Nathan Marcus, Stefan Nikolić and Tobias Straumann, 'Economic Policy 1918-1939', in Morys, *The Economic History of Central, East and South-East Europe*, pp. 189–98.

14   Patricia Clavin, *Securing the World Economy: The Reinvention of the League of Nations, 1920–1946* (Oxford: Oxford University Press, 2013).

15   Witold Szulc, 'Die Warschauer Agrarkonferenz (Aug. 1930) und die Formierung des Agrarblocks in Ostmitteleuropa', *Studia Historiae Oeconomicea* 20 (1993), pp. 169–77.

16   Marchildon, *War, Revolution and the Great Depression*, p. 152.

17   In 1931 and 1932, the global wheat trade was more than 800 bushels. Marchildon, *War, Revolution and the Great Depression*, p. 157 n.

18   Malenbaum, *The World Wheat Economy*, p. 188.

Bibliography

Belyaeva, Maria and Raushan Bokusheva. 'Will climate change benefit or hurt Russian grain production? A statistical evidence from a panel approach'. *Climatic Change* 149 (2018), pp. 205–17.

Curtis, Byrd C., Sanjaya Rajaram and Helena Gómez Macpherson. *Bread Wheat: Improvement And Production*, Rome: Food and Agriculture Organization of the United Nations (FAO), 2002; U.S. Department of Agriculture. Foreign Agricultural Service. *Romania reverses decision to ban grain exports. RO2020-0010*. Bucharest: USDA, 2021. https://apps.fas.usda.gov/newgainapi/api/Report/DownloadReportByFileName?fileName=Romania%20Reverses%20Decision%20to%20Ban%20Grain%20Exports%20_Bucharest_Romania_04-19-2020

Glauben, Thomas, Linde Götz and Ulrich Koester. 'Die Rubelkrise und Russlands Exportbeschränkungen für Getreide'. In *IAMO Policy Briefs 200289*. Institute of Agricultural Development in Transition Economies (IAMO), 2015.

Headey, Derek. 'Rethinking the global food crisis: The role of trade shocks'. *Food Policy* 36 (2011), pp. 136–46.

OECD-FAO. 'Agricultural Outlook 2020-2029'. https://stats.oecd.org/

Pingali, Prabhu. 'Green Revolution: Impacts, limits, and the path ahead'. *PNAS* 109 (2012) 31, pp. 12302–8. https://doi.org/10.1073/pnas.0912953109.

Reuters. 'Russia eyes 2035 grain crop boom with $70 billion investment plan'. https://www.reuters.com/article/us-russia-grains-forecast/russia-eyes-2035-grain-crop-boom-with-70-billion-investment-plan-idUSKCN1UB1W2

Svanidze, Miranda, Linde Götz and Florian Schierhorn. 'Analyse: Wie lässt sich das Getreideproduktionspotenzial Russlands mobilisieren?' https://www.bpb.de/internationales/europa/russland/analysen/298812/analyse-wie-laesst-sich-das-getreideproduktionspotenzial-russlands-mobilisieren.

Workmann, Daniel. 'Wheat Exports by Country'. http://www.worldstopexports.com/wheat-exports-country/

Further reading

Malenbaum, Wilfred. *The World Wheat Economy 1885–1939*. Cambridge, MA: Harvard University Press, 1953.

Marchildon, Gregory P. 'War, Revolution and the Great Depression in the Global Wheat Trade 1917–1939'. In *A Global History of Trade and Conflict since 1500*, edited by Lucia Coppolaro and Francine McKenzie. Basingstoke: Palgrave Macmillan 2013, pp. 142–62.

Morys, Matthias, Ed. *The Economic History of Central, East and South-East Europe. 1800 to the Present*. London and New York: Routledge, 2021.

Müller, Uwe. 'Eastern Europe in the Wheat Crises of Globalization and Deglobalization (1870–1939)'. In *Transregional Connections in the History of East-Central Europe*, edited by Katja Castryck-Naumann. Berlin: de Gruyter, 2021, pp. 37–83.

Topik, Steven C. and Allen Wells. 'Commodity Chains in a Global Economy'. In *A World Connecting: 1870–1945*, edited by Emily S. Rosenberg. Cambridge, MA: Harvard University Press, 2012, pp. 593–811.

Into 'History's Dustbin'? Visions of Economic Development (1917–89)

Max Trecker

11

Introduction

Leon Trotsky's famous remark about the Mensheviks, who were about to leave the All-Russian Congress of Soviets in October 1917, belonging to the 'dustbin of history' stood at the beginning of a bold experiment to transform the allegedly backward Russian empire into a beacon of material progress and public welfare.[1] Trotsky's one-liner was a harbinger of what was to come. Everyone who resisted the October Revolution – which was carried through just before the Congress started – and the Bolsheviks' vision of a new Russia was meant to be pushed aside, at least in principle. The old and the new could not, so it initially was propagated, exist side by side. At its beginning in 1917, this experiment seemed doomed to fail in its infancy. Embroiled in a civil war and still engaged in hostile activities against the two large Central European empires, Germany and Austria-Hungary, during the First World War, Russia's experiment had a marginal chance of survival. Yet, finally emerging from the turmoil both of the First World War and of the Russian Civil War, the Soviet Union survived until 1991. The Soviet experiment – seen as such by the actors themselves – which at times during the 20th century had a global outlook, entailed promises of reaching extensive economic development and erasing alleged backwardness.

Nowadays, to many North Atlantic observers, and a century or so after Trotsky's remarks, Eastern Europe seems to have relapsed back to its early-20th-century image: an allegedly underdeveloped region in the backwater of the West, emulating 'Western' concepts albeit in a vulgarized manner. If, for the larger part of the 20th century, the Soviet Union embodied a flawed version of the Western concept of socialism, so their narrative goes, then Russia since the 1990s epitomizes a flawed kind of Western liberalism; one with disastrous consequences for its region's inhabitants. An example of this widespread view can be found in the dialogue between the French historian (and ex-communist) François Furet and the liberal sociologist Ralf Dahrendorf, during which the former said, 'With all the fuss and noise, not a single new idea has come out of Eastern Europe.'[2]

We see here the tip of an iceberg of assumptions about Russia and East Central Europe, all based on the belief that the modern world was, and still is, largely shaped by the 'West'. This chapter opts to counter such notions. In doing so, it hopes to save the region from the 'dustbin of history', into which many with different ideological convictions have unfairly placed it.

Its focus lies in debates around socialism and development emanating from Eastern Europe, in actors from the Soviet Union as well as from East Central European countries. After all, one cannot separate the Soviet Union from the neighbouring regions, because after the Second World War it expanded its sphere of influence by working towards installing like-minded regimes in East Central Europe. Yet, at the same time, the emerging Cold War became entangled with decolonization in the 1950s. The Cold War allowed actors from Eastern Europe to propagate their own ideas on and experiences with development worldwide. Therefore, seen with an open mind, the post-1945 period showcases how flawed is the cliché of a passive and isolated Eastern Europe that, at best, was merely reacting to events that had their epicentre somewhere else.

As such, this chapter studies models of development. We need to be aware that these models do not exist per se. Many historical actors who pursued development had their own ideas about how it could and should be brought about. Yet very often, they did not frame their thoughts and actions as models. Such models are mostly a result of scholarly analyses of what these actors did. Modelling is an analytical tool used by scholars – whether they work on economic history or on virology – to highlight specific characteristics of the phenomena they study. The aim is to differentiate between different historical formations by highlighting some of their features and downplaying others. An ideal type in the Weberian sense – or model in our sense – exists in productive contrast to the real type – or practice. While the former is abstract in nature, the latter is rooted in empirical material. Models always offer interpretations and are always a simplification of reality. When we talk in this chapter about a socialist development model, we highlight characteristics of ideas and practices that were in fact much more complex and context bounded than the model would suggest. Socialist development models hardly existed as such but are an analytical lens which helps us to see common lines that guided development-oriented thinking and action in Eastern Europe. A closer look would show considerable differences in the practice both between different socialist countries as well as within a single socialist country over the course of time. The value of thinking in models, however, lies in the clarification of key lines of concepts and thoughts, of endeavours, plans and practices.

This chapter proceeds chronologically. First, it looks at the fundamental changes at the end of the First World War and, subsequently, during the interwar period. The Soviet developments did not have significant lasting influence on other world regions prior to 1945. However, the same cannot be said about Romanian intellectuals, who contributed to

Latin American discourses on economic development before and after 1945. The Soviet Union and its European allies saw themselves as decidedly anti-colonial powers. This facilitated an exchange between state-socialist Europe and former colonies that became independent states in the 1950s and 60s. The Cold War period represents the high-water mark of East–South interaction and exchange on concepts of economic development.

The chapter concludes with a section on the post-1989 world. The concept of 'co-transformation' is employed to highlight changes in the post-1989 world that originated from Eastern Europe. Most sections focus on East–South exchange. This does not mean that debates and events in the East had no influence on Western thinking about economic development, as shown in the last section on co-transformation. Yet, other examples from the 20th century, such as the cooperation in the United Nations Economic Commission for Europe (UNECE), can also very well be used to illustrate this point. What is important to note is that even during this short period under review, the region has seen rising and falling tides of economic integration. As much as the outbreak of the First World War split the region apart economically, so did initially the collapse of state socialism in 1989–91. The EU accession of eight East Central European countries in 2004 expanded this economic rift, as those countries cut their economic ties with Eastern Europe even further. This illustrates the complexities of talking of 'Eastern Europe' as one seemingly unified object of scholarly analysis.

Crumbling empires

In 1914, when the First World War broke out, large parts of Eastern Europe were partitioned among three empires, which had been on friendly terms with each other for the most part of the preceding century: the German, the Austro-Hungarian and the Russian empires. Of the three, the German empire was regarded as the most 'developed' in terms of economic prosperity back in 1914. When hostilities broke out in the summer of that year, the German and Austro-Hungarian empires fought together against the Russian. When the October Revolution occurred three years later, the Russian empire was on the verge of collapse – defeated by those same two empires, which had been almost completely isolated during the war due to the maritime blockade imposed by the British empire. Yet, despite its (in theory) vast reserves, the Russian empire had proved unable to mobilize enough resources to stem the tide.

When Lenin and the Bolsheviks orchestrated their revolution, they had no clear idea about what a planned economy – a hallmark of their socialist economic theories – should look like, how to run it in practice, or how to stage the transition from a (backward) semi-feudal and semi-market economy into socialism. They looked to the Russian and, particularly, to the German examples of war economy for inspiration, and combined their insights with the gist of economic debates in the transnational socialist community in the immediate prewar years. The emerging Soviet model for economic development was thus born out of the mobilization practices envisioned in the First World War. It took inspiration from the German industrialist Walther Rathenau and the socialist theoretician Rudolf

Hilferding alike. Its formation as a development 'model' was therefore born as much out of the particular circumstances the Bolsheviks were facing after the revolution as of theories about economic development. In general, socialist and particular Bolshevik economic thought sought to increase quality of life for all parts of society, especially for workers and peasants, by using the enteriety of available workforces and resources, all towards one general goal. Although this approach might sound eclectic today, the amalgamation of different ideas created something new – and, as such, already provides a counterproof to François Furet's dictum.

At first, the Bolsheviks tried to nationalize the financial sector, hoping that they could steer the economy in any direction desired to execute their plans for the economic development of the former Russian empire. Behind these measures stood the theories of Rudolf Hilferding, who, in his book *Finance Capital*, had stated that capitalism had transformed at the turn of the century and was not the same as it had been fifty years earlier. According to Hilferding, most economic sectors, which had been engaged in free global competition in the previous stage of capitalism, were now increasingly organized into cartels along national lines. These cartels were steered by a meta-cartel in the form of large financial corporations. These financial corporations controlling industry were not interested in free markets and free competition but in developing an economic structure that would maximize their profits. The national cartels were fighting on the global stage to expand their market share, thereby employing state power on the ideological lines of imperialism. What Lenin and leading Bolshevik economic expert Nikolai Bukharin did was to transform Hilferding's theories into a political agenda. If financial corporations were already consciously shaping the structure of the economy and even dominating politics, it would be logical to simply nationalize them in order to have the instruments necessary to bring a socialist society into being and to turn the hierarchy between state and cartel upside down. This attempt, however, did not work – not least due to the stiff resistance put up by old political and business elites.

What followed was a fight for survival and the radicalization of the Soviet economic model, since the actors who shaped this model had to deal with a change in circumstances. The strategy pursued during the civil war was later dubbed 'war communism'. This encompassed the nationalization of all economic activity, the introduction of strict military discipline in running the economy, and the allocation of goods by administrative mechanisms instead of market mechanisms. The consequences of these policy measures were disastrous. Output declined in all sectors of the economy, peasants refused to hand over their grain to governmental commissars, and large-scale famines broke out. Despite the obvious setbacks and tremendous human suffering, war communism was at times defended as a necessary stage to make the development of socialist society possible. The most famous defence was delivered by Bukharin himself in his book *Economics of the Transition Period* in 1920. Bukharin later rescinded his view that war communism was a necessary step in the development of socialism. Others – including the Hungarian economist and leading figure of the short-lived Hungarian Soviet Republic, Eugen Várga – took a different view. Like Bukharin back in 1920, Várga argued in the late 1920s that the destruction of the old capitalist order necessitated a cycle of expanded negative reproduction, as the old economic equilibrium was becoming increasingly unstable. Therefore, a total economic breakdown was, in his eyes, a precondition for establishing true communism. These debates on the necessity of something resembling war communism resurfaced later in socialist-inspired national liberation movements outside of Eastern Europe.

After the Bolsheviks won the Civil War, they introduced the New Economic Policy (NEP), which once again allowed for a stronger role for markets and money as well as private ownership of small- and medium-sized companies. The state, however, retained control of finance, foreign trade and large industrial and service companies. The market mechanisms introduced under the NEP co-existed with the first experiments in centralized planning embodied by the State Commission for the Electrification of Russia (GOELRO) under the leadership of the engineer Gleb Krzhizhanovsky. The GOELRO later became the nucleus for the State Planning Agency (Gosplan). Therefore, the Soviet Union of the mid-1920s resembled a mixed economy, in which state agencies exerted significant influence over the course of the economy but refrained from micromanaging all economic activity. To a certain extent, this meant going back to the first months of the revolution, when party and state agencies wanted to limit their control to the commanding heights of the economy.

From 1928 on, the economists at Gosplan became responsible for drafting the Five-Year Plans that were to guide the economic development of the Soviet Union. This coincided with a strong shift in economic policy by the new leader of the Soviet Union, Joseph Stalin. Under Stalin's leadership, most of the NEP reforms were abolished and agriculture was collectivized. The socialist development model in its Soviet and Stalinist variant, which would later be exported to East Central Europe and to parts of the world outside Europe after the Second World War, was established by the early 1930s. This development model relied on strict central planning, a very limited role for markets, no private entrepreneurship, forced collectivization of agriculture, and a strong preference for investing in heavy industries to the detriment of light industries and agriculture. These features have often been seen as synonymous with *the* socialist development model in contemporary perception, thereby ignoring its tumultuous genesis. The Soviet experiment had already garnered a lot of attention in the interwar period. This was particularly true for the Great Depression period in the 1930s, when the Soviet economy seemed to grow while all other regions of the world experienced an economic meltdown. Although this view was not entirely justified by the facts, it contributed to the prestige of the Soviet Union and its development model. The Soviet Union could profit from this rising prestige after the Second World War. Debates about the right developmental path to a socialist society would once again flare up in the post-1945 period, often with reference to the Soviet debates of the 1920s. For all practical purposes, however, the application of this development model remained basically limited to the Soviet Union in the interwar period.

East Central Europe saw the establishment of several new states after the First World War. These states were carved out of the former German, Russian and Austro-Hungarian empires. Envisaged to be nation-states, most of them had difficulties integrating national minorities and finding reliable paths to prosperity while resorting to protectionism or policy instruments bordering on autarchy. This does not mean that East Central Europe had been suffering from intellectual drought in the interwar period. With the exception of

Czechoslovakia, which had inherited the main industrial centres of the former Austro-Hungarian empire, all East Central European countries had been overwhelmingly agrarian. Combined with a relatively high population density, this meant severe underemployment of the countryside. A large number of poor peasants with no or almost no land stood against a tiny class of landed gentry. This constellation provided a fertile ground for debates about economic development that could resonate beyond the region.

Romania proves a good case in point. The country had more than doubled in size after the First World War. Despite having been on the side of the victors of war, the country had suffered much from fighting and been occupied by the Central Powers. After the war, the Romanian state had not only to rebuild the country but also to integrate the vast new territories annexed after the war, which included sizable minorities such as Germans, Hungarians and Jews. As 80 per cent of the population was engaged in agriculture, land reform became an important topic in interwar Romania. This coincided with a change in attitudes towards governmentality. The economic and social consequences of the war had severely undermined the belief in 19th-century laissez-faire liberalism. Instead, many actors on different levels of society began to believe in the possibility and duty of the state to intervene in economic affairs and to consciously shape society to achieve a desired outcome.

These debates led to the emergence of Romanian neoliberalism. Mihail Manoilescu and Stefan Zeletin were the two main representatives of this approach, with Zeletin having published a book titled *Neoliberalismul* in 1927. Not only an economist but also a sociologist and philosopher, Zeletin argued that Western foreign investment had transformed feudal Romania into a capitalist society and created a middle class. Yet, the same mechanism had fuelled a counter-reaction against Westernization and dependence on foreign capital and ideas. The only possible solution, he argued, would be to find a way to a capitalist modernity on Romanian terms without isolating the country entirely or receding back into the feudal past. Transforming Romania from an agricultural into an industrial country by liberal means could end a trade pattern of unequal exchange between Romania and the West and improve dismal living conditions in the countryside.

In contrast to Zeletin, Manoilescu was supportive of anti-Semitism and autocratic rule. Unsurprisingly, he was also more étatist in his thinking – that is, he relied more on the power of the state to transform society. According to Manoilescu, the state should help the domestic bourgeoisie to develop the country economically. Despite being highly interventionist, the government should act within the framework of a liberal understanding of the economy. Domestic capital should be shielded from foreign interference, thus necessitating protectionism. The aim, however, was not to shield the economy forever but to nurture particularly the development of domestic industries, with subsidies and other measures of political influence, until they became internationally competitive. The state was to encourage investment in industries that had a higher marginal productivity than the average national productivity, regardless of the situation on the world market. This amalgamation of state and business is also called 'corporatism'. Manoilescu's ideas found adherents not only in Southern Europe, e.g. Francoist Spain, but also across the Atlantic Ocean in Latin America.

The Latin American countries had been hit hard by the Great Depression of the 1930s. Their hitherto export-oriented economic model was rejected by local elites. Manoilescu's ideas became important in shaping the concept of industrialization by import substitution, which was adopted by most Latin American countries in the 1930s and 40s. This concept entailed fostering industrialization by state measures and trade controls by the government with a strong protectionist stance. In contrast to the Soviet model, full nationalization was off the table; markets and private entrepreneurship guided most decisions by economic actors. However, significant state intervention considerably distorted the market mechanism. Manoilescu's ideas found their way from theory into practice in Latin America via actors like the economist Raúl Prebisch and the UN Economic Commission for Latin America. The history of Romanian neoliberalism influencing debates on development and socio-economic practices is a further counterproof to Furet's statement that Eastern Europe produced no new ideas for most of the 20th century.

The dawn of a new era

The Soviet Union belonged to the victors of the Second World War. All East Central European states had been either occupied by German forces or allied with the Third Reich. As a consequence of the war, the Soviet Union expanded its sphere of influence westward, occupying all East Central European countries and regions. From 1948 on, the countries that the Red Army occupied were increasingly sovietized, thereby becoming sister republics of the Soviet Union. Their development and transformation were guided and controlled by the Kremlin. As long as Stalin lived, this control meant the forceful adoption of the Stalinist development model of the 1930s: with the partial exception of East Germany, all economic activity was nationalized, the role of markets was severely limited, and five-year planning by a central state agency was introduced together with a state monopoly on trade. As in the Soviet Union of the 1930s, private consumption and the development of agriculture were consciously depressed by the state in order to steer investment funds into the development of heavy industries and the production of (industrial) raw materials.

The result was a homogenized economic landscape between the river Elbe and the Pacific Ocean. The problem was that the economic structures created by the Stalinist development model, with the forced mobilization of all available workforce and material in the region, offered few comparative advantages. As every country had been building the same kind of iron and steel works, there was little opportunity for specializing production and generating gains in productivity by mutual trade. The economies of East Central and Eastern Europe were structured similarly but not integrated with each other. This proved a great obstacle for the future, since the hypothetically enormous gains resulting from such an envisaged large common market could not be harvested. Founded in 1949, the Council for Mutual Economic Assistance (CMEA) was tasked with harmonizing the economic space of Eastern Europe and fostering economic development in the subsequent years.

Despite great efforts, the CMEA was unable to fully overcome the negative consequences of the Stalinist development model imposed on the region in the immediate postwar years. Nevertheless, it provided a forum for discussion on economic development and integration for actors from the region, which had never existed before.

Following Stalin's death in 1953, towards the mid-decade, unrest began to materialize in the region. After Stalin's death, communist political elites never again dared to use his violent mobilization techniques to foster economic development. Despite these significant downsides, the application of the Stalinist development model also created a positive legacy – at least, partially. Formerly agrarian states had industrialized at breakneck speed within less than a decade. Agrarian underemployment and overpopulation had been done away with; an industrial proletariat created. The last point was ideologically important and an intended outcome. It showed the possibility for economic and social development in the form of a radical transformation of society by state intervention. This 'positive' legacy would resonate outside the region in the following decades.

The latter half of the 1950s and the 60s were laden with debates on the right developmental path to socialism in Eastern Europe, as virtually all state-socialist countries tinkered with economic reforms. What they had in common was a strengthening consumer goods sector, the reintroduction of some form of private ownership of small companies, increased trading with the West, and a stronger focus on the allocation of goods by market mechanisms. These measures greatly improved living standards in Eastern Europe in the subsequent years, and created a socialist consumer society. Up to the 1970s, economic growth rates in the region were among the highest in the world. These partial changes of the development model after Stalin's death, however, also contributed to a broadening rift with the People's Republic of China (PRC). The PRC and the Soviet Union had signed a friendship treaty in 1950. As a consequence, several thousand Soviet experts as well as experts from East Central Europe went to the PRC in the 1950s. The PRC hence became an important trading partner of all Eastern European countries. Yet, Mao Zedong and his allies did not appreciate the changes of the mid- and late 1950s. The Chinese leadership's answer to this perceived threat was the Great Leap Forward, which was basically a vulgarized version of the Stalinist development model of the 1930s. However, this failed to fulfil the economic performance expectations of the PRC leadership and was received negatively in Eastern Europe, contributing to the Sino-Soviet split of the 1960s.

This search for the right developmental path to socialism occurred simultaneously, and became partially intertwined, with decolonization. At the end of the Second World War, the future of the European colonial empires was unclear. India's independence from Britain in 1947 was a milestone of decolonization but not necessarily a game changer. It was, rather, a harbinger of imperial retrenchment, as the French tried to reassert their control over Vietnam with a massive military intervention at the same time. By the late 1950s, after the French had lost in Vietnam and the British had been unable to regain supremacy over the Suez Canal, decolonization was unstoppable. The societies of most decolonized countries were looking for not merely formal political freedom but also economic independence. This meant economic independence from their former colonial masters, who had left behind export-oriented economic structures and hardly developed internal markets. The fact that the PRC – increasingly at odds with Eastern European socialists – actively engaged in relations with the Global South was a factor that actively pushed Eastern Europeans to do the same.

The state-socialist countries of Eastern Europe became almost a natural partner of the newly independent states. Partnership, however, did not mean that the Soviet Union or one of its smaller Eastern European allies could control the internal affairs of a country like India. To stay with the Indian example, although Indian elites were keen to benefit from technological developments in the West, they had not fought for independence only to become totally economically dependent on the United States or any other Western (or Eastern) country. What brought them together with their Eastern European peers was a complementary understanding of economic development controlled by the state and not left solely to the forces of the free market. This common understanding of development entailed a focus on planning and industrialization with a bias towards heavy industries. The development of a heavy industries sector was seen as vital – not only by Indian elites – in transforming the country from an agricultural into an industrial one. Since most former colonies suffered from underemployment and overpopulation in the countryside, as well, the Eastern European development model was a possible, albeit radical, road to solve these problems. What the political elites in most newly independent states found fascinating in the Stalinist development model was its great socio-economic transformational power.

In general, the state-socialist countries of Eastern Europe were not interested in exporting their development ideas entirely, and neither were the potential recipients in the Global South in taking over the Soviet model unequivocally. Seen from a Southern perspective, contact with the East contained both a direct and an indirect advantage: The direct advantage was that the East offered credits with which to build factories and infrastructure as well as know-how on how to organize a state-led industrialization drive. The fact that the adoption of the Soviet model of development entirely was not a precondition contributed to the appeal of contacts with Eastern Europe. The indirect advantage was that the sheer existence of an alternative in the form of socialist Eastern Europe forced Western countries – particularly, the former imperial centres – to look for compromises when dealing with their former colonies. The Western European and North American countries had no internal incentive to give in to the demands for a more just world economic order, as uttered by representatives of the Global South. They were not interested in fostering the industrial development of their former colonies to the detriment of their own industries. Their primary self-interest was access to cheap resources either to rebuild their own economies, which was the case for Western Europe, or to retain their economic advantage over the rest of the world, as was the case for the United States.

The challenge that an internationalist Eastern Europe with a different development model and ideology posed to the West necessitated a more balanced approach by the Western countries that at least partially reconciled narrow self-interest with the interests of their potential partners. One outcome of this balanced approach was an international agreement on coffee that lasted as long as the Eastern European challenge after the end of the Second World War existed. Out of the fear of (primarily) Latin American coffee growers turning Soviet, Western politicians and consumers accepted higher prices for an otherwise very prestigious commodity. The International Coffee Agreement (ICA) came into being in 1962 and was supervised by the International Coffee Organization established one year later. It is no coincidence that the system of quotas that stabilized coffee prices collapsed in the summer of 1989 when state socialism in Eastern Europe was on the brink of collapse. The breakdown of the agreement resulted in rapidly deteriorating coffee prices in the early 1990s. This was beneficial for coffee consumers in the West yet detrimental for coffee planters in the Global South.

After Stalin's death, the state-socialist countries of Eastern Europe also played very active roles in international organizations and the UN. Representatives from Eastern Europe took part in the debates in various UN bodies on the future of the global economy after the demise of the old European colonial empires. The most important UN bodies concerned with these debates were the United Nations Industrial Development Organisation (UNIDO) and the United Nations Conference on Trade and Development (UNCTAD). The call for a New International Economic Order (NIEO) emerged out of these UN debates. In the early 1970s, the Soviet Union alone was a member of over two hundred political and non-governmental organizations. This, in itself, makes it clear that processes of globalization neither originated from the United States or the West alone nor were propagated solely by neoliberal economists and politicians in the 1980s and 90s. The Cold War era saw the emergence of a global interconnectedness actively shaped by many actors from Eastern Europe. We need to acknowledge a socialist globalization as one competing model in the Cold War era and an alternative to the West.

However, Eastern Europe was no strictly unified bloc on the international stage. Contemporaries recognized variations in ideas on what socialist development could mean. In economic terms, Hungary was perceived as a more liberal and market-friendly version of the Soviet model than the GDR or the Soviet Union itself.

As a consequence of the growing interconnectedness, trade increased as personal contacts multiplied. Trade between the East and South was often organized on a clearing or barter basis. According to modern economic theory, this is considered an archaic way of organizing trade. However, seen from the actors' perspective, it contained some advantages. Economic crises in so-called developing countries often took and still take the form of a balance-of-payments crisis. Economic development in a very basic sense demands the accumulation of a capital stock. This can take very tangible forms such as bridges, resource extraction sites and factories as well as intangible forms such as accumulation of knowledge. To bridge the development gap between the North and South after 1945, the countries in the Global South needed a lot of capital and they needed to accumulate it at a faster rate than the northern half of the globe. This often led to countries such as Brazil, India or Mexico importing sophisticated machinery on credit from public or private lenders. These credits had to be paid back in currencies like US dollars or British pounds, over which the debtor had no control. If the debtor could not pay on time, this triggered a wave of capital flight and the collapse of the economy.

The state-socialist countries of Eastern Europe offered to circumvent this mechanism by conducting trade in local currencies and agreeing on annual trade quotas. Credits – as long as they did not include importing Western technology as well – were paid back in local goods, not in internationally convertible currencies like the US dollar. These agreements could take such exemplary forms as a factory being erected by Eastern European engineers and delivering a certain percentage of its final produce for a fixed amount of time to the lending country. The downside of this system was that it was a rather inefficient mode of trading. On the upside, this mechanism was immune to traditional balance-of-payments crises. A further advantage was that this way of doing business, with pre-agreed annual trading quotas, created a relatively stable basic demand for the traditional export goods of countries such as India or Egypt. It therefore constituted a partial insurance against the short-term volatility of international export markets with prices being decided in London or New York. Furthermore, since trade had to be balanced, this created export markets in the East for goods from the Global South. This was also true for domestic goods that could not be sold easily to the West for various reasons.

Despite its relative inefficiency compared with Western technology – on average – Eastern machines and factories could be traded with the Global South. The prime reason was that economic development – in the eyes of contemporaries – meant more than producing steel or machines at the fastest possible rate with the latest technology. Economic development was about creating an industrial working class and national production lines, as well. Thus, it also meant becoming partially independent from 'unequal' economic exchange with the West. This did not necessitate the latest technology; at times, quite the contrary was the case. Sophisticated technology often demanded skilled craftsmen and engineers; both were scarce in predominantly agricultural societies. Eastern European technology was less capital and technology and more labour intensive. Sometimes, this suited the developing countries in the Cold War period better than Western modes of production since their economies possessed an abundance of (unskilled) labour but were capital scarce.

What Eastern and Southern economists could not overcome was the structural inequality of trade patterns between their respective countries. Despite numerous declarations to the contrary, Eastern policymakers were often unwilling to import machines from the South. They were content with importing mainly agricultural products and resources to preserve their own economic independence. This policy severely limited the potential mutual gains of East–South economic cooperation. It also points to a central weakness of the Eastern European development model in socialist times. The Eastern European economies proved very adept at transferring excess labour from agriculture to the industrial sector. This created extensive growth – that is, an increase in labour input in industry led to an increase in output. This model could only work up to a certain point. When all excess labour had been transferred to industry, there could be no more extensive growth. What remained was intensive growth: an increase in output with the same input – thus, an increase in labour productivity. This would have required a restructuring of industry in Eastern Europe, and sophisticated intra-industrial cooperation schemes both within Eastern Europe and between Eastern Europe and other parts of the world. This never happened on a sufficient scale. The difficulties encountered in creating large-scale intra-industrial cooperation between East and South were thus a symptom of the larger deficiencies of the state-socialist development model practised in Eastern Europe.

Some countries in the Global South not only traded extensively with the East in the Cold War period, or tried to profit from partially emulating its model of economic development, but actually became Soviet countries themselves. These were, namely, Cuba and Vietnam. Both became full members of the CMEA in the 1970s, making it a global organization for economic development. Cuba and Vietnam were now closely integrated with the Eastern European economies. Given its fragile security situation, Vietnam could profit less from this integration than Cuba. The other CMEA member states granted Cuba preferential prices for sugar – its main export commodity. The surplus generated by exporting sugar could in turn be used by Cuban planners to import Eastern European technology and consumer goods. This led to increasing levels of industrialization and rising living standards in Cuba in the 1970s and 80s.

In the 1980s, Angola, Ethiopia and Mozambique wanted to join the CMEA as well. This attempt failed due to political instability in these countries and political resistance in the smaller European CMEA member states. The former expected from membership in the CMEA material support and expertise for rapidly industrializing their countries, preferential and stable prices for their main export lines, and low-interest credits to finance the necessary imports to improve domestic living standards and to build up an industrial base. The latter feared that the accession of these three African nations could prove an economic burden for them in the foreseeable future.

Despite its rapid dissolution in the late 1980s and early 90s and despite its obvious failure, it should not be forgotten that the socialist world encompassed roughly one third of the world population in the early 1980s. This was not only, and not even primarily, due to the forceful suppression of resistance by a small socialist elite acting on Moscow's behalf. An important element of the appeal of state socialism was the promise of development. Although at no point in time was the Soviet Union able to control all these political movements, together with the other Eastern European states, it was an important focal point and a centre of intellectual and political gravity.

The socialist reception of the New International Economic Order

Bence Kocsev

The immediate sentiment of the newly independent countries in the early post-Second World War decades had largely been shaped by hopes and illusions related to the assumption that political independence would pave the way for economic growth and convergence. Although the 'development era' – as it was called by the historian Frederick Cooper – had provided seemingly favourable conditions for the economic advancement of the postcolonial states and, in fact, resulted in a number of positive achievements from an economic textbook point of view, many of the postcolonial states were unable to promote sustainable development. The Rostowian prophecy that all nations sail the same voyage and are destined to the same prosperity thus quickly turned out to be a false interpretation of global socio-economic processes. The post-independence development impasse substantially tempered the initial optimism of the newly independent countries and led to a dynamic polarization of interests between the North and South. Henceforth, the adjustment of the global economic system became a primary concern for a number of political leaders, activists and theorists. A concerted effort – later culminating in the so-called North–South dialogue – was initiated in the form of various summits, conferences and negotiations in order to mitigate the growing conflict. Issues pertaining to the alteration of the international economic hierarchy gradually emerged from these contexts in increasing numbers.

By making development a top priority on the international agenda and accumulating sufficient economic and political potential, developing countries eventually managed to pass the ambitious Declaration for the Establishment of a New International Economic Order (NIEO) during the 6th Special Session of the UN General Assembly in 1974. The passed resolution called for a reform of almost every aspect of the global economic structure and governance, and aimed at creating frameworks and mechanisms that could provide favourable conditions for the economic development of the Third World. As the most tangible dividing lines were those between the mainstream advanced capitalist countries and the developing ones, the common narrative tells the story of the NIEO within the framework of the North–South dialogue and habitually omits how Eastern European inputs influenced the course and fate of these negotiations. Neglecting the socialist bloc countries was, however, by no means without reason. Although the NIEO was probably the most widely debated issue within the international community during the 1970s and while the European socialist countries (with the exception of Romania and Yugoslavia) supported its aims on the surface, they nonetheless remained reluctant to mingle into the related negotiations when it came to actual decision making and implementation.

This ambiguous approach by the socialist countries seems particularly striking in the light of the fact that by the 1970s these countries had grown into a significant group in the international system and became increasingly entangled with both the capitalist and developing countries. Whereas cooperation in this latter regard yielded mixed results, given the intensity and variety of contacts as well as the new quality that this East–South nexus brought to global relations, it occupied a special position in the foreign policy of these socialist states. Consequently, while this bloc of countries could not dissociate itself from most of the demands of the developing world, they nevertheless insisted that the NIEO was simply a matter of conflict between developing and capitalist countries that had previously put them under exploited colonial control. This approach was often supplemented by positions that propagated the view that reforming the existing international economic order could only be accomplished through the spread of socialism on a global scale. This non-cooperative attitude eventually soured relationships with the developing countries, and substantially contributed to the disillusionment and distancing of this group of states from the socialist bloc.

Yet the global economic crisis that rippled across the socialist bloc with even worse consequences than in the capitalist hemisphere eventually highlighted the CMEA's inability to mitigate the mounting challenges posed by deteriorating economic conditions. The direct interest of some socialist economic experts in reforming international economic relations and creating a new world economic order (which might entail the opening up of the CMEA) became increasingly explicit. Their search for alternatives brought these economists closer to the idea of the NIEO, as they understood it. Despite differences, both the East and the South had to confront fundamental shared challenges and the fact that without the necessary implementation of structural and institutional reforms their peripheral positions would further deteriorate. In this sense, scrutiny of the reception of the NIEO by socialist expert circles can highlight how certain actors and stakeholders sought to cope with the failure of the Soviet Union's attempt to reshape the setting of the world economic order and the structure of global governance to its advantage.

It is within this context that the contribution of Hungarian economists features prominently. In order to analyse the concept from the perspective of CMEA countries, a separate research unit with internationally recognized development economists like József Bognár, Mihály Simai and Tamás Szentes, to name just a few, was created within the well-respected Institute for World Economics in Budapest. Despite the fact that, on the political level, the overwhelming majority of the European socialist countries eventually withdrew from any active participation in the NIEO negotiations, these researchers were able to join the global thinking on this initiative. This manifested itself, among other ways, in a wide array of publications as well as (co-)organized workshops and conferences concerning this global idea. Interestingly, although within a rather limited margin, the Institute was even able to oppose the views of the Soviet Union and approached the question in a more cooperative and pragmatic manner than the Soviets did. As contemporaries recall, rather than presenting general yet rather vague ideas on the table, their proposals contained a number of concrete practical recommendations that could help both the developing and the socialist countries to overcome their unequal economic positions; the common statement of the European socialist countries at the UNCTAD IV conference in Nairobi in 1976 was, for instance, generally based on the draft made by the researchers of the Institute.

Today's readers may be surprised by the extent to which researchers such as the long-time director of the Institute, József Bognár, were committed to issues that were close to the NIEO demands. His exceptionally broad interests and his engagement in drawing attention to the mounting problems that humanity was increasingly facing made Bognár one of the most well-received economic experts of the bloc, whose reputation radiated even beyond the Iron Curtain. Dedicated to making ways for a more resilient economic, social and environmental future, he consciously used his academic and public appearances (including those on television and radio) to raise awareness not only about global questions close to the NIEO demands but also on issues like non-renewable energies, food security and technical and environmental hazards.

Communism has fallen and the 'West' is victorious?

The Soviet bloc collapsed between 1989 and 1991. As a consequence, Eastern Europe lost the political and socio-economic cohesion that it had gained by force at the end of the Second World War. The Soviet Union was dissolved completely along the lines of its internal borders, with the Russian Federation forming the largest heir to the Soviet realm. The 1990s were marked by a peripheralization of the whole region. Many contacts established during the Cold War period vanished. Actors from Eastern Europe could hardly deliver a positive vision of development to the outside world after the dissolution of state socialism since their societies were themselves regarded as in need of outside guidance. This was to a certain degree a marketing problem and not due to a lack of intellectual substance in the region. The search for a third way to overcome the Stalinist heritage without turning capitalist had occupied not only dissident minds after Stalin's death but also the minds of quite a few critical thinkers who remained within the boundaries of what could be said and published without inviting closer scrutiny by the secret police. In 1989–90, a considerable number of regional actors wanted to reform socialism and advocated market socialism as a new economic doctrine.

The basic idea behind market socialism is that the state retains a dominant role in economic life but leaves significant room for market mechanisms and private enterprises to foster innovation and an efficient allocation of resources. Furthermore, the state is to soften the negative social consequences of technological change and markets. Such a system gives greater power to individual workers and weakens central bureaucracy. In the eyes of its advocates, it combines the social security and social justice approach of socialism with the efficiency of a market economy. To some degree, these ideas were connected to the very early phase of the Soviet Revolution in 1917/18 and the NEP. Advocates of reformed or market socialism did not harbour enough political acumen to gather the political power necessary to implement their ideas; 1989 could have been the great moment of these intellectuals and activists looking for a third way. In some countries, such as the GDR, they were even part of the government for a short period of time. But they failed for various reasons: former state-socialist elites wanted to secure their own transition to a better future and engaged in insider dealing and the asset-stripping of state companies to accumulate private wealth; large parts of society did not want to be associated any more with anything that had the name 'socialist' in it; and Western players on the international stage used a successful combination of carrot-and-stick arguments to nudge Eastern European actors into adopting their preferred Western economic behaviour.

The 1990s coincided with a wave of de-industrialization that hit the region. This was particularly bitter since many of the industries had been erected by a suppression of consumption in socialist times. Thus, the events of the 1990s discredited the state-socialist development model in the eyes of many observers. Similar processes happened in many formerly close economic and political partner countries in Latin America, Africa and Asia, as any development model relying on state-led industrialization and import substitution lost its appeal in the 1990s. This process had already started in the early 1980s, but the dissolution of state socialism in Eastern Europe was an event the shockwaves of which could also be felt in other parts of the world. The fallout was not only ideological; it also took very tangible forms. Countries like Cuba and Vietnam were hit the hardest, as they had the closest economic ties to and entanglement with Eastern Europe prior to 1991. Other countries including Syria, Egypt and India had to adapt their economies, as well. However, not all factories and infrastructures that were built with know-how and machinery from Eastern Europe during the Cold War went out of business in the 1990s. The case of India shows that companies, particularly in the heavy industries sector, could remain competitive after 1990 instead of turning their localities into giant rust belts. The heavy machine-building company Bharat Heavy Electricals Limited (BHEL) and Steel Authority India Limited (SAIL) are cases in point.

In Eastern Europe, the 1990s are often regarded as a period of transformation. The term signifies the adoption of the Western model of export-oriented free market economies. It implies a clear hierarchy, with the Western model seen as superior and the Eastern European societies as objects in a one-directional transfer of knowledge. The East therefore had to learn to emulate the Western development model. The question discussed by economists from inside and outside the region was not whether or not but how this transformation would happen. While some advocated shock therapy, others opted for a gradual transformation. The initial economic results of this process did not live up to the high expectations, as can be seen by the de-industrialization of the 1990s. This led to unemployment and the impoverishment of significant sections of the population. Hardest hit by these developments were women and minorities, who often were the first to lose their jobs.

In general, transformation implies that actors from Eastern Europe hardly possessed any agency in the process, as their roles were limited to implementing the Western development model with differing degrees of efficiency. This view was nurtured by the publications of mostly Western economic and political advisers involved in the process, who often blamed any obvious policy failures on the lack of will and ability of their Eastern European counterparts. It is important, however, to differentiate between mere speech acts aiming at discursive dominance and actual political and economic decision making. While most Western experts advocated a rapid transformation to a Western-style market economy, i.e. shock therapy, such measures were not implemented in any Eastern European country. The sharp contrast between radical and gradual approaches to market reforms existed in theory rather than in practice. This did not reduce the potential fallout from such measures. Mass privatization schemes of the 1990s could never live up to the expectations of economic experts. Although far less violent in a narrow sense, this mass privatization caused social upheaval on a scale comparable with the mass collectivization of the early Stalinist period in the Soviet Union, when the model of economic development was changed equally rapidly. Privatization procedures were often untransparent and flawed. They were marked by manipulation by insiders like former factory managers, and did not lead to widespread wealth and prosperity. In this regard, Eastern Europe became a rather negative example for economic development schemes.

An economic turn-around in the region started in the late 1990s and early 2000s, and affected the countries that had experienced the worst economic performance after

1989 – including Russia and Ukraine, as well as Hungary and Poland. The EU accession of East Central European states in 2004 lowered the economic cohesion of the region further. East Central Europe became the eastern periphery of the EU, which was in every respect dominated by the larger Western European states – not because of any specific EU regulation but because of the sheer political and economic power of France, Germany and Italy. Despite this peripheralization, Eastern Europe has influenced models of economic development in other regions, as well. After 1990, the region became a laboratory for economic concepts that could not be implemented in other regions, mainly in the West, because of the anticipated resistance of several political and social stakeholders. This applied particularly to the ideas of liberalization, deregulation and privatization to foster economic development. Despite their contested legacy, these concepts were later also applied in the West. This phenomenon of an East–West transfer is called 'co-transformation'.

Some political regimes in the region – this applies mainly to Hungary and the Russian Federation – have turned to more authoritarian forms of rule, particularly after the financial and economic crisis of 2007. In the case of the Russian Federation, this tendency has been accelerated following the occupation of Crimea. A common term used for these political systems – sometimes also used as self-description – is 'illiberal democracy'. These political changes were accompanied by transformations in the economic development model, as well. The Russian Federation, in particular, is still trading with other parts of the world but has taken substantial measures to seal itself off from changes in world trade. This move encompasses investments and nationalization campaigns in sectors that, according to the government, are deemed essential for national security and the future of the country. Far from being a complex programme for a state-led industrialization drive, these measures follow no systematic logic and are often ad hoc in nature. The primary promise of this development model is not to improve the material and social well-being of individuals but to protect the collective body of the nation from alleged outside interference. Nevertheless, it has led to a much more active role for the government in economic affairs – something that had seemed impossible in the early 2000s, when open markets, export-oriented growth and the attraction of foreign direct investments were the prime signifiers of economic development.

Conclusion

This chapter has shed light on thoughts on economic development in Eastern Europe since 1917 and their repercussions for other world regions. Far from being isolated and passive, Eastern European actors had an impact on debates and policies in other parts of the world during the whole period under consideration in this chapter. This process was not one-sided. As much as actors from Eastern Europe influenced debates in other parts of the world, so too were they influenced by debates and policies in other world regions and drew their own conclusions from them. Many, albeit not all, of these transfers are associated with state socialism. One important and underappreciated exception is Romanian neoliberalism. Thinkers like Stefan Zeletin and Mihail Manoilescu were dealing with questions of underdevelopment in a capitalist framework in the interwar period. They were asking how a largely agricultural society dependent on Western capital could deliberately foster national economic development and overcome structural imbalances in the global economy without being radically at odds with the surrounding world. Their thinking did not influence their home country in the long term but had a very long afterlife in Latin America. The emergence of both the Soviet economic system in the 1920s and the economic development model associated with illiberal democracy in Eastern Europe, from the 2000s onwards, show how actors from the region took up influences from other parts of the world and adapted them to their own needs.

Socialist thinking as it emerged in Eastern Europe was searching for alternative development outside the framework of capitalism. It became dominant in its Stalinist version in the region in the aftermath of the Second World War. Reform processes in socialist Eastern Europe overlapped and became entangled with decolonization in the Cold War period. Former colonies were looking to supplement their political freedom with economic independence. This necessitated some kind of break with the capitalist past that had often been imposed on them by their former colonial rulers. Socialist Eastern Europe was a logical partner for such undertakings. Experts from Eastern Europe worked in former colonies to foster economic development and find ways of cooperation beneficial for all parties involved. They left a legacy still tangible today in several countries in Asia, Africa and Latin America. Development thinking in Eastern Europe largely lost its positive appeal after 1991. What some countries in the region gained after 2007 was a negative appeal in the sense that their development model, chosen in the aftermath of the financial crisis, no longer aimed at providing the highest quality of life for its citizens but instead focused on preserving national autonomy and suppressing foreign cultural, political and economic influence. Trade relations between Eastern European countries and countries like India or Algeria still exist. However, as the Indian author Hari Vasudevan has titled his book on Indo-Russian economic relations after 1991, they are but 'shadows of substance'.[3] In the case of Russia, in particular, post-1991 economic relations have been concentrated mainly on the armaments sector and have no relation to any notions of development.

The often-neglected legacy of the active and direct involvement of Eastern European actors in, and influence on, other world regions lie in the indirect consequences of their activities. In the post-1945 period, this encompassed the West–South relationship. Because of the potentially global outreach of the Eastern European development model, Western actors had to consider the needs of their partners in the South to some degree. This can be seen in international treaties on the regulation of trade like the International Coffee Agreement. The formulations of the UN Development Goals and debt relief schemes to some of the economically poorest countries would have been unthinkable without the challenge of the Eastern European development model after 1945. Part of these indirect consequences of development thinking and practices in Eastern Europe is the concept of co-transformation and the repercussions of economic experiments in Eastern Europe in the 1990s. All these examples clearly point towards the false futility inherent to François Furet's dictum that 'not a single new idea has come out of Eastern Europe', and similar such statements.

Notes

1   Just as the Bolsheviks, Mensheviks were socialists, too, but they opposed the October Revolution, because – in their eyes – a revolution should be staged by the masses only after a bourgeois society had been established and not before – and certainly not by a self-styled avant-garde of a revolutionary party.
2   Ralf Dahrendorf, *Reflections on the Revolution in Europe: In a Letter Intended to Have Been Sent to a Gentleman in Warsaw* (London: Random House, 1990), p. 27.
3   Hari Vasudevan, *Shadows of Substance* (New Delhi: Manohar Press, 2010).

Further reading

Trecker, Max. *Red Money for the Global South: East–South Economic Relations in the Cold War.* London: Routledge, 2020.

Regional Development and Core–Periphery Divides

Thilo Lang

12

Introduction

In recent years, socio-spatial polarization has increasingly affected Central and Eastern Europe at the regional level. The result has been to ensure that economic growth, although considerable at the national level, has been very unevenly spread and that large parts of the population have become increasingly marginalized. EU-wide empirical studies using conventional GDP and population data reveal major North–South and East–West disparities as well as inequalities between core and periphery on the macro-regional plane. For instance, countries in the north and west of the European Union (EU) are faring better than those in the east and south, and there is still divergence between the core and the 'peripheries' of the EU. The picture is not simple, however: although Central and Eastern European countries are showing higher growth rates than the old member states, the catching-up process has been at the expense of cohesion between the regions within the Central and Eastern European member states. The aim of this chapter is to explain the emergence of new peripheries in terms of current forms of regional development and approaches to it, the relationship between centralization and peripheralization and the regional policy background, using the countries of Central and Eastern Europe as examples.

The long-term de-coupling of a growing number of non-metropolitan regions in Central and Eastern Europe (and elsewhere) has caused concern that the EU is proving ill-equipped for the task of redistributing wealth across all its regions and is, in fact, transforming into an elitist project that is far removed from the majority of its inhabitants and which is, in effect, producing even more 'left-behind places'.[1] The populations of these spaces sense that development support is focused on other regions and that their voices are going unheard because power is concentrated in a few core areas. This means that improving our understanding of the kind of demographic, economic and discursive-political processes that constitute these new peripheries is a matter of some urgency. Similarly, we must also explore the processes through which these peripheries interrelate with the dynamic core regions in Central and Eastern Europe.

The increasing socio-spatial polarization immanent in Central and Eastern Europe and throughout the EU is seen as a bi-directional process. On the one hand, we can observe political-economic metropolization which draws social, cultural, economic and political activity to a limited number of increasingly globalized city regions. On the other hand, a growing number of less densely populated and post-industrial regions are being further peripheralized by the devaluation of social and discursive means. The suggestion is that these two processes are closely interrelated and affect each other. In other words, the emergence of new peripheries cannot be understood without taking equal account of the increasing allure and centralization of core regions. In addition, the current shape of regional development in Central and Eastern Europe must also be seen as a product of a dominant political discourse which favours large agglomerations and the 'West' over the 'East' in policymaking. A corollary is that the goal of making metropolitan regions globally competitive tends to be prioritized in economic development over more holistic approaches which aim to improve quality of life. Furthermore, it is in the nature of core–periphery dependencies to exacerbate the peripheralization of areas outside major agglomerations. This is a consequence of the value-laden discourses at the heart of the dependencies which usually portray metropolitan regions as dynamic, attractive, diverse, innovative and creative, whereas other regions are perceived as backward, less dynamic and problematic in terms of demography, infrastructure and quality of life. Current approaches to regional policy and regional development have not addressed these conflicts appropriately; indeed, the overall policy rationale in the EU in general and in Central and Eastern Europe in particular seems to give disproportionate weight to competitiveness and economic growth and too little to overall well-being and social and territorial cohesion.

The first part of this chapter looks at the latest work on understanding and conceptualising socio-spatial polarization, while the following section describes current processes on the basis of a descriptive analysis of a small number of relevant and applicable indicators. In the third part, recent turns and longer-term trends in regional policy in Central and Eastern Europe are presented on the basis of recent scholarship. This is followed by a discussion of potential alternative avenues for regional policy in part four. Finally, the conclusion proposes a broader understanding of regional development based on ideas of social and spatial justice.

Making the global city: The case of Riga

Guido Sechi

Since the Middle Ages, Riga has been the most important settlement in Latvia thanks to its strategic location at the crossing of important trading routes. As part of the Russian empire in the second half of the 19th century, it also became an advanced industrial city, retaining its pre-eminence during the first years of national independence (1918–40) and throughout the Soviet era. Today, Riga is the most important city in the Baltic states – more prominent than either the less well situated and less industrialized Vilnius or the significantly smaller Tallinn. After the collapse of the USSR, the centrality to Latvia of its capital city has even increased thanks to the decline of other key centres that suffered more significantly from the implosion of the Soviet economy and planning structure.

Since 2016, Riga has been classified by the European Spatial Planning Observation Network as a Metropolitan European Growth Area with a significant knowledge base – in particular its well-educated workforce – but constrained in terms of size and relatively weak in terms of competitiveness. On the other hand, connectivity is relatively strong and is constantly improving. Riga's airport has gradually expanded its role as a gateway between the EU and former USSR countries, with a 30-per-cent growth in passenger traffic between 2016 and 2018. Cargo traffic through the airport and the city's port has also increased in recent years, with a growth of 12.1 per cent and 8.2 per cent between 2017 and 2018, respectively – making Riga a major trade hub between the EU and Russia, which is Latvia's third largest export market after Lithuania and Estonia (as of 2019).

Today, Latvia – and Riga, in particular – scores highly in terms of its business environment and financial attractiveness (according to the 2019 Kearney Global Services Location Index) and enjoys a stable credit rating. A significant expansion of the banking sector, overwhelmingly concentrated in Riga, is forecast in the next few years; as of June 2020, only 17.5 per cent of all banking assets in Latvia were controlled by divisions of foreign banks. All these factors contribute to a positive business climate and to Riga's overall attractiveness as a location for international economic activities.

Since 2010, national and urban economic development strategies have emphasized Riga's role as the 'driving force of Latvia', the 'bearer of Latvia's name in the world' and as the country's economic and cultural capital (Riga City Administration Planning Department 2014). City marketing has focused on branding Riga as a 'Northern European metropolis' with a claim to being a global city in the Baltic Region (ibid.). Current and future megaprojects – such as the Riga Northern Transport Corridor connecting Riga Freeport to the Trans European road network and re-routing traffic away from the city centre – are focused primarily on reinforcing transport infrastructure and improving environmental sustainability. Urban development policy guidelines emphasize compactness and targeted, diversified policies for city neighbourhoods (with regard, for example, to municipal, social and recreational services) and identify transport and logistics, IT, creative industries and advanced manufacturing as strategic economic fields. Most of the country's R&D capacity is concentrated in Riga, although the sector is limited by the low levels of both public and private investment in Latvia as a whole compared with older EU member states.

While Riga's claim to be a global city has advanced greatly over the past few years (see Figure 12.2 below), the concentration of investment activities in and around the capital has tended to block the prospects for polycentric development, which would strengthen other cities in Latvia. The 2014–20 National Development Plan made no mention of polycentricity, emphasizing instead 'trickle-down' benefits that would derive from the growth and development of the capital city region. Today, the Riga metropolitan area is home to almost half of the national population, contributes 69 per cent to national GDP, and is growing at a faster rate than the national average.

Figure 12.1 Skyline of Riga as seen from the new University of Latvia campus (Swedbank office tower and national library in the foreground); photo by author

Understanding socio-spatial polarization

Although regional polarization is an 'old' topic within regional studies,[2] the formation and re-production of powerful metropolitan regions and world cities and the emergence and re-production of peripheral regions are generally discussed as if there was no relationship between them. This is highly problematic because the growth and increasing prominence of particular core regions cannot be conceptualized without reference to the sources of this growth and the processes of decline involved in that development, and these lead to the re-production of existing peripheralities and the creation of new ones. Instead, we find a large body of literature which talks about 'lagging', 'peripheral', 'structurally weak', 'shrinking' or 'rural' regions and about their development often perceived as being problematic in nature. Similarly, there is a wealth of scholarship about global and world cities and metropolitan regions, and much is written about the importance of large cities for society, knowledge production and innovation; these topics are typically portrayed in relatively positive terms. In fact, interrelations exist between 'the core' and 'the peripheries', and between the processes constituting them – as the example of Riga (see text box, above) shows – meaning that the formation of regional, national and even global peripheries can be best understood by examining the processes of polarization and imbalanced relations between the core and the peripheries.

The term 'periphery' is a static concept, however, and so an examination of regional development that incorporates current dynamics and reflects the processes constructing peripheries requires a process-based social science perspective rather than focusing on the indicators of what constitutes a periphery. The Greek root of the word (*periphereia* meaning 'circumference') implies a relationship to a centre, and peripheries certainly cannot exist without at least a conceptual reference to a centre. Regional studies and social sciences have added other components to conventional definitions of peripheries as areas on the edge of a larger region – and distant, rural and sparsely populated areas – to include features such as a lack of infrastructure and public services, economic marginalization, political insignificance and social heterogeneity.[3] In the context of world-systems theory and other postcolonial approaches, and at a supra-national level, whole countries and macro-regions can be seen as peripheries within a polarized world-system. This is, for example, the case for global trade, which is dominated by North America, the EU and Asia and sidelines and peripheralizes entire global macro-regions such as sub-Saharan Africa. In short, the term 'periphery' can be applied to regions on different and intersecting levels. Consequently, the term will be used here in a way that includes these multidimensional and multiscalar senses.

Not only does focusing on peripheries as a static notion divert our attention from the processes that lead to their emergence, it also tends to mask other dynamic changes within multiple and complex core–periphery relations. Examining the processes of peripheralization and its counterpart – centralization[4] – may not only reveal how peripheries emerge and are (re)produced but can also shed light on the social processes that constitute these (re)production processes. To this we can add another relevant aspect – namely, the discursive construction of space.[5] At its root is the observation that space, regions, centres and peripheries do not exist without our presence as human beings; in other words, spaces are products of our social (inter)action. The process of space-making through discursive practice associates different values with different (types of) spaces, and this spatial or territorial stigmatization is also a factor in the emergence of peripheries.[6] Groups of people or communities denigrate particular spaces or even spatial categories by attributing particular (negative) properties and features to them. The value-laden negative connotations linked to these spaces and places generate negative spatial images and promote their construction as peripheries.

As the two co-constitutive processes of socio-spatial polarization, peripheralization and centralization are mutually interdependent and embedded in regional, national and global relations. They embody a dynamic impulse and cannot be seen as the result of a natural order, meaning that regions should not be branded as unavoidable victims of a globalization process; instead, they are the products of conscious decisions taken on the multiple scales and levels that constitute our current world society and world economy. In this sense, the logics and dynamics of spatial concentration and centralization constitute the peripheralization of other areas. The more core regions attract capital, people, economic activity, infrastructure and public functions, the more other regions become marginalized and dependent. Often, these processes induce self-reinforcing virtuous cycles of growth (in which positive development attracts further growth) and vicious cycles of decline (in which negative development leads to further decline). Their effect can be intensified by particularly positive or negative discursive and value-laden connotations linked to certain features found in both developing and declining regions. In this sense, the perceived disadvantages of one region directly interrelate with the perceived advantages of others.

Socio-spatial polarization and core–periphery divides in Central and Eastern Europe

Let us now look more closely at recent undercurrents in regional development in Central and Eastern Europe and try to identify core–periphery dynamics. Counterintuitive though it may seem, we will first look at processes of centralization. One measurement that can be used to depict the growing economic importance of metropolitan city regions in Central and Eastern Europe is the relative position of Central and Eastern European world cities based on the presence of advanced producer service (APS) firms in 2018 compared with their presence in 2000 (see Figure 12.2, below).[7] The presence of APS firms in a city is often used as an indicator of its strategic position within the global economy as – with their global office networks offering essential amenities such as financial services, management consultancy, law, accountancy and advertising – they are linked to and used by companies which operate on international markets. Accordingly, researchers from the Global and World Cities Research Network (GaWC) used the presence of APS companies to rank world cities on a 12-step scale which ranges from 'sufficiency' to 'alpha++'. The greater the number of APS companies, the higher the ranking. Emerging world cities with only a small number of APS firms are ranked as having a 'sufficiency', while only London and New York are in the 'alpha ++' category.

With the exception of Prague, which maintained its already pre-eminent position in the 'alpha-' category, all Central and Eastern European capital cities saw their profile among world cities rise significantly in the period to 2018 (see Figure 12.2, below), and three cities (all in Poland) entered the GaWC ranking for the first time: Krakow, Poznan and Wroclaw. The increasing presence of APS firms in these locations can be seen as an indicator of economic centralization and concentration in a few dominant cities. While Poland's cities seem to be developing into a polycentric metropolitan network, all the other Central and Eastern European countries have become more mono-centric in character – much to the disadvantage of other regions.

The tendency towards mono-centrism in Central and Eastern Europe is particularly evident if recent economic and demographic development is analysed at NUTS 3 level.[8] Over the past two or three decades, we have seen a constant process of concentration of both economic activity and demographic development in a small number of dominant core regions – mainly capital city regions – to the disadvantage of nearly all other regions. The already strong position of the metropolitan regions as economic powerhouses has been strengthened further as jobs increase, incomes rise, productivity improves and populations grow.

Although all Central and Eastern European countries have shown stronger economic growth than older, core European countries on average and at national levels, the benefits of this growth have been rather unevenly distributed.[9] While the weakest NUTS 3 regions show only moderate growth or even a decline in GDP per capita, all capital regions in

Figure 12.2 World cities in Central and Eastern Europe (CEE) 2018 in comparison with the year 2000.

Data: GaWC-Research Network, https://www.lboro.ac.uk/microsites/geography/gawc/gawcworlds.html

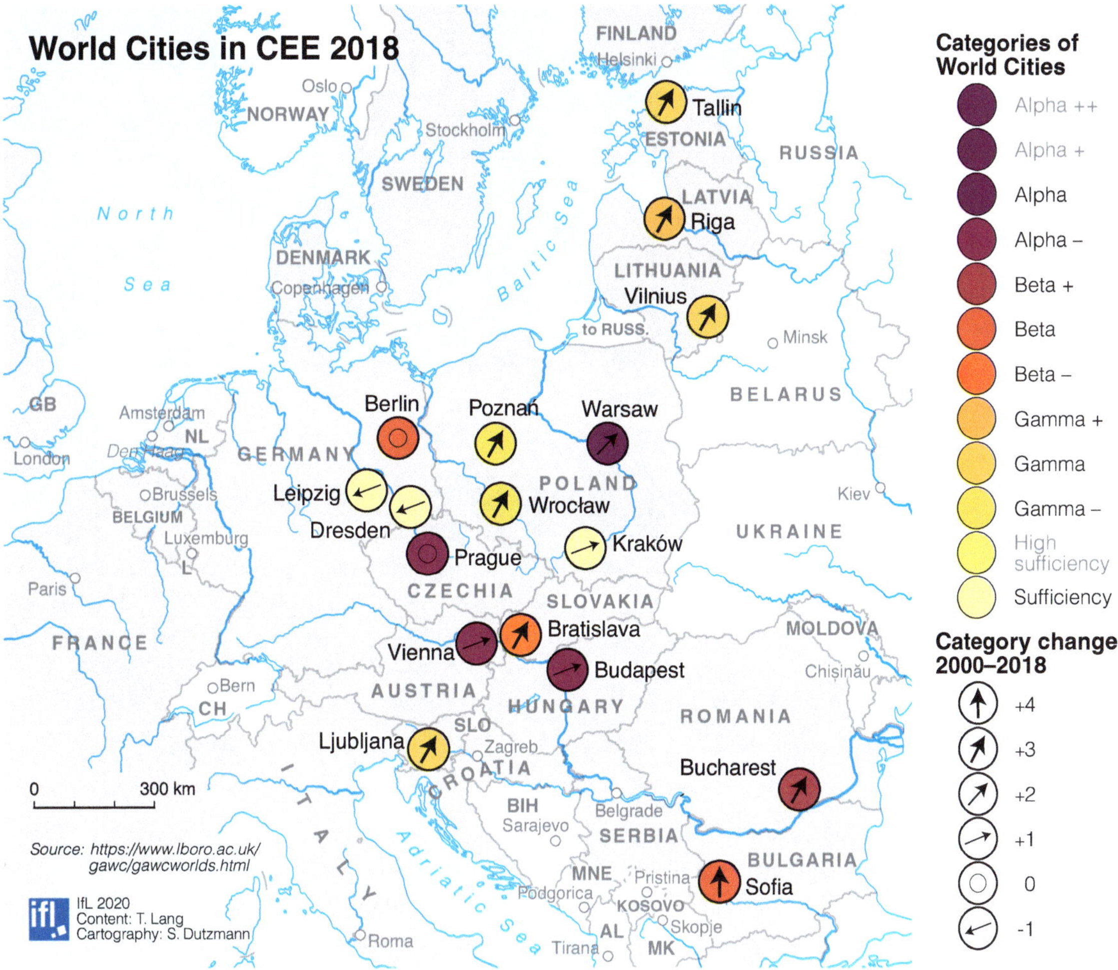

Central and Eastern Europe (with the exception of Ljubljana in Slovenia) have grown considerably. In purchasing power standards – a metric which acknowledges differences between countries in price levels – these capital regions have reached levels far above the European average. For instance, the numbers for Warsaw are more than double the EU28 average, and the two Romanian NUTS 3 regions forming the capital region surpass even the ten most dynamically growing regions in the EU. Unlike in countries elsewhere, the stronger position of capital regions in Central and Eastern Europe in terms of income (GDP per capita) also equates to a better quality of life in these regions.[10] (For a general criticism of using GDP as a metric of development, see the text box, below.)

Figure 12.3, below, shows the GDP per capita in NUTS 3 regions in terms of purchasing power standards in selected Central and Eastern European countries for the years 2007 and 2017. The columns illustrate the spread of all NUTS 3 regions' economic output (GDP)

Figure 12.3 Gross Domestic Product (GDP) in selected countries 2007 and 2017.

data source: Eurostat data explorer [nama_10r_3gdp]

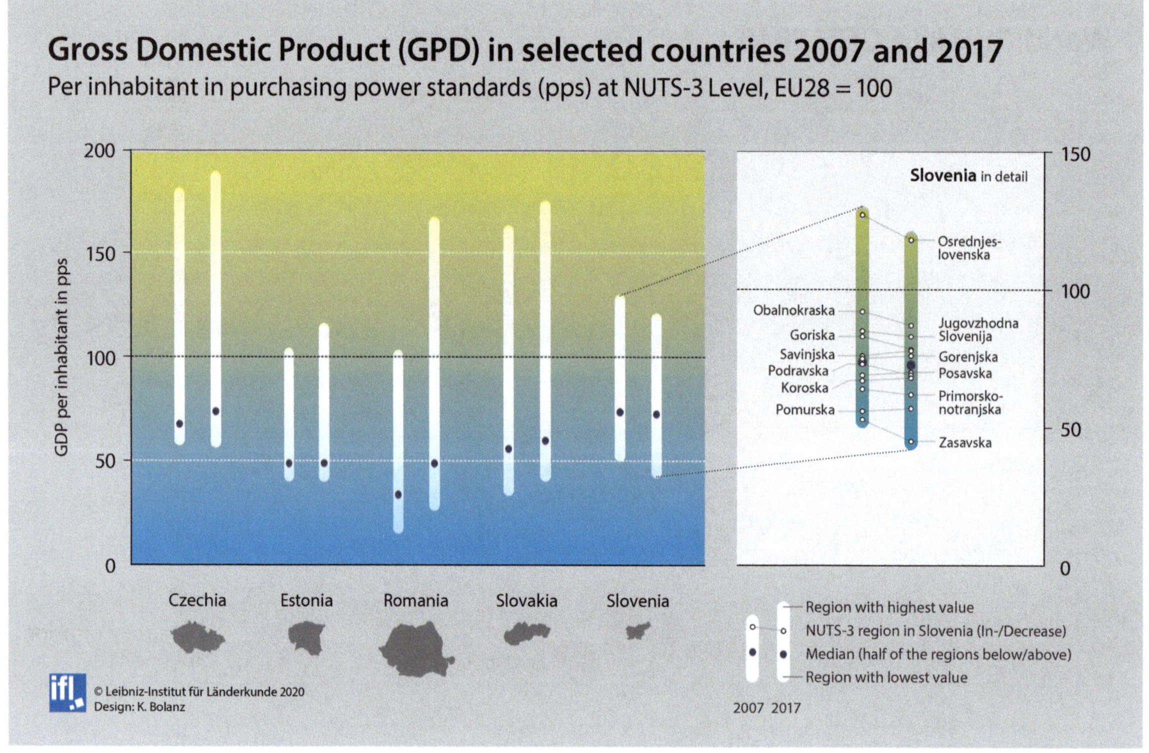

per capita, giving an indicator by which we can assess regional prosperity by country. The position of the median tells us that very few regions enjoy high prosperity while most other regions are far less affluent. The figure mainly illustrates the extent to which disparities developed between regions in the years 2007 to 2017. The changing position of the median can be seen as an indicator of the overall development of all regions; a significant increase in median value illustrates an improvement of economic conditions for a larger number of regions, while a lack of change illustrates economic stagnation for most regions – both compared with the EU average. Most countries in Central and Eastern Europe show a pattern of a rising median value and an increasing spread of regional values (Czechia, Bulgaria, Hungary and Latvia). Estonia and Slovenia show a constant (Estonia) or falling (Slovenia) median value with a widening (Estonia) or constant (Slovenia) spread coupled with below average economic development in Slovenia. The differences between the region with the lowest value and that with the highest value are most extreme in Romania and Poland, but these two examples show that more regions can benefit from economic growth, as the rising median value illustrates. In Estonia, the region with the lowest value remained stable, but in Slovakia and Lithuania economic growth was seemingly most equally distributed – with rising values in all dimensions.

Looking beyond GDP: Well-being in Central and Eastern Europe

Tomas Hanell

In an effort to break free from the overwhelming dominance of GDP as a metric for societal progress, in 2009 the EU Commission launched an initiative called 'Beyond GDP' containing a road map outlining key actions to improve the EU's indicators of progress and how these could be integrated into decision-making processes.

The limitations of GDP as a metric for well-being are well known. Its shortcomings have been thoroughly discussed by researchers such as Harvie et al. (2009), Stiglitz et al. (2009), and Van den Bergh (2009). Yet despite their heavy criticisms GDP is still so widely utilized today, and prevails as a metric also in the context of regional development. The allocation criteria for EU regional policy has hitherto been based solely on GDP per inhabitant. In the current programming period (2021–7), it retains its primary role in fund distribution but is now also complemented by new criteria such as youth unemployment or low education levels.

There are several ways in which to operationalize the measurement of well-being. A commonly utilized approach rests on subjectively reported well-being outcome metrics such as happiness or overall satisfaction with life. As depicted in Figure 12.4, below, at the aggregate level for the entire EU population, the growth in GDP no longer correlates with changes in life satisfaction.

There are, however, clear indications at the regional level in Europe (cf. Pittau et al., 2010; Ferrara and Nisticò, 2015) that GDP, income or other corresponding aggregates do correlate positively with subjective well-being up to a certain level of economic development. This was the case in Central and Eastern European countries until very recently, and residents of capital metropolitan regions were generally much happier or more satisfied with their lives than were the more rural residents in the respective countries. However, as prosperity has increased, that link now appears to have broken.

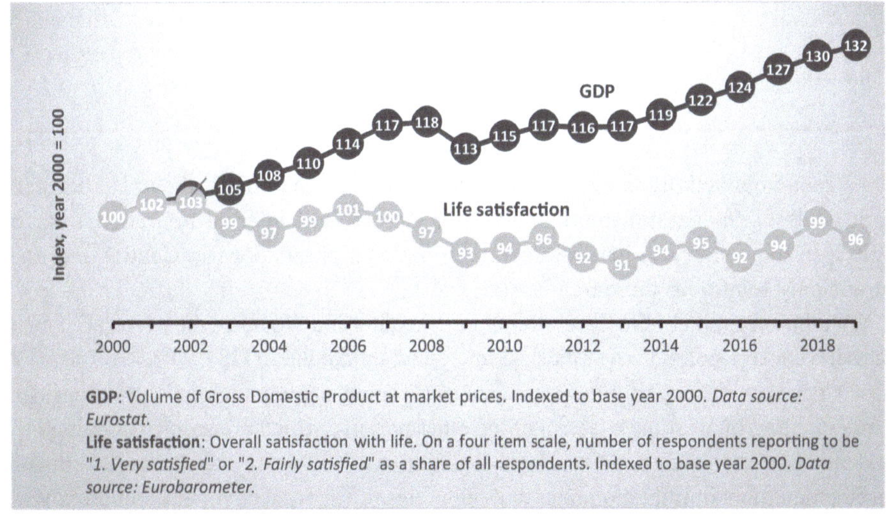

GDP: Volume of Gross Domestic Product at market prices. Indexed to base year 2000. *Data source: Eurostat.*
Life satisfaction: Overall satisfaction with life. On a four item scale, number of respondents reporting to be "*1. Very satisfied*" or "*2. Fairly satisfied*" as a share of all respondents. Indexed to base year 2000. *Data source: Eurobarometer.*

Figure 12.4 Evolution of GDP and life satisfaction in the EU 2000–19 (author's elaboration).

Data on life satisfaction from the European Quality of Life Survey (European Foundation for the Improvement of Living and Working Conditions, 2018) illustrates this. In all Central and Eastern European countries in which regional data is available, apart from Romania and Slovenia, the capital metropolitan region is no longer home to the most satisfied residents. Overall, regional variations in life satisfaction appear rather large in many Central and Eastern European countries, with Poland showing the greatest variation.

There is, however, a major drawback when it comes to happiness or satisfaction – and this is that outcome variables for well-being, happiness or life satisfaction are very difficult to affect by means of policy (and there is no Ministry of Happiness in any EU member state). To achieve that goal requires analysis of the factors that create happy or satisfied individuals – or, as in our case, regions with high average happiness or life satisfaction. A recent study (Hanell n. 10, below) compiled variables which act as drivers of well-being in 195 regions in the EU. There were sixty-four variables, and all are proven to affect subjectively reported well-being, either directly or indirectly. Examining individual indicators, we note that many Central and Eastern European regions – urban and rural alike – perform rather well on several factors related to high subjective well-being in comparison with many regions in southern and western EU member states. Income distribution is fairly uniform in many Central and Eastern European regions, job stability tends to be high, mental stress is recorded as lower than elsewhere, access to social support from relatives and friends is high, perceived societal tensions are low.

Regional variations in Central and Eastern European countries are, nonetheless, substantial. Regions in East Germany, Slovenia, the Czech Republic and Slovakia generally fare fairly well on many indicators, whereas many Bulgarian, Romanian and Hungarian regions are at the opposite end of the scale. Comparing the aggregate performance across all sixty-four variables, only three of the ten worst-performing regions in the EU are in Central and Eastern European countries (in Romania, Bulgaria and Poland); the remaining seven are either Greek or Italian.

Among Central and Eastern European countries, Poland in particular appears extremely divided with, e.g., the north-eastern Warminsko-Mazurskie region performing roughly on a par with, e.g., Northern Ireland or Hamburg, whereas the Opolskie region in the south-west scores very low and on the level of regions such as Calabria or Campania in Italy, where well-being is generally among the lowest in the EU. Regional polarization in the other Central and Eastern European countries is much less pronounced.

As economic activity concentrates in the large agglomerations, they also become the main goals of (moderate) immigration from abroad and internal migration from other regions in the country. A general decline in national populations in Central and Eastern Europe only reinforces these trends.

With the exception of the Czech Republic, Slovenia and Slovakia, the newest EU member states have lost population over the past few years, unlike the EU28 (*c.* +2.4%, 2007–17). In most Central and Eastern European countries, some capital regions show considerable demographic growth at the expense of the other regions, which are seeing declining or only moderate growth in their populations. This pattern is driven by negative natural demographic development, low immigration rates and high rates of (age-selective) emigration to Western Europe combined with interregional migration to the respective metropolitan regions. Consequently, in most Central and Eastern European countries, more than half of NUTS 3

Figure 12.5 Change of population from 2007 to 2017 in selected countries.

data source: Eurostat data explorer [demo_r_gind3], population figures 31.12.2017

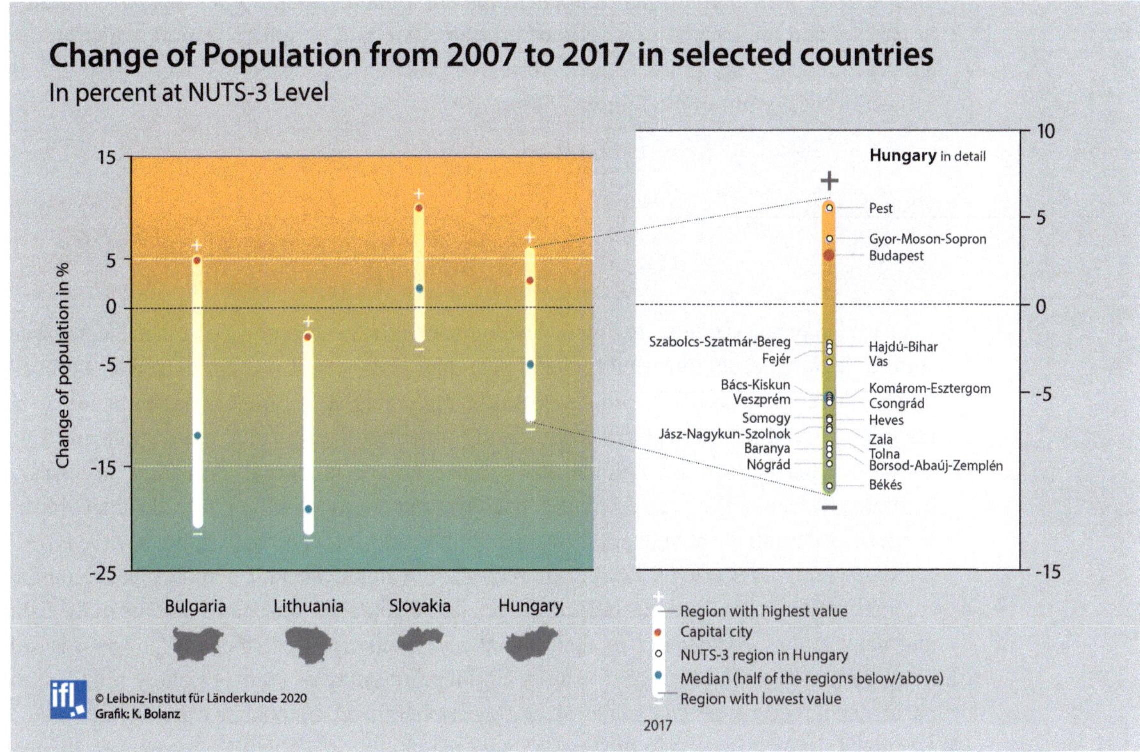

regions are shrinking in terms of population. Demographic polarization is strongest in Bulgaria, Estonia, Poland and Romania, with many peripheralizing regions showing rates of decline as high as 20 per cent and the capital regions recording rapid population growth. In Lithuania and Latvia, all regions are affected by population decline – including the capital regions. Of the ten most rapidly shrinking regions in the EU28, four are located in Romania, four in Lithuania, and one each in Bulgaria and Latvia. Conversely, the most rapidly growing NUTS 3 region is also located in Romania: Ilfov county, surrounding the capital, Bucharest. In Slovakia, the Czech Republic and Slovenia, the majority of regions show population increases with median growth rates between 1 and 2 per cent. In most Central and Eastern European countries, the capital cities or the surrounding districts, such as the county of Pecs in Hungary, show the greatest population growth. In Poland, the metropolitan region of Poznan shows the largest population growth (+15.8%, 2007–17).

The above data confirms observations that socio-spatial polarization has increased in Central and Eastern Europe over the past decade or two. It seems that there are two main driving forces behind this: the first is globalization, as illustrated in this chapter in the form of changes in the world city network. As we will see below, this form of globalization is clearly mediated through EU and national policies. The second driving force is demographic change (natural population decrease) in combination with European integration through the single labour market (encouraging international mobility). Both of these forces cause socio-spatial polarization in newly emerging as well as continually reproduced peripheral and core regions. The many forms of polarization are dynamic social processes co-constituted in parallel and multiscalar processes of centralization and peripheralization, which in turn are reinforced by the political and discursive processes of space making. These are the subject of discussion in the following section.

Regional development, regional policy and territorial cohesion

Like regional polarization, regional development is also a very 'old' theme in regional studies, regional economics and regional planning. However, it is often treated as a process that is inherent to a particular region, downplaying or neglecting multiscalar embedding and relations as well as political dimensions and normative frameworks, reducing them to the simplistic question of how regional development can be supported. Instead, it promises to be more productive if we perceive regional development as a highly political subject rooted in specific normative considerations and paradigms which significantly influence the type of regional policy advocated.[11] Studies on regional development have certainly become more sophisticated in recent years, stressing the relational character of regions and the multiscalar and network-based character of their social constructions. Nevertheless, the topic is still often discussed without reference to the complex interplay of core–periphery relations. In particular, development challenges faced by peripheralized regions are often viewed from a locational perspective within the region rather than in terms of relational processes. In more recent years, however, many scholars have begun to raise concerns regarding spatial justice and the political economy of regional development, and have called for more attention to be paid to socio-spatial marginalization and polarization at various levels. So far, however, these calls have had little impact on the foundations and practices of regional policy.[12]

Socio-spatial polarization at the regional level should not be seen as a natural consequence of processes beyond our control, however, but as linked to deliberate political spatial strategies.

Most Central and Eastern European countries are currently following neoliberal approaches to regional development, focusing development support on regions with the highest growth rates with the political aim of increasing the global relevance of a small number of metropolitan cities in the hope that spill-over effects will benefit the country as a whole.[13] The approaches taken include selective public investment in technical and social infrastructures, the concentration of public institutions, and the targeted allocation of resources and subsidies for economic development – all of which are to the disadvantage of less-developed, non-core and marginalized regions.

This focus on high-growth regions chimes with the strategy of supporting the development of competitive city regions which are globally recognized. It is a strategy which can be seen as a deliberate metropolization backed by national and European policy agendas and promoted by organizations such as the OECD, the World Bank and the

ESPON programme. These agendas and road maps also reflect changing paradigms of spatial policy in which the dominant themes currently are competitiveness, growth and innovation. Other aspects of cohesion, such as its social and territorial attributes, tend to be given short shrift. However, metropolization can be understood as:

> a multiple process combining empirical dimensions such as the concentration of population and (economic) activities, normative-political dimensions such as policy frameworks supporting the formation of metropolitan regions, and discursive dimensions adding particular values (e.g. about a good life) and relations (e.g. urban-rural dichotomies) to the general debate.[14]

Here, we focus on the normative-political dimension – and many scholars have already identified the rise of metropolization policies across Europe, and their origins in normative ideas about competitiveness and growth in an increasingly globalized world. In this paradigm, spatial policy is driven by the belief that economic development at the European, national and regional levels is best supported by forming and strengthening a number of metropolitan city regions which then function as 'hotspots' and focal nodes in the global economy. Better integration into the global economy via these hotspots is the main strategy for promoting economic growth and, ultimately, regional development throughout the country as a whole. In this sense, the formation of metropolitan regions is pushed to a greater extent by European and national policy agendas than by regional impulses to self-organize with the goal of more efficient governance. Regional policy across the EU, and in Central and Eastern Europe particularly,[15] seems to be dominated by the goal of integrating into the world economy via the bigger metropolitan city regions as nodal points with disproportionate 'gateway' functions. Promoting balanced spatial development and social, economic and territorial cohesion is clearly subordinated, or even contradictory, to this metropolitan focus on growth and innovation policies. Minor cities and rural areas face increasing challenges to their survival in this 'metropolitan world'.[16]

This 'widespread big city enthusiasm' seems to reflect current economic and demographic trends as well as constituting a range of positive images, and this adds a powerful discursive dimension to the metropolization process. Perceptions about the economic supremacy of global cities linked to hegemonic narratives portraying larger city regions as 'international, cultural, innovative and economic hot spots' began to cause concern some time ago that increased socio-spatial polarization would further marginalize areas outside the large agglomerations.[17] With the shift in spatial development priorities towards competitiveness and growth rather than cohesion, policies directed at disadvantaged and peripheralized areas received even less political attention than they had before. Moreover, the idea of focusing development on a small number of metropolitan regions with high growth potential and the aim of achieving a European or even global profile seems to have become the dominant paradigm shaping regional policy within a hegemonial neoliberal discourse of competitiveness or a 'competitive city-regional narrative'.[18] Instead of foregrounding the political dimension of this metropolization process and the calculated support it receives from policy (and opening these topics up to debate), the growth-oriented approach is portrayed as a natural consequence of changes in the world economy – furthering socio-spatial polarization and the emergence of new peripheries.

Increasing polarization as a source of nationalism and populism?

Thilo Lang

In the past few years, political commentators have often linked the new strength of conservative-nationalistic as well as xenophobic or anti-LGBT movements and the rising support for 'populist' parties to the issue of increasing social and spatial polarization. Indeed, across the countries of the Visegrád Group in particular, but also in other countries, the populist-conservative voting grounds have been in rural and peripheralized areas whereas metropolitan populations have tended to vote instead for liberal and progressive parties.[19]

While there is consensus about the shifts in the political landscapes of Central and Eastern European countries, it would be too simple to root the rise of populism solely in rising inequalities. There is at least one further prominent hypothesis, which sees the main drivers as lying in the cultural sphere. The argument is that for some populations, the turn towards something like progressive values has been over-stretched – kicking off conservative counter-movements. A recent study about the geography of populist support (Wishlade, 2019) suggests that the picture is even more complex. Both hypotheses (focusing on inequalities or cultural reasons) seem too static, and the evidence from spatial analyses is too mixed to fully explain these trends. The new divides are not clearly urban–rural, neither they are purely cultural/attitudinal. However, increasing demographic change, combined with economic disadvantage, will certainly be a growing source of political discontent (Dijkstra et al., 2020) in the future.

Rethinking regional policies and alternative avenues to regional development

It has become obvious that these kinds of neoliberal competitiveness-based regional policies have tended to further socio-spatial polarization, in Central and Eastern Europe in particular, and so the urgency of rethinking them and exploring alternatives has only increased. Concepts such as post-development, de-growth and spatial justice that are at the centre of scholarly debate seem to offer promising perspectives for development opportunities for regions struggling to find their place in global capitalism. A key objective for policymakers must be to find a way past the dominance of the economic dimension in evaluating regional development and instead to take a more holistic and societal approach,[20] foregrounding quality of life and individual happiness. This must go hand in hand with a relational perception of development which avoids handing regions sole responsibility for their own success or failure. As well as integrating ecological, social and cultural elements in approaches to development, the doors should also be opened to experimenting with more radical policies for the benefit of 'left-behind places'.[21] This more courageous approach seems particularly relevant given that the policies adopted so far have clearly been unable to address this issue in peripheralized regions (and among their populations) with any degree of success. Cohesion and (transnational) solidarity must be given more weight and must be coupled with supporting strategies designed to promote sustainable development, including the exploration of alternative social and solidarity economies.[22]

'Left-behind' places

Erika Nagy

Hungary, as a European (semi)peripheral economy, could be considered a laboratory of uneven spatial development driven by changing modernization strategies. The systemic crisis of the 1980s and the post-socialist transition of the 1990s entailed the repositioning of spaces (including the local assets of firms, households and municipalities) within the context of the emerging capitalist regime. Spatial inequalities emerged along fault lines that had existed before state socialism, reproducing urban/rural and metropolitan/non-metropolitan dichotomies that were rooted in late-19th-century peripheral modernization (e.g. railway construction), yet that also reflected the centralized, hierarchical, industrialization-driven spatial logic of state socialism.

Socio-spatial polarization grew into such a complex, formidable and ubiquitous problem in the 1990s that it led to the formulation of a new regional policy in 1996. Nevertheless, despite the allocation of massive levels of EU and national funding to regional development and the adoption of sophisticated methodology in defining spaces in need, inequalities persisted – for instance, differences in household income have remained unchanged since the late 1990s. The most cogent explanation for this persistence lies in the neoliberal agenda adopted by national political and economic elites with the goal of promoting economic growth and stability (Bockman and Eyal, 2002). This was further compounded by EU-funded spatial projects in line with the Lisbon Agenda principles, which have informed regional policies throughout the EU since the early 2000s. Moreover, massive state debt (which revealed the dependent-peripheral status of the Hungarian economy) limited the scope for development policy. Additionally, the institutional cultural context reduced regional access to scarce development resources as bargaining processes took place in non-transparent ways. Both circumstances were powerful mechanisms in reproducing the position of powerlessness experienced by poorer regions. State intervention was increasingly centralized, selective and dominated by interest groups (e.g. transnational corporations in the automotive industry), and was thus less than responsive to territorial problems. As a consequence, new dimensions and spaces of marginality emerged, and contagious rural and/or industrial ghettoes began to form in eastern, north-eastern and south-western Hungary.

Marginality not only grew increasingly complex but also became spatially fixed. South Békés (a LAU1 region in East Hungary) is a good example: it has been affected by the country's largest population loss by proportion (17 per cent since 2000) and faced the greatest poverty (two thirds of its primary school children come from low-income households).[23] The region was hit badly by the transition crisis even though its high agricultural potential could in fact have been a basis for local well-being. However, control over local assets such as land, development funds and labour was usurped by a few powerful actors (domestic landowners and transnational corporations), who have constrained the local workforce to low-paid and increasingly precarious jobs such as seasonal work, informal employment and temporary public work programmes in order for them (the landowners and corporations) to be competitive in global food networks. As incomes fell, locals were also marginalized as consumers. Shops and pubs closed down (see Figure 12.6, below), leaving ageing villagers without local access to daily supplies. Moreover, half of local households were excluded from the formal credit market due to their 'no-value' housing stock, and this gave rise to incidences of usury. Finally, the residents of South Békés also suffer from being considered second-class citizens. This is a lived experience of locals which is materialized in the shortcomings of public services such as a poor road system, health care deficits (leaving 30 per cent of the population without locally available basic services) and a decline in public education. The state acts here more as an agent reproducing multiple dependencies (e.g. through public work programmes and the social care system) and creating clientism than as a benevolent actor (counter)balancing inequalities and injustice.

Figure 12.6 The 'left behind' places: Kevermes in Hungary.

The main street of Kevermes, Hungary (1,844 inhabitants): one third of the houses in the village have been abandoned; photo by author

The case of South Békés suggests that, with current power structures, marginalized spaces are destined to function as reservoirs of cheap labour (exploited as contract labour, long-distance commuters, etc.) and also as pools where social, economic and environmental marginalities are entangled, lived out and kept under control. This spatial strategy is likely to be challenged by an emerging urban leftism that aims to address the diverse marginalities of left-behind spaces in Hungary.

Concluding Remarks

This chapter has argued that we cannot understand the emergence of peripheries without studying the constituting processes and consequences of centralization. Hence, it seems reasonable to look at the different kinds and scales of periphery-forming forces in terms of socio-spatial polarization. This places the focus on the complex, multidimensional and multiscalar societal processes that lead to the creation and re-production of core–periphery relations rather than on structural forces as determinants of development in particular regions. As a result, it becomes clearer that regions cannot be held responsible for their own misfortune. Peripheralized regions, in particular in Central and Eastern Europe, do in fact need the attention of political decision makers and should be perceived in the context of the centralizing forces which have led and are continuing to lead to an extreme concentration of development in the capital and metropolitan regions of Central and Eastern Europe.

Most Central and Eastern European states exhibit strong socio-spatial polarization with a limited number of very attractive, globally networked city regions (usually the metropolitan capital regions) counterbalanced by a growing number of stagnating and shrinking regions, many of them new peripheries or left-behind regions facing precarious development prospects. The widespread policy shift towards the neoliberal paradigm of growth and innovation-based regional development across the EU only reinforces the socio-spatial polarization caused by a radical market liberalism that was particularly sharp in Central and Eastern Europe. Regional policy is increasingly based on the premises of competitiveness and economic growth, despite the formal adoption of European-level documents emphasizing territorial cohesion and sustainability.[24] Several authors have argued that the hegemony of the neoliberal paradigm in Central and Eastern Europe is a consequence of state-led planning experiences in the past, with any kind of similarity with socialist planning continuing to be treated with suspicion.[25]

Nevertheless, the narrow focus on competitiveness and the promotion of metropolitan regions at European and national level has been criticized by both development practitioners and academics. Given the unprecedented levels of polarization and the emergence of new peripheries, this criticism should be taken more seriously and regional development should be repoliticized with a strong focus on understanding and moderating core–periphery relations. Uneven regional development and regional polarization must be accepted as intrinsic features of today's capitalist societies, and as such, regulatory intervention by state power and the EU is called for.[26]

In the light of these conclusions, and in order to better deal with new patterns of regional disparities and polarization, support for territorial, social and economic cohesion needs to be given more weight in future regional policies – both at the European and national level throughout Central and Eastern Europe. There is a growing wealth of scholarship on the concepts of spatial justice and balanced spatial development, and we can take these as a basis for widening our understanding of what development means – going beyond mere economic growth and promoting alternatives which integrate social, ecological, political and cultural concerns into future policy agendas while still acknowledging diverse potentials of development beyond agglomeration and encouraging more reflective policies as an opportunity for change. The result could be that uneven social and spatial development would be better addressed as the idea of providing good living conditions and well-being in different spatial settings grows stronger and supplants the orthodoxy of promoting extraordinary growth and development in only a few regions to the disadvantage of many others – including those newly emerging peripheries in Central and Eastern Europe.

Notes

1 Andrés Rodríguez-Pose, 'The revenge of the places that don't matter (and what to do about it)', *Cambridge Journal of Regions, Economy and Society* 11 (2018) 1, pp. 189–209.

2 Gunnar Myrdal, *Economic Theory and Underdevelopment* (London: Duckworth, 1957). See also Paul Krugman, *Geography and Trade* (Leuven: Leuven University Press, 1991).

3 Manfred Kühn und Thilo Lang, 'Metropolisierung und Peripherisierung in Europa: eine Einführung', *Europa Regional* 23 (2017) 4, pp. 2–14.

4 Manfred Kühn, 'Peripheralization: Theoretical concepts explaining socio-spatial inequalities', *European Planning Studies* 23 (2014) 2, pp. 367–78. See also Thilo Lang et al. (eds), *Understanding Geographies of Polarization and Peripheralization. Perspectives from Central and Eastern Europe and Beyond* (London: Palgrave Macmillan, 2015).

5 Henri Lefebvre, *The Production of Space* (Oxford: Blackwell Publishing, 1991).

6 Frank Meyer and Judith Miggelbrink, 'The Subject and the Periphery: About Discourses, Loopings and Ascriptions', in *Peripheralization: The Making of Spatial Dependencies and Social Injustice*, ed. Andrea Fischer-Tahir and Matthias Naumann (Wiesbaden: Springer, 2013), pp. 207–23.

7 Peter Taylor and Ben Derudder, *World City Network – A Global Urban Analysis* (2nd ed.) (London: Routledge, 2016).

8 Eurostat's NUTS classification (Nomenclature of territorial units for statistics) is a hierarchical system for dividing up the economic territory of the EU and the United Kingodm for the purpose of collecting, developing and harmonizing European regional statistics; socio-economic analyses of the regions; and framing EU regional policies. NUTS 3 relates to small regions for specific diagnoses.

9 Thilo Lang and Stefan Haunstein, 'Wachsende regionale Polarisierung in Europa [Increasing regional polarisation in Europe]', *Nationalatlas aktuell* 11 (2017) 8 [27.09.2017]. Leipzig: Leibniz-Institut für Länderkunde (IfL).

10 Tomas Hanell, *Regional Quality of Life in the EU. Comprehending the European space beyond GDP through the capability approach* (Espoo: Aalto University press, 2018), p. 191 n.

11 Franziska Görmar and Thilo Lang, 'Acting Peripheries: An Introduction', *ACME: An International Journal for Critical Geographies* 18 (2019) 2, pp. 486–95.

12 Andrew Pike et al., 'Shifting horizons in local and regional development', *Regional Studies* 51 (2017) 1, pp. 46–57.

13 Thilo Lang et al., 'Socio-spatial polarisation and policy response: Perspectives for regional development in the Baltic States', *European Urban and Regional Studies* 29 (2022) 1, pp. 21–44.

14 Thilo Lang and Ibolya Török, 'Metropolitan region policies in the European Union: Following national, European or neoliberal agendas?', *International Planning Studies* 22 (2017) 1, pp. 1–13, here at p. 2.

15 See Lang et al., 'Socio-spatial polarisation', pp. 21–44.

16 For an example on Hungary, see Gabor Lux, 'Minor Cities in a Metropolitan World: Challenges for Development and Governance in Three Hungarian Urban Agglomerations', *International Planning Studies* 20 (2015) 1–2, pp. 21–38, here at p. 23. On Romania, see Daniel Dranca,

'Cluj-Napoca Metropolitan Zone: Between a Growth Pole and a Deprived Area', *Transylvanian Review of Administrative Sciences* 40 (E) (2013), pp. 49–70, here at p. 54.

17 Lang and Török, 'Metropolitan region policies', p. 1.

18 Kevin Morgan, 'The Rise of Metropolitics: Urban Governance in the Age of the City-Region', in *Governing Urban Economies: Innovation and Inclusion in Canadian City Regions*, ed. Neil Bradford and Allison Bramwell (Toronto: Toronto University Press, 2014), p. 301 n. 1.

19 The so-called Visegrád Group is a cultural and political alliance of four Central European countries: the Czech Republic, Hungary, Poland and Slovakia.

20 Andy Pike, Andrés Rodríguez-Pose and John Tomaney, 'What Kind of Local and Regional Development and for Whom?', *Regional Studies* 41 (2007) 9, pp. 1253–69.

21 Rodríguez-Pose, 'The revenge of the places', pp. 189–209.

22 Aram Ziai, 'Post-development 25 years after The Development Dictionary', *Third World Quarterly* 38 (2017) 12, pp. 2547–58.

23 To meet the demand for statistics at a local level, Eurostat maintains a system of Local Administrative Units (LAUs) compatible with NUTS (see note 1, above).

24 Garri Raagmaa and Dominic Stead, 'Spatial Planning in the Baltic States: Impacts of European Policies', *European Planning Studies* 22 (2014) 4, pp. 671–9.

25 Epp Annus, 'The Problem of Soviet Colonialism in the Baltics', *Journal of Baltic Studies* 43 (2012) 1, pp. 21–45, here at p. 21.

26 Costis Hadjimichalis and Ray Hudson, 'Contemporary Crisis Across Europe and the Crisis of Regional Development Theories', *Regional Studies* 48 (2014) 1, pp. 208–18. See also Neil Brenner, 'Urban governance and the production of new state spaces in Western Europe: 1960-2000', *Review of International Political Economy* 11 (2004) 3, pp. 447–88.

Bibliography

Dijkstra, Lewis, Hugo Poelman and Andrés Rodríguez-Pose. 'The geography of EU discontent'. *Regional Studies* 54 (2020) 6, pp. 737–53.

European Foundation for the Improvement of Living and Working Conditions. *European Quality of Life Survey Integrated Data File, 2003–2016*. [data collection]. UK Data Service. 3rd ed., 2018. SN: 7348. http://doi.org/10.5255/UKDA-SN-7348-3

Harvie, David, Gary Slater, Bruce Philp and Dan Wheatley. 'Economic well-being and British regions: The problem with GDP per capita'. *Review of Social Economy* 67 (2009) 4, pp. 483–505.

Pittau, M. Grazia, Roberto Zelli and Andrew Gelman. 'Economic disparities and life satisfaction in European regions'. *Social Indicators Research* 96 (2010) 2, pp. 339–61.

Riga City Administration Planning Department. *Sustainable Development Strategy of Riga until 2030 and Development Programme of Riga for 2014–2020*. Riga: Riga City Council City Development Department, 2014. https://www.rdpad.lv/wp-content/uploads/2014/11/ENG_STRATEGIJA.pdf

Stiglitz, Joseph E., Amartya Sen and Jean-Paul Fitoussi. *Report by the Commission on the Measurement of Economic Performance and Social Progress*. Paris: L'Institut national de la statistique & des études économiques, 2009.

van den Bergh, Jeroen C. J. M. 'The GDP paradox'. *Journal of Economic Psychology* 30 (2009) 2, pp. 117–35.

Wishlade, Fiona. 'The rise of populism, regional disparities and the regional policy response'. *European Policy Research Paper* 109 (2019). European Policies Research Centre, University of Strathclyde, Glasgow. https://eprc-strath.org/wp-content/uploads/2021/09/The-rise-of-populism-regional-disparities-and-the-regional-policy-response-EPRP-109.pdf

Further reading

Bockman, Johanna and Gil Eyal. 'Eastern Europe as a Laboratory for Economic Knowledge: The Transnational Roots of Neoliberalism'. *American Journal of Sociology* 108 (2002) 2, pp. 310–52.

Harvey, David. *The Limits to Capital*. Oxford: Blackwell, 1982.

Lang, Thilo and Franziska Görmar (eds). *Regional and Local Development in Times of Polarisation*. Singapore: Palgrave Macmillan, 2019.

Peck, Jamie. *Construction of Neoliberal Reason*. Oxford: Oxford University Press, 2010.

Eastern Europe and China
Lela Rekhviashvili

13

Introduction

In August 2020, over forty Indian workers went on hunger strike in a mid-sized Serbian city, Kraljevo. They were requesting their long-unpaid salaries from a Serbian construction company, which had hired them on behalf of an American corporate entity to work on the construction of the Chinese- and Russian-funded Budapest–Belgrade railway project. This Eastern European rail line is a flagship project in China's Belt and Road Initiative (BRI), connecting Europe and Asia via land and sea routes and heralded as the 'largest coordinated investment in infrastructure in history'.[1] This seemingly marginal snippet of news on Indian labourers nonetheless hints at complex circulations of capital and labour stretching from the People's Republic of China (PRC) to the United States, and then into Eastern Europe (see text boxes on p. 313 and p. 314). In tandem with this incident, August 2020 also saw a media report on another Serbian building company – this time, owned by one of Europe's largest construction conglomerates (Austrian Strabag) – that had been employing prison inmates to rebuild a bridge in the Serbian town of Knjanzevac. Avoiding paying taxes or social contributions, the company paid one euro per inmate's hourly work to the county jail – with barely 20 cents of that being delivered to the working inmates themselves.[2] Such abuses of workers' rights and shady business deals might be linked to European or Chinese actors, but the challenge facing literature that focuses on Chinese investments in the infrastructures of Eastern Europe lies in its stubborn unwillingness to discuss such stories side by side. This reveals the problematic consequences of singling out China and treating Chinese engagements strictly as an isolated, threatening and historically unprecedented phenomenon.

I attempt here a critical analysis of existing, contested knowledge on Chinese investments in Eastern Europe, pointing out the limits of existing approaches and suggesting further possible paths for research. First, I review existing empirical knowledge on infrastructure investments in various sub-regions of Eastern Europe and also in Russia, the Caucasus and Central Asia, revealing substantial diversity in local and regional responses to the rise of China's influence. Second, I examine how Chinese infrastructure investments and economic diplomacy are currently interpreted in academic and semi-academic literatures, revealing a problematic overemphasis on a perceived Chinese threat while representing the EU and a broadly conceived West as benevolent, innocent or normatively superior powers. Third, I attempt to deconstruct the narrative of a benevolent EU in order to uncover its hitherto hidden role in creating open and FDI- (Foreign Direct Investment) dependent economies on its eastern periphery; I then suggest linking research on Chinese investments in Eastern Europe with data about the broader spatial reorganization under global capitalism. Overall, I argue that large, debt-driven infrastructure projects can pose significant challenges for the region, and that Chinese investments might further undermine existing regulatory settings and accountability mechanisms. Yet, these processes cannot be thoroughly examined without rethinking the existing developmental paradigm historically and currently instituted by, and still mostly benefiting, the Western (former) imperial centres.

The Belt and Road Initiative

Kean Fan Lim

The Belt and Road Initiative (BRI) is an influential development plan driven by the Chinese state. It was first proposed in 2013 by current Chinese president Xi Jinping to enhance transcontinental connectivity and collaboration. It has since become a broad and rolling blueprint enabling the Chinese government to expand its geo-economic sphere of influence. Whether or not the BRI delivers on its stated goals has become a major focal point of social-scientific research. Much has been written about the geopolitical intentions and international security implications of the BRI. Attention has focused primarily on what is now widely known as 'debt trap diplomacy' – namely, the extension of excessive credit that could subject debtor countries to a loss of sovereign control over their key resources. Whether this critique is credible is still unclear, but there are at least two palpable economic logics to the BRI.

1. It involves a new form of market capture that goes beyond the traditional practice of price dumping. This does not mean that Chinese firms are primarily aiming to sell finished products at ultra-low, state-subsidized prices in foreign markets in order to 'crowd out' competitors. Rather, these firms help to facilitate the export of Chinese expertise and technology to infrastructure, logistics and energy sectors abroad. This not only enables the absorption of domestic surplus capacity but also allows China to exert long-term technological influence over the collaborating countries.

2. It enhances an extant global-scale project also targeted at expanding geo-economic influence – the internationalization of the renminbi (RMB). While the exact figures are not announced, loans to collaborating countries have been issued in RMB. This is useful because the monies can then be used to pay Chinese firms and workers participating in the projects as well as for the import of Chinese-made equipment. Because the RMB is not fully convertible or freely traded in global currency markets, the BRI provides a concrete platform for the Chinese state to internationalize its currency and further its political commitment to reduce usage of the US dollar while still controlling its supply, flow and use.

Figure 13.1 The Belt and Road Initiative (BRI)

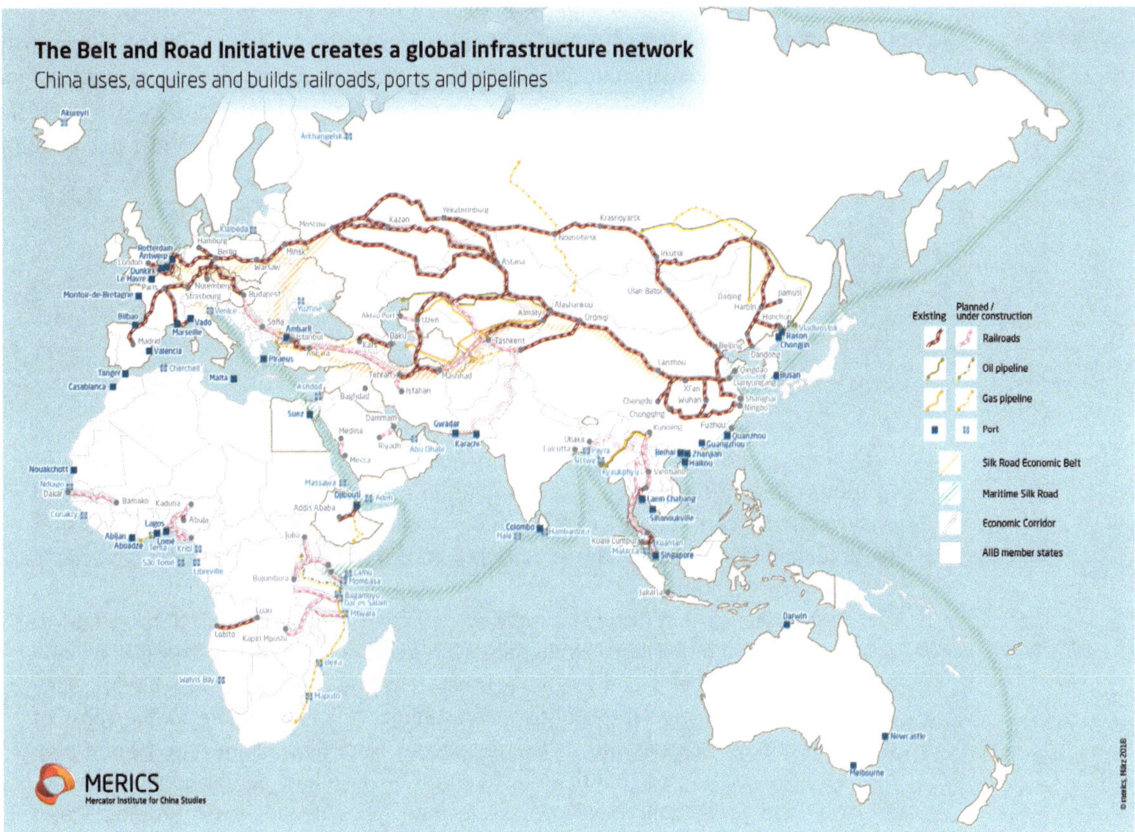

The 2010s witnessed an unprecedented rise in China's economic presence – via trade, infrastructural connectivity and investment flows – in the whole of Europe and Eurasia, as an eventual result of the country's 'going-out' strategy (initiated in 1999 by the PRC government to promote Chinese investments abroad). By 2020, the PRC had replaced the United States as the European Union's most important trading partner. Chinese investments grew from marginal to major transactions, amounting to $248 billion in 2010–19 with more than 40 per cent of these projects involving the EU's critical infrastructures (see text box, below, for a definition of 'infrastructure'). EU institutions, the continent's media and its academic commentators all express worries about the growing role of China as a trade-and-investment partner for the whole of Europe. Yet, despite the fact that the vast majority of Chinese investments on the continent are made in Western European economies, Chinese infrastructure investments and political-economic engagement with Eastern Europe have attracted by far the larger share of attention and sparked anxieties. Concerns were especially triggered by flagship, large-scale infrastructure projects such as the aforementioned Budapest–Belgrade railway (a 1.8 billion euro Chinese loan, purely for the Hungarian leg of the project), Piraeus Port in Greece (a 600 million euro investment), and the Trans-Anatolian gas pipeline project in the Caucasus (a 600 million US dollar loan in 2016, the largest loan issued at the time by the PRC-led Asian Infrastructure Investment Bank). To many, the Eastern European peripheries represent China's Trojan Horse, with this region seeming fertile ground for the PRC's 'authoritarian advance' whereby China allegedly exploits Eastern Europe's infrastructural needs so as to advance its own interests, using 'divide-and-rule' strategies, while threatening new 'East–West' divides and creating new dependencies.

Defining 'infrastructure'

Andy Pike

Infrastructure systems provide the services on which people rely for their everyday lives. Heat, light, hydration, shelter, connection and mobility enable the basic daily tasks of cooking, eating, resting, washing, communicating with each other, and moving around on bikes, boats, cars, foot, trains and trams. Infrastructure underpins and connects sites for fundamental human and social activities worldwide – in the home and in places to live, learn, work and play.

The term has a long history of evolving definitions. It was first used in relation to railway engineering in France in the late 19th century, and later to describe military assets including airfields and roads. In urbanizing and industrializing societies, early definitions focused on the physical manifestations of infrastructure in the form of bridges and power, water and sewerage systems. Later distinctions have been drawn between 'economic' (or 'hard') infrastructures – including digital communication, energy, flood protection, transport, waste management and water systems – and 'social' (or 'soft') infrastructures – including those for education, health, legal, medical and security purposes. Some degree of blurring occurs between 'hard' and 'soft', especially across the categories of commercial and residential property – and activities have become increasingly connected in places by state, financial and other actors.

Academic disciplines and professions have different, and sometimes competing, definitions and understandings of infrastructure. Economists see infrastructure as public goods that can only be provided by governments in response to 'market failure' in which the private sector cannot or will not supply such goods. Engineers understand infrastructure as 'systems of systems' that provide critical or essential services. In addressing the mitigation and adaptation needed to cope with climate change, engineers increasingly seek integration and interdependencies in order to minimize resource use and service provision, and to make them more sustainable. Financiers see infrastructure as assets and revenue streams capable of generating returns over the longer term. Their growing involvement in the field has been part of the financialization of infrastructures, a process through which infrastructure assets are conceived of as financial assets. This process of financialization has in turn contributed to the fragmentation and 'unbundling' of infrastructure systems and services, and to the transformation of infrastructure from public goods into financial assets.

China's diverse engagements across Eastern Europe

An overview of Chinese infrastructure investments and economic diplomacy in Eastern Europe indicates that the PRC relies on different strategies when engaging with the sub-regions of Eastern Europe and Eurasia. In turn, the political elites at national and regional levels also show diverse predispositions, preferences, motivations and bargaining powers when negotiating exchanges with China. This section is organized according to this regionally patterned logic of Chinese investments. What emerges are the visible differences in China's approaches and local political responses across EU-member and non-EU-member economies. We begin with experiences in Central Asia – which, while not strictly part of Eastern Europe (according to most flexible definitions of this region), does hold lessons for it.

Russia and Central Asia

Central Asia is commonly understood as a frontier region between China and Eastern Europe, which has experienced far longer engagement with the former than with Eastern European states. Bilateral links between China and five Central Asian republics have been strengthening since the 1990s, culminating in the establishment of a multilateral collaboration framework – the Shanghai Cooperation Organisation – in the early 2000s. The resource-rich, open economy of Kazakhstan has been a significant economic and political partner for the PRC. Chinese investments are also important for the governments of poorer economies in the region, such as those of Kyrgyzstan and Tajikistan. China is, in fact, emerging as the most powerful partner and investor in the region, primarily focusing on the energy and infrastructure sectors. It invests in and expands on Soviet-era projects, especially in mining and natural-resource extraction.[3] Being the most exposed to Chinese investments, Central Asian societies show high levels of resistance to their adverse environmental consequences, accompanying economic dependency and labour exploitation. In response to such widespread social discontent, PRC-based investors are increasingly hiring local, rather than Chinese, labour in Central Asian republics.

Unlike the Central Asian states, Russia only started deepening ties with China after the annexation of Crimea (2014), in the light of Russia's disillusionment with its prospects of integrating with the West. Since then, 'China has become Russia's closest ally in a range of activities spanning from hydrocarbon business projects in the Far East and wood extraction in Siberia to marine transportation via the Northern Sea Route in Arctic'.[4] Yet, Russia remains wary of Chinese investments. While energy-related projects succeed more often, many of the large transport-infrastructure ventures remain stalled – especially if they have been planned near the Russia–China border. Impediments on transportation projects are explained by Russia's 'implicit view that national security depends on national oversight and operation of transportation networks'.[5] Such caution sets Russia apart from its Eastern European and Central Asian neighbours, which have longer-established experience of their infrastructures being planned and financed from imperial centres and are also currently more open to debt-driven infrastructure development – even when it comes to critical or essential infrastructures.

Non-EU-member in Eastern Europe and the South Caucasus

The member countries of the EU's Eastern Partnership scheme – the non-EU-member Eastern European states of Moldova, Ukraine and Belarus, and the South Caucasian states of Azerbaijan, Armenia and Georgia – 'represent a vital link [for the BRI] simply by virtue of their geographic position'.[6] China initially excluded these countries from its multilateral collaboration scheme with Central and Eastern European countries in acknowledgement of Russia's claims of influence over the region. Nevertheless, investment volumes have been increasing throughout the 2010s, and the three South Caucasian states are engaging particularly eagerly with the BRI. They have signed free trade agreements with the PRC, are attempting to position themselves as a connectivity hub between China and Europe, and are invested in the development of the 'middle corridor' of the BRI, which is a potential transit route between Central Asia and Europe through the Caucasus (in contrast to the BRI's 'northern corridor' which runs through Russia). Among other energy- and transport-infrastructure projects, the Trans-Anatolian gas pipeline stands out for its scale – connecting Azerbaijan, through Georgia, to Turkey and further to Europe. The China-led Asian Infrastructure Investment Bank (AIIB) issued a 600 million US-dollar loan in 2016 for this project, the largest loan issued at the time by the AIBB. Ukraine, Moldova and Belarus are somewhat more modestly, but still increasingly, welcoming Chinese investments – with Belarus hosting the largest industrial park with Chinese investment outside China (the Great Stone Industrial Park) near Minsk, and Chinese companies modernizing the Port of Yuzhni near Odesa in Ukraine. It appears that Eastern Partnership countries seem particularly enthusiastic about Chinese investments. Yet, despite the fact that some large projects are being executed there, China's interest in these countries seems less marked than its enthusiasm for Central and Eastern Europe or Central Asia.

Central and Eastern Europe

In 2012, China established a political collaboration scheme (now known as '14+1') with Central and Eastern European countries to deepen collaboration when it comes to infrastructure, and 'green' and advanced technologies. Observers refer to the scheme as 'multilateral bilateralism' on the part of the PRC: a platform which China utilizes as a hub to strike bilateral rather than multilateral deals with individual participating countries. The Central and Eastern European political elites' willingness to engage with the PRC is ascribed to their wish of catching up 'on relations with China as a rising global power and in that sense upgrading [Central and Eastern Europe]'s political position in Europe and within the EU'.[7] Further sub-regional differences are apparent both in China's investment preferences and in the local political responses to Chinese engagement across Central and Eastern Europe.

South-east Europe, or the so-called Balkan states, hosts the highest number of infrastructure investments in the region, with non-EU-member Balkan governments being particularly keen to advance such ventures. The largest infrastructural investments in the Balkans with Chinese involvement run the gamut from coal-fired power plants to transport infrastructures such as highways, railways and ports. If we are to counter mainstream narratives on the region as China's Trojan Horse, we should bear in mind the agency of local political elites in steering such infrastructure projects. Some commentators point out that these host elites manage to guide 'Chinese finance towards politically expedient projects of their own choosing: roads with no Western financial backing and lignite power plants facing Western institutions' defunding of coal'.[8] Others argue that South-east European countries welcome Chinese infrastructure projects given their weak or non-existent access to EU infrastructure-financing schemes such as structural funds.[9] China has become a particularly prominent investor in Greece, with Piraeus port playing a strategic role in the BRI. Interestingly, the Baltic states used to be also open and welcoming to Chinese investments – yet seem, thus far, to have received neither significant infrastructure loans nor FDI.

Chinese investments in the Port of Piraeus

Paschalis Samarinis and Theodore Styliadis

In 2008, the concession of the Piraeus Port Container Terminal Piers II and III was made by the Piraeus Port Authority (OLP) to the Chinese state-owned company, China Ocean Shipping Company (COSCO). In the ensuing years, the Chinese sought to further increase their presence at the port. Its strategic location (the first major container port westwards after the Suez Canal) as well as the prospects of increasing transshipment and transit volumes through European freight corridors were the primary reasons China desired Piraeus to be a crucial node within its Belt and Road Initiative (BRI). The dire economic situation of Greece from 2010 onwards, and its implementation of a massive privatization programme focusing on publicly owned assets and state-run services, served as a catalyst to pursue this objective. In 2016, following a competitive tender for the master-concession of Piraeus port, COSCO won the bid for a 67-per-cent stake in OLP – held until then by the Greek state. In return, COSCO would implement mandatory investments of 293.8 million euros within the 2016–20 period and 56 million euros in 2021–5.

Critical commentators suggest that the bid was extremely low bearing in mind the well-known intangible characteristics that comprise Piraeus port's actual value, rendering it one of China's flagship infrastructural projects. Its geostrategic importance aside, Piraeus is a vibrant multipurpose urban-port in functional contact with the country's largest metropolitan area (Greater Athens), the largest passenger port in Europe connecting the mainland to the Aegean islands (with an annual traffic of more than 15.5 million passengers) and an important cruise port. Furthermore, OLP's land property offers great opportunities for real-estate development. This diversification of services has been a strong incentive for Chinese investors as it allows the port system to be more flexible and agile to changes in demand and in external environments.

The Port of Piraeus therefore functions at different scales, from the local (the metropolitan complex) to the national (the Hellenic Republic) to the regional (the Aegean and eastern Mediterranean) to the global (the BRI). Accordingly, both through the privatization process and the port's current administration under the management of Chinese investors, various stakeholders are involved: COSCO, the EU, the Greek government, the local community, workers' unions, maritime and logistics businesses, and the shipbuilding and tourism sectors, to name but a few. In this respect, the case of Piraeus is indicative not only of the expansion of Chinese investment interests but also of the emergence of a new, multifaceted and antagonistic, political and economic environment.

In contrast to South-east Europe, the EU-member Visegrád countries (the 'V4') and Slovenia receive fewer infrastructure-related loans and more FDI. This is hardly surprising given that these countries already have better access to infrastructure funds and also host more complex industries than their south-eastern neighbours do. It is estimated that the V4 has so far secured over 75 per cent of Chinese FDI in the region – primarily targeting transportation, telecommunications, electronics and the chemical industry. PRC state-owned as well as private companies have been making greenfield investments in the V4 countries since the early 2000s, while since 2010 they have pursued mergers, acquisitions and joint ventures there.[10] Nevertheless, the Visegrad countries also receive significant Chinese infrastructure-related investments – for example, a number of Polish cities host Chinese logistic hubs related to the China–Europe Railway Express. In addition, the afore-mentioned Budapest–Belgrade railway represents one of the most visible infrastructure projects in Central and Eastern Europe.

The Budapest–Belgrade Railway Project

Csaba Jelinek and Linda Szabó

The upgrading of the Budapest–Belgrade railway line, including 183 kilometres of lines from Belgrade to Kelebia on the Serbian side and 152 kilometres from Kelebia to Budapest in Hungary, is one of the major flagship projects of the BRI and is being carried out at the intersection of local, European and global politics. It is claimed to form the final segment of the track from the majority Chinese-owned port at Piraeus, in Greece; and ostensibly designed to transport Chinese-manufactured goods to locations throughout Central, South-eastern and Eastern Europe, where Hungary would serve as the base for a distribution centre (yet to be constructed).

Even though the international media often frame the project, financed mostly through loan payments, as yet another potential instance of China's 'debt-trap diplomacy', the project's financial portfolio – especially in the Serbian case – proves to be much more complex. First, some of the feasibility studies and the environmental-impact assessments of the reconstruction in Serbia were financed by an EU pre-accession grant during the 2010s. Second, a loan amounting to at least 800 million US dollars was provided by the Russian state both for construction work and for the related investments in railway modernization. Third, as part of the reconstruction works, begun in 2017, the main railway station in the heart of Belgrade was shut down and replaced by a new station in a different part of the capital – entailing a huge urban-development project financed mainly by the Kuwait Fund for Arab Economic Development. This mixture of financial sources shows that an EU-neighbourhood state with limited access to EU funds (exacerbated by the withdrawal of Western firms from the country) cannot help but look for alternative external sources to finance local large-scale infrastructure developments. It is also a fitting example of how the common, simplified image of Chinese involvement may overshadow the real complexity of such a project – which in actuality involves local, EU, Russian and Middle Eastern sources, let alone the US-registered company employing Indian workers to carry out the construction work mentioned in the Introduction, above.

On the Hungarian side, the Budapest–Belgrade project, attracting a c. 1.8 billion euro Chinese loan (85 per cent of the total budget), is a clear example of how the interests of domestic politics may run up against China's geo-economic expansionism. At the local scale, the project has never been reconciled with any other strategic plans for infrastructure development, while reconstruction works are guaranteed to be carried out by a consortium of Chinese state-owned enterprises and a Hungarian company closely connected to members of that country's ruling party. The investment is used strategically as a channel to access economic sources outside of the Western European region in order to gain some political as well as economic leverage on the scale of the European Union.

Despite a great deal of talk around the issue, the economic engagements between China and Central and Eastern Europe are actually viewed as somewhat insignificant. Central and Eastern Europe in fact receives far less Chinese investment than the primary recipients of Chinese FDI in Western Europe. Furthermore, the most significant outcomes of economic ties are not FDI or infrastructure loans but an increasing trade surplus for China – and hence, a trade deficit for the partner region. Finally, Chinese investments are not particularly impressive when compared with Central and Eastern Europe's integration with and dependence on Western Europe.

The image of the Chinese threat in the media, political responses and academia

Chinese involvement in Eastern Europe has raised a series of concerns expressed in media, political and academic commentary. The perception of a threat, and anxieties about geopolitical divides and economic dependency, has consumed the media, the EU's institutional responses and academic writings alike. They all single out the PRC as an exceptionally dangerous actor, and portray the West – particularly EU institutions and its core, Western members (former colonial powers, we should not forget, and currently the exporters of capital to the EU's internal and external peripheries) – as benevolent or normatively superior. However, it would be naïve, if not dangerous, to propose that Chinese engagements with Eastern Europe and Eurasia should not be cautiously scrutinized. When criticizing hypocrisy in such attitudes towards China, we should not romanticize the PRC, depict it as a revisionist or emancipatory force, or disregard the new imperial dynamics that China engenders.[11] Yet, we do need to question whether the dual assumptions of Chinese threat and Western benevolence are accurate in relation to Eastern Europe.

Demonizing China in 'Western' Media

US- or Europe-based liberal media outlets are dominated by straightforward demonization of increasing Chinese influence in Eastern Europe and Eurasia, as reflected in headlines such as 'Chinese Octopus: How China is Taking Over the Post-Soviet Space'.[12] Others state that Chinese investments are not as significant as portrayed, but do not contest the representation of the PRC as a particular threat. At times, even sexualized language and belittling analogies of prostitution are employed to cement images of the penetrability and vulnerability of the region. Such media reports primarily point out two types of danger allegedly stemming from engagement with China. First, they report hazards of an economic nature such as increasing indebtedness on unfavourable terms. Second, they emphasize political hazards such as a deepening of political tensions within European countries due to 'the "divide-and-rule" politics of the BRI', which threatens 'a new East–West divide in Europe'.[13] Chinese involvements are then implicitly and explicitly contrasted with the EU's involvement on its internal and external peripheries, suggesting that its political and economic offers of engagement with the region are superior.

It is claimed that EU funds for infrastructure are larger as well as cheaper than their Chinese counterparts, and offer more non-repayable grants instead of loans. China is said to use the 'debt trap' – a situation in which the debt is hard for the lender to repay – to gain various concessions and favours from the indebted governments. Eastern or South-eastern European politicians' willingness to pursue Chinese funding is explained by their wish to avoid EU regulations, which were introduced in the first place to rescue just such corruptible politicians from their own possible wrongdoings and to 'save countries from reckless governments'.[14] Such politicians are not only said to be ungrateful but also blamed for actively undermining the European project by supporting 'a counter-narrative to European cooperation and the liberal values underpinning the European project'.[15]

The EU's political anxieties and changing regulatory regimes

Much like the aforementioned media reports, EU institutional statements betray disquiet that China wishes to spread authoritarian governance modes conflicting with the EU's liberal values, as well as fear of unreciprocal and unfair economic engagement from the Chinese side. Such anxieties resurface in relation to both the EU's internal (EU-member) and external (non-member-state) peripheries. Fear of the PRC and mistrust towards local political elites is particularly amplified when it comes to the Balkan and Eastern Partnership countries. European Commissioner Johannes Hahn, for example, openly declares that non-EU-member Balkan countries are being exploited by the PRC as Trojan Horses to penetrate EU-member economies, and worries that 'China's "combination of capitalism and a political dictatorship" could appeal to some leaders in the region'. In a similar vein, it is emphasized that Chinese loans can impose restrictive fiscal burdens on Eastern Partnership countries, 'thereby also reducing the likelihood of recipient countries being able to acquire more funding from other international players, such as the World Bank'.[16]

European governments, as well as EU institutions, have also begun taking some steps to address the aforementioned fears. From 2017, a number of EU member states including Germany, France, Hungary, Italy, Latvia and Lithuania have tightened FDI screening regulations and many others are planning to strengthen their investment-review mechanisms. Prior to the 2008 financial crisis, and increasingly amid the 2020 global pandemic, EU institutions have also grown wary of non-domestic investments. The European Commission issued guidance in March 2020 calling for greater control over FDI in order to protect its critical and essential infrastructures. In parallel, the EU is becoming increasingly cautious regarding the PRC – with the European Commission portraying EU–China relations as 'simultaneously, in different policy areas, a cooperation partner [...], an economic competitor in the pursuit of technological leadership, and a systemic rival promoting alternative models of governance'.[17]

In short, the EU 'should robustly seek more balanced and reciprocal conditions governing the economic relationship'. This shows that fear of Chinese investments might be behind the EU's increasing protectiveness in relation to non-European or non-Western FDI.

Academic reinforcement of popular anxieties

Even the research-based non-academic and academic literature has a tendency to reiterate the EU's 'higher moral ground' and the 'China threat' narrative. Only a few years ago, the largest European think tank exclusively focusing on the PRC, the Mercator Institute for

China Studies (Merics), offered relatively neutral reporting and pointed out the opportunities accompanying Chinese investments in Europe. Shortly thereafter, studies coming out of the Mercator Institute started emphasizing the dangers of China's '[a]uthoritarian advance' and expressed concerns that the PRC was exploiting European openness while restricting foreign capital and information flows into China.[18]

Much academic writing also reproduces the 'China threat' narrative. Such accounts question the official Chinese narrative on the win-win, harmonious and well-intentioned character of Chinese economic diplomacy, and discuss the PRC's advance as 'offensive mercantilism'.[19] The BRI infrastructure projects are criticized for low environmental standards. Contrasting Chinese infrastructure investments with the allegedly 'sound and sustainable' lending policies of the World Bank, such research warns Chinese partner states that if they 'do not wish to become the pollution "dumping ground" for China's ecological civilization, they need to push for the adoption of meaningful social and environmental standards'.[20]

Even those who contest different elements of the mainstream negative depictions of engagements between Eastern Europe and China rely on a statist framework of analysis, single out the PRC for criticism, fail to account for the agency of different Eastern European actors, and reiterate the EU's superiority.[21] Some suggest that the portrayal of the China–Central and Eastern Europe relationship as an 'empty shell' is misplaced, and cite the deepening and wide-ranging nature of relations between the PRC and Central and Eastern Europe.[22] Others contest the narrative of the Balkans representing a Trojan Horse, and illustrate the ways in which the EU is successfully reinforcing its hegemonic role in the region. Yet others claim that Chinese infrastructure investments do not necessarily reflect the PRC's geopolitical intentions but simply benefit specific Chinese companies.[23]

Certain commentators even explore how Eastern European economies might benefit from integration with China. Optimistic claims are based on the alleged insignificance of Central and Eastern Europe in global hegemonic struggles: 'Logically, it is not in China's interest to profit at the expense of [Central and Eastern European] economies, because these economies are emerging rather than fully developed.'[24] This statement not only contradicts all accumulated knowledge on how hegemonic capitalist powers benefit from and reproduce the semi-peripheral and peripheral positions of so-called less developed economies, it also reproduces the perception of Central and Eastern European economies as insufficiently significant for China to even care about taking advantage of. The same sentiment is expressed in a more straightforward, and belittling, manner by Dragan Pavlićević, who suggests that China is far from challenging the EU-centred regional order because the EU is a far more important partner for the PRC than Central and Eastern European countries are, arguing that 'China would be careful not to "trade a horse for a donkey"'.[25] While not all accounts of China's presence in Eastern Europe would use such condescending metaphors, overall the academic literature on the topic suffers from a reliance on Eurocentric and statist frameworks.

In summary, the media, political commentary and academic accounts postulate a range of economic and political threats stemming from Chinese investments and political-economic engagement with Eastern Europe. While some of their concerns merit further examination, the patronizing tone of these accounts is alarming. Assuming normative superiority on the part of the EU, they portray Eastern Europe and its political elites as ungrateful, corrupt and opportunistic vis-à-vis the virtuous EU. They choose easy explanations, blaming the corruption or outright stupidity of Eastern European political elites and fail to ask: What has led to existing East–West divisions in the EU? How has Eastern Europe come to depend on external capital? What kind of global political-economic settings have enabled China to export its capital to the region?

Beyond the 'China threat': The historical and spatial contextualization of Chinese engagements with Eastern Europe

To overcome the limits of the dominant interpretative frames on China–Eastern Europe relations, this section aims to deconstruct the 'China threat' narrative. There are sound reasons to continue scrutinizing China–Eastern Europe relations and to be cautious of such engagements. All we know from the previous research indicates that Chinese infrastructure loans might not necessarily benefit recipient governments or locally impacted societies.[26] However, insisting on Western supremacy, while singling out China without understanding its place within the dynamics of global capitalist accumulation and shifts in hegemonic power structures, and reducing examination of the topic to geopolitical rivalry, is not only empirically unsubstantiated but also closes down possible avenues for further research. Such accounts are based on evasion and a lack of reference to already existing research; they externalize and divert attention from structural problems. Here, I aim to provide alternative 'entry points' for a historical and spatial contextualization of China–Eastern Europe relations. It highlights thus-far dismissed and silenced strands of literature on the role of the West in the financialization of infrastructures and in shaping FDI-dependent economies on its eastern peripheries, and on China's place in the restructuring of global capitalism. I suggest that we need to remain cautious of the PRC's engagement with Eastern Europe, not because China represents an exceptional threat but because Eastern Europe's engagements with it take place in a broader context of political and economic risks, uneven development geographies, and dependencies co-constituted by the contending hegemonic powers of contemporary capitalism.

Beyond the seeming superior infrastructure financing of the EU

The existing literature underlines ways in which China is a risky donor; finances socially, economically and environmentally unjustified projects; and how the EU or, more broadly, Western donors make superior infrastructure-financing offers to Eastern Europe and

Eurasia. Such diagnoses entirely skip over existing long-standing research on broader systemic changes in infrastructure financing, funding and governance in Europe and beyond, which has yielded three main tendencies.

First, the whole of Europe has been grappling with infrastructure financing over the past few decades – and especially since the 2008 financial crisis. Extensive research on the financialization of infrastructures traces the drying up of public investment in infrastructures (in Western and Eastern Europe alike) and the transformation of infrastructures 'from a public and collective good into an alternative asset class within the international investment landscape'.[27] Beyond Europe, European or, more broadly, Western finance capital and financial institutions have supported financially extractive infrastructure developments and reaped the benefits of the financialization of infrastructures in the Global South.

Second, although the EU has played an important role in promoting (particularly transport) infrastructures as a key developmental strategy, EU-supported projects have often failed to deliver on their promises. Documented cases of 'underused motorways, closed high-speed railway lines, and empty airports' in various European regions have led observers to suggest that many such projects 'have been a complete waste of public resources that could have been used more effectively for other purposes'.[28] The example of Spanish High Speed Rail (HSR) – one of the most notorious large-scale, environmentally costly infrastructure projects of little economic or public value – shows how such projects are 'rooted in capital's tendency to geographical expansion' and enabled by the export of overaccumulated capital from Europe's core to its (semi-)peripheries.[29] Projects like Spanish HSR are often given impetus through non-refundable EU grants. These grants tend to cover about 25 per cent of costs while the rest of the expenditure is debt financed.

Finally, the EU's mechanisms of financing infrastructures, primarily in Eastern Europe, are highly controversial. The EU-level mega-infrastructural project Trans-European Transport Network has been contested by Eastern European civil-society groups for its averse local social and environmental consequences. Furthermore, EU cohesion policy and related EU funds in Eastern Europe have been found to contribute to the increasing indebtedness of local governments in the region. Eastern European local governments, being the biggest beneficiaries of EU funds, have relied on EU grants for the provision of social services and local physical infrastructure. The attendant co-financing requirements, ranging from 50 to 85 per cent prompt those local governments to secure debts on private capital markets or to rely on funds from central government. This contributes to the increasing dependence of local governments on their respective central administrations, and to the deterioration of local-government finances.[30] In other words, the West – and, primarily, the EU – has contributed to the creation of a structural condition in which large economic infrastructures are accepted as a developmental 'heyday', are largely private-debt financed, and undermine fiscal stability and marginalize social infrastructures on the EU's eastern peripheries. Needless to say, China tapping into and benefiting from such conditions carries the risk of further aggravating the aforementioned challenges. Yet, the problem starts not with China's exceptionality but, more broadly, with the dangers of infrastructure financialization and the uneven geographies of infrastructure-led development.

Beyond the discourse of new 'East–West' divides

The literature on China and Eastern Europe contemplates whether China is engendering new East–West divides – as if social, spatial and economic divides were not in place already, as can be seen in two ways. First, the so-called transformation from socialism to a market economy has led to new, unprecedented socio-spatial inequalities and divides across post-socialist Eastern Europe. With neoliberal capitalism being the 'only game in town', local political elites often pushed reforms further than transnational actors anticipated, pursuing 'even more radical neoliberal reforms than the EU advised, including the flat tax, pension privatization, slashing corporate tax rates, extreme monetarism, and central bank independence'.[31] This process, understood as local political elites' response to competitive pressures in attracting capital, was accompanied by a deep regional socio-spatial polarization, a lack of urban planning, gentrification and the encroachment of private interest on public spaces. Alongside deepening sub-national and regional inequalities and spatial disparities, cross-regional East–West divides also prevailed. Such divides were articulated not only in material and political-economic but also in discursive and ideational terms. While Western Europe has been 'hailed' as 'developed', Eastern Europe has been defined through its relative backwardness, and institutional or cultural deficiencies vis-à-vis the West.

Second, divides between EU-member Eastern and Western Europe not only prevail but are being (re-)produced and deepened by the EU's economic-integration policies. European integration policies have created clear winners and losers, favouring Western export-centred capitalist thinking. In Eastern Europe, the EU has played a key role in shaping the direction of economic reforms. Eastern European states initially viewed FDI with a degree of scepticism – yet the EU actively promoted openness to FDI, and did so by supporting the setting up of national investment-promotion agencies (already under way in the mid-1990s), making FDI openness an important membership condition and even by 'specifically suggest[ing] privatisation via foreign ownership in a number of strategic sectors'.[32] While FDI inflows and EU cohesion policy have supported overall economic growth in the region, they have also 'produced dual economies in which some privileged, FDI-based, competitive sectors thrive along[side] less prosperous, domestically-owned ones', while 'FDI has also been the main driver of rising territorial disparities'.[33] It has been argued that the failure of EU cohesion policy to support peripheralized regions was a result of it drifting away from its cohesion goals in favour of promoting growth and competition, thereby constructing asymmetrical interdependence between Eastern and Western Europe.

The fear that China might exploit pre-existing divides, or even play a part in further deepening those divides, cannot be conflated with solely blaming the PRC for the emergence and re-production of socio-spatial and economic inequalities. Even more importantly, before emphasizing the superiority of European or, more broadly, Western financing and investment schemes it has to be noted that the EU and Western financial institutions have played a crucial role in shaping the FDI-dependent, open economies of Eastern Europe as well as their (semi-)peripheral embedding in a global capitalist economy. If China, as a hegemonic rival to the West, looks set to exploit the kind of developmental model dominant in Eastern Europe and Eurasia, it might be worth questioning the developmental model itself.

Understanding the Chinese presence in Eastern Europe as part of the spatial reorganization of global capitalism

The literature on China–Eastern Europe and Eurasia debates whether China represents an opportunity or a threat – in the process, largely treating Chinese loans and investments as a unique, unprecedented phenomenon. Yet, the PRC is embedded in global capitalism, and historical and contemporary workings of debt, foreign investment and large infrastructure projects lie behind the re-production of capitalist accumulation in all its classed, racial and gendered aspects. All this, we know from the history of Western imperialism – however, two aspects in particular stand out.

First, Chinese engagement with Eastern Europe might be a relatively recent phenomenon, but what China does through its 'going-out' strategy and the BRI is not exceptional but rather repeats paths that other contending capitalist hegemons have pursued. Despite the country's own specificities as an authoritarian and still partially socialist polity, it is well established that 'China's rise – as driven by its unprecedented economic growth – is premised upon its embrace of capitalism and the opening up of its economy to global markets, production chains, and (if less so) financial flows'.[34] The BRI in turn is seen as one of the most powerful expressions of the PRC's embedding in the global capitalist economy, as it is a symptom of a capital overaccumulation problem – the challenge of investing surplus capital in a productive manner. The BRI embodies a typical capitalist response to the overaccumulation crisis: geographic expansion and spatial reorganization. For some, the BRI aligns overall with the dominant capitalist developmental mode. For others, it engenders important new spatial reorganizations of global capitalism.[35]

Second, once we move beyond singling out China, it becomes easier to determine what threats and challenges it can pose, based on the examples that the history of capitalist accumulation offers. On the broadest level, the geographical expansion of capital has never proceeded painlessly and has habitually involved dispossession, exploitation, the racialized dehumanization of entire communities, the enclosure of commons, and the erasure of alternative forms of production and consumption. Debt has also been key to capitalist accumulation. Following the financial crisis of 2008, we have witnessed how Western banks, engaged in predatory lending as they were, were bailed out using public funds – and there has been no escaping the austerity politics that followed the crisis. History shows us plenty of similar examples, with the 1980s debt crises also heavily impacting on Eastern European (then, socialist) countries, which

> borrowed heavily from Western [. . .] banks in the 1970s, on terms that seemed too good to refuse. Following recession and interest rate hikes in the 1980s, they could no longer pay the interest and started to default on the loans; this yielded structural adjustment, accompanying a shift to neoliberal agendas as defined by the Bretton Woods institutions.[36]

In this sense, the concept of the debt trap, used pejoratively in relation to China, has actually been a norm in the capitalist policies of lending. The devastating social consequences of such lending, and the accompanying IMF bailouts and structural adjustment programmes, have been well documented. With the BRI being primarily a debt-financed project, the question stands: Who will be paying off the debts? Given that

> we've seen from typical capitalist behaviour, [. . .] usually the people who end up paying the debt are the least privileged and most marginalized population. The same questions have to be posed regarding the return on China's foreign loans and investments.[37]

The exclusive focus on nation-states means that even if the political elites of Eastern Europe might at points benefit through engagements with Chinese or other debt-driven infrastructural projects, specific social classes, communities and locales are likely to be unevenly affected and bear high socio-economic and environmental risks as a result.

Conclusions

In Eastern Europe and Eurasia, something significant and worth examining is taking place. Chinese engagement with the region warrants further research and scrutiny – on the one hand, due to the volume and depth of these exchanges; on the other, because of their geopolitical and geo-economic implications, with the EU declaring the PRC to be its 'systemic' rival and local political elites in the region adopting diverging stances. However, as we have seen, current interpretative lenses are quite misleading: Western media, policy commentary and academic research on the topic have all imposed major limits on themselves and their discourse, obscuring potentially fruitful possibilities for further research. Existing analyses construct China as an exceptional political and economic threat for the continent; reinforce the EU's and, more broadly, the West's higher-moral-ground posture; and adopt statist analytical frameworks, dismissing the uneven consequences of engagement with the PRC for different classes, social groups and locales. Ultimately, Chinese engagements with Eastern Europe and Eurasia are not so exceptional. For one thing, the dominance of foreign investments in their economy and infrastructures is nothing new for most states in Eastern Europe and Eurasia. Furthermore, East–West material and discursive divides are also not new, and in the past three decades have been exacerbated through the Europeanization project. Lastly, China's outward investments and its mega-infrastructure project the Belt and Road Initiative are also not unique but, rather, represent one of the widely studied systemic characteristics of capitalism: the tendency of overaccumulated capital towards geographic expansion. Existing research could learn much simply from the history of the world capitalist system – thus far shaped overwhelmingly by Euro-Atlantic hegemony.

With regard to China's *démarche* in Eastern Europe, there is still much else that future research can draw from in terms of pre-existing processes of the financialization of infrastructures, pre-existing causes of East–West divides, and the role of the EU in shaping

Eastern Europe's development policies. Chinese infrastructure loans and direct investments within and beyond the BRI pose real challenges for their recipient countries. Yet, this is not because China is so exceptional but precisely because we know from Western imperial and colonial history the social and environmental risks of similar developmental politics and the logics of borrowing and foreign investments.

Such historical and spatial contextualization of Chinese engagements with Eastern Europe and Eurasia opens up possibilities for further research to ask: Who exactly within and across countries, which communities and which social classes will reap the benefits and who will have to carry the burdens of debt repayment and environmental destruction? What is being done and what can be done to address those risks? How can we draw from existing knowledge and experiences regarding the challenges of large, debt-financed infrastructure projects? Activation of such critical research agendas can hopefully enable us to use the research on China's presence in Eastern Europe for rethinking existing developmental paradigms, dependencies and deep inequalities in the region.

Notes

1   Joe Williams, Caitlin Robinson and Stefan Bouzarovski, 'China's Belt and Road Initiative and the emerging geographies of global urbanisation', *The Geographical Journal* 186 (2020) 1, pp. 128–40, here at p. 128.

2   Sasa Dragojlo, 'Serbian Inmates Hired for a Pittance by Subsidiary of Austrian Construction Giant. Balk', *Balkan Insight*, 20 August 20 2020, https://balkaninsight.com/2020/08/20/serbian-inmates-hired-for-a-pittance-by-subsidiary-of-austrian-construction-giant.

3   Irna Hofman, Oane Visser and Artemy Kalinovsky, 'Introduction: Encounters After the Soviet Collapse: The Contemporary Chinese Presence in the Former Soviet Union Border Zone', *Problems of Post-Communism* 67 (2020) 3, pp. 193–203.

4   Gaziza Shakhanova and Jeremy Garlick, 'The Belt and Road Initiative and the Eurasian Economic Union: Exploring the "Greater Eurasian Partnership"', *Journal of Current Chinese Affairs* 49 (2020) 1, pp. 33–57, here at p. 2.

5   Fanqi Jia and Mia M. Bennett, 'Chinese infrastructure diplomacy in Russia: the geopolitics of project type, location, and scale', *Eurasian Geography and Economics* 59 (2018) 3–4, pp. 340–77, here at p. 368.

6   Nadège Rolland, 'China's Ambitions in Eastern Europe and the South Caucasus', *Notes de l'Ifri (Institut français des relations internationales)* 112 (December 2018), p. 10. Available at: https://www.ifri.org/en/publications/notes-de-lifri/russieneivisions/chinas-ambitions-eastern-europe-and-south-caucasus.

7   Justyna Szczudlik, 'Seven Years of The 16+1: An Assessment of China's 'Multilateral Bilateralism', *Central Europe' in Notes de l'Ifri (Institut français des relations internationales)* 107 (April 2019), p. 3. Available at: https://www.ifri.org/en/publications/notes-de-lifri/asie-visions/seven-years-161-assessment-chinas-multilateral-bilateralism.

8   Igor Rogelja, 'Concrete and coal: China's infrastructural assemblages in the Balkans', *Political Geography* 81 (2020), MS 102220, pp. 1–10, here at p. 3.

9   Ivana Karásková et al., *Empty shell no more: China's growing footprint in Central and Eastern* Europe. Policy paper by China Observers in Central and Eastern Europe (CHOICE) (Prague: Czech Republic's Association for International Affairs (AMO), April 2020). Available at: https://chinaobservers.eu/wp-content/uploads/2020/04/CHOICE_Empty-shell-no-more.pdf.

10 Karásková et al., *Empty shell no more.*

11 Alison J. Ayers, 'Beyond Myths, Lies and Stereotypes: The Political Economy of a "New Scramble for Africa"', *New Political Economy* 18 (2013) 2, pp. 227–57.

12 Michael Lambert, 'Chinese Octopus: How China Is Taking Over the Post-Soviet Space', *Russian International Affairs Council*, 18 June 2019, https://russiancouncil.ru/en/analytics-and-comments/columns/asian-kaleidoscope/chinese-octopus-how-china-is-taking-over-the-post-soviet-space/.

13 Małgorzata Jakimów, 'China's grand geopolitical project threatens a new East-West divide in Europe', *The Conversation,* 30 June 2017, https://theconversation.com/chinas-grand-geopolitical-project-threatens-a-new-east-west-divide-in-europe-79477.

14 Valbona Zeneli, 'China in the Balkans: Chinese investment could become a challenging factor for the European future of the Western Balkans', *The Globalist*, 9 April 2019, https://www.theglobalist.com/balkans-china-fdi-belt-and-road-eu/.

15 Jan Gaspers, 'Divide an Rule', *Berlin Policy Journal (German Council on Foreign Relations – DGAP)*, 2 March 2018, https://berlinpolicyjournal.com/divide-and-rule/.

16 Ryan Heath and Andrew Gray, 'Beware Chinese Trojan horses in the Balkans, EU warns', *Politico*, 27 July 2018, https://www.politico.eu/article/johannes-hahn-beware-chinese-trojan-horses-in-the-balkans-eu-warns-enlargement-politico-podcast/.

17 EU Commission High Representative for Foreign Affairs and Security Policy, *Joint Communication To The European Parliament, The European Council And The Council: EU-China – A Strategic Outlook, Policy Brief, 12 March 2019*, p. 1. Available at: https://commission.europa.eu/publications/eu-china-strategic-outlook-commission-and-hrvp-contribution-european-council-21-22-march-2019_en.

18 Thorsten Benner et al., *Authoritarian Advance: Responding to China's Growing Political Influence in Europe* (Berlin: Mercator Institute for China Studies (MERICS), February 2018). Available at: https://merics.org/en/report/authoritarian-advance-responding-chinas-growing-political-influence-europe.

19 Jeremy Garlick, 'China's Economic Diplomacy in Central and Eastern Europe: A Case of Offensive Mercantilism?', *Europe-Asia Studies* 71 (2019) 8, pp. 1390–1414.

20 Elena F. Tracy et al., 'China's new Eurasian ambitions: the environmental risks of the Silk Road Economic Belt', *Eurasian Geography and Economics* 58 (2017) 1, pp. 56–88, here at p. 78.

21 For exceptionally critical readings on this topic, see Evelina Gambino, 'The Georgian logistics revolution: questioning seamlessness across the New Silk Road', *Work Organization & Labor Globalization* 13 (2019) 1, pp. 190–206. See also Igor Rogelja, 'Concrete and coal'.

22 Karásková et al., *Empty shell no more.*

23 Mladen Grgić, 'Chinese infrastructural investments in the Balkans: political implications of the highway project in Montenegro', *Territory, Politics, Governance* 7 (2019) 1, pp. 42–60, here at pp. 55–7.

24 Garlick, *China's Economic Diplomacy*, p. 20.

25 Dragan Pavlićević, 'A Power Shift Underway in Europe? China's Relationship with Central and Eastern Europe Under the Belt and Road Initiative', in *Mapping China's 'One Belt One Road' Initiative,* ed. Li Xing (Cham: Palgrave Macmillan, 2019), pp 249–78, here at p. 271.

26 Giles Mohan and May Tan-Mullins, 'The geopolitics of South–South infrastructure development: Chinese-financed energy projects in the global South', *Urban Studies* 56 (2019) 7, pp. 1368–85.

27 Peter O'Brien, Phil O'Neill and Andy Pike, 'Funding, financing and governing urban infrastructures', in *Urban Studies* 56 (2019) 7, pp. 1291–303, here at p. 1293.

28 Andrés Rodríguez-Pose, Riccardo Crescenzi and Marco Di Cataldo, 'Institutions and the Thirst for "Prestige" Transport Infrastructure', in *Knowledge and Institutions*, ed. Johannes Glückler et al. (Cham: Springer 2018), pp. 227–46, here at p. 228.

29 Natalia Buier, 'The Second Coming of Rail: The Spanish High-Speed Rail-Finance Complex', *Antipode* 52 (2020) 6, pp. 1603–23, here at p. 1604.

30 Gergő Medve-Bálint and Dorothee Bohle, 'Local Government Debt and EU Funds in the Eastern Member States: The Cases of Hungary and Poland', in *Maximizing the integration capacity of the European Union: Lessons of and prospects for enlargement and beyond – MAXCAP Project*

Working Paper series No. 33 (Berlin: Freie Universität, November 2016), p. 23. Available at: https://userpage.fu-berlin.de/kfgeu/maxcap/system/files/maxcap_wp_33.pdf.

31 Hilary Appel and Mitchell A. Orenstein, 'Why did Neoliberalism Triumph and Endure in the Post-Communist World?', *Comparative Politics* 48 (2016) 3, pp. 313–31, here at p. 316.

32 Dorothee Bohle, 'European Integration, Capitalist Diversity and Crises Trajectories on Europe's Eastern Periphery', *New Political Economy* 23 (2018) 2, pp. 239–53, here at p. 242.

33 Gergő Medve-Bálint and Dorothee Bohle, 'More Integrated but Also More Divided: Intended and Unintended Consequences of Foreign Direct Investment and the Cohesion Policy in Eastern Europe', in *Maximizing the integration capacity of the European Union: Lessons of and prospects for enlargement and beyond – MAXCAP Project Working Paper series No. 34* (Berlin: Freie Universität, September 2016), p. 4. Available at: http://userpage.fu-berlin.de/kfgeu/maxcap/system/files/maxcap_wp_34.pdf.

34 Nana de Graaff, 'China's rise in a liberal world order in transition – introduction to the FORUM', *Review of International Political Economy* 27 (2020) 2, pp. 191–207, here at p. 193.

35 Williams et al., *China's Belt and Road Initiative*, p. 129.

36 Karen P. Y. Lai, Shaun Lin and James D. Sidaway, 'Financing the Belt and Road Initiative (BRI): research agendas beyond the "debt-trap" discourse', *Eurasian Geography and Economics* 61 (2020) 2, pp. 109–24, here at p. 123.

37 David Harvey and Paik Nak-chung, 'How capital operates and where the world and China are going: a conversation', *Inter-Asia Cultural Studies* 18 (2017) 2, pp. 251–68, here at p. 253.

Bibliography

Jia, Fanqi and Mia M. Bennett. 'Chinese infrastructure diplomacy in Russia: the geopolitics of project type, location, and scale'. *Eurasian Geography and Economics* 59 (2018) 3–4, pp. 340–77.

Summers, Tim. 'China's "New Silk Roads": Sub-national regions and networks of global political economy'. *Third World Quarterly* 37 (2016) 9, pp. 1628–43.

Tracy, Elena F. et al. 'China's new Eurasian ambitions: The environmental risks of the Silk Road Economic Belt'. *Eurasian Geography and Economics* 58 (2017) 1, pp. 56–88.

Further reading

Hildyard, Nicholas. *Licensed Larceny: Infrastructure, Financial Extraction and the Global South*, Manchester: Manchester University Press, 2017.

Schindler, Seth, Jessica DiCarlo and Dinesh Paudel. 'The new cold war and the rise of the 21st-century infrastructure state'. *Transactions of the Institute of British Geographers* 47 (2021), pp. 331–46.

Szabó, Linda and Csaba Jelinek. 'State, capitalism and infrastructure-led development: A multi-scalar analysis of the Belgrade-Budapest railway construction'. *Environment and Planning A: Economy and Space* 55 (2023) 5, pp. 1281–304.

van Veelen, Bredje et al. 'Interventions on Democratizing Infrastructure'. *Political Geography* 87 (2021) 102378, pp. 1–10.

Contributors

Chapter authors and volume editors

Azar Aliyev
Azar Aliyev, LL.M. is junior professor for International Economic Law and Comparative Law of the Martin Luther University of Halle-Wittenberg. His research is focused on post-socialist countries, especially on the region of Central Asia and the Caucasus. Aliyev studied Law in Baku and Heidelberg and holds a PhD degree from the University of Kiel. Dr Aliyev lectures in Civil Law, IT Law and International Dispute Settlement in Halle, and Azerbaijani Civil Law at the Baku State University. Besides academic activities Aliyev is involved as legal expert in numerous legal reform and capacity building projects of the UNCTAD, UNCITRAL, GIZ, USAID and other international organizations. He publishes in Azerbaijani, English, German and Russian.
azar.aliyev@jura.uni-halle.de

Gilad Ben-Nun
Gilad Ben-Nun is professor of global studies at Leipzig University's Global and European Studies Institute where he teaches history of international law and Muslim-Jewish relations.
gilad.ben-nun@uni-leipzig.de

Benjamin Beuerle
Benjamin Beuerle is a researcher at the Centre Marc Bloch in Berlin (CMB) and co-responsible for the CMB's new research focus 'Environment, Climate, Energy'. Until February 2022 he worked for the German Historical Institute Moscow, where he was the scientific coordinator of the interdisciplinary and transnational network project 'Russia's North Pacific'. His research interests include climate policy approaches, energy issues and urban transport with a focus on the late Soviet Union, Russia and Ukraine. Recent publications include 'Urban Air Pollution and Environmental Engagement in the Russian Far East', in Benjamin Beuerle, Sandra Dahlke and Andreas Renner (eds), *Russia's North Pacific. Centres and Peripheries* (2023), as well as 'From Continuity to Change. Soviet and Russian government attitudes on climate change', *Climatic Change* 176 (2023) 36.
benjamin.beuerle@cmb.hu-berlin.de

Katja Castryck-Naumann
Katja Castryck-Naumann is senior researcher at the Leipzig Leibniz Institute for the History and Culture of Eastern Europe (GWZO). She worked as guest researcher at the ENS Paris and GHI

Warsaw, as guest professor at Science Po Lyon and Arhus University, and was a fellow of the GHI Washington. Her research deals with the history of international organizations, global connections of East Central Europe, and world history writing. Her latest publications include the edited volume 'Transregional Connections in the History of East Central Europe' (2021) and the article 'Competing Politics in Regionalizing the Social Sciences. UNESCO, CODESRIA, and the European Research Council' (2022).
katja.castryck@leibniz-gwzo.de

Lena Dallywater

Lena Dallywater is researcher at the Leibniz Institute for Regional Geography Leipzig and coordinator of the Leibniz ScienceCampus 'Eastern Europe – Global Area' (EEGA). In her dissertation and project-based publications, she has focused on transregional entanglements, particularly in the area of intellectual engagement and emancipatory activism in the middle of the 20th century. Most recently, she published *Eastern Europe, the Soviet Union, and Africa: New perspectives on the era of decolonization, 1950s to 1990s* (2023, co-edited with Chris Saunders and Helder Adegar Fonseca).
l_dallywater@leibniz-ifl.de

Mónika Dánél

Mónika Dánél is assistant professor at Eötvös Loránd University (Budapest) and was postdoctoral researcher at the University of Oslo (2018–21). Her research interests lie in contemporary Eastern European Studies (especially Hungarian and Romanian Literature and Film), theory of intermediality, multilingualism, space and body theory, memory and gender studies connected to post-socialist societies. She led the international project *Space-ing Otherness. Cultural Images of Space, Contact Zones in Contemporary Hungarian and Romanian Film and Literature* (http://contactzones.elte. hu/). She has co-edited two scholarly volumes, *Event-Trauma-Publicity* (2012) and *Space – Theory – Culture. An Interdisciplinary Handbook of the Space* (2019), and published two monographs in Hungarian, *Transparent Frames: The Intimacy of Reading* (2013) and *Language-Carnival: The Poetics of Hungarian Neo-Avant-Garde Artworks* (2016).
danel.monika@btk.elte.hu

Michael G. Esch

Michael G. Esch is a freelance historian, translator and adjunct professor for Comparative European Social and Cultural History at the University of Leipzig. He has worked and published extensively on German occupation policies in Poland, population policies in East Central Europe and on the social, cultural and discursive history of migration. An additional research focus is the history of 'popular' music and subversion in the long 1960s. His more recent publications include 'Migrants from East-Central Europe in South America: Discourses and Structures between Mission, Pogrom Escape, Human Trafficking, and "Whitening"', in Katja Castryck-Naumann (ed.), *Transregional Connections in the History of East-Central Europe* (2021); 'Refugees and Migrants: Perceptions and Categorisations of Moving People 1789–1938', in Włodzimierz Borodziej and Joachim von Puttkamer (eds), *Immigrants and Foreigners in Central and Eastern Europe during the Twentieth Century* (2020); 'Music and Revolt: A Breakneck Ride through the Transnational Production and Significance of Jazz and Rock', in Matthias Middell (ed.), *The Routledge Handbook of Transregional Studies* (2018).
kontakt@michael-esch.de

Zaur Gasimov

Zaur Gasimov is a historian of Eastern Europe and the Middle East. He co-runs the Faculty of Economics and Administrative Sciences at Turkish-German University in Istanbul, on behalf of the German Academic Exchange Service (DAAD). He completed his habilitation project at the

University of Mainz in 2020, and joined the Russian Studies Department of the University of Bonn as a DFG Principal Investigator. He studied international relations, international law and history in Baku, Berlin and Eichstaett-Ingolstadt, and has published extensively on Russian-Turkish relations and the entangled history of Eastern Europe and the Middle East.
gasimov@uni-mainz.de

Stefan Keym

Stefan Keym is professor of musicology at Leipzig University. He has been visiting professor at the Universities of Zürich and Berlin (Humboldt) and full professor at Université Toulouse Jean Jaurès. He has published monographs on the transfer of symphonic music between Germany and Poland in the long 19th century and on Olivier Messiaen's religious opera *Saint François d'Assise*. His research focusses on 18th-, 19th- and 20th-century music with its political and cultural contexts (especially intercultural transfers and the search for national identity), on musical institutions and repertoires (concerts and publishers), large instrumental genres (sonata, symphony), and modern music theatre. Recent publications include *Eastern European Emigrants and the Internationalisation of 20th-Century Music Concepts* (2022, co-edited with Anna Fortunova).
keym@uni-leipzig.de

Stephan Krause

Stephan Krause is senior researcher at the Leibniz Institute for the History and Culture of Eastern Europe (GWZO) in Leipzig. He holds a PhD in German literature from Humboldt University Berlin. He worked as a guest professor at the University of Pécs, ELTE Budapest and the University of Szczecin. His research focuses on literatures in East Central Europe (Hungarian, French, German, Romanian, Polish) and on film. Recent publications include *Klassiker des rumänischen Films* (2024, co-edited with Dana Duma and Anke Pfeifer) and 'The "Gift of Memory" and the "Gift of Oblivion": Holocaust and World War II in Contemporary Hungarian Literature', in M. Schwartz, N. Weller and H. Winkel (eds), *After Memory. World War II in Contemporary Eastern European Literatures* (2021).
stephan.krause@leibniz-gwzo.de

Thilo Lang

Thilo Lang is head of department at the Leibniz Institute for Regional Geography (IfL), and professor for economic geography at the Global and European Studies Institute Leipzig University. He is a member of the Collaborative Research Centre 1199 'Processes of Spatialisation under the Global Condition' and directs the research group 'Multiple Geographies of Regional and Local Development' at IfL. His research interests include polarization processes at multiple scales, innovation outside of agglomerations, local and regional development with a focus on institutional change in 'peripheral' regions and alternative economies. Previously he held positions at the Leibniz Institute for Research on Society and Space and the Regional Development Agency ZukunftsAgentur Brandenburg GmbH, as well as fellowships at the Universities of Sheffield and Durham, , and a guest professorship for globalization and development at the Latvian University in Riga.
t_lang@leibniz-ifl.de

Uwe Müller

Uwe Müller is an economic historian and has been senior researcher at the Leibniz Institute for the History and Culture of Eastern Europe (GWZO) since 2011. Before that he researched and taught at the Humboldt University in Berlin, the European University Viadrina in Frankfurt (Oder) and the Saarland University in Saarbrücken. His research interests include the economic history of Eastern Europe from the middle of the 19th century to the present day with a special focus on the integration of this region in the European and world economy. In this context, he has published on issues of transport history, trade history and agricultural history. He has recently published *The*

Middle-Income Trap in Central and Eastern Europe: Causes, Consequences and Strategies in Post-Communist Countries (2024, co-edited with Yaman Kouli).
uwe.mueller@leibniz-gwzo.de

Lela Rekhviashvili

Lela Rekhviashvili is researcher in political economy and regional geography at Leibniz Institute for Regional Geography. Her work focuses on infrastructure-led development and infrastructure's role in (re-)claiming socialist and capitalist modernities. She has also been published on issues as marketization, social embeddedness, urban mobility, informality and social movements.
l_rekhviashvili@leibniz-ifl.de

Max Trecker

Max Trecker is a visiting associate professor at the University of Pittsburgh. He studied history and economics at LMU Munich and CEU Budapest. His dissertation on the coordination of East–South economic relations in the Council for Mutual Economic Assistance was published as *Red Money for the Global South: East-South Economic Relations in the Cold War* (2020). His most recent book, on the birth of a new entrepreneurial class in East Germany after 1989, was *Neue Unternehmer braucht das Land: Die Genese des ostdeutschen Mittelstands nach der Wiedervereinigung* (2022).
MAT595@pitt.edu

Elizabeth White

Elizabeth White is associate professor of Global History at the University of the West of England, Bristol. Her current research focuses on the history of children's rights. She was awarded a British Academy Small Grant Award in 2021 to support researching a monograph on the role of the socialist bloc in internationalizing children's rights in the UN. Her most recent publication was *A Modern History of Russian Childhood: From the Late Imperial Period to the Collapse of the Soviet Union* (2020) and she has published widely on the history of refugee children and humanitarianism in the 20th century, as well as on Soviet children and the Great Patriotic War.
Elizabeth6.White@uwe.ac.uk

Visualizations team

Kristin Bolanz

Kristin Bolanz is trained in geo-information, cartography and graphic design. With her innovative map-creations and layout she brought research data to life and shaped the visual appeal of the textbook.

Jana Moser

Jana Moser is head of the department 'Cartography and Visual Communication' and coordinator of the research area 'Geovisualisations' at the Leibniz Institute for Regional Geography Leipzig. Her key activities and research interests include developing and editing of maps and atlases, map design, and the history of cartography, with a special regional focus on Saxony, Central Germany and Southern Africa. Moser supervised the overall design and cartographic accuracy, i.e. adequacy, of the book's maps and visualizations.
j_moser@leibniz-ifl.de

Text box authors

Kristine Beurskens

Kristine Beurskens, is senior researcher and director of the research group "Geographies of Belonging and Difference" at the Leibniz Institute for Regional Geography (IfL) Leipzig

Konstantin Branovitskii
Konstantin Branovitskii is visiting professor at the Martin-Luther-Universität Halle-Wittenberg and was fellow of the Alexander von Humboldt Foundation from 2021 to 2023. His research focuses on civil procedure and comparative law.

Ulf Brunnbauer
Ulf Brunnbauer is professor in the historical anthropology and social history of South-eastern Europe and scientific director of the Leibniz Institute for East and Southeast European Studies in Regensburg.

Bettina Bruns
Bettina Bruns is senior researcher and deputy director of the research group "Geographies of Belonging and Difference" at the Leibniz Institute for Regional Geography (IfL) Leipzig

Jessica Graybill
Jessica Graybill is a geographer and professor of Russian and Eurasian Studies at Colgate University (Hamilton, NY)

Tomas Hanell
Tomas Hanell is senior research fellow at the Migration Institute of Finland.

Beáta Hock
Beáta Hock is senior researcher at the Leibniz Institute for the History and Culture of Eastern Europe (GWZO), Leipzig, focusing on art and cultural history of East Central Europe (20th and 21st cent.)

Csaba Jelinek
Csaba Jelinek is researcher in urban and regional policies at Periféria Policy and Research Center in Budapest.

Bence Kocsev
Bence Kocsev is researcher at Otto-von-Habsburg Foundation in Budapest.

Kean Fan Lim
Kean Fan Lim is senior lecturer in economic geography at the Centre for Urban & Regional Development Studies, Newcastle University.

Fabian Lüscher
Fabian Lüscher is scientific librarian at the Université de Fribourg.

Dietmar Müller
Dietmar Müller, is historian, teacher and researching the comparative cultural and social history of Europe at Leipzig University.

Erika Nagy
Erika Nagy is researcher at the Centre for Economic and Regional Studies at the Hungarian Academy of Sciences.

Andy Pike
Andy Pike is Henry Daysh Professor of Regional Development Studies at the Centre for Urban & Regional Development Studies, Newcastle University.

Paschalis Samarinis
Paschalis Samarinis is researcher of urban and regional development, holding his PhD from National Technical University of Athens.

Susann Schäfer
Susann Schäfer is an economic geographer, researching and teaching at the University of Jena.

Guido Sechi
Guido Sechi is researcher at the Department of Human Geography at the University of Latvia in Riga.

Theodore Styliadis
Theodore Styliadis is researcher in transportation and economics, holding his PhD in Port Economics from the University of Piraeus.

Linda Szabó
Linda Szabó is an anthropologist working as a researcher at Periféria Policy and Research Center in Budapest.

Pavel Szobi
Pavel Szobi is an economic historian and contemporary historian. He works at the Institute of International Studies at the Charles University in Prague and currently also at the Department of Contemporary History at the University of Vienna.

Onur Yildirim
Onur Yildirim is an economic historian and professor in the Department of Economics at Middle East Technical University in Ankara.

Abbreviations

AA	EU (q.v.) Association Agreements
AIIB	Asian Infrastructure Investment Bank
APS	advanced producer service
BiH	Bosnia-Herzegovina
BRI	Belt and Road Initiative
CEDAW	Convention on the Elimination of All Forms of Discrimination Against Women
CEES	Central and Eastern European States
CIA	*Commission Internationale d'Agriculture* (International Commission of Agriculture)
CMEA	Council for Mutual Economic Assistance
CO2	carbon dioxide
COMECON	Council for Mutual Economic Assistance (*Sovet ekonomičeskoj vzaimopomošči*)
COP	Conference of the Parties (supreme decision-making body of UNFCCC [q.v.])
COSCO	China Ocean Shipping Company
CSW	UN Commission on the Status of Women
DEDAW	Declaration on the Elimination of Discrimination Against Women
ECD	European Commission of the Danube
EEC	European Economic Community
EU	European Union
FDI	Foreign Direct Investment
FNPP	floating nuclear power plant
FRELIMO	*Frente de Libertação Moçambique* (Liberation Front of Mozambique)
FRG	Federal Republic of Germany (West Germany)
GaWC	Global and World Cities Research Network
GDP	Gross Domestic Product
GDR	German Democratic Republic (the former state of East Germany)
GHG	greenhouse gases
GHI	German Historical Institute
GOELRO	State Commission for the Electrification of Russia
ICA	International Coffee Agreement
ICEF	International Children's Emergency Fund
IDPs	internally displaced people
IfL	Leibniz Institute for Regional Geography
IIASA	International Institute for Applied System Analysis
IMF	International Monetary Fund
IPCC	(UN) Intergovernmental Panel on Climate Change
ISCM	International Society for Contemporary Music
ISCU	International Save the Children Union
IUCW	International Union of Child Welfare
KUTV	*Kommunisticheskii Universitet Trudiashchikhsia Vostoka* (Communist University of Toilers from the East)

LAU	Local Administrative Unit
LNG	liquefied natural gas
LoN	League of Nations
Merics	Mercator Institute for China Studies
NATO	North Atlantic Treaty Organization
NIS	Newly Independent States (of the former Soviet Union)
NDEA	National Defence Education Act
NEP	New Economic Policy (in the post-civil war Soviet Union)
NGO	Non-governmental Organization
NIEO	New International Economic Order
NMO	Neighbouring Military Occupation
NPP	nuclear power plant
NPT	Nuclear Non-Proliferation Treaty
NUTS	*Nomenclature des Unités territoriales statistiques* (Nomenclature of territorial units for statistics)
NWFZ	Nuclear-Weapon-Free Zones
OECD	Organisation for Economic Co-operation and Development
OLP	Piraeus Port Authority
OPEC	Organization of the Petroleum Exporting Countries
OSCE	Organization for Security and Co-operation in Europe
PCAs	Partnership and Cooperation Agreements (between EU [q.v.] and NIS [q.v.])
PHARE	Poland and Hungary Aid for Reconstruction of the Economy programme
PoW	Prisoner of War
pps	purchasing power standards
PRC	People's Republic of China
R&D	research and development
SALT	Strategic Arms Limitation Talks
SED	*Sozialistische Einheitspartei Deutschlands* (Socialist Unity Party of Germany [GDR (q.v.)])
TACIS	Technical Assistance to the Commonwealth of Independent States
UDHR	UN Universal Declaration of Human Rights
UK	United Kingdom (of Great Britain and Northern Ireland)
UN	United Nations
UNCRC	UN Convention on the Rights of the Child
UNCTAD	United Nations Conference on Trade and Development
UNECE	United Nations Economic Commission for Europe
UNEP	United Nations Environment Programme
UNESCO	United Nations Educational, Scientific and Cultural Organization
UNFCCC	United Nations Framework Convention on Climate Change
UNICEF	United Nations Children's Fund
UNIDO	United Nations Industrial Development Organisation
UNRRA	United Nations Relief and Rehabilitation Administration
USA	United States of America
USSR	Union of Soviet Socialist Republics ('Soviet Union')
WHO	World Health Organization
WMO	World Meteorological Organization
WTO	World Trade Organization
WWF	World Wide Fund for Nature

Index

Page numbers in **bold** refer to figures, page numbers in *italic* refer to tables.